The British School at Athens
with
The British Museum

SPARTA IN LACONIA:

THE ARCHAEOLOGY OF A CITY AND ITS COUNTRYSIDE

SPARTA IN LACONIA

Proceedings of the 19th British Museum Classical Colloquium
held with the British School at Athens
and King's and University Colleges, London
6–8 December 1995

W. G. Cavanagh and S. E. C. Walker (Editors)

BRITISH SCHOOL AT ATHENS
STUDIES 4

Published and distributed by
The British School at Athens
Senate House, Malet Street, London WC1E 7HU

First published in Great Britain 1998
ISBN 0 904887 31 6

This book is set in Ehrhardt 11/12pt
Designed by Charlotte Westbrook Wilson
Printed in Great Britain by Technical Print Services Ltd, Nottingham

Contents

List of illustrations

FIGURES

TABLES

List of abbreviations

PG	Protogeometric
G	Geometric
O	Orientalizing
EO	Early Orientalizing
Cl	Classical
Hl	Hellenistic
R	Roman
ER	Early Roman
N	north
S	south
E	east
W	west
masl	metres above sea level

BIBLIOGRAPHICAL ABBREVIATIONS

AAA	*Athens Annals of Archaeology (Αρχαιολογικά Ανάλεκτα εξ Αθηνών)*
AA	*Archäologischer Anzeiger*
A. Delt.	*Archaiologikon Deltion*
AJA	*American Journal of Archaeology*
AR	*Archaeological Reports*
BCH	*Bulletin de Correspondance Hellénique*
BSA	*Annual of the British School at Athens*
PAE	*Πρακτικὰ τῆς ἐν Ἀθήναις Ἀρχαιολογικῆς Ἑταιρείας*
RE	Pauly-Wissowa, *Realencyclopädie der klassischen Altertumswissenschaft*

Abstracts

H. W. CATLING
The work of the British school at Athens at Sparta and in Laconia.

The British School at Athens has worked in Laconia and at Sparta since 1904. While research by individual scholars has been continuous since that date (apart from the interruptions created by the two World Wars) the School's work as an institution belongs to three phases—the first 1904 to 1910, the second 1924–28, the last from 1973 until the present. There has been much excavation in Sparta itself (on the acropolis, at the Great Altar, the Heroön, the sanc-tuary of Artemis Orthia) and beyond—at the Menelaion, the Eleusinion at Kalyvia Sochas, at the Zeus Messapeus sanctuary at Tsakona.

Further afield, the Bronze Age settlement at Ayios Stephanos in the Helos plain has been excavated, the underwater Bronze Age site at Pavlopetri, Elaphonisi surveyed and small sites at Koutiphari and Angelona tested. Much topographic work has been undertaken notably the survey of prehistoric Laconia before and after the Second World War by Waterhouse and Hope Simpson, and the Laconia Survey of the 1980s by the School in collaboration with Amsterdam University. All branches of study continue at the present time.

THEODOROS G. SPYROPOULOS
Pellana: the administrative centre of prehistoric Laconia.

Pellana, a remote and forgotten village near Mt. Taygetos, is proving today to be a prehistoric centre of paramount importance. In the 1930s two rock-cut tholoi of modest size had been cleared at Pelekete by T. Karachalios. Fifty years later three monumental tholoi were excavated there by the author. These date to the LH II–IIIB/CI period. On the acropolis of Pellana important finds testify to the significance of the site during the EBA and the LH period: a large road ascending the eastern slope of the hill; two, possibly more, tumuli; a Mycenaean settlement (LH IIIA–IIIB/CI); and most recently a group of shaft graves of the MH III/LH I period.

Pellana is very probably the Homeric Lakedaimon, royal residence of Tyndareos and Menelaos. What has still to be found is the Mycenaean palace, which lies most probably near the Pellanis Spring to the s of the acropolis of historic Pellana.

PAUL CARTLEDGE
City and *chora* in Sparta: Archaic to Hellenistic

Whereas the normal and normative Greek *polis* united town and country in a harmonious political symbiosis, Sparta in this respect as so often was atypical, if not unique. The Spartan system of urbanization was consciously designed to emphasise and reinforce the centre's separation from and hierarchical domination over the periphery. The presence or (until the mid-Hellenistic era) absence of a city wall was a clear ideological and spatial marker of Sparta's difference.

REINHARD FÖRTSCH
Spartan art: its many different deaths

The refutation through archaeological evidence of the picture of a Sparta without art does not satisfactorily explain the role of art at Sparta. The decline in the production of Laconian art is explored by means of a synopsis of formally defined 'type' series.

A change-point occurs in the third quarter of the sixth century bc. The number of new products declines and the number of products coming to an end reaches a maximum but the number of products co-existing is, for the time being, only slightly reduced. At the same time there appear three of the five most important forms which were to continue into the fifth century BC. I interpret this as a statistical consequence of a constitutional change of paradigm: an aristocratic, luxurious society, with representational art, is displaced by the egalitarian, anti-luxurious ideology of the homoioi.

STEPHEN HODKINSON

Patterns of bronze dedications at Spartan sanctuaries, *c.* 650–350 BC: towards a quantified database of material and religious investment

This essay advocates a new approach to Laconian material culture, examining the bronze finds from Spartan sanctuaries *c.*650–350 BC as a record of material and religious investment.The fundamental requirement for this approach is a complete database of the finds. Obstacles to the construction of such a database are noted. Nevertheless, even incomplete data currently avcailable demonstrate the value of a quantitative approach which permits comparison of Spartan votive offerings with those elsewhere in Greece. Spartan dedication patterns largely conform to general Greek trends and offer little support for the supposed development of a uniquely austere society in the late Archaic and Classical periods.

CONRAD M. STIBBE

Exceptional shapes and decorations in Laconian pottery

Given the fact that Sparta occupies a rather exceptional place among the Greek city states in pre-Hellenistic times, we might expect to find some reflection of this special cultural and political status in its minor arts, in particular in its pottery. This paper attempts to show that this is a realistic expectation. The following exceptional pieces, some of which have unusual decoration, are considered: five tubes or stands (one of which was exported); a fragment of an inscribed olpe; two lekythoi with elongated bodies (one exported); a series of lekythoi with globular bodies (many of which were exported); a giraffe-necked jug; and an Attic C-cup with a curious inscription, found in a Laconian sanctuary. The interpretation of these shapes and decorations should contribute to our understanding of the archaic culture of the Spartans.

TYLER JO SMITH

Dances drinks and dedications: the archaic komos in Laconia

The komast figure appears in Laconian art throughout the sixth century BC. The bottom-slapping reveller common to Corinthian and Athenian vase-painting takes his characteristic form in the arts of Archaic Laconia.

This paper examines the iconography of the Laconian komos in vase-painting and in other media, including lead figurines and bronze objects. Archaic Sparta presents the first and only instance of the komast figure employed for religious or dedicatory purposes. The possibility that komast dancers maintain a special local function in Archaic Spartan life is questioned.

MARIA PIPILI

Archaic Laconian vase-painting: some iconographic considerations

An interesting category of archaic Laconian vases are those decorated with scenes which seem to have a religious character: symposia attended by small winged daemons, komasts surrounding an imposing musician, a rider accompanied by winged daemons, gods on their own or approached by worshippers.

Of the five major Laconian vase-painters it is the Naukratis Painter who probably introduced most such scenes, giving to Laconian iconography much of its eccentric character. It is suggested here that these works were produced mainly for the needs of particular sanctuaries, especially the Samian Heraion, where a large number of such vases was found. Other Laconian vases, which may also have been special commissions for cult purposes, are examined, and the relation between subject-matter and find-spot considered.

G. B. WAYWELL, J. J. WILKES AND S. E. C. WALKER

The Ancient Theatre at Sparta

Recent studies of the remains of the stage and stage-building of the Sparta Theatre have shed more light on their structural history. The cavea and orchestra, contructed *c.* 20 BC, were originally faced by a Doric colonnade (Waywell). In front of this was a stage-platform which could be moved on stone runnels out of sight into the west parados (Wilkes). This arrangement was replaced in the Flavian period (an inscription of AD 78 is the key evidence) by a permanent stage fronting a stage-building with a two-storey projecting columnar facade in the Corinthian order (Walker). Though extensively repaired on more than one occasion, this arrangment survived until the Theatre ceased to function at the end of the 4th century.

ANASTASIA PANAYOTOPOULOU

Roman mosaics from Sparta

Sparta maintained a prominent position in the production of mosaic pavements. This paper presents the evolution of mosaic art in Sparta, from the Hellenistic to the early Christian period, the characteristic features to be recognized in each period, and decoration both with geometric patterns and figurative scenes. Spartan mosaics of the Roman period are noteworthy for the figurative scenes which usually appear in the centre of the room. The rest of the pavement is covered with varied, multicoloured geometric patterns.

Comparison with contemporary mosaics, whether from other Greek cities or the rest of the Roman empire, provides evidence that a local workshop was active in Sparta, whose acme may be identified in the second half of the third century and the first decades of the fourth century AD.

ANNA KARAPANAYIOTOU

A Roman portrait from Monemvasia of the early second century AD

This paper discusses the stone carving of a man's head, found at Monemvasia, dating to the first quarter of the second century AD. The style and its sources are identified, and its significance brought out for our understanding of social and cultural attitudes in one corner of the Roman world. The technique and the hair-style place the sculpture in the Trajanic or even early Hadrianic period, with striking similarities to the portraits of Trajan and an early type of Hadrian, as well as several associated works, such as the Arch of Trajan at Benevento, and examples of imperial portraiture found at Athens. A closer examination of the style and technique point to an Athenian product, inspired by the latest fashions in style and taste, emanating from Rome itself. The quality and context of the Monemvasia head suggest that the subject might be identifiable as the senator Herculanus, the last of the well-known Spartan family, the Euryclids.

STELLA RAFTOPOULOU

New finds from Sparta

This paper offers a brief overview of the finds from rescue excavations, conducted during the period 1991–1995 in house-plots and roads in the modern town. The results, which range in date from Proto-Geometric to Early Christian, and reflect all aspects of the life of the city, are grouped according to category: public buildings, sanctuaries, houses, villas and tombs. Although the public buildings are not common, there are some large deposits from sanctuaries, which betray the existence of sacred buildings. The scanty remains of domestic architecture are counterbalanced by the impressive mosaic pavements. Geometric burials follow the norm for the S Peloponnese, but the archaic type and the later type of two-storey, free-standing, family sepulchres, with ossuaries, are peculiar to Sparta.

The archaeological record reveals Sparta as a prosperous and important centre, which, in most material aspects, kept pace with the other city-states of mainland Greece. It is hoped that, however fragmentary this evidence may be, it will eventually contribute towards our understanding of the material appearance of the ancient city of Sparta.

WILLIAM CAVANAGH AND CHRISTOPHER MEE

Diversity in a Greek Landscape: the Laconia survey and rural sites project

The Laconia Rural Sites Project aimed to investigate small rural sites and the rural economy of Laconia in the prehistoric and historic periods. A set of twenty sites from the 400 discovered in the course of the Laconia Survey were selected for very intensive treatment. Our understanding of the nature of these sites is of critical importance to research into the rural economy of Greece over this very long span of time.

The sites have been investigated as fully as possible short of actual excavation. Thus all surface remains were closely plotted, geophysical survey investigated sub-surface features, soil, and magnetic and chemical characteristics were tested. The archaeological questions addressed are of great interest, not least given the prominence of archaeological field survey projects in recent years.

Small rural sites have been discovered in their hundreds, and this project investigates precisely the limits of interpretation given the extremely exiguous and fragmentary nature of the evidence. Our field methods were designed ex-pressly with these aims in mind. This article reviews the history of research and illustrates our results with one example.

KEITH WILKINSON

Geoarchaeological studies of the Spartan Acropolis and Evrotas Valley: some preliminary conclusions

This paper discusses the results of ongoing geoarchaeological work within the Evrotas Valley. Although the valley, and in particular the town of Sparta are comparatively well-known archaeologically, relatively little is known of the landscape history of the area prior to the nineteenth century. The geological history of the valley is also only understood on a broad level, with most significant events taking place in the Pliocene and Pleistocene. The importance of the deposits produced during these time frames is highlighted and the sedimentology is discussed in an attempt to outline 'background characteristics' of the local parent material. It is suggested that alterations from these properties are most likely to be the result of human activity or relatively recent diagenesis, both of which are of archaeological interest.

Attention is then focused upon a single sedimentary environment, that of Sparta's Roman Theatre. The results of detailed sedimentological investigation are presented showing that the theatre was deliberately located on clay strata of Pliocene/Pleistocene date, ideal for the location of foundations. Evidence is also put forward for the existence of a *terra rossa* soil predating the theatre which was largely removed during its construction. Post Roman deposits dating from the 8th to the 10th centuries contained within the theatre bowl are then discussed, and it is concluded that the characteristic green colour of these is inherited from Pliocene/Pleistocene parent material which has since eroded away.

Finally it is argued that the next stage of research should be a detailed study of the sub-surface stratigraphy beneath the central part of the Evrotas Valley, which could preserve evidence for landscape change since the Upper Palaeolithic.

DONALD NICOL

Byzantine Mistra—Sparta in the mind

Sparta was an archaising name for Mistra. No Byzantine writer, however, not even Gemistos Plethon, would have agreed with the learned M. de Pouqueville who, about 1800, declared that, while the ancient city of Sparta was little more than a name, yet 'it is evident that the modern town of Mistra is built upon its ruins'. The Byzantines knew better than that. To them Mistra was a real and lively place. Sparta was a historical fact or a political and philosophical abstraction; and it never occurred to Byzantine scholars to climb down and investigate its mortal remains. Better let it stay in the mind.

Περιλήψεις

H. W. CATLING

Το έργο της Αγγλικής Αρχαιολογικής Σχολής Αθηνών στη Σπάρτη και Λακωνία.

Η Αγγλική Αρχαιολογική Σχολή εργάζεται στη Λακωνία από το 1904. Ενώ η έρευνα από μεμονωμένους ερευνητές είναι αδιάκοπη από τότε (εκτός από τα διαλείματα των δύο Παγκοσμίων Πολέμων), η εργασία της Σχολής ως Ιδρύματος ανήκει σε τρείς φάσεις—η πρώτη από το 1904 έως το 1910, η δεύτερη από το 1924 έως το 1928, η τελευταία από το 1973 έως σήμερα. Πολλές ανασκαφές γίνονται στην ίδια τη Σπάρτη (στην Ακρόπολη, στον Μεγάλο Βωμό, στο ιερό της Ορθίας Αρτέμιδος) και επιπλέον στο Μενελαΐο, το Ελευσίνιον στα Καλύβια Σόχας, στο ιερό του Διός Μεσσαπέως στην Τσακώνα. Στην ευρύτερη περιφέρεια, ανασκάφτηκε ο προϊστορικός οικισμός στον ΄Αγιο Στέφανο, στην πεδιάδα του Έλους, ερευνήθηκε η ενάλια προϊστορική θέση του Παυλοπετρίου στο Ελαφονήσι, και εξετάσθηκαν μικρές θέσεις στο Κουτιφάριο και την Αγγελώνα. Τοπογραφικές εργασίες, επίσης, έχουν πραγματοποιηθεί, ιδιαίτερα η έρευνα της προϊστορικής Λακωνίας πριν και μετά τον 2° Παγκόσμιο Πόλεμο, και η Laconia Survey της δεκαετίας του '80, πραγματοποιηθείσα από τη Σχολή σε συνεργασία με το Πανεπιστήμιο του Amsterdam. ΄Ολοι οι κλάδοι της μελέτης συνεχίζονται μέχρι και σήμερα.

ΘΕΟΔΩΡΟΣ ΣΠΥΡΟΠΟΥΛΟΣ

Πελλάνα· το διοικητικό κέντρο της Λακωνίας

Η Πελλάνα, ένα απομακρυσμένο και ξεχασμένο χωριό κοντά στο όρος Ταΰγετος, αποδεικνύεται σήμερα ένα προϊστορικό κέντρο ιδιάζουσας σημασίας. Κατά τη διάρκεια της δεκαετίας του 1930 δύο λαξευτοί θολωτοί τάφοι, μετρίων διαστάσεων, καθαρίστηκαν από τον Τ. Καραχάλιο. Πενήντα χρόνια αργότερα, τρείς μνημειώδεις θόλοι ανασκάφησαν από τον γράψαντα. Αυτοί χρονολογούνται κατά την ΥΕ ΙΙ–ΙΙΙΒ/Γ1 περίοδο. Στην Ακρόπολη της Πελλάνας σημαντικά ευρήματα ήρθαν στο φως, που μαρτυρούν τη σημασία της περιοχής κατά τη διάρκεια της Πρώϊμης Εποχής του Χαλκού και της Υστεροελλαδικής περιόδου· ένας μεγάλος δρόμος που ανέρχεται την ανατολική πλευρά του λόφου, δύο ή ίσως περισσότεροι τύμβοι, ένας Μυκηναϊκός οικισμός (ΥΕ ΙΙΙΑ–ΙΙΙΒ/Γ1) και πρόσφατα ένα σύνολο κάθετων λακκοειδών τάφων της ΜΕ ΙΙΙ/ΥΕ Ι.

Η Πελλάνα πιθανόν ταυτίζεται με τη Μυκηναϊκή Λακεδαίμονα, τη βασιλική κατοικία του Τυνδάρεω και του Μενέλαου. Απομένει να βρεθεί το Μυκηναϊκό ανάκτορο, το οποίο πιθανότατα κείται κοντά στην πηγή Πελλανίδα, νοτίως της Ακρόπολης της Πελλάνας των ιστορικών χρόνων.

PAUL CARTLEDGE

Πόλη και χώρα στη Σπάρτη από την αρχαϊκή στην ελληνιστική περίοδο

Ενώ η συνήθης και πρότυπη Ελληνική πόλη-κράτος συνδύαζε το άστυ με την ύπαιθρο σε μία αρμονική συμβίωση, η Σπάρτη από αυτή την άποψη ήταν μη τυπική, αν όχι μοναδική. Το Σπαρτιατικό σύστημα αστικοποίησης ήταν συνειδητά σχεδιασμένο για να τονίζει και να ενισχύει το διαχωρισμό του (αστικού) κέντρου από την περιφέρεια, καθώς επίσης και την ιεραρχική κυριαρχία του πάνω σε αυτή. Η ύπαρξη ή η απουσία (μέχρι και τη Μέση Ελληνιστική περίοδο) ενός τείχους που περιέκλειε την πόλη, ηταν ένας σαφής ιδεολογικός και χωροταξικός δείκτης της Σπαρτιατικής διαφοροποίησης.

REINHARD FÖRTSCH

Η Σπαρτιάτικη Τέχνη: οι πολλοί τρόποι της εξαφάνισής της

Η ανασκευή μέσω των αρχαιολογικών τεκμηρίων της εικόνας μιάς Σπάρτης χωρίς τέχνη δεν εξηγεί ικανοποιητικά το ρόλο της τέχνης στη Σπάρτη. Διερευνάται η παρακμή της Λακωνικής τέχνης με μέσο μια σύνοψη μιας σειράς ορισμένων 'τύπων'. Στο τρίτο τέταρτο του $6^{ου}$ αιώνα π.Χ. συμβαίνει μια αλλαγή. Ο αριθμός των νέων προϊόντων λιγοστεύει, τα προϊόντα που εξαφανίζονται φθάνουν στο μάξιμουμ, ενώ ο αριθμός των προϊόντων που συνυπάρχουν είναι, προς το παρόν, μόνον ελαφρώς μειωμένος. Ταυτόχρονα εμφανίζονται τρεις από τις πέντε μορφές που επρόκειτο να συνεχιστούν μέσα στον 5ο αιώνα π.Χ. Ερμηνεύω αυτό το φαινόμενο ως στατιστική συνέπεια μιας ριζικής αλλαγής του πολιτεύματος· μια αριστοκρατική, πολυτελής κοινωνία, με εικονιστική τέχνη, μετατοπίστηκε από την ιδεολογία των 'όμοίων', που υποστήριζε την ισότητα και κατέκρινε την πολυτέλεια.

STEPHEN HODKINSON

Είδη χάλκινων αναθέσεων στα Σπαρτιακά ιερά 650–350 π.Χ.: προς μια ποσοτική βάση δεδομένων του υλικού και της θρησκευτικής επένδυσης

Αυτή η παρουσίαση συνηγορεί προς μια νέα προσέγγυση στο Λακωνικό υλικό πολιτισμό, εξετάζοντας τα χάλκινα ευρήματα από Σπαρτιατικά ιερά της περίοδου 650–350 π.Χ. με αναφορά στην υλική και θρησκευτική επένδυση. Η θεμελιώδης προϋπόθεση για αυτήν την προσέγγυση είναι μια πλήρης βάση δεδομένων από τα ευρήματα. Σημαίνονται τα εμπόδια που υπάρχουν στη δημιουργία μίας τέτοιας βάσης. Ωστόσο τονίζεται ότι ακόμη και τα ελλειπή στοιχεία που έχουμε στη διάθεση μας σήμερα αποδεικνύουν την αξία μιας ποσοτικής προσέγγισης που επιτρέπει σύγκριση των Σπαρτιατικών λατρευτικών αναθημάτων με παρόμοια από άλλες θέσεις της Ελλάδας. Τα είδη των Σπαρτιατικών αναθέσεων συμφωνούν με τις γενικές τάσεις στην Ελλάδα και παρέχουν ελάχιστη υποστήριξη για την υποτιθέμενη εξέλιξη μιας εξαιρετικά λιτής κοινωνίας των υστεροαρχαϊκών και κλασσικών χρόνων.

CONRAD M. STIBBE

Ασυνήθη σχήματα και διακοσμητικά θέματα στη Λακωνική κεραμεική

Δεδεδομένου ότι η Σπάρτη καταλαμβάνει μία ιδιαίτερη θέση ανάμεσα στις ελληνικές πόλεις-κράτη κατά τους προ-ελληνιστικούς χρόνους, θα περιμέναμε να βρούμε κάποιου είδους αντανάκλαση αυτού του ιδιαίτερου πολιτιστικού και πολιτικού καθεστώτος στη μικροτεχνία της, και κυρίως στην κεραμεική. Το παρόν άρθρο επιδιώκει να δείξει οτι αυτή είναι μία ρεαλιστική προσδοκία. Τα ακόλουθα εξαιρετικά αντικείμενα μελετώνται, μερικά εκ των οποίων έχουν ασυνήθη διακόσμηση: πέντε σωληνοειδή ρυτά (tubes) η υπόστατα (ένα προϊόν εξαγωγής), ένα θραύσμα ενεπίγραφης όλπης, δύο λήκυθοι με επίμηκες σώμα (εκ των οποίων η μία είχε εξαχθεί), μία σειρά ληκύθων με σφαιρικό σώμα (πολλές προϊόντα εξαγωγής), μία πρόχους με εξαιρετικά επιμήκη λαιμό και μία αττική κύλιξ τύπου C με παράξενη επιγραφή η οποία βρέθηκε σε ένα Λακωνικό ιερό. Η ερμηνεία των σχημάτων και των διακοσμητικών θεμάτων θα συντελέσει στην κατανόηση του αρχαϊκού πολιτισμού των Σπαρτιατών.

TYLER JO SMITH

Χορός, πιοτό και αφιερώσεις· ο αρχαϊκός 'κωμός' στη Λακωνία.

Το μοτίβο του κωμαστή εμφανίζεται στη Λακωνική τέχνη κατά τον 6 αιώνα π.Χ. Ο κυβιστής γλεντοκόπος, συνήθης στην Κορινθιακή και Αττική αγγειογραφία, παίρνει τη χαρακτηριστκή του μορφή στην τέχνη της αρχαϊκής Λακωνίας. Το παρόν άρθρο εξετάζει την εικονογραφία του Λακωνικού 'κωμου' στην αγγειογραφία και τις άλλες μορφές της τέχνης, συμπεριλαμβανομένων των μολύβδινων ειδωλίων και των χάλκινων αντικειμένων. Η αρχαϊκή Σπάρτη παρουσιάζει την πρώτη και μοναδική περίπτωση χρήσεως του ειδωλίου του κωμαστή για θρησκευτικούς ή αναθηματικούς σκοπούς. Αμφισβητείται ότι οι χορευτές-κωμαστές μπορεί να διατηρούν μία ιδιαίτερη τοπική λειτουργία στην αρχαϊκή Σπάρτη.

ΜΑΡΙΑ ΠΙΠΙΛΗ

Αρχαϊκή Λακωνική αγγειογραφία· μερικές εικονογραφικές παρατηρήσεις

Μία ενδιαφέρουσα κατηγορία αρχαϊκών Λακωνικών αγγείων ειναι αυτά που φερουν παραστάσεις που φαίνεται πως έχουν θρησκευτικό χαρακτήρα·συμπόσια στα οποία μετέχουν μικροί φτερωτοί δαίμονες, κωμαστές που χορεύουν γύρω από μία επιβλητική μορφή μουσικού, ο ιππέας που συνοδεύεται από φτερωτούς δαίμονες, θεοί μόνοι τους ή με λατρευτές που έρχονται προς αυτούς. Από τους πέντε κύριους Λάκωνες αγγειογράφους, ο Ζωγράφος της Ναυκράτεως ήταν εκείνος που εισήγαγε τις περισσότερες από αυτές τις παραστάσεις, προσδίνοντας στη Λακωνική εικονογραφία μεγάλο μέρος του εκκεντρικού της χαρακτήρα. Προτείνεται εδώ ότι αγγεία με τέτοιες παραστάσεις κατασκευάζονταν κυρίως για τις ανάγκες συγκεκριμένων ιερών, ιδίως του Ηραίου της Σάμου όπου έχουν βρεθεί πολλά τέτοια αγγεία. Εξετάζονται επίσης άλλα Λακωνικά αγγεία, που ίσως ήταν και αυτά ειδικές παραγγελίες για λατρευτικές ανάγκες και θίγεται το πρόβλημα της σχέσης μεταξύ του θεματολογίου των αγγείων και του τόπου εύρεσής τους.

G. B. WAYWELL, J. J. WILKES KAI S. E. C. WALKER

Το Αρχαίο Θέατρο της Σπάρτης

Οι πρόσφατες μελέτες των λειψάνων της σκηνής και της σκηνικής κατασκευής του Θέατρου της Σπάρτης έχουν διαφωτίσει την κατασκευαστική τους ιστορία. Το κοίλον και η ορχήστρα, που κατασκευάστηκαν περίπου το 20 π.Χ., αρχικά είχαν στην πρόσοψη μία Δωρική κιονοστοιχία (Waywell). Έμπροσθεν υπήρχε μία εξέδρα, η οποία μπορούσε να μετακινηθεί εκτός θέας, πάνω σε λίθινες αύλακες, προς τη δυτική πάροδο (Wilkes). Αυτή η διαρρύθμιση αντικαταστάθηκε κατά τη Φλάβεια περίοδο (μία επιγραφή του

78 π.Χ. αποτελεί την κυρία απόδειξη) από μία μόνιμη σκηνή μπροστά από μία κατασκευή (σκηνικό) με διώροφη, προεξέχουσα, κιονωτή πρόσοψη κορινθιακού ρυθμού (Walker). Αν και εκτενώς επισκευασμένη επανελειμένα, η διαρρύθμιση αυτή επιβίωσε μέχρι την παύση της λειτουργίας του θέατρου στα τέλη του 4^{ου} αιώνα.

ΑΝΑΣΤΑΣΙΑ ΠΑΝΑΓΙΩΤΟΠΟΥΛΟΥ
Ρωμαϊκά Ψηφιδωτά από τη Σπάρτη

Η Σπάρτη κατέχει εξέχουσα θέση μεταξύ των πόλεων που παρουσιάζουν παραγωγή ψηφιδωτών. Παρουσιάζεται εδώ η εξέλιξη της τέχνης του ψηφιδωτού, από την ελληνιστική εποχή ως την ύστερη αρχαιότητα, τα χαρακτηριστικά γνωρίσματα της κάθε περίοδου, ο πλούσιος γεωμετρικός διάκοσμος και τα εικονογραφικά θέματα που έχουν χρησιμοποιηθεί.

Τα ψηφιδωτά της Σπάρτης των ρωμαϊκών χρόνων είναι αξιοσημείωτα για τις παραστάσεις, που συνήθως απεικονίζονται στο κέντρο του δωματίου. Το υπόλοιπο δάπεδο καλύπτεται με γεωμετρικά κοσμήματα, θαυμαστής πολυχρωμίας και ποικιλίας. Η σύγκριση με σύγχρονα ψηφιδωτά, που προέρχονται από τον υπόλοιπο ελληνικό χώρο ή από άλλες ρωμαϊκές επαρχίες, υποδηλώνει ότι στην Σπάρτη υπήρχε εργαστήριο παραγωγής ψηφιδωτών και η μεγάλη ακμή του τοποθετείται στο δεύτερο μισό του τρίτου και τις πρώτες δεκαετίες του τέταρτου αιώνα.

ΑΝΝΑ ΚΑΡΑΠΑΝΑΓΙΩΤΟΥ
Ένα Ρωμαϊκό Πορτραίτο από τη Μονεμβασιά του Πρώϊμου 2^{ου} αιωνα π.Χ.

Το παρόν άρθρο εξετάζει ένα ανδρικό πορτραίτο από τη Μονεμβασιά, που χρονολογείται στον πρώϊμο 2^{ο} αιώνα μ.Χ. και διερευνά το στυλ, την προέλευση καθώς και τη σημασία του έργου για την κατανόηση του κοινωνικού και πολιτιστικού πλαισίου σε μία γωνιά του ρωμαϊκού κόσμου. Η τεχνική και η διάταξη της κόμης τοποθετούν το γλυπτό στην τραϊάνια–πρώϊμη αδριάνεια περίοδο. Ιδιαίτερες ομοιότητες επιδεικνύει το έργο με την εικονογραφία του Τραϊανού και ένα πρωϊμο τύπο του Αδριανού, όπως επίσης και με μορφές από την ανάγλυφη διακόσμηση στην Αψίδα του Τραϊανού στο Benevento κάθως και με παραδείγματα αυτοκρατορικής εικονογραφίας από την Αττική. Στενότερη εξέταση της τεχνοτροπίας και της τεχνικής οδηγεί στη συνδέση του γλυπτού μ'ένα αθηναϊκό εργαστήριο παραγωγής με σαφείς επιδράσεις από νεώτερα μητροπολιτικά ρεύματα στην τέχνη του πορτραίτου. Η ποιότητα και το περιεχόμενο του δημοσιευμένου έργου υποδηλώνουν πιθανή ταύτισή του με τον συγκλητικό Ηρακλανό, τον τελευταίο απόγονο της φημισμένης σπαρτιατικής αριστοκρατικής οικογένειας των Ευρυκλειδών.

ΣΤΕΛΛΑ ΡΑΥΤΟΠΟΥΛΟΥ
Νέα Ευρηματα από τη Σπάρτη

Η ανακοίνωση περιγράφει σύντομα τα αποτελέσματα σωστικών ανασκαφών σε οικόπεδα και δρόμους της Σπάρτης κατά τα έτη 1991–95. Τα ευρήματα των ανασκαφών, που καλύπτουν το χρονικό διάστημα από τα πρωτογεωμετρικά μέχρι και τα παλαιοχριστιανικά χρόνια, περιγράφονται κατά κατηγορίες: δημόσια και ιδιωτικά κτήρια, ιερά, ταφοι. Τα περισσότερα δημόσια κτήρια είναι ύστερορωμαϊκές βασιλικές, από τα ιερά βρίσκονται κατά κανόνα μεγάλοι αποθέτες αναθήματων, ενώ από τα σπίτια σώζονται ψηφιδωτά δάπεδα. Τα ταφικά έθιμα παρουσιάζουν ιδιαίτερο ενδιαφέρον, διότι ενώ κατά την πρωτογεωμετρική και γεωμετρική εποχή ακολουθούν τον διαδεδομένο τύπο, από τα αρχαϊκά χρόνια και μετά εμφανίζονται τοπικοί τύποι: είναι χαρακτηριστικοί οι διώροφοι, κτιστοί ελληνιστικοί οικογενειακοί τάφοι, που έχουν ανασκαφεί σε διάφορα σημεία. Τα ρωμαϊκά νεκροταφεία είναι μεγάλα και κανονικά οργανωμένα. Τα αρχαιολογικά ευρήματα μαρτυρούν με σαφήνεια ότι η Σπάρτη ήταν ένα σημαντικό και πλούσιο κέντρο, που ακολοθούσε σε πολλά σημεία τον κανόνα των πόλεων της κυρίως Ελλάδας. Τα λιγοστά και καταρχήν αποσπασματικά στοιχεία της ανακοίνωσης συμβάλλουν στη μελέτη της τοπογραφίας της Σπάρτης, και διαφωτίζουν αρκετά σκοτεινά σημεία της ιστορίας της.

WILLIAM CAVANAGH ΚΑΙ CHRISTOPHER MEE
Διαφοροποίηση στην Ελληνική Ύπαιθρο: η Laconia Survey και το Rural Sites Project

Το Laconia Rural Sites Project είχε σαν σκοπό τη διερεύνηση μικρών αγροτικών θέσεων και της αγροτικής οικονομίας της Σπάρτης κατά τους προϊστορικούς και ιστορικούς χρόνους. Μία ομάδα από 20 θέσεις (εκ των 400 που αποκαλύφθηκαν στα πλαίσια της Laconia Survey) επελέγησαν για περαιτέρω λεπτομερή μελέτη. Η κατανόηση της φύσης αυτών των θέσεων έχει εξαιρετική σημασία για τη διερεύνηση της αγροτικής οικονομίας της περιοχής κατά αυτό το μεγάλο χρονικό διάστημα. Οι θέσεις έχουν ερευνηθεί όσο το δυνατό πληρέστερα, ελλείψει πραγματικής ανασκαφής. Ωστόσο όλα τα επιφανειακά λείψανα αποτυπώθηκαν, η γεωφυσική μελέτη διερεύνησε τα υπό την επιφάνεια χαρακτηριστικά και του εδάφους, και εξετάστηκαν τα χημικά χαρακτηριστικά του. Τα αρχαιολογικά ερωτήματα που ετέθησαν ειναι μεγάλου ενδιαφέροντος, όσο και η σημασία των επιφανιακών ερευνών τα τελευταία χρόνια. Μικρές αγροτικές θέσεις έχουν βρεθεί κατά εκατοντάδες, και αυτό το πρόγραμμα διερευνά με ακρίβεια τα περιθώρια της ερμηνείας, δεδομένης της εξαιρετικά μικρής και αποσπασματικής φύσης των μαρτυριών. Οι μέθοδοι σχεδιάστηκαν ρητώς έχοντας υπ' όψη αυτούς τους στόχους. Το παρόν άρθρο κάνει μία ανασκόπηση του ιστορικού της έρευνας και παρουσιάζει τα αποτελέσματα με την ανάλυση ενός παραδείγματος.

KEITH WILKINSON
Γεω-αρχαιολογικές μελέτες στην Ακρόπολη της Σπάρτης και στην Κοιλάδα του Ευρώτα: προκαταρκτικά συμπεράσματα

Η παρούσα μελέτη σχολιάζει τα αποτελέσματα της εν εξελίξει γεω-αρχαιολογικής έρευνας στην κοιλάδα του Ευρώτα. Αν και η κοιλάδα, και ιδιαίτερα η πόλη της Σπάρτης είναι αρκετά γνωστή αρχαιολογικά, γνωρίζουμε σχετικά λίγα για την ιστορία του τόπου πρίν από το 19ο αιώνα. Η γεωλογική ιστορία της κοιλάδας είναι κατανοητή σε γενικές γραμμές, με πιο σημαντικά τα φαινόμενα της Πλειοκαίνου και της Πλειστοκαίνου περίοδου. Φωτίζεται η σημασία των καθιζήσεων που δημιουργήθηκαν κατά τη διάρκεια αυτών των περιόδων και συζητάται η ιζηματολογία σε μια προσπάθεια να δοθεί το περίγραμμα του γονικού τοπικού υλικού. Προτείνεται ότι οι μεταβολές από αυτές τις ιδιότητες είναι πιο πιθανό να αποτελούν αποτέλεσμα ανθρώπινης δραστηριότητας ή μιας πρόσφατης διαγένησης, δύο σημεία ιδιαίτερου αρχαιολογικού ενδιαφέροντος. Δίνεται ιδιαίτερη προσοχή σε ένα μοναδικό ιζηματογενές περιβάλλον, αυτό του ρωμαϊκού θεάτρου της Σπάρτης. Παρουσιάζονται τα αποτελέσματα της λεπτομερούς ιζηματολογικής έρευνας που δείχνουν ότι η επιλογή της θέσης του θεάτρου ήταν σκόπιμη και έγινε σε ιδανικά για τη θεμελίωση στρώματα πηλού της Πλειοκαίνου και Πλειστοκαίνου. Προβάλλονται επίσης τεκμήρια για την ύπαρξη terra rossa που χρονολογείται πριν από το θέατρο η οποία αφαιρέθηκε σε μεγάλο μέρος κατά τη διάρκεια της κατασκευής του. Στη συνέχεια σχολιάζονται τα μεταρωμαϊκά στρώματα χρονολογούμενα από τον 8ο ως το 10ο αιώνα μ.Χ. που περιέχονται στο κοίλο του θέατρου και συμπεραίνεται ότι το χαρακτηριστικό πράσινο χρώμα είναι συμφυές με το γονικό υλικό της Πλειοκαίνου-Πλειστοκαίνου που διαβρώθησαν. Τέλος προβάλλονται τα επιχειρήματα για το επόμενο στάδιο της έρευνας που θα πρέπει να είναι μία λεπτομερής μελέτη της υπόγειας στρωματογραφίας κάτω από το κεντρικό μέρος της κοιλάδας του Ευρώτα που θα μπορούσε να προβληθεί σαν αποδείξη για τις μεταβολές στο τοπίο από την εποχή της Ανώτερης Παλαιολιθικής.

DONALD NICOL
Ο Βυζαντινός Μυστράς και η Σπάρτη

Το όνομα Σπάρτη είχε δοθεί στο Μυστρά από τάση αρχαϊσμού. Όμως κανένας βυζαντινός συγγραφέας, ούτε καν ο Γεμιστός Πλήθων, δεν θα είχε συμφωνήσει με τον λογιώτατο M. de Pouqueville, όταν γυρω στο 1800 παρατηρούσε ότι, ενώ η αρχαία πόλη της Σπάρτης δεν ήταν πιά τίποτα περισσότερο από ένα όνομα, 'είναι φανερό ότι ο σύγχρονος Μυστράς έχει κτιστεί πάνω στα ερείπια της αρχαίας Σπάρτης'. Οι Βυζαντινοί είχαν καλύτερη αντίληψη των πραγμάτων· γιαυτούς ο Μυστράς ήταν ένας πραγματικός και ζωντανός τόπος. Η Σπάρτη ηταν ένα ιστορικό γεγονός ή μία πολιτική και φιλοσοφική αφηρημένη έννοια, και οι Βυζαντινοί λόγιοι δεν σκέφτηκαν ποτέ να κατέβουν χαμηλότερα και να αναζητήσουν τα θνητά λείψανά της. Προτίμησαν να την φυλάξουν έτσι στο μυαλό τους.

Preface and Acknowledgments

This volume presents the proceedings of the XIXth Classical Colloquium held at the British Museum on 6–8 December 1995. The success of the Colloquium owes much to its initiator and organiser, Dr Susan Walker (Deputy Keeper, Department of Greek and Roman Antiquities), who worked in collaboration with Professor G. B. Waywell of King's College and Professor J. J. Wilkes of the Institute of Archaeology, University College London, and with the British School at Athens. The British Museum is particularly grateful to the Managing Committee of the British School at Athens for agreeing to publish this volume. The task of preparing the papers for publication has been undertaken by Dr W. G. Cavanagh of the University of Nottingham, aided by Charlotte Westbrook Wilson (designer) and Susan Walker (co-editor).

The Department of Greek and Roman Antiquities is also pleased to record its thanks to the British Academy, King's College London and the Institute of Classical Studies, University of London for providing grants that enabled Greek scholars to attend and give papers. Here are published Maria Pipili's convincing demonstration of the religious purpose of much of the finest archaic Laconian vase-painting, Anastasia Panayiotopoulou's superbly illustrated survey of the workshops of mosaicists in Roman Sparta, and Stella Raftopoulou's exciting report of recent finds from rescue excavations. We are grateful to Dr Theodore Spyropoulos, Ephor of Classical Antiquities for Arcadia and Laconia, for permitting the publication of these and many other new finds, and for submitting his own most interesting paper on the important and little-known site of Pellana. In addition, the Caryatids, an international group of supporters of the Department, provided further support for the Colloquium, a fitting tribute to Artemis Caryatis of Laconia.

The future of Spartan archaeology depends on a precarious balance between hard-pressed archaeologists recording in the face of destruction from modern development and an international community of scholars, themselves working with very limited resources and opportunities for fieldwork. One of the benefits of a colloquium such as this is to bring together scholars from many countries with a common interest in Sparta, and to draw to the attention of their audience the enormity of the task in recording and understanding a great and previously underestimated heritage. As Donald Nicol brilliantly evokes in his contribution on Byzantine Mistra, ancient Sparta was much in the mind, but not investigated in the soil. Like the sages of Mistra, modern tourists know that the great site they see is not ancient Sparta, but few have the inclination or time to seek it out. We hope that the publication of these colloquium papers will show readers the nature of what has been missed, and that they will urge action to raise Sparta's profile for archaeologists and visitors alike, and, not least, for the community of modern Sparta, which takes a lively interest and pride in its remarkable past.

Dyfri Williams,
Keeper of Greek and Roman Antiquities,
The British Museum.

I

The work of the British School at Athens at Sparta and in Laconia

H. W. Catling

We are all most grateful to the Greek and Roman Department of the British Museum, and especially to the Keeper, Dr Dyfri Williams, and to Dr Susan Walker, for organising this Colloquium on 'Sparta in Laconia', the interest of which is so full of promise. How splendid to see so many colleagues who have taken the trouble to come from abroad to participate. We are much disappointed, nevertheless, that Dr Th. Spyropoulos, Ephor of Antiquities for Arkadia-Laconia, should have been prevented from joining us, at the very last minute. Happily, however, he has sent his paper on his work at Pellana for a colleague to read on his behalf. We welcome members of his staff, including Ms Stella Raftopoulou, who has recently done a great deal to help those of us here currently working in Laconia. I can think of no more appropriate way in which to begin this Colloquium than by a warm and sincere expression of gratitude to them and all our other Greek colleagues who have been responsible for approving and supporting British work in Laconia over many years. At the same time, let me express our warm appreciation of the *philoxenia* which continues to be shown to us in all Laconian quarters.

As an introduction to this Colloquium's serious business on Thursday and Friday, I have been asked to give a survey of work in Laconia in general, at Sparta in particular, undertaken by the British, especially by the British School at Athens, over the past nine decades (Catling H. W. 1986b). I must, of course, disclaim any particular virtue for British work and remind you of the great importance of other work, notably that by generations of Greek scholars, the weight and significance of which will certainly be highlighted during the days ahead.

While the word 'Sparta' has a major role in our Colloquium's title, there is work to which I must refer on a wider Laconian canvas since, from the beginning, British scholars have been active in many parts of Laconia, as well as at many points in Sparta. This may to some degree have been the result of the narrow financial constraints under which the British School operated in its early years, preventing it from undertaking any one massive field commitment—massive in terms of the cost of land acquisition on a grand scale, massive in terms of the corresponding operational costs commensurate with, say, those of the French School at Delphi, or of the German Institute at Olympia. There has also been a far from contemptible British tradition of research programmes designed and executed by individuals—scholars who have preferred to follow their own lines of inquiry, by their own methods, rather than join a monolithic enterprise with a permanent commitment to it. In saying this, I am neither applauding nor deploring the phenomenon, merely referring to it as a factor that has played a part. As part of this tendency, there is a very strong British affection for topographic work, stronger than financial considerations on their own are sufficient to explain. Perhaps, for Laconia in particular, this has been an inheritance from the towering figure of Colonel Martin Leake (Wagstaff 1992).

In any event, as I hope to show, British work in Laconia since the beginning of the century has undertaken both extensive and intensive topographic study, excavation of both single-period and multi-period sites, urban, rural, religious, as well as study and analysis of categories of Laconian material remains, with pride of place perhaps going to epigraphy, but important work having also been done in ceramic studies. More recently, the British have taken the lead in the application of scientific techniques, applying, for instance, geo-physical procedures to site-location and investigation, as well as utilising a wide range of techniques in materials analysis (Jones *et al.* 1986). The existence of the Fitch Laboratory as an integral part of the Athens School has much to do with this.

Although outside my brief this evening, it must not be forgotten that British scholars who have worked in Greece under the aegis of the British School have played a significant role in elucidating the complexities of Spartan history. I think of G. L. Huxley (Huxley 1962), Paul Cartledge (e.g. Cartledge 1979), J. T. Hooker (Hooker 1983), Paul Cartledge and Tony Spawforth (Cartledge and Spawforth 1989), not to mention fundamental studies of Spartan land management and inheritance by Stephen Hodkinson (Hodkinson 1986, 1989, 1992).

Though British interest in Sparta and Laconia has been continuous during the present century, for a number of extraneous reasons with which I shall not trouble you, the institutional interest of the British

School has been concentrated in three periods, the first from 1904 to 1910, the next from 1924 to 1927, the third and current phase from 1973 onwards. From the outset, this interest has been catholic, embracing a chronological spectrum of study from the Bronze Age, via the pinnacles of Archaic and Classical Sparta, to the Imperial Roman epilogue and its Late Antique and Medieval aftermath. Circumstances have created gaps in this sequence, it is true. Some of them may be attributed to site-location shift, a phenomenon to which Sparta has been particularly subject. The earliest 'Sparta' seems to have been the low mound site at Kouphovouno, half-way between Sparta and the village of Ayios Ioannis (Hope Simpson and Dickinson 1979: 110, no. C. 6). Bronze Age Sparta lay on the Menelaion spur, E of the river, two miles or so from the modern town (Hope Simpson and Dickinson 1979: 107–08, no. C. 1) Dark Age, Archaic, Classical through to Imperial Roman Sparta stood on and around the complex of low hills whose existence (excepting the acropolis) is now muffled by the modern town. The successor, Lakedaimonia, was restricted to the acropolis area, until the move to Mystras, under the walls of Villehardouin's citadel. Most recently, Sparta returned to its present site, at the end of the War of Independence.

Before we embark on a general account of work and discoveries, there is a significant extraneous factor of which account must be taken, for it significantly affects the quality and quantity of information about Sparta recoverable from archaeological procedures, for it may not occur to those coming fresh to the subject. The forces of nature over the centuries have exacted a terrible toll from the region's ancient sites and their surroundings. Without first-hand experience of the extent to which sites can be ravaged and degraded by storm-water in a region of soft geology such as the sediments on the E bank of the Eurotas it is difficult to understand how loss can be suffered on such a scale. I have myself had personal experience of this destructiveness from all parts of the Menelaion site (e.g. Catling 1978) and from the sanctuary at Aphyssou, Tsakona (Catling 1990b). But the most potent illustration of the degree of destruction achievable in a single episode comes from John Cook's account (Cook and Nicholls 1950) of the work he did in 1949 at Kalyvia tis Sochás, up against the Taygetos foothills, not far S of Sparta, at the site of the Eleusinion, in which there had been earlier British interest (Dawkins 1911). Cook had been invited to investigate a find made in extraordinary circumstances. This is what he says:

> 'The river broke its left bank at the mouth of the gorge and a torrent swept through the village (Cook is speaking of October, 1947), washing away 30 houses and scores of trees on its way. Just below the point where it broke out the torrent gouged out a new bed about 10 metres wide to a depth of three metres and more, exposing a row of foundation blocks in either bank . . . Heavy marble blocks and stelai were dislodged from the bed and carried as much as 1000 yards downstream, while miniature vases and other light debris were washed across the main Sparta-Gytheon road to the Eurotas.'

A few weeks ago, I made my first visit to the Archaeological Museum of Taranto where a number of justly famous Archaic Laconian vases from the ancient cemeteries of Taras are displayed (Curci *et al.* 1994). Their great beauty is enhanced by their pristine condition, a condition that is in marked contrast to the deplorable state in which much Laconian pottery is found in and around Sparta, making study laborious and frustrating. Local soil chemistry is particularly malignant.

Before the British School began its work in Laconia in 1904, it had achieved distinction elsewhere in Greece for its work at a number of prehistoric sites, including Knossos, Zakro and Palaikastro on Crete and Phylakopi on Melos. Work in the post-Bronze Age field seemed less assured and lacked commitment. If we exclude F. C. Penrose's investigation at the Temple of Olympian Zeus in Athens (work, indeed, on which he had already been engaged before the opening of the School), and the work in Cyprus of 1887–88, at Paphos, Marion and Salamis, there had been a School undertaking at Megalopolis in the years 1890–93, a short involvement (1893) at Aegosthena, inconclusive digs in 1894 at Abae and Hysiae in Phokis, and the now almost forgotten 1896–97 work in the Kynosarges area of Athens, under Cecil Harcourt-Smith, during his Directorship of the School (Waterhouse 1986). We may be certain that those who began the Sparta undertaking in 1904 fully intended to put behind them these less than convincing undertakings, and produce something of substance, coherence and lasting value in Laconia.

The School's original strategy for Laconia in the early 1900s was in many ways a preview of procedures now *de rigueur* for working in a new area, or on a new site. Marcus Tod and Alan Wace reviewed the existing material *testimonia* by examining the contents of the Sparta Museum, leading to the publication of Wace and Tod, 1906. Tod was responsible for inscriptions, Wace for sculpture and minor antiquities. Each man wrote a general introduction to his own section, showing a mature and thorough grasp of the interest and importance of the material. Tod, certainly, was already recognised as an accomplished epigrapher. Alan Wace's astonishing versatility is seen to advantage in his account of the sculpture. Had the same thoroughness been maintained throughout the course of this phase of the Sparta work, it would have been hard to criticise.

The School's first phase at Sparta lasted for seven years. The *Annuals* of the School for those years contain a miscellany of articles in which aspects of the work were described, with varying degrees of authority. Some articles are no more than interim accounts of the stages of the excavations undertaken (e.g. Bosanquet 1907), though in a number of cases these interim accounts have proved the only published record of particular excavated sites (e.g. Dickins 1907b). Other papers, such as Wace's classification of lead votive offerings from the Menelaion (Wace 1909) were definitive, and of permanent value (for a more recent approach to the study of these lead offerings see Cavanagh and Laxton 1984).

The First World War must have been at least partly responsible for the failure of those involved in Phase One to have published more than a single monograph describing their results. The monograph in question was Dawkins *et al.* 1929, describing the sanctuary of Artemis Orthia, certainly the most important single site investigated in the period 1906–10.

Before turning to Artemis Orthia, however, there are some early papers published in *Annual of the British School at Athens*, 10–17, (covering the years 1903–1911) to be considered, for they offer an *aide-mémoire* for a miscellany of activities.

Tod, 1904 is a very professional study of a number of *sphaireis* inscriptions, found in Sparta before the beginning of British work (later supplemented by Tod 1907). His mantle as epigrapher was then assumed by H. J. W. Tillyard (e.g. Tillyard 1906); his place was later taken by A. W. Woodward (e.g. Woodward 1909). E. S. Forster described ancient sites in S. W. Laconia (Forster 1904a), and inscriptions that he had recorded (Forster 1904b). His work was characteristic of his time, beginning with his thorough knowledge of the literary *testimonia* for the ancient sites which *ought* to exist in a particular area, leading to the attempt to identify such sites in the field. Neither he nor his contemporaries thought this might be to put the cart before the horse, and opted, instead, to make a thorough examination of the terrain, before reaching for a well-thumbed copy of Pausanias.

Three small excavations in widely separated parts of Laconia were reported in *Annual of the British School at Athens* 10 and 11. Guy Dickins described his search for the site of the dream-oracle of Ino-Pasiphaë, placed by Pausanias near the town of Thalamae, the site of which Dickins believed he had found near the modern village of Koutiphari (Dickins 1905). He considered his finds supported the identification, but the evidence is not compelling.

At Geraki (ancient *Geronthrae*), Wace, Tillyard and Hasluck, with Pausanias once more to help them, made trial excavations in search of the Temple of Ares and its grove, the Agora and its springs, and a temple of Apollo on the acropolis (Wace and Hasluck 1905b). These efforts were unsuccessful, but the party took full note of a great defensive wall surviving on the acropolis, remarking on the primitive character of its construction and raising, at least, the possibility that it might date to the Bronze Age. Their evident disappointment at their results suggests they did not fully appreciate the interest of what they *had* found, which included prehistoric deposits on the acropolis, and an important Middle Helladic cist grave, to which Wace was to do greater justice in a later publication (Wace 1910). It is revealing that at Geraki the chance finds of inscriptions (Tillyard 1905) and sculpture (Wace 1905) made before the excavation were studied and reported with a care and confidence that is missing in the account of the fieldwork. As many of you will know, the British School has recently ceded any claim that it might be considered to have to future work at Geraki to our Dutch Colleagues. Later in this meeting we look forward to hearing from Professor Joost Crouwel, of Amsterdam University, concerning the results of his first season's work at Geraki this year.

The third minor excavation took place at Angelona, not far from Epidauros Limera, where Wace and Hasluck salvaged material from a small Archaic and later heroön which had been brought to light by cultivation. This last seems largely to have destroyed the site (Wace and Hasluck 1905a). The site, which now lacks surface indications, is in an area of considerable, but largely untapped, archaeological potential.

Other papers demonstrate the very wide range of Laconian interests in the British School in those first years. In one, Wace considered Frankish reliefs at Parori and at Geraki (Wace 1905b). Elsewhere, Traquair gave an account of mediaeval fortresses (Traquair 1906a). Considering the richness of Sparta itself in Byzantine and Mediaeval remains, it is disappointing that interest in these periods of its history was almost entirely suppressed in the work carried out there. A six-page article on the Byzantine pottery of Sparta (Dawkins and Droop 1911) is only a small consolation.

Full-scale work began at Sparta in 1906, in the hands of many individuals who were to follow it to its end, individuals who would be responsible for much that was to be written about it. The Director of the School, R. C. Bosanquet, was in charge, assisted by R. M. Dawkins, who the following year was to succeed him both as School Director and director of the Sparta undertaking. With them were Guy Dickins, J. P. Droop, H. J. W. Tillyard and A. J. B. Wace. This first year was a very active one. Its prime objective was the definition of the city's topography (Bosanquet 1906a; Dickins 1906c). Work centred on the acropolis, and the Late Period fortification surrounding it (Traquair 1906); this led to a rather slight study of a large stoa within the SE quadrant of these fortifications (Traquair 1906), a stoa of which more will shortly be heard. The first examination was made of the Theatre

(Dickins 1906b). Both these great Imperial Roman buildings—Theatre and Stoa—have very recently been re-examined by Professor Geoffrey Waywell and Professor John Wilkes, who have published accounts of their results (Waywell, Wilkes *et al.* 1993; Waywell and Wilkes 1994), and from whom we shall have news of their most recent work during the Colloquium.

An elegant topographic study was made during 1906 of the earlier fortification circuit, dated to the third century BC. In this, as in much else, A. J. B. Wace played a leading role (Wace 1906a, 1907a). The wall was found to have been between 2.50 and 3.00 metres wide, had been built of mud-brick on a stone socle, its top weather-proofed by a coping of ceramic tiles, many of them stamped at manufacture to show they had been made for this particular contract (and, in so doing, to discourage their misappropriation by the unscrupulous). Wace was able to show that even where the remains of the wall had totally vanished below ground, its course could be established by surface finds of these distinctive tile-stamps (Wace 1906b, 1907b).

The E sector of this defensive circuit lay near the W bank of the Eurotas, where in the scarp cut by riverine incursions, several important sites were identified, chief amongst them the sanctuary of Artemis Orthia (Bosanquet 1906b), of which more will be said below. Before this, however, we may remark upon a site identified and excavated by Guy Dickins close to the river, not far S of the modern bridge. Here he found and cleared a massive masonry platform, nearly 24.0 metres long, over 6.60 wide, still standing nearly 2,00 metres high. He sought a date in the style of masonry, no later than mid-second century BC and an identity by comparison with the Great Altar at Megalopolis (Dickins 1906a).

Still further S, within the circuit of the earlier fortification wall and close to it, a succession of deposits was found containing pottery, terracotta relief plaques and other finds from Geometric to Classical times, including fragments of a very fine Archaic relief pithos decorated with battle scenes (Wace 1906b). On the strength of the hero-relief plaques, Wace identified this as the remains of a heroön. It is regrettable that more work was not attempted here, and that the publication of the material was so eclectic, for early deposits unencumbered by later remains are rare at Sparta. The site included a pithos burial containing two vases. Professor Conrad Stibbe has recently reported that the remains of this site are no longer to be identified.

Burials of any period are rare, not only in Sparta itself, but everywhere in Laconia. That the British found no cemeteries made it much more difficult to construct a relative sequence of decorated and other pottery. It has also greatly limited what can be said about Dark Age Sparta (Desborough 1952; Coldstream 1968; Coulson 1985). To this day understanding of the earliest development of the site is very restricted, as would be our knowledge of early Athens without its Protogeometric and Geometric cemeteries.

Wace and Dickins did in fact identify and excavate a small number of built tombs that they dated from the mid-second to the late first century BC. They lay not far from the so-called Tomb of Leonidas. The report, including an account of an interesting series of clay vases and lamps, was summary (Wace and Dickins 1907).

After working on the Great Altar, Dickins transferred to the acropolis where, above (to the N that is) and close to the theatre, he identified the site of the shrine of Athena Chalkioikos, one of the most noted of Spartan religious centres, well attested in the literary sources (Dickins 1907, 1908). Pathetically little of the sanctuary remained; associated deposits divided into a Geometric stratum, and a 'Classical' level. The site, whose identification was confirmed by tile stamps, had been levelled when the theatre was built; it was further slighted by superincumbent Late Roman structures. Geometric pottery and later offerings (including good Archaic bronzes), and a fine Archaic relief dedicated by one Anaxibios (Dickins 1908) were found in wash levels. As we shall see, the area was further excavated under Woodward in the 1920s.

But it will be for the excavation of the sanctuary of Artemis Orthia that British work at Sparta will almost certainly longest be remembered (Bosanquet 1906b; Dawkins 1907, 1908, 1909, 1910a, 1910b; Dawkins et al. 1929). The work was prolonged and difficult, yielding enormous quantities of material of all categories; it seems to have taken heavy toll not only of the School's material resources, but of the stamina and resolution of the participants. The site was one of those exposed in the scarp of the river-bank. The early levels owed their relatively good state of preservation to the construction of a theatral building over them in the third century AD. In brief, excavation uncovered a succession of Archaic and later deposits, containing decorated pottery (Droop 1907, 1908, 1909; Dawkins *et al.* 1929), terracotta statuettes (Farnell 1908; Dawkins *et al.* 1929) and masks (Bosanquet 1906c; Dawkins *et al.* 1929), carved ivories (Dawkins 1907; Dawkins *et al.* 1929; Marangou 1969), bronze ornaments, etc., (Droop 1907a; Lamb 1928b; Dawkins *et al.* 1929), and tens of thousands of small lead figures and objects (Dawkins 1906; Dawkins *et al.* 1929) that had been offered to a female deity originally called, simply, Orthia, later Artemis Orthia (Bosanquet 1906c).

Recent views on the date of the successive phases of the decorated Laconian pottery found at the Orthia site (Boardman 1963) suggest that cult began rather later than Dawkins and his colleagues had calculated (Dawkins 1910; Dawkins *et al.* 1929). The cult may have started during the eighth century BC, but the first altar and temple seem no earlier than 700 BC, when a temenos wall was also built. The site was completely reorganised in the sixth century, perhaps in the wake of a damaging flood (Dawkins 1910b). As a part of the reorganisation, a larger temple and a new altar were built, the temenos was enlarged, and the earlier remains were covered and sealed by a layer of sterile sand. The new Archaic temple had *cella* and porch, with two columns *in antis* (Dawkins *et al.* 1929). Though hardly any of the superstructure survived, there is a hint that the pediment contained the sculptured stone figures of antithetic lions (Dawkins 1907). One or other, or both of the successive temples were finished with decorated terracotta disk-acroteria (Dawkins *et al.* 1929), most famously seen at Olympia, from the Hera temple. As Dr Nancy Winter has recently shown, such acroteria were almost certainly Laconian in origin (Winter 1993).

No finds from Sparta have played a more telling role than those from the Orthia site in demonstrating the artistic excellence of Archaic Sparta, and its merited place among contemporary Greek achievement. Perhaps the most important British contribution in Laconia will have been this demonstration of Sparta's involvement in the evolution of mainstream Archaic Greece (Waterhouse 1986).

Unlike some Laconian cults, devotion to Orthia remained popular down to, and during Roman times. It may have been little or no earlier than this that the notorious flogging of the ephebes became a feature of the cult. The first literary reference to this offensive practice—the *diamastigosis*—is in a Roman source of the first century BC. The final reconstruction of the shrine was its most monumental. During the third century AD the temple and altar were encapsulated within an amphitheatre, the ruins of which still survive. Until the later nineteenth century, this amphitheatre had been one of the most prominent of Sparta's ancient buildings (Bosanquet 1906). The Kabirion at Thebes was a not-dissimilar complex. The suggestion that this elaborate reconstruction was a response to the popularity of the *diamastigosis* seems far-fetched. In this new form, the Orthia sanctuary may have survived substantially undamaged until the sack by Alaric of AD 396.

As this first phase of British work at Sparta drew to its close, there came a sense of incipient *ennui*, and perhaps the participants were by now, if not disappointed with their results, by no means elated. After the first two years there had been no further casting about throughout the confines of the city for promising new sites. Instead, in 1909, some of them moved across the river up to the standing monument on the bluff overlooking the E bank of the Eurotas, long ago plausibly identified as the Menelaion by Ludwig Ross. Here they investigated a site which had already caught the imagination of several others (Wace, Thompson and Droop 1909). In a useful first season, they made an excellent plan and elevation of the shrine-building, and excavated previously untouched deposits containing votive debris on the E side, where they were rewarded by finding an important early bronze statuette of a woman (Wace, Thompson and Droop 1909: Pl. X). They returned in 1910 further to explore traces of Mycenaean buildings found the previous year. This led to R. M. Dawkins' part-excavation of a Mycenaean 'house', 200 metres from the Archaic shrine, and rather unproductive trenching in the vicinity. The work was not well done; the subsequent report was perfunctory (Dawkins 1910a). It was, indeed, time to stop.

Phase Two of British work at Sparta began in 1924, the year in which A. M. Woodward followed A. J. B. Wace as Director of the School, the year in which the Managing Committee of the School apparently decided that a period of work in classical sites should follow Wace's brilliant work at Mycenae (Waterhouse 1986). The decision was taken to return to Sparta, under Woodward's direction. He was assisted by J. P. Droop from the original Sparta team, and a number of newcomers, not least among whom was Piet de Jong, as architect-draughtsman. The return to Sparta must, surely, have been congenial to Woodward, whose epigraphic interests were almost certain to be fuelled by the decision to work on the acropolis, particularly on the Theatre (Woodward 1926a, 1926c, 1927a, 1928a; Woodward and Hobling 1926). If the manner of reporting the results of the work of Phase Two is a reliable indicator, Woodward in the 1920s played the role of project-director far more obviously than Bosanquet, or Dawkins look to have done in the earlier work. From the outside, it seems each of these acted as a *primus inter pares*, a situation reflected in the allocation of publication responsibilities in the Sparta sections of *Annual of the British School at Athens* 10–17. A comparison with Woodward's publication role in *Annual of the British School at Athens* 26–30 is instructive. Be that as it may, the resumption of work at the Theatre was rewarded by a very rich harvest of inscriptions cut on the E *parodos* wall, and on a number of blocks fallen from it (Woodward 1926c, 1927b). One of his assistants began the excavation of a church E of the Chalkioikos site and, near it, of the remains of a Roman house. An area to the N of the acropolis was tested, and a long sequence of occupation from Geometric times onward was noted (Woodward 1926a); it has to be regretted that nothing more was done at this last site. The chief pull, it is clear, continued to come from public buildings, and the implicit hope of yet more inscriptions.

Woodward's assistants returned to the very complicated area between the Chalkioikos site and the uppermost part of the theatre (Woodward and Hobling 1926; Woodward 1926d, 1928b). In four seasons' work an extensive wash level rich in early material was studied, together with the badly damaged remains of a portico close by S of Chalkioikos and parallel with it, and, further SW, the fragment of a building that Woodward suggested could have been another sanctuary; fragments of disk-acroteria found near it might have come from its roof, but could equally have been debris from Athena Chalkioikos (Woodward 1928b). In general, the early deposits were found much contaminated by later building; the upper levels seem largely to have consisted of material redeposited after the construction of the theatre. Small amounts of early Imperial pottery were found among much larger quantities of Archaic and Classical material (Droop 1928; Woodward 1929). It was from the SW area of this site that came the justly famous fragmentary Late Archaic statue of a warrior—the so-called 'Leonidas'—and parts of other monumental sculptures (Woodward and Hobling 1926; Woodward 1926d) that have been very fully studied (see references Palagia 1993: nn.13,14). Recently Professor Olga Palagia has published marble fragments of a decorated shield from this complex which she attributes to an Archaic Athena, not from the Chalkioikos shrine, but the shrine of Athena Er-gane, mentioned by Pausanias in the same breath as his account of Chalkioikos (Palagia 1993). It is very unfortunate that the archaeology of the whole Chalkioikos-theatre *cavea* wall area was so opaque, and that it was not reported in greater detail by its excavators.

Woodward worked on the Theatre throughout Phase Two (Woodward 1926b, 1927a, 1928a), and published a detailed account of the architecture (Woodward 1930a). Resources available to him during Phase Two were insufficient to permit the building's complete excavation, even had he wished to make the attempt. Further clearance has been undertaken by the Greek Archaeological Service (e.g. Christou 1962), including Mr George Steinhauer's excavation in the 1970s of Byzantine-period houses built on the NW arc of the *cavea*. And now, as I mentioned a moment ago, it has been thoroughly re-examined during the course of current British School work, by Professors Waywell and Wilkes (Waywell, Wilkes *et al.* 1995).

Throughout the first two phases of British School work at Sparta there was intense interest in epigraphy, reference to some of the results of which has already been made. Many new inscriptions came to light in both phases; these were promptly reported (Tillyard 1906; Tod, Tillyard and Woodward 1907; Woodward 1908, 1909, 1910, 1926c, 1927b, 1929, 1930b; Woodward and Robert 1929). Of more than 1600 pages of the eleven volumes of the *Annual of the British School at Athens* in which the Sparta work was reported, over a third were devoted to epigraphy. The three principal sources of lapidary inscriptions were, first, the third-century AD amphitheatre at Artemis Orthia, where many dedications were found in secondary use. These had been set up by victors, chiefly boys, in musical and athletic competitions. They have considerable prosopographic interest. A second rich source has been the Late Fortification Wall, in whose construction is much *spolia*, (eg Woodward 1908). Thirdly, the *parodos* wall of the Theatre provided a rich quarry of texts, including lists of magistrates, and the *cursus* of individual Spartan officials (Woodward 1926). These date from the first half of the second century AD, and, again, provide an important source of prosopographic reference. A vivid illustration is provided by the eighteen-line *cursus* of C. Julius Theophrastos, Ephor in the year of Hadrian's second visit to Sparta, on two occasions member of an embassy to Rome, among a long line of distinctions which reveal him as a tireless, well-connected, well-to-do man of affairs who, in his prime, may well have aspired to even greater distinction (Cartledge and Spawforth 1993).

Many of the Archaic and Classical inscriptions are very concise dedications cut on pottery (Woodward 1930b) or bronze (e.g. Lamb 1928a) offerings, telling us relatively little. An exception is the so-called Hymn to Athena, found near the Chalkioikos site in 1927. Ann Jeffrey considered the mutilated text (which she dated 530–500 BC) is more probably a dedication to Athena made by the victor in some contest, than a Hymn (Jeffrey 1990).

Although it would be 45 years from the last year of Woodward's work at Sparta before the School again undertook a prolonged period of Spartan work, much happened, piecemeal, in the intervening years. Arthur Lane published what was for long to be the standard study of Laconian vase-painting (Lane 1936), in which he combined a re-examination of the British material from Sparta with other finds, not least those from Magna Graecia. Other contributions to the difficult topic of post-Bronze Age Laconian ceramics were made by V. R. Desborough (Desborough 1948), R. M. Cook (R. M. Cook 1972) and J. N. Coldstream (Coldstream 1968).

Though A. J. B. Wace's chief interests had distanced him from Laconia from the Great War onwards, he never forgot or lost interest in it. Dr Elizabeth French has told me, indeed, that her father would much have liked to have returned to the Mycenaean site at the Menelaion. Other preoccupations prevented this, but Wace was certainly responsible for encouraging Helen Thomas (now Lady Waterhouse) before the Second World War, and Richard Hope Simpson, after it, to make a topographic study of prehistoric Laconia, exploring it on foot, and recording all the Bronze Age sites that came to notice. This they did, severally, and subsequently jointly reported their results in a two-part paper (Waterhouse and Hope Simpson 1960, 1961). Here was an extensive survey of the region with results and supporting evidence described in a much more sophisticated way than had previously been attempted. The importance of their findings for our present understanding of Bronze Age Laconia must be given unstinting recognition and admiration, even if, by comparison with current surface survey theory, their procedures seem simplistic. With O. T. P. K. Dickinson, Hope Simpson would later expand the Laconia work in the appropriate section of their *Gazetteer* (Hope Simpson and Dickinson 1979). and another version of the same from his pen alone (Hope Simpson 1981).

The British School was very briefly involved in Laconian rescue-excavation in 1949 at Kalyvia tis Sochás (J. M. Cook) and in Sparta itself (R. V. Nicholls), but the times were difficult, and work was not continued (Cook and Nicholls 1950). Another ten years passed before the School undertook excavation in Laconia. When it came, the stimulus had been provided by the Waterhouse-Hope Simpson topographic work. In 1959, Lord William Taylour began to excavate the important Bronze Age settlement at Ayios Stephanos, on a low hill on the very W edge of the Helos plain, in the lands of the modern village of Stephaniá (Hood 1960, 1961; Taylour 1962; Megaw 1964; Taylour *et al.* 1972). The site is close to the quarry source, in the lands of Krokeai, of *lapis lacedaemonius*, the highly decorative hard dark green stone much sought after at different times in antiquity (Warren 1992). In the same year, soundings were made at another Bronze Age site at Asteri, in the opposite, E side of the Helos plain. The Ayios Stephanos results were as encouraging as those at Asteri were disappointing; work was temporarily discontinued after the 1963 season, but was resumed in the 1970s (Catling 1974a, 1975, 1978; Taylour 1970). Of particular interest is the strong Minoanising influence on the site's pottery at the beginning of the Mycenaean period, *c.* 1600 BC. Much of this material has been separately published by S. and J. Rutter (Rutter and Rutter 1976). Not surprisingly, the Rutters were able to point to links between Ayios Stephanos finds and the results of the excavation of the 1960s at the Kastri settlement on the island of Kythera by G. L. Huxley and J. N. Coldstream (Coldstream and Huxley 1972). There is a shared link with Crete. Work on the final publication of the Ayios Stephanos excavation has reached an advanced state; it is sad that Lord William Taylour did not live to see its completion.

In 1968, A. M. Harding, G. Cadogan and R. J. Howell collaborated in the survey of a submerged Bronze Age settlement site and associated cemetery at Pavlopetri, Elaphonisi, close to Neapolis, in SE Laconia. Their report (Harding, Cadogan and Howell 1969) is illustrated by excellent plans of the flooded town. Perhaps because of the inevitable uncertainties concerning the chronology of the site (pottery gave a wide bracket of Early to Late Helladic for its occupation), this work has received less attention than it deserves, and it should certainly be retrieved from its relative obscurity.

An event took place in Oxford in 1970 which has turned out to have exercised a profound influence on the work of the British School in Laconia. Towards the end of my service at the Ashmolean Museum, Miss Katie Demakopoulou, as she then was (now Dr K. Demakopoulou-Papantoniou, Director of the National Museum in Athens), Epimeletria in the Arkadia-Laconia Ephoreia, came to Oxford with a British Council scholarship to further her work on Mycenaean Laconia. I was asked to meet Miss Demakopoulou to discuss her work on a regular basis. During this period it became known that I was to move to the School in Athens, news which prompted Katie Demakopoulou to remonstrate with me over British neglect of the Mycenaean site at the Menelaion, in the importance of which she firmly believed, and in the unfinished state of the excavation of which she was convinced. I took note of this advice and, once established in Athens, with my wife and R. N. L. Barber, made a first visit to the Menelaion, where I was completely captivated by the ambience, and struck by the potential of the Mycenaean site. To cut a long story short, the School's Managing Committee accepted my recommendation that excavation should be resumed there, and the Greek authorities granted a permit for work to begin in 1973. In this manner Phase Three—the current phase—of British School work in Laconia began, and I must honour the memory of Spyridon Marinatos, who was instrumental in bringing this about.

There is no need for a detailed account of our work at the Menelaion, which ended by investigating several discrete locations on what has proved to be a very large Bronze Age settlement (Catling 1974a, 1975a, 1975b, 1976a, 1976b, 1977a, 1977b, 1978, 1979a, 1979b, 1981, 1982, 1983a, 1983b, 1984a, 1984b, 1985, 1986a, 1988, 1989) on a long N–S ridge above the E bank of the Eurotas, and parallel with it. More work has also been done at the much excavated Menelaion site itself (esp. Catling 1977a). The Late Helladic (Mycenaean) settlement succeeded an extensive Middle Helladic site on the same spur, fragments of which have been found, including isolated walls, two small pottery kilns, and a number of inhumation burials (esp. Catling 1981). Finds of Late Helladic I and IIA pottery in later fills strongly suggest site occupancy during the period 1600–1450 BC, but all trace of it was removed in an root-and-branch reconstruction of the site, certainly on the Menelaion and Aetos hills. Full excavation of the complex opened by Dawkins (Dawkins 1910a) revealed the remains of a proto-palace, a building for which the less emotive term 'mansion' may be preferred (Catling 1977a, 1979b). This was built in the second half of the fifteenth century. The specific design (which foreshadows the palace-plans of Pylos and elsewhere in the thirteenth century) of the mansion was apparently of such overriding importance that those responsible insisted the available building platform at the edge of the hill be artificially enlarged. This seems to have been a bad decision, since it seems clear that in no time at all the NE corner collapsed, thanks to the inexperience of the site-engineer. The building was almost immediately replaced, what survived of the old house having been carefully dismantled, and much of its material reused in the construction of its successor which, though built on a wholly different orientation (Catling 1977a: Plan) repeated the plan of the old house as closely as circumstances permitted. This time, every conceivable precaution was taken to ensure the building's stability. All these events had taken place by 1375 BC, at latest. Its later history is less clear (largely as the result of the Dawkins excavation), except that it was evidently fire-destroyed *c.* 1200, and not re-occupied. Elsewhere, however, on the Prophitis Elias and Aetos Hills (Catling 1978, 1981) a short-lived re-occupation continued into the twelfth century (Catling and Catling 1981). Then nothing more.

There is disagreement concerning the location of the major Mycenaean site in the general vicinity of Sparta. Many suppose it was at Palaeopyrghi, the Bronze Age settlement adjacent to the Vaphio tholos tomb (Hope Simpson and Dickinson 1979: Site C.4; Waterhouse and Hope Simpson 1960; Hope Simpson 1981). Dr Spyropoulos is impressed by the claims of Pellana, NNW of Sparta several miles up the Eurotas valley (Hope Simpson and Dickinson 1979: Site C.56; Spyropoulos 1982), where there is a very impressive cemetery of Mycenaean rock-cut tombs, some of them of truly monumental dimensions. Despite these alternatives, I am sure that Mycenaean Sparta was at the site we now call the Menelaion. I take this view in part because of the great size of the Mycenaean settlement there (Catling 1977a: Plan), partly because of the kinds of buildings we have found there (Catling 1974a, 1988), but chiefly because that was where the Spartans themselves, well over 2500 years ago evidently believed it to have been. The steps in the supporting argument are few, and straightforward. At a date close to 700 BC, the Spartans began a hero-cult up on this ridge, in the immediate vicinity of a small natural knoll on the edge of the bluff, which they could be forgiven for thinking was a tomb from the heroic past; the shrine prospered, was enlarged and given idiosyncratic architectural form (plan and section in Wace, Thompson and Droop 1909), attracting huge numbers of votive offerings. Who was the Hero? We found inscribed votives to answer that question (Catling and Cavanagh 1976; R.W.V. Catling 1986)—it was the shrine of Menelaos and Helen, as most scholars, from the time of Ludwig Ross at least, had anyway assumed. Why locate it here, at such an inconvenient distance from Sparta, and in such an inaccessible spot? Because, I believe, at the end of the eighth century there was a well founded tradition that in days long past the ridge had been the home of the rulers of the region, the greatest of whom had been the Hero Menelaos, and his semi-divine and rather erratic wife, Helen. These were the figures to honour whom it was the duty of the Spartans, in so doing demonstrating the descent through which they came to possess the lands once the property of these great ones. Bronze Age town, Archaic sanctuary complement and illumine one another.

Other research programmes have followed the return to the Menelaion. From 1985, Dr W. G. Cavanagh, Nottingham University and Dr (now Professor) J. H. Crouwel of Amsterdam co-directed a joint British School–Amsterdam University intensive surface field survey (Cavanagh and Crouwel 1988) of a large specimen tract of land on the E side of the Eurotas bounded by Sellasia in the N, Chrysapha in the E and the Menelaion ridge to the S. Several hundred previously unknown sites, dating from Neolithic times to Ottoman, were identified and recorded, their sizes estimated by a variety of techniques, their possible identities assessed against the evidence of location, size and surface finds, and their period(s) of occupation calculated from scrutiny of datable pottery (Cavanagh, Crouwel, Catling, R. W. V. and Shipley 1996). In some areas this work was done in the nick of time, just before great tracts of land, especially the marginal land on the Chrysapha plateau were deep ploughed in advance of planting olive trees. Many small sites, especially Early Helladic farms—or something of the kind—recorded by the Survey teams, have now vanished for ever. Interest attaches to changing patterns of settlement revealed by the Survey—signs of synoikism in the later Bronze Age, when the scatter of small Early Helladic sites was replaced by larger and fewer Middle Helladic sites, and larger sites still (of which the Menelaion settlement is much the largest) in the Late Helladic period. No Dark Age sites were found, but the number of small rural sites grew steadily from Archaic time to Hellenistic. In a second phase of the Survey, Dr Cavanagh and Dr C. Mee (Liverpool University) have in collaboration selected a small number of the sites found earlier for much more rigorous study, making use of a range of experimental techniques, aiming to push out further and further the boundaries of what can be established about an ancient site by non-invasive procedures.

In 1988, as we have seen, a fresh start was made on the study of the late monuments of the acropolis of Sparta and its immediate environs, under the joint direction of Professor Geoffrey Waywell, of King's College London, and Professor John Wilkes of the London Institute of Archaeology, with the assistance of Dr Susan Walker in matters architectural and of Dr A. J. S. Spawforth, Newcastle University, as epigrapher (Catling 1989; French 1990, 1991, 1992, 1993,

1994; Tomlinson 1995). The Roman stoa, SE of the acropolis hill has been partly re-excavated, restudied and re-interpreted, emerging as one of the most important Imperial Roman buildings of Sparta, probably constructed *c.* AD 130, 'no expense spared' (Waywell and Wilkes 1994). The stoa's relationship with the enigmatic 'Round Building' has been defined more precisely. The possibility that this stoa is the reconstructed Persian Stoa remains open. Byzantine reoccupation of the stoa has been interpreted as the site of the church and conventual buildings of the Monastery of Ayios Nikon Metanoeites, correcting the already suspect identification of a much earlier basilican church nearer the theatre as that of Ayios Nikon.

The same team has been working on the Theatre, by test trenching, careful resurveying, and study of the architectural members, particularly those belonging to successive *scaenae frontes*. Two phases have been identified—early Augustan and Flavian. Close examination of the upper part of the *cavea* suggests there were seventeen usable rows of seats, rather than the twenty proposed by Woodward, 65 years ago (Waywell, Wilkes *et al.* 1995).

One of the sites identified by the Laconia Survey, at the locality Tsakona, in the lands of Aphyssou, some way ENE of Sparta, on high ground until recently the property of the nearby Monastery of the Ayii Tessarakonta, seemed from surface finds to be a sanctuary, and to have had a building whose tiled roof had been embellished by architectural terracottas (Cavanagh, Crouwel, Catling, R. W. V. and Shipley 1996, Site N415). Many handmade terracotta figures of ithyphallic humans and grotesques were found on the surface. Soon after its discovery the site was doubly damaged, first by deep ploughing (it had lain unmolested for decades previously), then by forest fire. Re-examination of the site after these misfortunes suggested that immediate excavation was imperative if any further information was to be retrieved from the site. This was done, thanks to Dr Spyropoulos' sympathetic understanding of the situation, in 1989. It proved to have been very, very nearly too late, though it provided an object lesson in the various causes of site destruction (Catling 1990a–c). We recovered—just—the plan of a long, narrow stone construction, roofed with terracotta Laconian tiles, cover-tiles with antefixes, the gables picked out by disk-acroteria. Among Late Archaic and Classical offerings were bronze weapons and shield fittings. Thousands of complete and fragmentary handmade terracotta statuettes were found, and a large number of miniature aryballoi. Several bronze scalpel-like tanged blades have aroused our curiosity. Tile stamps and other evidence attribute this shrine to Zeus Messapeus. The apparent concern with male fitness to procreate has led us to wonder whether this cult had gained favour in response to the perceived threat to Sparta of *oliganthropia*. The site was deserted in Late Hellenistic times; activity of an uncertain kind and scale was renewed in the third and fourth centuries AD.

That is enough, and more than enough from me. There is no need, in this company, to plead the cause of Spartan and Laconian studies, only to remind you of the infinite satisfaction that awaits those who are willing and able to come to work in surrounding of majestic beauty and incomparable grandeur, where, indeed, the differing qualities proper to Menelaos and to Helen are for ever in equipoise.

2

Pellana, the administrative centre of prehistoric Laconia

Theodoros G. Spyropoulos

Today Pellana is a small, humble village in northern Laconia, some 30 km from Sparta half way along the ancient road from Sparta to Megalopolis. To the S and W the site is dominated by the spectacular barrier of Mt. Taygetos, to the E it is open to a fertile and hollow plain, well watered and irrigated by a chain of copious springs, the most famous of which, named Pellanis, is located at the site of Pellana, just to the S of the ancient acropolis, which lies to the E of the hill occupied by the modern village.

The strategic position of the site, controlling the passage from Laconia to the Megalopolitis and Messenia, was recognised by the Spartans, who built there a tower, called Charakoma, the ruins of which are located to the S of the village. Pausanias, who made only one excursion towards Northern Laconia, after mentioning the tomb of Ladas, a renowned Olympic victor, notes 'Προϊόντι δὲ ὡς ἐπὶ τήν Πελλάναν χαράκωμα ἔστιν ὀνομαζόμενον καὶ μετὰ τοῦτο Πελλάνα, πόλις το ἀρχαῖον' (iii 21 2).

The passage through Pellana was safely guarded by the Spartans during the critical events which preceded the famous battle at Mantinea in 362 BC, and the site was used as the base of operations by King Agesilaos against Epameinondas. Xenophon calls the town Πελλήνη (*Hell.* vii 5 9), though the geographer Strabo speaks of a small Laconian village, named τὰ Πέλλανα πρός τὴν Μεγαλοπολίτιν νέυον, i.e. lying towards Megalopolitis (viii 7.5). Finally Plutarch calls the town Πελλήνη (*Agis* 8). The identification of the hill called Palaiokastro with the ancient site and the acropolis of Pellana, is strengthened by the remains of a circuit wall, which surrounds the hill; parts of this wall are now visible on the SE side of the hill, and they are datable to fourth or early third century BC. The fields on and around Palaiokastro are covered today with innumerable sherds, dating from EH to Mediaeval times. The same hill was also inhabited in the Mycenaean period, as we shall see below. The gradual decline of the site has been well portrayed by

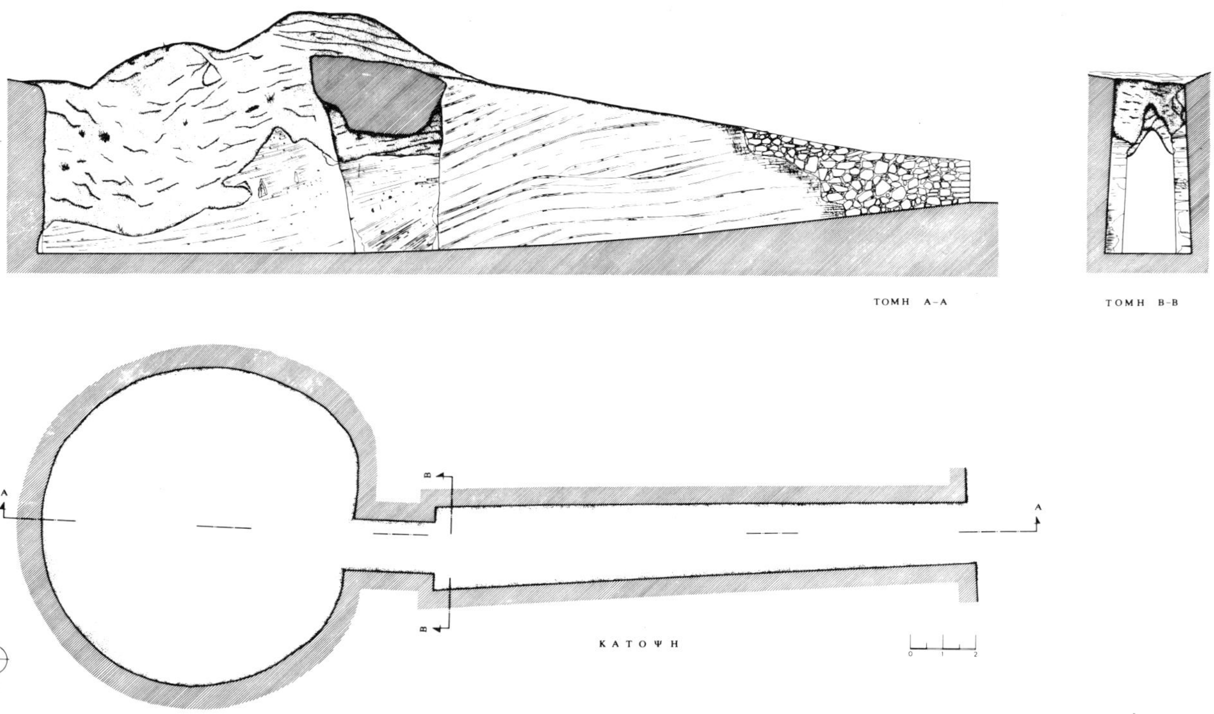

Fig. 2.1 (above) *Plan and sections of the Great Tomb at Pellana (Tomb 1)*

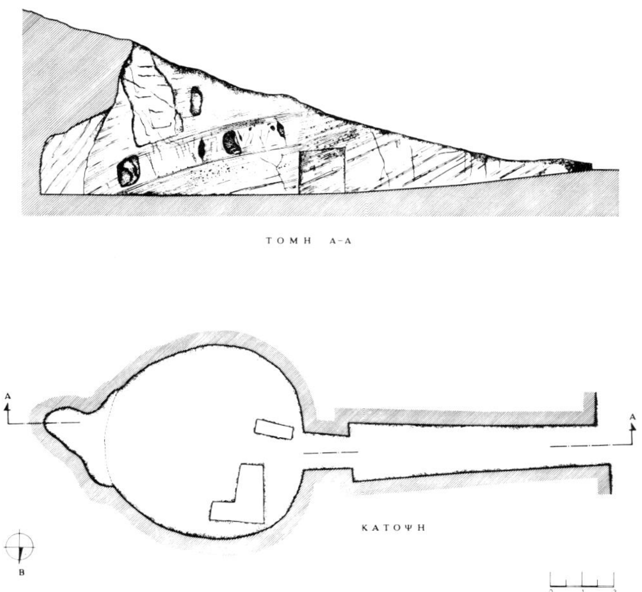

Fig. 2.2 (above) *Plan and section of Tomb 2 at Pellana.*

Fig. 2.3 (below) *Plan and section of Tomb 3 at Pellana.*

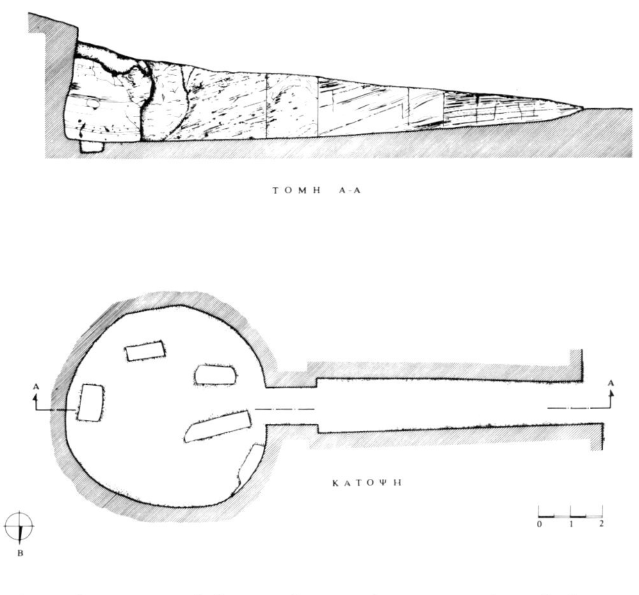

the references of the ancient writers mentioned above. The last to consider it worthwhile visiting the place was Pausanias, after the middle of the second century AD, who devoted some paragraphs to it recalling its earlier fame rather than stressing its contemporary importance. I refer to two passages in his text. The first refers to the sanctuary of Asklepios and the spring Pellanis. The site of the spring is well-known, although it was encased some forty years ago in concrete, the beautiful plane trees were cut down, and many ancient finds were removed or destroyed during the construction of irrigation channels for the fields. The site of the sanctuary is still unknown, but we may assume that it lies somewhere on the hill of Palaiokastro. This assumption is based on the following reason. The Asklepieion was the main, if not the only sanctuary at Pellana, and it seems reasonable to look for it in the area of the Mycenaean palace, which is supposed to lie on the acropolis.

H. Waterhouse and R. Hope Simpson, in their important study on Prehistoric Laconia (1961: 125 ff.), note three places with Mycenaean finds in the area of Pellana. The first is the cemetery of tholos tombs, the second the plateau of Tryporrachi, 400 m to the E, where some Mycenaean chamber tombs are still visible, and the third place is the hill of Palaiokastro itself. The first excavations at Pellana were conducted by the Ephor Konstantinos Rhomaios and immediately after him by the Ephor Theodoros Karachalios in 1926. At the site called Spelies (Caves) or Pelekete they cleared two chamber tombs, lying on the N bed of a torrent, which flows in front of the entrances to the tombs. The first was almost empty (FIG. 2.4), except for some sherds of Mycenaean vases, the second was filled with rubble and contained four cist graves cut in the floor of the chamber. The graves had been plundered long before their excavation and contained only disordered skeletal remains, though some of the offerings were found dispersed around the floor. The last as described by the excavator (see *A. Delt.* 10 (1926) par. 42) were mainly vases and fragments of vases, a female figurine, one sealstone of amber (with its device effaced), another seal of semi-precious stone (without any device), 25 small and round glass-beads of violet colour, several stone buttons of different colours and some other beads of various materials and colours. The tomb measures: diameter of the

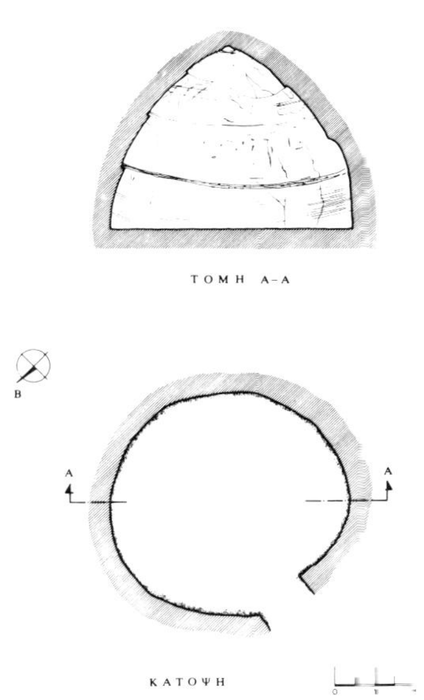

Fig. 2.4 Plan and section of the tomb excavated by Karachalios, Pellana.

Fig. 2.5 (right) *The* dromos *(entrance-passage) of the Great Tomb of Pellana, from the S.*

tholos 6 m, height of the tholos 5 m, length of the entrance-passage (dromos) 4.50 m, depth of the dromos 2.50 m and the height of the stomion (entrance) 2.50 m. The tomb has a relieving triangle over its stomion.

Research into prehistoric Pellana was halted and only after 60 years was reopened by the author of this article (FIGS. 2.1–3). Our first excavation took place in the area of the Cemetery of the Tholos Tombs. Our trial trenches brought to light three rock-cut tholos tombs. The biggest lies in the middle, the other two are placed either side. All of them were found plundered and disturbed in ancient times, their roofs had collapsed and the two lateral tombs were found hardly damaged. The central one—the biggest in the whole cemetery—deserves special mention and description.

Fig. 2.6 (above) *An amber bead from the* dromos *of the Great Tomb.*

Fig. 2.7 (right) *The entrance to the Great Tomb with the remains of the stone blocking-wall.*

We may refer in some detail to the Great Tomb of Pellana, the excavation of which lasted several months (FIG. 2.5). The long dromos leading to the Tomb is oriented from SW to NE. Its state of preservation is excellent. Both walls of the dromos converge gradually upwards without, however, meeting, and this observation offers the first chronological indication for the construction of the tomb. It is well-known that the dromoi of the earlier tombs of this type (fifteenth and fourteenth century BC) have almost vertical walls, while, from the thirteenth century on, the walls of the dromos tend to converge and almost join one another at the top.

The maximum preserved height of the dromos near the entrance attains 5.60 m. The width of the dromos starts at 2.10 m and reaches 2.55 m by the entrance to the tomb. The length of the dromos is preserved to 12.70 m and is small when seen in comparison with the chamber of the tomb, which exceeds 10 m. This is because a deep torrent cut into the hill out of which the tomb was excavated, thereby shortening the dromos.

Some very important finds of the early Mycenaean period were found in the dromos, among them a button made of amber (FIG. 2.6). It is lens-shaped and perforated; probably imported from the Baltic.

At the inner end of the dromos there was found the monumental façade of the Tomb. Its stomion, set in the middle of the façade, forms a rectangular opening, sloping slightly at the top, where it is crowned by a relieving triangle. The stomion leads to the chamber, where the burial of the dead took place, and was sealed with large stones, in dry-stone walling (FIG. 2.7). The fact that the

Fig. 2.8 Lamps of the Hellenistic period found in the Great Tomb.

stones had been dismantled, when the tomb was excavated, suggested that the tomb had already been robbed.

In different parts of the tomb and more specifically by its entrance we found numerous objects of later date, among them figurines, animal bones and vases dating to the late Hellenistic and early Roman period (FIGS. 2.8 and 2.9–10), which testify to the use of the tomb in later periods for cult purposes.

The vases as well as the figurines are cult-objects, perhaps used as offerings to heroised ancestors.

Among the exquisite finds in the tomb we may mention two remarkable piriform jars (FIGS. 2.11–12). They are decorated with a marine landscape and seaweed and with rich ivy-leaves, tenderly drawn. Other finds such as alabastra (FIGS. 2.13–14), amber beads, fragments of gold foil (FIG. 2.15) and fine pottery sherds witness the original richness of the tomb. These brilliant finds present similarities with the well-known finds from Mycenae, Vapheio and Kakovatos in Trifilia, dated to around 1500 BC.

We have already mentioned that our investigations uncovered three tombs in the cemetery at the site known as Spelies or Pelekete. In addition to the Great Tomb two others of the same shape but of smaller size were placed to the left and to the right of it. It is probable that these two smaller tombs belonged to members of the royal family and this theory is further supported by the fact that the graves of the 'ordinary' people were placed at a different site and more specifically on a slope called Tryporrachi, 400 m E of the cemetery for the royal family. During our first excavations we had the opportunity to dig one of the smaller tholos tombs, that to the left of the Great Tomb. It proved to resemble the Great Tomb in shape and construction: dromos with vertical walls, tholos chamber, and a conical vault (not intact). It is generally admitted that this particular grave was used as a shelter during medieval times. By the entrance of the tomb we found a small number of bronze coins struck during the reign of the Emperor Phokas (AD 602–610). This is of great importance, considering that coins representing the Emperor Phokas in particular and more generally coins of the seventh century AD, are very rare in Greece, due to the Slavic invasions. On the floor of the tomb we found five cist graves with skeletal remains (FIG. 2.16–17). The dead were placed in cist graves cut into the floor of the tomb, in accordance with a well-known Mycenaean custom.

Fig. 2.9 A cup of Roman date found in the Great Tomb.

Fig. 2.10 A pot of Roman date found in the Great Tomb.

Fig. 2.11 Palace style jar from the Great Tomb, decorated with marine landscape and sea-weed.

Fig. 2.12 Piriform palace style jar from the Great Tholos, decorated with ivy-leaves.

The contents of these cist graves provide chronological evidence for the construction of the tomb as well as for the surrounding Mycenaean cemetery. The finds, exclusively ceramic, date between 1350–1200 BC. Thus this tomb was in use 1350–1200 BC, and we may reasonably conclude that the whole Mycenaean cemetery of Pellana was in constant use from 1500–1200 BC; this also applies to the Great Tomb. In the light of this, we are led to the conclusion that Pellana was an important Mycenaean centre in continuous use, a conclusion which will help our understanding of LBA society in Laconia, as reflected in the Homeric epics and the Linear B tablets. Pellana was then at its acme during the period of the Trojan war and during the reigns of Tyndareos, Menelaos and Helen.

As far as the identity of the Great Tomb at Pellana is concerned, we note that it belongs to the same

Fig. 2.13 Alabastron from the Great Tholos.

Fig. 2.14 Another alabastron from the same tomb.

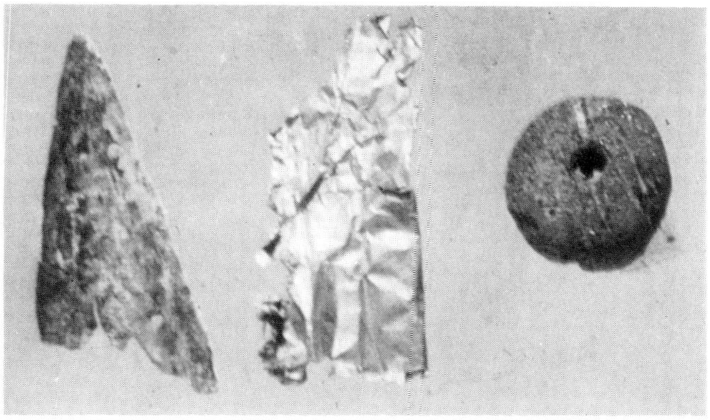

category of communal or family vaults as the chamber tombs and tumuli. These graves are very common in Greece from the Early Helladic period onwards.

During the Middle Helladic period (1950–1580 BC) the prevailing type of grave is the cist tomb, though during the Mycenaean period (1580–1100 BC) the type of tomb with chamber and dromos reappears. The two main forms of family graves during the Mycenaean period are the tholos and chamber tomb. The first type is usually constructed in stone slabs in the so-called corbelled technique (beehive tombs), whereas the other is always hewn out of the soft rock. It has

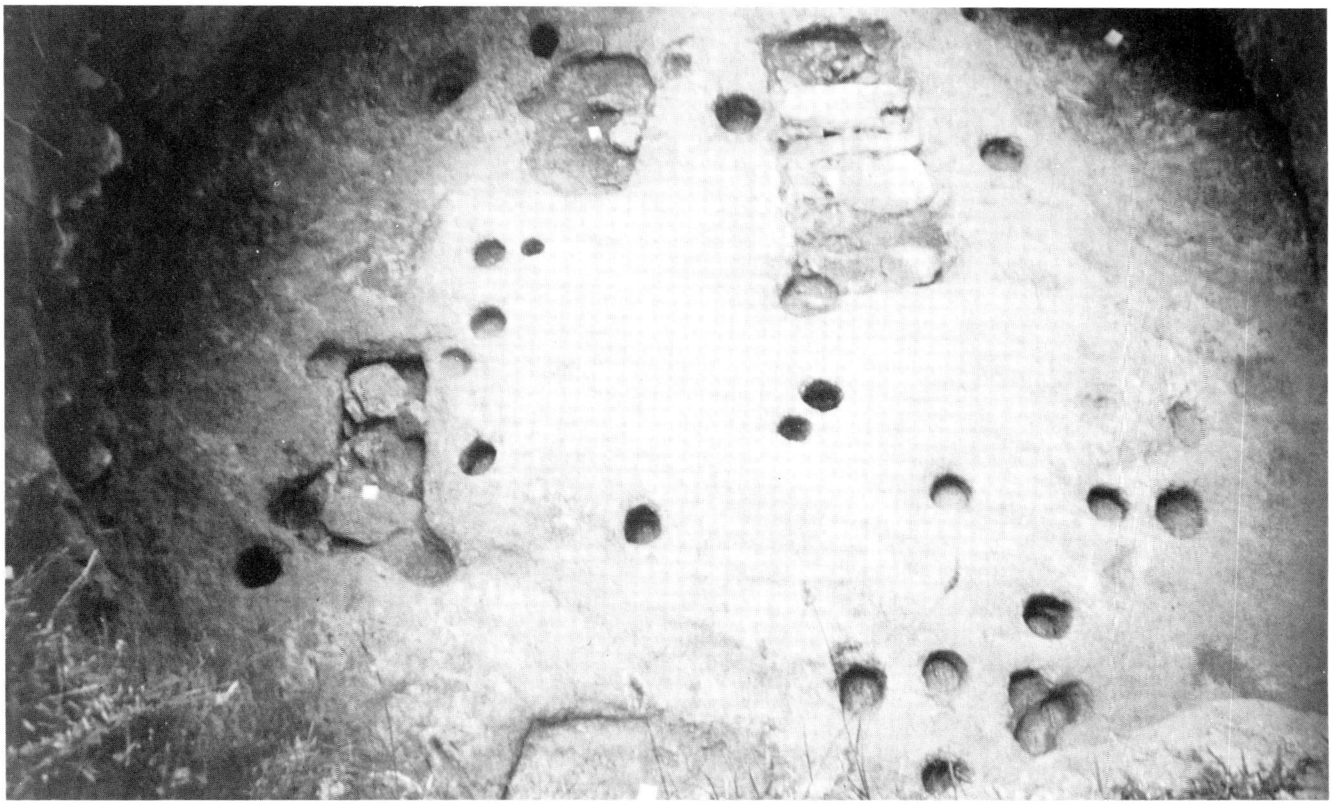

Fig. 2.15 (top) *A fragment of a bronze arrow-head, a fragment of gold foil and an amber bead, from the Great Tholos.*

Fig. 2.16 (above) *The floor of the tomb to the left of the Great Tholos. The post-holes probably supported wooden posts for a shelter. Near its entrance a hoard of Byzantine coins was found.*

Fig. 2.17 (left) *One of the cist graves cut in the floor of the tomb. (See also Fig. 2.21).*

generally been held that the tholos tombs represent the majestic funeral monuments destined for royal burials. To this variety belong the megalithic monuments of mainland Greece, such as the famous tombs at Mycenae, at Orchomenos in Boeotia, in the Pylos region, the tomb at Kapakli near Volos, those at Marathon and at Vapheio in Laconia and so on. The chamber tombs on the other hand have been found in their thousands from Thessaly to Crete and Rhodes and they were the graves of the ordinary people. The tombs at Pellana belong to a specific category or a variation of the above main types. They are cut out of the rock like the chamber tombs, but their chambers take the beehive shape, like the tholos tombs.

The creator of this type of grave must have been well aware of the techniques used in the chamber and tholos tombs. In the tholoi the linear and the curved components of the tomb are successfully harmonized.

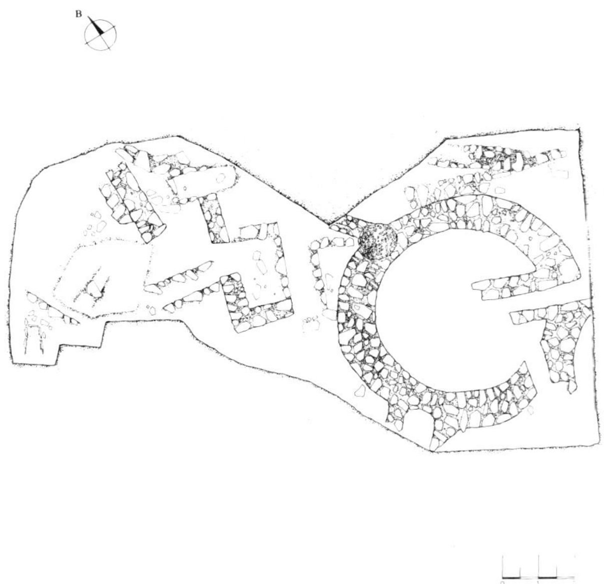

Fig. 2.18 (above left) *The Great Tholos Tomb at Pellana seen from the interior.*

Fig. 2.19 (above) *Plan of the EH tumulus at Pellana.*

Fig. 2. 20 (left) *The stone krepis of the tumulus of the EH II period.*

The dromos, the façade, the side walls of the stomion and the lintel are rectilinear and straight and wherever they join, they form right-angles, for example at the junction with the dromos, behind the stomion, with the relevant parts of the beehive chamber (FIG. 2.18). These features are necessary in constructing a normal tholos tomb, both from the technical and the static point of view, but when they occur in the rock-cut tholos tombs, like the tombs at Pellana, they are properly characterised as stylizations, which show the efforts of the craftsman to imitate, with the greatest possible accuracy, the shape and appearance of the normal tholos tombs (see Iakovidis 1966: 98 ff.). Imitation is also shown in the cutting of a relieving triangle, which does not offer any significant relief for the lintel above the stomion of the rock-cut tholos tombs. It is only a skeuomorph. On the other hand, the irregularity in the circumference of the chamber of the tomb is due to the nature of the monument (FIG. 2.1). In the case of the Great Tomb at Pellana the diameter of the chamber from the stomion to the opposite side of the tomb is 0.60–0.80 m. shorter than the other diameter of the chamber, which runs from N to S.

The stomion in the normal tholos tombs is rectilinear, the side walls perpendicular and the lintel straight and linear; because of that the starting point of the dome lies much higher than on the opposite side of the chamber; the result is that, in section, the two arcs of the dome are not equal and the point of their intersection, at the apex, is nearer to the entrance of the tomb. If this were not the case static problems could arise, even the collapse of the structure's roof. Therefore the cavity which is encountered in the inner part of the roof of the Tombs at Pellana is not found in the very centre of the 'ideal' circle of the chamber but nearer to the entrance of the tomb. This cavity has no constructional significance for these rock-cut tholos tombs; on the other hand, it is an organic component of the normal tholos tombs, because their upper courses converge at an angle of 30° and then a big horizontal stone, (the so-called key-stone) closes the opening, giving the shape of a shallow cavity.

The above proves that the rock-cut tholos tombs have adopted several constructional features from the stone-built tholos tombs. It is then possible that the craftsmen who made the Great Tomb at Pellana were familiar with the technical specifications of the normal tholos tombs, some of which are contemporary or earlier.

We can refer to Tholos Tomb I at Peristeria, to the two tombs at Koukounara, to one of the tombs at Koryfasion, to the tombs at Vapheio and at Kampos in Mani, to the tomb at Analipsis in Arcadia etc. The imitation of certain constructional elements found in the stone-built tholos tombs does not prove, however, that their rock-cut counterparts are of lesser monumentality and significance. The construction of a huge tholos tomb at Pellana during the LH IIB period, testifies to great expertise and technical virtuosity, of a kind not found in any other funeral monument of this type in the whole Greek mainland. Note, on the other hand, that the Royal Tomb of Mycenaean Thebes, the administrative and political centre of Boeotia, was also rock-cut, i.e. it was not made after the manner prevailing in other parts of Greece. The tomb at Pellana is then a Royal Tomb, and Pellana was an administrative centre during the period. This period at Pellana, on the evidence of the finds from the Great Tomb and the other princely tombs beside it, extends from the LH II to the LH IIIC period, a chronological span of continuous habitation, which is encountered in other places in Laconia, even at the Menelaion itself. Some tombs of the same type have been excavated by Marinatos at Volimidia in Messenia, some 5 km N of the Palace of Nestor. The smallest of those tombs has a diameter of 3.13 m and the largest, which has been characterised as monumental, has a diameter of 6.13 m. They are also dated in the LH II period (Marinatos 1952; 1953; 1954; *Das Altertum* 1 (1955): 141 ff.). A similar tomb was found some years ago at Agrapidochori in Elis and has a diameter of *c.* 4 m (see Parlama 1971; Pelon 1976: 443, note 7). At the same time that the Great Tomb at Pellana was made, another great tholos tomb was constructed at Vapheio in Laconia (see Tsountas 1889: p. 130–171; Vermeule 1964: 90 ff. and 127 ff.). Two more similar tombs of the same date have been found in a wider area, at Kambos in Messenia and at Analypsis in Arcadia.

Without doubt this was a period of great prosperity and a climax in Mycenaean civilisation. During the thirteenth century BC, when the Mycenaean kingdoms in the Peloponnese were consolidated and their geographical borders were stabilised, as they are portrayed in *Iliad* ii, one of the princes of Laconia became the king (wanax) of the whole territory. The most probable place for this to take place was Pellana, which presents, among other evidence, to be discussed below, continuous habitation and continuous funerary use of the great Tombs until the beginning of the twelfth century BC.

The prehistoric and the classical acropolis of Pellana was undoubtedly situated on the hill of Palaiokastro, which lies opposite and to the E of the modern village. My excavations at the site during the last 15 years have brought to light ruins of an extensive settlement of the Early and the Middle Bronze Age Periods. On the summit of the acropolis only ruins of a spacious building were unearthed, which was destroyed by fire during the EH II Period. Everything above this layer was removed, probably during the Frankish occupation of the acropolis, to judge from a tower and other buildings erected over and amid the prehistoric ruins. Whether there was a

Fig. 2.21 (above left) *A burial found outside the krepis of the Tumulus.*

Fig. 2.22 (above) *The EH II Tumulus and, in front of it, the bothros.*

Fig. 2.23 (left) *Part of the settlement at the S slope of the Acropolis of Pellana*

Fig. 2.24 (below left) *Excavated part of the late settlement at the S slope of the Acropolis of Pellana.*

Fig. 2.25 (below) *Plan of the Mycenaean settlement at Pellana.*

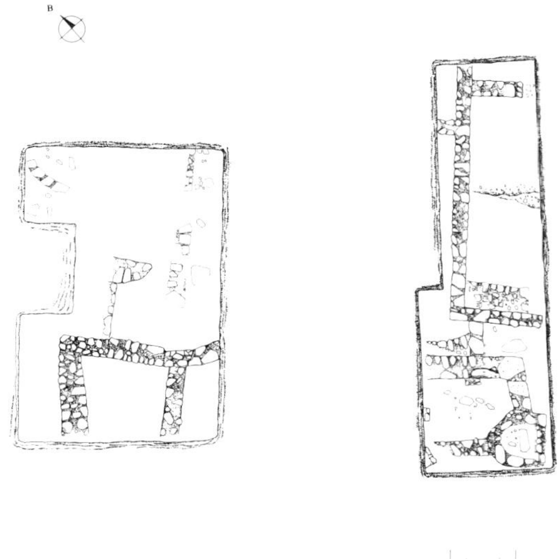

royal residence built on the top of the acropolis during the Middle Helladic or the Mycenaean period will remain a matter of speculation. On the next terrace down, just below the summit of the hill, where some signs of artificial terracing are visible, the stone krepis and the interior of a tumulus was excavated (FIGS. 2.19–21); this contained burials of the EH II period, unfortunately without grave offerings. Next to it, however, a bothros was located (FIG. 2.22), containing ashes and a couple of vases of the same period. The bothros was attached to the tumulus and contained the ashes from the sacrificial rites and the bowls for offerings to those buried under the tumulus. A channel runs through the interior of the sepulchral monument and recalling the blood-channels in Tomb II at Dendra and other funerary monuments of Mycenaean and later date in Greece (Andronikos 1968: s.v. 'Blutrillen'). We have good reasons to believe that the tumulus at Pellana, the first to be found in Laconia, was not a single funeral monument. The size of the terrace suggests that more tumuli might have been erected there, a whole cemetery of tumuli, like that at Stavros in Lefkas (Dörpfeld 1927; *A. Delt.* 27 (1972) *Chr.*: 211–6). The place where the tumulus, or tumuli, at Pellana, were situated, has a broad view over the whole plain, the beautiful mountain of Taygetos and the mountains of Arcadia. The tumulus occupies the best situation on the acropolis, just below the houses on the top of the hill, and undoubtedly contained the remains of the chieftains, who ruled over Pellana and perhaps over Laconia during the Early and Middle Bronze Age Periods. The siting of the tombs is another argument in favour of Pellana's special position and significance in the prehistoric civilisation of the whole area and argues for the primary role of the site and its development as an administrative centre in the later Mycenaean period as well. The line of chieftainship remained probably unbroken until the Early Mycenaean Period, when the royal tholos tomb was constructed nearby and survived up to the end of the Mycenaean period.

A small excavation on the second lower terrace of the acropolis to the S (FIGS. 2.23–25), opposite the copious spring Pellanis, has brought to light part of a settlement of the Late Mycenaean period (LH IIIA2 to LH IIIB2/C1). Despite the very small area excavated the discovery of a Mycenaean settlement at Pellana becomes a very important element for the topography of the site and presages further valuable finds and results (FIGS. 2.26–27).

The last, but not the least, important find at Pellana is a monumental road (FIG. 2.28), which starts at the foot of the acropolis to the E and ascends to the acropolis itself. It is one of the largest and best preserved roads ever found in Mycenaean Greece and we have good reasons to believe that it led either to a royal residence or to some other important installation on the acropolis.

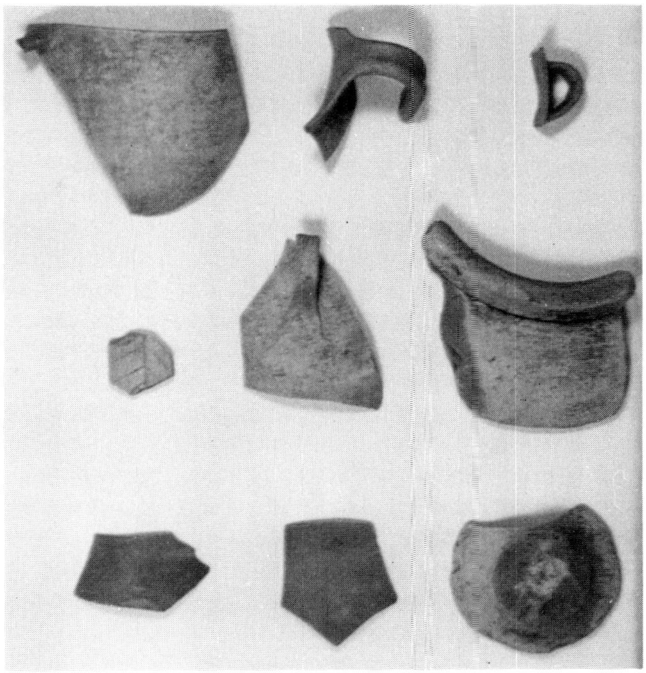

Fig. 2.26–27 (above and below) *Sherds from the settlement* (*both groups same scale*).

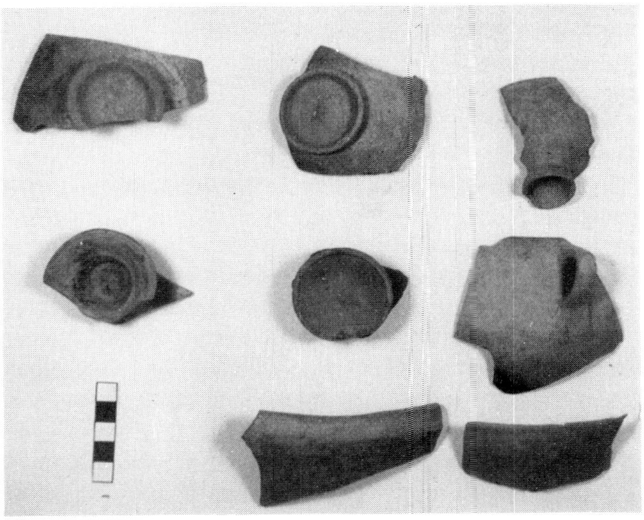

If we now turn to the epic tradition and more specifically to *Iliad* ii (581–7) we are informed that the following cities of Laconia took part in the expedition against Troy, under the leadership of Menelaos. Lakedaimon, Sparta, Pharis, Messe, Brysseai, Augeai, Amyklai, Helos, Laas, and Oitylos. The Homeric poems never refer to Sparta as the seat of King Menelaos, on the contrary the *Odyssey* (book iii) makes it clear that the palace of Tyndareos and Menelaos was in Lakedaimon, which, in both poems is characterised as 'κοίλη' and 'κητώεσσα' that is 'hollow' and 'with subterranean trenches'.

Pellana is, in our opinion, Mycenaean Lakedaimon, and the traditional epithets of κοίλη and κητώεσσα fit its geographical situation and its geological structure

Fig. 2.28 The monumental road ascending to the acropolis of Pellana from the E.

very well. Other Mycenaean sites in Laconia, which have been investigated or excavated have not yielded positive finds or indications for the identification or the discovery of a palatial centre of the fourteenth and the thirteenth centuries BC. Only a few sites date to the sixteenth and fifteenth centuries BC. Twenty sites were inhabited during the fourteenth century BC, 39 in the thirteenth and 17 places in twelfth century BC (Hooker 1976: 60 ff.; Furumark 1972: 49). Two of these sites seemed to hold most promise for the discovery of a Mycenaean palatial centre: the site of Menelaion and the Palaeopyrgi near Vapheio, which is generally identified with the Homeric city of Pharis. Unfortunately neither of these places supports the existence of a palace of the thirteenth century BC. The case consequently remains open and the palace of Tyndareos and Menelaos is still to be found.

The excavations at Pellana over the last 15 years have opened a new chapter and a new perspective on this question. We still do not have the palace there, but we can point to the impressive finds and to the royal and administrative ideology, which underlies the chieftains' tumulus, the magnificent tholos tomb, the majestic road, and the undoubtedly royal residences which existed at Pellana-Lakedaimon during the prehistoric and Mycenaean periods of Laconia (Kilian, 1988; Wright 1987).

3

City and *chora* in Sparta: Archaic to Hellenistic

Paul Cartledge

EXORDIUM

The vexed problems of the rise, evolution and devolution of the state are ones to which ancient Greek historians and classical archaeologists may reasonably claim to have a special contribution to make. Thanks to the *polis* (however precisely it be defined) and to Aristotle, we are in there at the very beginning of the debate, so to speak (Cartledge 1996a; *cf.* Snodgrass 1977; Runciman 1982; Morris 1987; Runciman 1990; Hansen 1993). Forty years ago Ernst Kirsten set the whole issue in its proper geographical framework, mapping the political ecology of the *polis* as a Medi-terranean phenomenon (Kirsten 1956; *cf.* Kirsten 1984; Murray and Price 1990; Gschnitzer 1991). Yet—such are the vagaries of scholarship—it remained stubbornly the case that 'A generation ago it was rare for British scholars writing about ancient history to bring the landscape into play alongside political accounts of antiquity' (Shipley 1996: 4).

Since then, however, the situation has happily changed. Human landscapes have become a central preoccupation of British ancient historians and classical archaeologists, with particular attention to the issue of core-periphery or town-country relationships (e.g. Rich and Wallace-Hadrill 1991; Shipley and Salmon 1996). This problematic has been greatly enlightened in recent years both by an English translation of de Polignac's seminal volume on 'the birth of the Greek city' (de Polignac 1984/1995) and by the proper publication, at last, of some of the intensive field-survey work of the 1970s and 1980s, not least the British School/University of Amsterdam Laconia Survey (Cavanagh *et al.* 1996–7; *cf.* Cavanagh and Crouwel 1988) and the Southern Argolid survey (Jameson *et al.* 1994/1995; *cf.* Cavanagh 1991; Snodgrass 1991). In what follows I shall attempt to bring to bear the fruits of these complementary historical and archaeological approaches on the relationships between city and countryside (chora) at Sparta during the last millennium BC. Specifically, I shall be asking how the Spartans of the centre or core settlements represented and conducted themselves as against the periphery of perioikic and helot inhabitants of Laconia (and Messenia).

POLITICAL BACKGROUND: TERMINOLOGY AND DEFINITION

In my earlier work on Greek self-definition (now Cartledge 1997), I preferred to emphasise cultural, symbolic and intellectual, rather than material, economic or social aspects. Here, I shall attempt to bring the material dimension closer to parity with the cultural, though the two are of course mutually implicated and conditioned. Topography, as Artemis Leontis has recently reminded us, is in the mind as well as on the ground (Leontis 1995; *cf.* Hirsch and O'Hanlon 1995; von Reden, forthcoming). Moreover, in the shape of the religious sanctuary, on which there has been a quite exceptional concentration of high-quality research published over the past quinquennium (Cartledge 1996b), the material and the cultural become almost one and the same—within the overarching framework of the political, to which I turn first of all.

Whether or not the ancient Greeks invented 'the political' or 'politics' (Meier 1990 [originally 1980]; Finley 1983), they certainly used them as a basic framework of theory and practice within which to define themselves. For them, it was of the essence of their self-definition as Greek citizens that their primary political loyalty and political identification, their 'nationalism' so to speak, were focused almost exclusively, not on the nation, let alone the nation-state, but on their own separate and radically self-differentiated political communities—as separate and different from each other as, say, Slovenia and Serbia, or France and England, are today (Walbank 1985; Cartledge 1995). I say 'political communities' advisedly. Comparative study suggests how difficult it is, if not impossible, to define 'state' or even 'city' with sufficient generality and precision. Nor does sticking to the Greek word *polis* altogether help. In our terms, that word was used to denote both what some of us would call a 'city' and what some of us would call a 'state' (Sakellariou 1989; Hansen 1993; Hansen and Raaflaub 1995), and it served also both to distinguish 'town' from countryside and to signify the Greeks' distinctive melding in one political entity of both town and country (Finley 1981b, 1985; Morris 1987; Osborne 1987, 1991, 1996; Snodgrass 1993).

The *polis* of Sparta, as we shall see, affords unusual interest and typically complex variations from this point of view.

On the other hand, attention to the Greeks' own theoretical and practical usage, most notably in Aristotle's *Politics* (a title that means very specifically 'matters relating to the *polis*'), does reveal their overridingly concrete understanding. The *polis* was for them a question not only or primarily of some abstract entity but rather of men, specifically citizen men (*politai*). Put differently, the *polis* was a citizen-state (Runciman 1990; Hansen 1993), in which citizens were, more precisely, those who enjoyed the public rights and duties of judgment and office. There was usually little or no State, capital S, in our modern sense of a governmental, judicial and military-police apparatus set apart from and above the common run of citizens (or subjects). Nor—to introduce a specifically archaeological or artefactual dimension—was the *polis* necessarily and sufficiently defined by, though it might be optionally or optimally equipped with, certain material attributes. Several ideologically freighted texts (e.g., Thuc. vii 77.7) explicitly distinguish between the *polis* in the sense of its living citizenry and the walls of a *polis* (in the material sense of 'city'). The special relevance of this distinction will transpire as we bring out the peculiarities of Sparta by comparison or rather contrast with Athens.

ATHENS V. SPARTA

There were in the Archaic to Hellenistic periods with which I am specially interested perhaps a thousand or even more Greek *poleis* scattered almost all round the Mediterranean and Black Seas from the Pillars of Herakles (Gibraltar) in the W to Phasis (in ex-Soviet Georgia) in the far NE. But there are only two, Sparta and Athens, about which we have anything like the requisite sort of detailed evidence to conduct a fruitful analysis within our appointed framework of city-chora relationships. And it is precisely in terms of the politics of urbanization that Thucydides introduces the polar opposition between Sparta and Athens that underlies his entire History. Suppose, he wrote in the so-called Archaeology, that the central places, or civic centres, of Athens and Sparta were at some time in the future to be utterly destroyed apart from the foundations of some public and private buildings, observers would then be quite unable to retrodict accurately the former power of the Peloponnesian War's protagonists. Instead, they would overestimate that of Athens and underestimate that of Sparta.

Thucydides' prediction is in one sense quite accurate: there is no comparison between the physical remains of the central places of the two antagonists. But in another sense it is self-refuting, since the survival of the literary work in which the prediction is contained is by itself sufficient to establish an *a priori* case that there had once been some sort of parity of power between the two. However, what interests me principally here are the grounds for Thucydides's prediction regarding Sparta: 'the *polis* is not regularly planned and contains no shrines or other buildings of great cost or magnificence, but is simply a collection of villages (*komai*) after the ancient Hellenic manner' (i 10; *cf.* Hansen 1995: 52–3, 53–4). Modern scholars have sometimes suspected that Thucydides was here indulging in artistic license, for the sake of his Athens-Sparta polarity. Certainly, as a self-declared Athenian (i 1) Thucydides was guilty of some chauvinist or ethnocentric special pleading. His definition of civilisation in terms of citification, placing 'archaic' Sparta at the opposite pole from 'modern' Athens, does reflect a thoroughly Athenian viewpoint, and one with which Aristotle, for example, the metic from Stageira, would surely have taken strong issue. On the other hand, archaeology apparently bears Thucydides out. There would seem to have been a real difference between the urban development of central Athens (Travlos 1971; Wycherley 1978) and that of Sparta (Stibbe 1989; pace Hansen 1995: 54). What concerns me now are the origins and implications of this distinction and opposition, which—following the argument of the preceding section—ought to have been located primarily in the political rather than the cultural or economic sphere. There is no better place to begin with than the cities' very different constructions of citizenship.

To become a Spartiate, one had to pass successfully through the educational cycle known as the *agoge* (Kennell 1995) and be elected to a dining society or 'common mess'; and, in order to retain one's citizen status, one had to be able to contribute a certain minimum of natural produce to one's mess as 'dues'. In all these ways, the Spartan citizens' qualifications and way of life contrasted with those of the Athenians, for whom it was sufficient to be born Athenian and registered as such at the age of majority. A further differentiating requirement was daily attendance by all Spartans at the evening meal eaten communally in the messes, which, like the *agoge*, was designed primarily to inculcate group solidarity, to the detriment of family and other ties and values. This universal dining requirement (coupled with an over-night sleeping obligation for the under-thirties) had a cardinal spatio-political correlate. Not only did all adult male Spartan citizens act together politically in the central place but most of them also resided there more or less permanently. But why were there these centrally positioned communal messes and living quarters?

FUNCTIONS OF URBANISM

Leaving aside speculation as to the ultimate origins of messing as a social practice (one not unique to Sparta), the answer briefly is that Sparta was in origins and essence a 'conquest' state (Finley 1983: 61–4). Its territory, some 8000 square km. in all, was easily the largest in the entire Greek world, and Sparta town was mapped ideologically in the image of an armed camp on constant military alert. This state of alert was directed not primarily against any external enemies, from whom they were cushioned and buffered by the so-called *perioikoi*, who 'dwelt round about' them within the borders of the Spartan state, in personal freedom but political subservience (Shipley 1992; Lotze 1994). The alert was directed rather against their enemy within, the many times more numerous helots, though this was not without a certain paradox. For it was thanks to the labour of the helots that Spartan citizens were enabled to reside permanently in Sparta, often at a considerable distance from their helot-worked estates. Yet, equally, it was because of the diehard hostility of at least the helots of Messenia that the Spartans felt constrained to live or endure a military-style barracks existence in the central place (Ducat 1990).

Sparta town, in other words, functioned politically to keep the non-citizens out—and down; to mark off the centre sharply from its periphery. Why, then, did

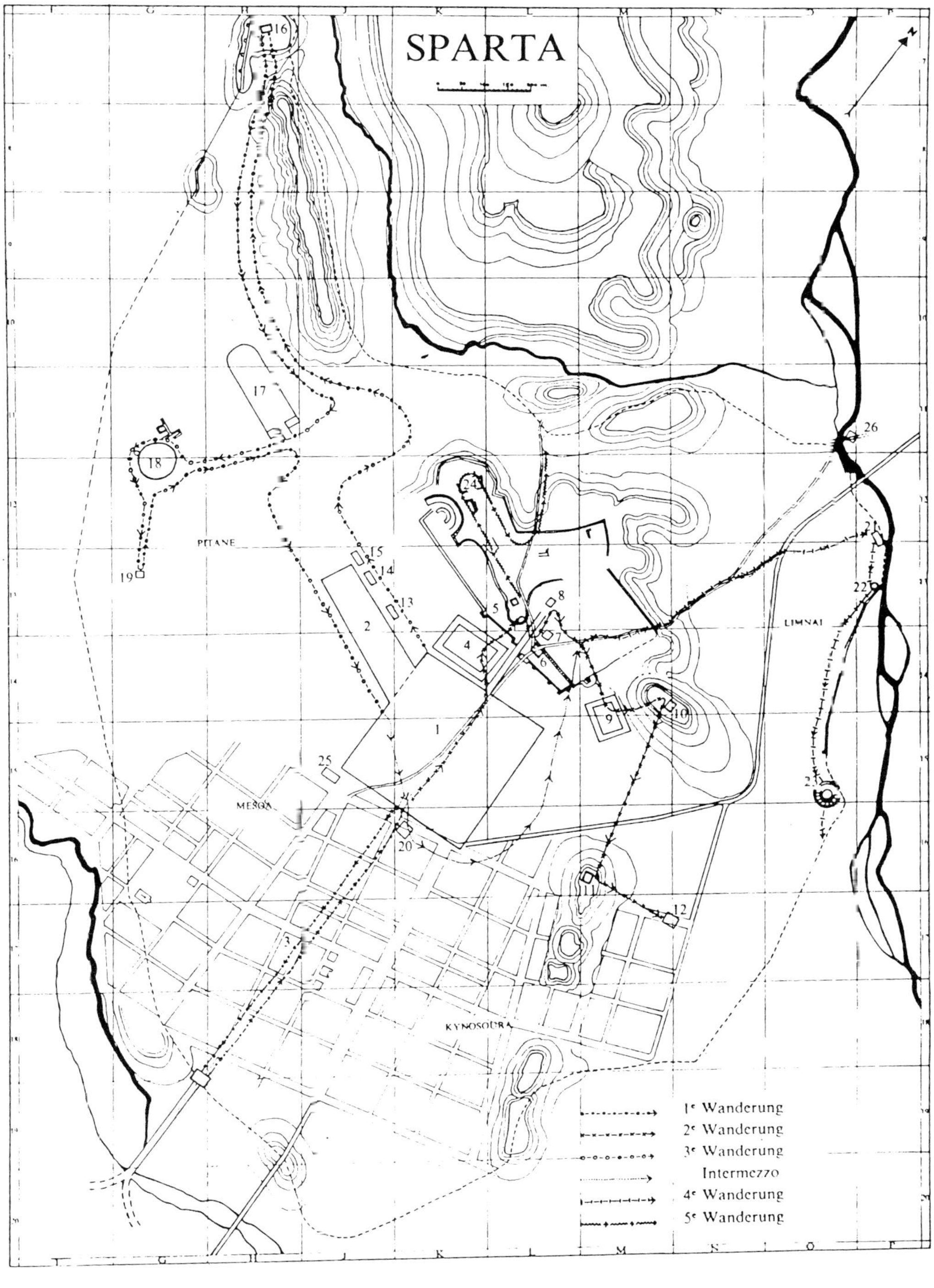

Fig. 3.1 The Sparta of Pausanias (second century AD*).
16 Temple of Artemis Issoria, 23 Temple of Artemis Orthia,
24 Temple of Athena Chalkioikos. (After Stibbe 1989)*

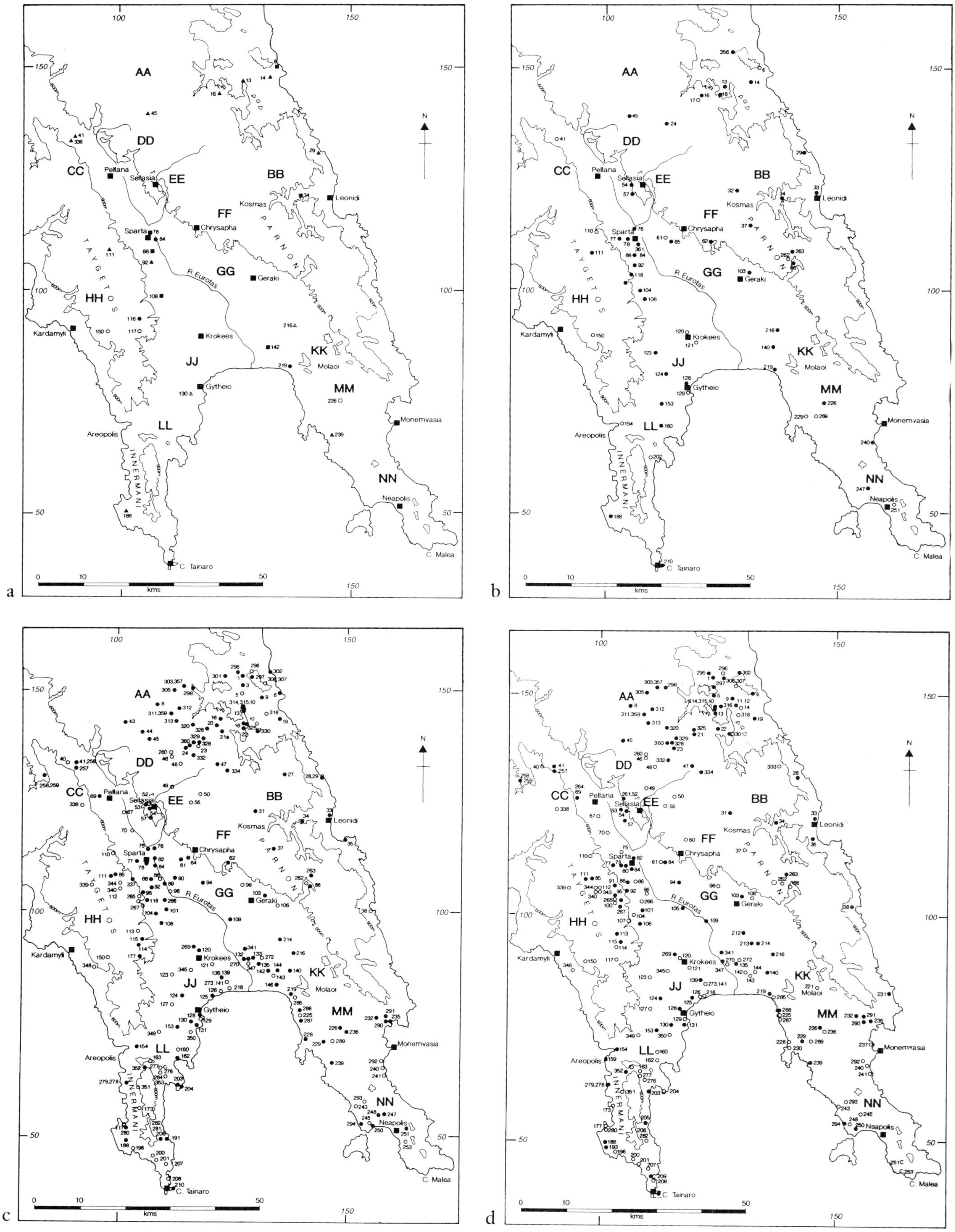

Fig. 3.2 (a, b, c and d) Sites in Laconia: (a) Protogeometric, (b) Archaic, (c) Classical and (d) Hellenistic (Cavanagh et al. 1996)

it not acquire what Thucydides clearly believed to be the normal accoutrements of urbanization, and in particular why did the Spartans not surround their central place, or part of it, with one of those normal accoutrements, an enceinte wall? Several reasons suggest themselves. First, the weight of tradition. The Spartans notoriously over-valued the past and, in part precisely because they too were not immune from change, liked to represent their way of life as having been frozen like a fly in amber from the earliest mists of their city's history. Part of this Spartan ideological myth-history involved the principled disdain of a city-wall, as a stigma of effeminacy, in favour of the citizens' strong right arms. But actually not every *polis* had had an enceinte wall to begin with, and by the time city-walls had become a normal feature of the Greek landscape the Spartans had evolved complicated alternative modes of central self-protection, partly material and partly symbolic.

The *perioikoi* have been introduced above; their strategic presence required an enemy from outside Laconia or Messenia to fight through this substantial first line of resistance before reaching Sparta itself, as no enemy in fact did before 370/69, when crucially some of the *perioikoi* of northern Laconia defected. A less obvious but none the less efficacious wall-substitute was provided by a cluster of religious sanctuaries around or in the close vicinity of Sparta town. A Greek sanctuary's basic function as a place of human-superhuman intercommunication was effected most conspicuously through a variety of sacrificial rituals, and most lastingly through the dedication of a multiplicity of votive offerings (Alcock and Osborne 1994; Cartledge 1996b). But although human-superhuman communication was a necessary feature of each and every sanctuary, this did not constitute a sufficient definition of all Greek sanctuaries' many and varied functions. For they were not merely places of worship and pilgrimage. Indeed, they were not always primarily, let alone exclusively, religious (as we would put it) in their functional significance. They might function also—or rather—as political entities in something like a secular sense.

Most relevant to us in the present context is the category of the limitary sanctuary. This comprised sanctuaries that were borderline in a literal as well as metaphorical sense, being located on natural or artificial boundaries within or between communities (including territories overseas: Malkin 1994). As such, they might serve a variety of purposes: to articulate the necessary organic relationship between countryside (the economic basis) and urban centre (the political superstructure), or to mark ritually the symbolic passage of citizens from 'wild' adolescence to 'tame'

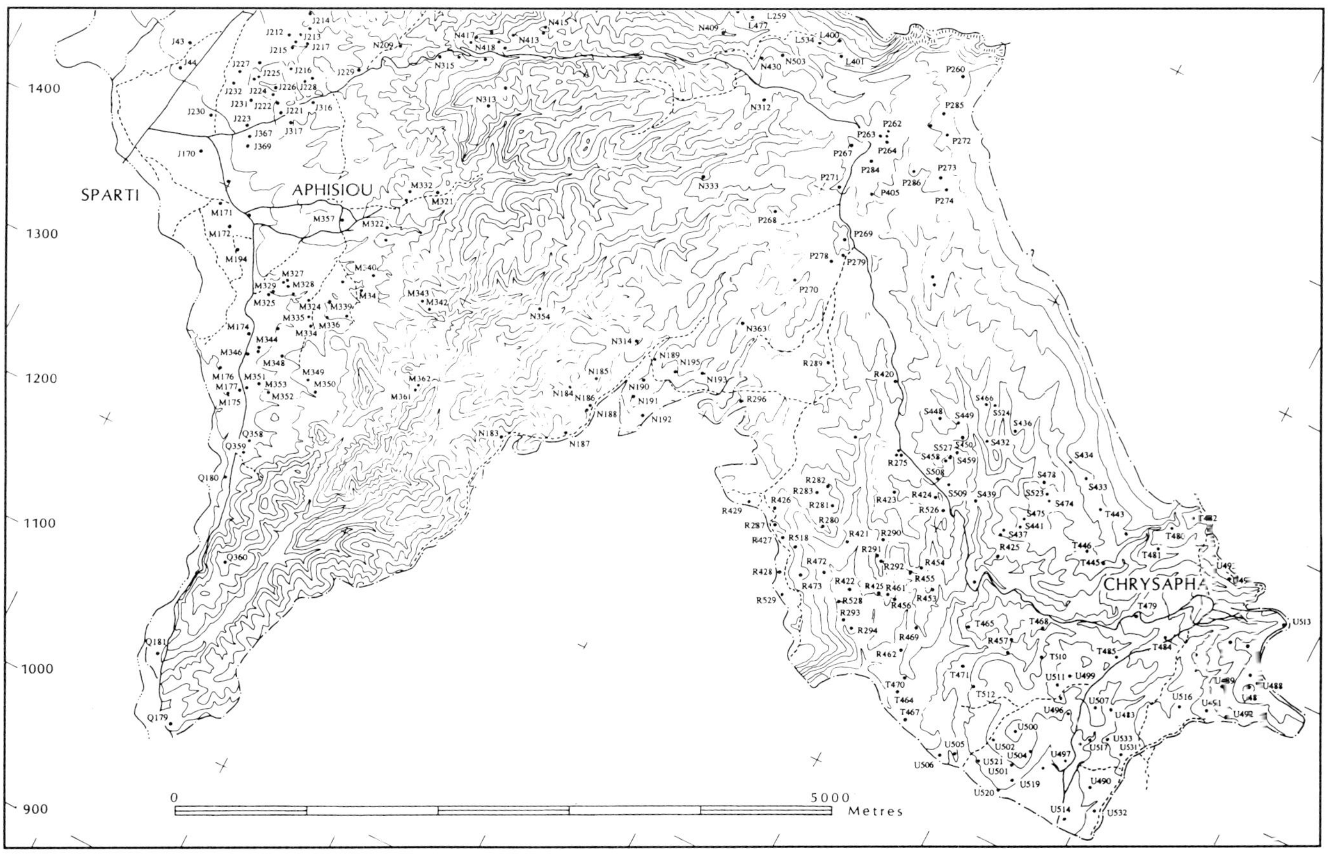

Fig. 3.3 Laconia Survey: the S *and* SE *of the survey area (Cavanagh et al. 1996)*

Fig. 3.4 Terracotta figurine (Archaic) from the sanctuary at Tsakona

civic maturity (as in several Artemis sanctuaries), or to establish, consolidate or promulgate a state's claim to border-territory against a neighbour, always the prime cause and context of ancient Greek interstate warfare (cf. Sartre 1979; Daverio-Rocchi 1988). The limitary sanctuaries that concern us here are of two main sorts: first, those which formed a kind of *pomerium* (to borrow the Roman term) or sacred boundary around Sparta itself and, second, those which served to define Spartan citizen territory, the πολιτικὴ γῆ, against the territory of the perioikoi.

So far as Sparta's '*pomerium*' is concerned, special attention should be drawn to the two Artemis sanctuaries—surnamed Ortheia and Issoria—on E and W, respectively. (FIG. 3.1) Artemis was herself among other things a goddess of boundaries, separating the wild from the tame or cultivated. Regarding the area in the immediate vicinity of Sparta town (FIG. 3.2), attention may be directed first to the Menelaion sanctuary (devoted to Menelaos and Helen, together with Helen's brothers, the Dioskouroi) in the NE (Laconia Survey, GG 84), and to the Eleusinion (sacred to Demeter and Kore) rather further to the S (Laconia Survey, GG 95). Both of those sanctuaries have long been known and, in the former's case at any rate, very well excavated. Much more recently, however, a most interesting sanctuary of demonstrable social and political significance, plausibly identified as a sanctuary of Zeus Messapeus, was discovered by the Laconia survey at Tsakona some 4km to the N of Sparta towards the perioikic town of Sellasia (Laconia Survey N405; *cf.* Catling 1990a, 1990b). (FIG. 3.3).

Finds here include an unusual and distinctive plethora of ithyphallic terracotta votives that might well be accorded a monitory, territory-marking interpretation (FIG. 3.4). Sir Kenneth Dover has characteristically cited in a comparable connection not only the statues of Priapus that dotted Roman orchards and fields but the threatening, boundary-marking ithyphallicism of 'watchful males' in 'some primate species' (Dover 1978: 105). Given Tsakona's location so close to the centre of Sparta and to Sellasia, the nearest perioikic town across the border from Sparta's 'civic land', this sanctuary was surely a Spartan rather than a perioikic shrine, and it would not be implausible to see it as primarily serving a limitary political function.

However, by far the most important of these limitary sanctuaries in the immediate environs of Sparta was that of Apollo and Hyakinthos located at Amyklai a few kilometres SE of Sparta town (Laconia survey GG88, *cf.* 92). Significantly, it was here, at the Amyklaion, and not in Sparta town that the Spartans' principal 'national' religious festival was celebrated. To this we shall return. More immediately to the point, this physical separation of Amyklai, a constituent kome or 'village' of Sparta on a par with the four contiguous villages of the central place (pace Kennell 1995: 162–9; see rather Tausend 1992: 103ff.; and now Thommen 1996: 15 and n. 38), was of course another reason why the Spartans did not at first build a city-wall round their central settlement. For by the time that Sparta did finally decide to do so, in the early second century BC, its geopolitical situation had altered, drastically, for the worse. All the *perioikoi* and most of the helots had acquired their independence, and Sparta's *polis* territory had been reduced to 'normal' Greek proportions, comprising the terrain immediately surrounding the central place in the Spartan plain (Cartledge 1979; Cartledge and Spawforth 1989). A wall was therefore no longer a mere luxury or frippery that might be pragmatically dispensed with, and whose absence could be ideologically glossed. It had become an imperious necessity—regardless of the politico-military and symbolic cost of Amyklai's inevitable exclusion from its protection.

AN ATHENIAN COMPARISON

In order to bring out further the peculiarities of Sparta's treatment of its *chora*, we may briefly return to our comparison and contrast of the politics of urbanization at Athens, where they managed these things very differently, especially in the democratic period (fifth-fourth centuries). For a start, most of the 30,000 or so (on average) Athenian citizens did not reside permanently within the City (Astu) and Peiraieus area, enclosed as this usually was by walls of various kinds and periods. They lived instead in the surrounding chora of Attica, in which were situated the vast majority of the 140 constituent *demes* or villages (Whitehead 1986). Thus whereas Spartan citizens compulsorily ate together every day in the central place as members of a citizen corporation, Athenians did so voluntarily and only on high days and holidays. And whereas presumably all fit Spartans always attended the Spartan assembly, at its relatively infrequent sessions, never did more than a maximum of half the citizenry attend the Athenian assembly, even though that was a truly decisive organ of government (Hansen 1987). The Athenian Assembly, in other words, was not located centrally in the City (on Pnyx hill) in order to differentiate and emphasize the hierarchy of centre and periphery. Most Athenian citizens were independent rural small farmers, and such town-country antagonism as did exist was as much a matter of elite snobbery as a structural factor integral to the functioning of Athenian political institutions—with the admitted exception of the strains imposed by Periclean policy during the Peloponnesian War period.

The reasons for the Athenian Assembly's central location were partly historical and symbolic—the Pnyx, like the Agora, was not far from the Athenian Acropolis, which had served as a central refuge and rallying-point as well as the heart of Athenian religious life since at least the foundation of the historical polis; and partly practical—Athens was by Greek standards a remarkably large and heterogeneous *polis* and absolutely required centralized governmental institutions. Hence Athens City was truly the seat of a 'national' assembly. Yet even that would not by itself have accounted for the remarkable urbanization of Athens attested by Thucydides. For this, two further factors, neither of which applied to Sparta, were chiefly responsible: the self-aggrandizing Peisistratid tyranny of the sixth century; and the Athenian empire of the fifth. As a result, huge quantities of public and private resources were devoted to a largely religious building-programme rivalled in cost only by the secular reconstruction of the city-walls and walls linking Athens to Peiraieus at the beginning of the fourth century.

On the other hand, the Athenians' urbanism lacked one of the principal motivations behind Sparta's centripetal concentration. Despite the undoubtedly large numbers of slaves they possessed both individually and collectively, they had no serious cause to fear a servile enemy within. A continuing and probably unresolvable debate rages over the precise nature and extent of the connection, if any, between slavery and democracy at Athens. What is generally agreed, however, is that the Athenian slave body, being a heterogeneous polyglot mass, did not pose the constant threat to the stability, let alone the continued existence, of the Athenian *polis* that the helots did to the *polis* of the Spartans.

THE FESTIVE DIMENSION

From urbanism, with its vital religious components, I move finally and specifically to the politics of religion, with reference to civic festivals. Religion in ancient Greece was essentially, not just accidentally, civic in nature, the Greek *polis* being constituted as a city of gods as well as of men (Bruit and Schmitt 1992). Indeed, according to a famous but controversial thesis of de Polignac (1984/1995), the very origin of the Greek *polis* was owed to a primarily religious development, the integration of the central place with a major peri- or extra-urban shrine or cult-place. Whether that thesis holds universally or not—and de Polignac himself (1994) has significantly modified his own original position—religious festivals were indeed the beating heart of ancient Greek religion, and festivals somehow linking centre and periphery could thus perform a vital civic political function (Cartledge 1985; Robertson 1992). I have chosen therefore to compare and contrast one Athenian and one Spartan civic religious festival in order to illustrate the very different meanings and functions they could have for centre-periphery interaction.

The Panathenaia or 'All-Attican/Athenian' festival annually celebrated the birthday of the polis's patron deity Athena Polias (Neils *et al.* 1992). By its very name the festival was overtly designed both to celebrate and to reinforce the political homogeneity and integrity of the entire *polis* territory, which was both unusually large by Greek standards and by no means unitary in its origins. When the festival was founded in its 'classical' form, traditionally in the 560s, homogeneity and integrity were probably a pious hope rather than an unmistakable actuality. Genuine politico-territorial unity was not to be achieved until the Cleisthenic reforms over half a century later, and even thereafter unity might still be seriously (con)tested at the margins. Those reforms placed the foundations of Athenian citizenship on the twin bases of birth and locality, and it was as members of their local demes that Athenians participated in the Panathenaia. Every four years the celebrations were conducted with especial magnificence, partly for the benefit of the non-citizens entitled or even required to participate. Yet the festival remained a triumphantly Athenian occasion, employed to present the desired face of Athens both to itself and to others. At the centre of that image lay the Acropolis, the hub of the Attic wheel. But just as a hub is useless without the wheel, so the Acropolis derived its significance from its location at the spiritual centre of the *polis* territory, and indeed of the wider Greek world within which Athenian citizens might be temporarily or permanently domiciled (Loraux 1993; *cf.* 1986).

Sparta had no precise equivalent of the Panathenaia, with its international as well as national connotations and reverberations. Its nearest thing was the

Hyakinthia, in that that was the principal annual festival of Spartan 'national' or rather civic identity. But in almost all other respects it offers a clattering contrast. Sparta's patron deity, like that of Athens, was an Athena of the Polis (Piccirilli 1984), but although Spartan Athena enjoyed at least one important festival, the Promakheia, the Hyakinthia was dedicated instead to Apollo, as were all Sparta's major festivals (Pettersson 1992). The Hyakinthia likewise took place in the political centre of the Spartan state, but it was significantly not a centripetal or monocentric occasion. Sparta town was, as we have seen, a dispersed scatter of five villages, only four of which were directly contiguous. The fifth was Amyklai, and it was here, eccentrically, just out of town, that the Hyakinthia were held.

Moreover, it seems to have remained a significantly Amyklaian as well as a 'pan-Spartan' festival. Thus only serving Spartan soldiers from Amyklai, and not also those from the other four villages, were automatically released from campaign to return home to celebrate it——in what was after all the height of the campaigning season. The non-Amyklaian Spartans processed solemnly from Sparta town down the Hyakinthian Way, symbolically marking thereby the political unity but at the same time also the separate identity of Sparta and Amyklai. Sparta, in other words, did not strictly have a festival which like the Athenians' Panathenaia consciously united in a single shared cult the entire civic territory of the Spartan *polis*. Indeed, the Hyakinthia, though national, yet retained a strongly separatist and local flavour—harking back perhaps to the contested origins of the Spartan *polis* in the eighth century.

One final contrast with the Panathenaic festival concerns eligibility for participation at the Hyakinthia. The procession and associated games of the former were open not only to Athenian citizens but also to resident aliens and foreigners; indeed, the participation of the latter two groups was in certain aspects required. The Hyakinthia's military-style procession and musical and athletic contests, however, were open only to Spartan citizens. Indeed, the only non-Spartans present at the Hyakinthia—in contrast especially to the Gymnopaidiai festival, at which distinguished foreign guests were made welcome, or the Promakheia, at which *perioikoi* were given a significant role—were helots. It was not merely for geographical convenience, therefore, that the common messes in Sparta town, those quintessentially Spartan civic structures, were situated along the Hyakinthian Way.

CONCLUSION

The Hyakinthia, in short, like the Spartan system of urbanization as a whole, was consciously designed to emphasise and reinforce the centre's separation from and hierarchical domination over the periphery. Whereas the normal and normative Greek *polis* united town and country in a harmonious political symbiosis, Sparta in this respect as so often was atypical, if not unique. The presence or (until the mid-Hellenistic era) absence of a city wall was a clear ideological and spatial marker of Sparta's difference.

CODA: BRITISH LACONIAN STUDIES: PAST, PRESENT AND FUTURE

'Historical Studies'

Unless Brutus the Trojan stopped off in Sparta en route to becoming the First Briton, the first authentic Briton whose visit to Laconia has left significant literary trace is the late 17th-century merchant Bernard Randolph (an extract describing Mistra—subject of an elegant monograph by Sir Steven Runciman, 1980—from his *The Present State of the Morea* [1689] is printed in Richard Stoneman's Penguin *A Literary Companion to Travel in Greece*, p. 65; other reports by Randolph feature also in Martin Garrett's no less companionable *Greece: A Literary Companion*). Randolph had of course been long anticipated in visiting Laconia by early modern scholarly travellers from other countries, beginning with Cyriac of Ancona in the mid-15th century, and it was to be almost a century and a half after Randolph before Britain seriously staked a claim in the burgeoning field of Laconian, or more accurately Morean, studies—thanks to Sir William Gell (1823) and (Colonel) W. M. Leake (1830): see Hooker 1980: 24 [ref. below]. Even so, the early honours for the 'scientific' exploration of the Morea including Laconia in the 19th century went chiefly not to Britain but to France (Puillon Boblaye, Bory de Saint-Vincent) and Germany (Ross, Stein, Philippson). It was presumably a mercy, though, that Schliemann in 1888 could find 'not even a rubbish-dump' on the Spartan Acropolis and 'no trace of antiquity' in the hills bearing the main Mycenaean settlement and the historical Menelaion sanctuary . . . [all refs again in Hooker 1980: 20–24].

The 20th century, however, does belong to Britain, well, more so rather than less. Desperate for a historical site that would rival the German Institute's Olympia and the French School's Delphi, not to mention the Greeks' Athenian Acropolis and environs, and that would complement their own prehistoric Knossos and Phylakopi; and alarmed perhaps by the incursions into Laconia of Tsountas (prehistoric, esp. Vapheio) and Furtwängler (Amyklaion, mainly historic), the BSA settled in the first decade of our century on Sparta—or rather, what is crucial for our purposes, on Sparta as the centrepiece of Laconia, the jewel in the crown. For before beginning excavations in Sparta, especially but not only at the sanctuary of Orth(e)ia, members of the School had first conducted extensive surface exploration in sw Laconia and sunk their spades, picks and trowels at Geraki (ancient Geronthrai) and Angelona (a heroon site). In the year that work at Orthia itself began, 1906, M. N. Tod and A. J. B. Wace published their *Catalogue of the Sparta Museum* (still not superseded ninety years later).

So the pattern was set for the first quinquennium of campaigns (1906–1910) under R. C. Bosanquet and then R. M. Dawkins. The list of those participating both inside and outside Sparta reads like a roll-call of honour of British archaeological and ancient historical scholarship in the first half of the century—including as it does, besides those already named, G. Dickins, R. J. H. Jenkins (later an eminent Byzantinist) and A. M. Woodward. The ultimate fruit of work at the major site of concentration, publication of which was delayed by the First War among other factors, was R. M. Dawkins (ed.), *Artemis Orthia* (1929, a supplementary volume of the JHS). By then, however, the School had also completed, under Woodward, a second quinquennium (1924–28) of archaeological-cum-historical research in and around Sparta, the most significant results of which were the excavations on the Acropolis and in the theatre below it, and further extensive topographical surveys, all promptly published in the School's *Annual* (vols. 26–30).

It is no exaggeration to say that the School's labours in the first and third decades of our century transformed not only Laconian studies as a whole but also general perceptions of the nature and significance of early Sparta and especially Spartan culture. Guy Dickins (killed in World War I) could even get an article on Spartan art (sic) published in the connoisseurs' *Burlington Magazine* (1908), while Woodward's general summation of the implications of the new archaeological picture for the history of early Sparta published in the most widely read British historical journal (*History* 1923) set the agenda and tone for the spate of reappraisals that has barely ceased to flow from the 1930s (Alan Blakeway, A. Andrewes) and 1940s (H. T. Wade-Gery) to this day.

Selection of representative examples from those fertile six-plus decades is of course invidious, but two interlinked chains of research and researchers seem to me more than averagely significant. First, a prehistoric chain started before World War II, at the prompting of Alan Wace, by Helen Waterhouse (née Thomas). Her research, expanded by the indefatigable legwork of Dick Hope Simpson, issued in a two-part publication in BSA 1960 and 1961 that was the immediate source of all postwar prehistoric extensive survey in Greece. It was largely due to their inspiration that Hector Catling chose to devote the principal energies of his Directorship of the School to Laconia, a wise choice which justly earned him the sobriquet used as the title of his 1992 Festschrift by grateful colleagues, pupils and friends: Φιλολακων.

The second chain is a historical one. It begins with John Boardman's seminal re-examination of the (for its day) pioneering stratigraphy of Orthia. From him the torch was passed to his graduate pupil Cartledge, who in turn was fortunate to be able to collaborate with one of the leading experts in the epigraphy of Roman Greece, Tony Spawforth. Developing and (more often) revising Cartledge on Archaic and Classical Sparta has been Hodkinson, originally a pupil of Finley, latterly of Cartledge, whose current research focuses principally on Sparta's Archaic archaeology.

Hodkinson will now, as will we all, have to take into account the heaps of new data and ideas being piled up by the interdisciplinary intensive Laconia survey. But I conclude this too rapid résumé with a mention, *honoris causa*, of work in progress. Joost Crouwel is almost a 'British' scholar by adoption—following on from his labours on the joint British School/University of Amsterdam survey, he has gone back to where the British left off at Geraki over 90 years ago. Also resuming and developing much earlier excavations, but in this case back in the central place, are Geoff Waywell and John Wilkes: much is hoped for from their current work both on top of and alongside the Spartan Acropolis.

A Selection of British Research

Andrewes 1954; Badian 1966; Boardman 1963; Cartledge 1979; Cartledge 1987; Cartledge and A. Spawforth 1989; Cavanagh, J. Crouwel, G. Shipley, *et al.* 1996; Chrimes 1952; Dawkins 1929; de Ste. Croix 1972; Finley 1981a; Forrest 1968; Hammond 1973; Hodkinson 1983; Holladay 1977; Hooker 1980; Huxley 1962; Jeffery 1990; Jones 1967; Lazenby 1985; Lewis 1977; Powell 1989; Powell and Hodkinson 1994; Rawson 1991; Sanders 1992; Toynbee 1969 [note that AJT's work on Sparta began with topographical autopsy in 1911]; Wade-Gery 1958; Walbank 1985; Waterhouse and Hope Simpson 1960–61.

ACKNOWLEDGEMENTS

The ultimate origins of this short paper lie in a contribution to the 1991 Anglo-American Conference of Historians, in a panel on '*Capital Cities and the State*'. Another version was delivered at Durham University in November 1995. Thanks are due to members of the audiences at all three presentations, especially Hector Catling and Joost Crouwel, for helpful comments and suggestions. But my main debt is to Susan Walker both for organising the B. M. colloquium so skilfully and for inviting me to participate.

4

Spartan art: its many different deaths

Reinhard Förtsch

In the fourth century BC Sparta was considered a state where visual art had long since been abolished (Nafissi 1991: 227 f.). Remarks made by Herodotus (ii 167) confirm that artists as a social group were more despised in Sparta than in other poleis. According to Thucydides (i 10 2), the urban appearance of Sparta would not allow any conclusions to be drawn about its present or future military and political power. The arts, which were flourishing at the time of Alkman and others in the late seventh century, seemed to have come to an end before the days of Herodotus and Thucydides.

The archaeological response to this picture is no longer new and for this reason one might expect more than the repeated representation of Spartan material culture as a purportedly new discovery (Christ 1996). So the basic question to be raised is the role that the visual arts played in Sparta. This is too complex a problem to be dealt with in one short paper, so I wish here to focus on a detailed problem, namely the decrease in the production of Laconian art. In the minds of modern researchers Spartan art has died many different deaths. Its death is a topic which is closely connected with the question of how art was conditioned by the development of the Spartan constitution. In the first part of this paper I shall consider the history of research, and in the second the archaeological evidence.

In the development of the Spartan constitution there is a clear process of change. An earlier period was characterized by a taste for luxury and appreciation of art by the Spartan aristocracy. This was then suppressed by the levelling ideology of the Homoioi, hostile to any form of luxury and visual art. Thus, from approximately 600 BC, the visual arts became subject to increasing censorship. That does not mean, however, that art came to a sudden halt.

Research carried out so far may be divided into three positions:

(i) The *separation* of historical and archaeological criteria.
(ii) The *direct connection* of historical and archaeological criteria.
(iii) The *dialectic connection* of historical and archaeological criteria, i.e. the proposal of a specific status for the visual arts.

POSITION I: SEPARATION OF HISTORY AND ARCHAEOLOGY

It was the British archaeologist R. M. Cook who adopted a provocatively agnostic position (Cook 1962). He maintained that not only have the literary records of Spartan austerity been exaggerated but, in addition and principally, he denies that there ever was any correlation between art and austerity. The interest of Finley in 1975 focused just on the development of the constitution (Finley 1975: 161 f.). He denied the reliability of archaeological sources altogether. His hostility towards the 'extremely subjective judgment of the archaeologists' and the 'fashionable allusions to archaeological evidence, which, in the end, do not really prove anything', is quite understandable. However, Finley was not absolutely up to date with the latest research, for example in the field of Laconian vase-painting (Stibbe 1972). In his analysis of the development of the Spartan constitution published in 1975, Bringmann did not include archaeological sources, which may be regarded as the continuation of the aporistic tendency already expressed by Finley (Bringmann 1975). Untouched by all discussions about visual art, a standard interpretation of Greek history, the German 'Propyläen Weltgeschichte' by Alfred Heuss, even in its 1979 edition maintained that Sparta became 'Tyrtaic' in the second half of the seventh century BC (Heuss 1979).

POSITION II: A DIRECT CONNECTION BETWEEN HISTORY AND ARCHAEOLOGY

Impressed by their new discoveries in the sanctuary of Artemis Orthia, Dickins and Woodward (in 1912) connected the evident interruption in the production of art in Laconia, around the middle of the sixth century, with a Spartan move towards austerity (Dickins and Woodward 1912; Dickins 1913). They saw this upheaval as a distinct event that took place in a relatively short time. This could not fit the conventional dates of the reformist Lykourgos, who was said to have lived in the ninth or eighth century BC. So their main interest focused instead on the figure of the Ephor Chilon, who was proposed as the initiator of the *volte-face*. And it soon became clear that neither the theory of a sudden death, nor that of an end of production towards the middle of the sixth century, could be maintained.

The assessment of Dickins and Woodward, though, had already become a standard theme. Even today the tendency persists to date certain monuments before the middle of the sixth century, higher than is stylistically possible, in order to make them 'pre-Chilonian', so the picture of Chilon as *Lycurgus redivivus* can be kept up. Examples are the bronze kraters and the architectural fragments of the Amyklaion (Stibbe 1996: 128 f.; Faustoferri 1996). In 1935 A. Blakeway tried to explain this phenomenon on economic grounds since it was obvious that the theory proposed by Dickins did not extend late enough. The supposed end of Laconian art presented itself as a longer process—even taking into account the constitutional development, a radical change was no longer conceivable. In 1983 Clauss expressed his doubts about the validity of the archaeological evidence (Clauss 1983: 24, 179 ff.). He questioned the notion of the 'decline' of Laconian art and pointed to types continuing. Furthermore he was sceptical about any relationship between political development and the production of art.

POSITION III: THE DIALECTIC CONNECTION BETWEEN HISTORY AND ARCHAEOLOGY

In 1965 Starr considered the relationship of austerity to art. He compared the end of the Laconian black-figure workshops with the end of the much more significant Corinthian ones. Furthermore he pointed to the persistence of Laconian bronze statuettes into the fifth century. Spartan militarism did not necessarily lead to the decline of art. Starr recognized that one had to define the interaction of both factors, thus coming closer to a dynamic concept of culture. In 1977 Holladay replied to Cook's contribution. In his view growing austerity, which acted as a stimulus for the *damos* of hoplites, also represented a return to an *agoge* revived from ancient times. Regarding the date, he suggested that the military crisis with Tegea in the early sixth century provoked the development. He saw no clear-cut break in the production of art, because, due to Sparta's isolation, this rather slow process was noticed only in retrospect and as late as the fourth century BC, when the writers of the time had to explain the striking situation by historical constructions. Holladay measured the impact on art and culture in terms of a partial militarization of the subject-matter and a cut in production.

In 1979 Cartledge summarized the current state of research, using a data-base that was unequalled (Cartledge 1979: 155 f.). He too did not date the move towards austerity any earlier than the sixth century, and did not recognize a deep cut in the production of art *c.* 550. He proposed a displacement of the displays of luxury by rich Spartan citizens as a consequence of this process. Since 'conspicuous consumption' in the symposium, as well as extravagant clothing, private property or rich votive offerings became ever more problematical, the Spartans shifted their investment in the display of personal status to quadriga races at Olympia, at that time the most prestigious *agon* in the ancient world. In 1980 Fitzhardinge outlined an important counter-model, which took into account the question of the patrons of art. According to him the immediate consequence of the victory in the Second Messenian War was not austerity but, on the contrary, an increase in luxury and the production of art. He referred to Alkman, to the ivories and the bronze statuettes. Events of the first half of the sixth century, the unsuccessful war against Tegea and the immediately consequent change of orientation from a policy of conquest to one of consolidation, did not have any noticeable influence on the development of art. Indeed, this period saw the beginning of the export of Laconian black figured pottery, and the Olympic victories continued as well. After the middle of the sixth century production in Laconia, as in other centres, was reduced to supplying the local market, mainly as a result of the intense competition from Athens. At the same time, the production of stone sculpture had increased, there were public commissions for artists such as the new construction in the sanctuary of Apollo at Amyklai and the *Skias* in the agora at Sparta. After the Persian wars the last sculptures were created: the Stoa of the Persians, new monuments at the Menelaion and dedications by the politically reduced nobility on the occasion of their victories in Olympic quadriga races. In the most recent analysis M. Nafissi tries to specify the production and export of certain forms into certain areas by quantification (Nafissi 1991: 11, 13, 24, 99). He sees austerity as a process of slow effect growing out of a need for social integration. It is determined less by law or political decisions than by the mutual control of two social groups of equal importance. In opposition to Fitzhardinge, he sees the thriving Hoplite *damos* as the main market for artistic production in the sixth century. However, one might raise the question why the production of art eventually fell, if the social groups who were its main consumers were still flourishing. Could it be that the *damos*, although it had for a time imitated the former aristocracy, in the end readopted an attitude of hostility against all art?

PRODUCTION DATA

The models defined above outline the principal approaches to understanding the role of art in Sparta. In the second part of my paper I wish to confront these models with the available data concerning the course of artistic production. The picture given here may differ from a more precise analysis of votive-complexes in certain sanctuaries (Hodkinson, this conference), and it differs also from a quantified analysis of production (Nafissi 1991: 252), but its main aim is to encompass the greatest possible range and consequently the data comprise a wide variety of forms and shapes produced over a long span of time. Only in the areas of basic needs, for example pottery and terracotta, does it not cover the overall activity of workshops.

In considering the chronology of works of art in parallel with the political situation, one will have to proceed with caution. The main turning points in the development of Sparta are described in the top line of TABLE 4.1.

(i) Second Messenian War, about 650–600 BC (a profound crisis, affecting the future definition of the Spartan state).
(ii) Reforms of the second half of the seventh century BC and the Great Rhetra (a reaction to the Second Messenian War).
(iii) Reigns of kings Leon and Agasikles soon after 600 BC (a phase of consolidation after the victory in the Second Messenian War).
(iv) Military crisis with Tegea 580–560 BC (a new crisis acting, like (i) above, as a catalyst in the constitutional development of Sparta).
(v) Sparta's military-orientated consolidation around 550 BC (the cultural situation recorded in the fifth/fourth century BC sources is now reached).
(vi) The Spartans change from athletic contests to quadriga races 576–550 BC (an indication of a deep-rooted change in the attitude of the Spartans).

(For the following see TABLE 4.1.) In the first half of the eighth century the earliest form of vessel relevant for the archaic period came into being—the Lakaina. In this case there may have been an unbroken transition from a geometric predecessor to the archaic examples.

Approximately 700 BC, the production of cut-out animal figures in ivory started (Marangou 1970: 125 Cat. No. 72).

In the second quarter of the seventh century BC the formation of a symposium culture becomes apparent, with important and, as in the case of the stirrup-kraters, very long-lived shapes. Given that the predominance of the aristocratic order in Sparta following the victory in the First Messenian War is ascribed to this phase, the different kinds of art that now emerged do not really seem to be as numerous as one might expect.

In the third quarter of the seventh century BC, nine different branches of production came into being, which is more than twice the number in the preceding quarter of a century. Even if one does not really have a clear view of the whole situation, the marked intensification in production cannot be denied; leading artistic forms include standing female statues—the precursor of the bronze statuettes—as well as female protomes and ivory *kouroi*. Combs of type A and daedalic representations add important votive objects to the repertoire of ivories. More and more Sparta now becomes a centre of ivory carving in Greece. The range of symposium vessels is increased by the addition of the relief krater and two Lakaina types, one of which is the significant and long-lived 'canonical' type. Increasing in size, the relief kraters now mark the appearance of the first real luxury objects.

The obvious increase in production, already evident during this stage, is not consonant with the model offered by Fitzhardinge, according to which this increase did not come about before the end of the Second Messenian War. Moreover, the general scale of production does not reflect a fundamental Spartan crisis, and visual art does not seem to be repressed by a sense of austerity.

Eleven new branches of production emerge in the last quarter of the seventh century BC, which again indicates a slight increase compared with the preceding quarter. The symposium pottery is enriched both by the earliest groups of black figured cups, and also by the bronze hydrias of the Telestas group, which are of precious material and decorated with handle protomes. The earlier Laconian acroteria, now emerging, are a form of monumental architectural decoration.

The number of newly introduced types increases dramatically in the second half of the seventh century BC, from one and a quarter to nine, a tendency that continues into the first half of the sixth century. Another change was brought about by innovations in vase painting, which up to that time had not changed since the Late Geometric phase. It is to this period that the Second Messenian War, the reforms associated with the Great Rhetra and the rise of the Hoplite *damos* are dated. The introduction of the Hoplite phalanx in Sparta about the middle of the seventh century BC could even be seen as a process supporting the initial rise in the production of art.

In the first quarter of the sixth century the large-scale sculptures, the bronze tripods and the volute kraters appear, representing important genres of art. Relief kraters are followed by bronze kraters indicating increased luxury in the symposium. The production of metal vessels acquires an almost pivotal position both on a local and on an interregional scale. In this field a tremendous increase in quantity and quality takes place. The greatest variety is to be found in bronze statuettes, including *kouroi*, figures in motion, animals in motion, naked girls serving as mirror supports and running figures wearing the short chiton. Ivory production, however, with its final genre, the little tablets showing an 'ajouré' pattern, comes to an end towards the last quarter of the century. The further typological development of the drinking cups does not show any marked divergences; in the case of the black figure cups, Stibbe groups 3 and 4 are introduced. Group 4, showing for the first time a body on a slightly higher foot, holds some promise for future development; the black glazed and black figured Lakainai appear for the first time. The introduction of fourteen new forms represents the highest rate of increase ever reached; at the same time no less than thirty of the chosen forms are in contemporary use. This crescendo built up almost continuously from the third quarter of the seventh century and did not happen all of a sudden at Sparta's victory in the Second Messenian War. In any assessment, the standard that was reached at this time represents a high demand for and acceptance of art within Spartan society.

In the second quarter of the sixth century, the terracotta acroteria are joined by a new monumental genre made of marble, a form that lasted right into late Hellenism. The black figure cups of Stibbe groups 5–9 show the greatest variation, although there is at the same time a decrease in quality and quantity foreshadowing the end of production in the following quarter of the century. The bronze statuettes are enriched by several new basic types: female figures wearing the peplos, *korai* wearing chiton and *Schrägmantel*, goddesses and wreathed *kouroi*. In the class of bronze hydriai the groups with anthropomorphic handles and female handle protomes are introduced; the kantharoi include groups 3 and 4.

The number of new types reaches four, as in the first quarter; the number of types in contemporary use peaks at 37. The development of the black figure cups, described above, shows that these numbers, however representative they are for the whole situation, give few signs of an incipient decrease. The military crisis of the conflict with Tegea does not have any impact on this situation, at least not immediately. The rate of decline in the number of forms increases once more: at 25 year intervals from 650–575 one records the loss of five, five, seven and ten forms. At first sight this might be interpreted as an effect of the growing capacity of overall production: the greater the number of forms produced, the more they can disappear again. At this point however, the first phase of the three great 'phases of cessation', a period that saw the end of an exceptionally large number of types, makes itself felt: in the period 575–525 one records ten, fifteen and eleven forms. Here a far-reaching change of production becomes evident. For these reasons I would suggest a relationship between the crisis with Tegea and the underlying fundamental change in Sparta, leading to the strict discipline of the fifth and fourth centuries.

In the third quarter of the sixth century, the later Laconian terracotta acroteria emerge and the main production of marble acroteria now begins. The last group of black figured cups emerges, developing in form out of the preceding types. Representations of hoplites are introduced as the last but one type of bronze statuette. Further lines of production, which extend right into Roman times, are started in the form of the first stone reliefs showing heroes and the Dioskouroi. Already earlier research has established that in this period production had undergone a change in subject-matter chosen. Most striking is the accentuation of a traditional theme (namely the hoplite) in association with the types of relief (showing the Dioskouroi or heroes), which, once established at this time, was repeated relatively unchanged. Furthermore marble acroteria, having fully displaced the terracotta acroteria, prove to be monumental and long-lived forms. A change is shown by the crossing of statistical thresholds. There is a clear decrease in the introduction of new types: whereas in the preceding quarter centuries nine, eleven, fourteen and fourteen categories had been introduced, only five new ones emerged during the third quarter of the sixth century. The number of types disappearing rises to the maximum value of fifteen.

In the absence of a wider base of observation, the research carried out in the past has led to a contradictory assessment of the question 'termination or continuation'. In my view it seems to be of special significance that this process is in a way ambivalent. However great the number of types whose production has terminated may appear, they do not have an immediate impact on the whole spectrum, as the number of existing forms diminishes only from 37 to 32. This may indicate the combination of a far-reaching structural change coinciding with a delay in its consequences. Only in the following century does the recession make itself felt; the continuing abundance of types, however, is an inheritance from the past. This does not in the least lead to a halt in the production of art. On the contrary, the start of a new epoch is heralded, the origins of which are partially hidden by the density of the total number of types: three of the five most important forms, which continue into the fifth century, and some of them even into the Hellenistic period, start exactly at the point when the greatest decrease so far known is recorded. Especially in that general context, the new forms could hardly have achieved their numbers and persistence without strong support from the public authorities. The new forms emerge with a more distinct orientation towards traditional and military aspects. Here is the point at which Spartan art is thought to have died. How did it live on afterwards?

The last quarter of the sixth century brings only one new type of bronze statuette: the athlete. At this time there are still 18 different types existing alongside each other compared to the 32 in the preceding quarter of a century. But public projects like the bronze krater for Kroisos decorated with figures, the throne at Amyklai and the temple of Athena Chalkioikos are still being undertaken. This is proof that it is an anachronism to expect a general decline in

TABLE 4.1 Forms of Spartan art in chronological sequence

≈ 735–715 First Messenian war — Kings Theopompos and Polydoros (distribution of land) — ≈ 630–620 Second Messenian war — Kings Leon and Agasikles — Consolidation of power, militarization

Dates BC	725	700	675	650	625	600	575	550	525	500	475
New forms:	1	1	3	9	11	14	14	5	1		
Parallel existing forms:	1	2	5	14	21	30	37	32	18	7	5
Ceasing forms:				5	5	7	10	15	11	2	

Form	Span
Lakainai: "late geometric group" (Stibbe 1990, 75)	>**************
Ivory: rectangular fibula plates (Marangou 1970, 13)	**************
Craters: stirrup craters (Stibbe 1989, 14, 22, 91)	***************************************>
Craters: volute craters (Stibbe 1989, 14, 91 Cat.-Nr. B 1)	*********************
Ivory: lying animals (Marangou 1970, 117 f.)	*****
Kantharoi: Stibbe group 5 (Stibbe 1978, 29, 37 Cat.-Nr. 16 f.)	*******************
Bronze statuettes: female figures (Herfort-Koch 1986, 19 f.)	*********
Lakainai: Stibbe "Laconian 1 group" (Stibbe, 1990, 77)	******
Ivory: female protomes (Marangou 1970, 151 f.)	*****
Ivory: kouroi (Marangou 1970, 163 f.)	*****
Lakainai: Stibbe "canonical group" (Stibbe 1990, 94 f.)	*********************
Ivory: combs type A (Marangou 1970, 94 f.)	*******
Ivory: daedalic figures (Marangou 1970, 130 f.)	****
Craters: relief craters (Schleiffenbaum 1991, 28 f.)	*********
Kantharoi: Stibbe group 1 (Stibbe 1978, 23, 37 Cat.-Nr. 6)	**************
Bronze hydriai: Telestas-group (Stibbe 1992, 14 f.)	******************
Kantharoi: Stibbe group 2 (Stibbe 1978, 37 Cat.-Nr. 8)	*****************
'Ivory': reliefs made of bone (Marangou 1970, 171 f.)	******
Lakainai: Stibbe "group with experimental decoration" (Stibbe 1990, 78 f., 91 f.)	**********
Older Laconian acroteria (Kästner 1990, 251 f.)	************
Bronze statuettes: female figures with chiton (Herfort-Koch 1986, 19 f.)	*******
Lakainai: Stibbe "black and coloured group" (Stibbe 1990, 103 f.)	*************

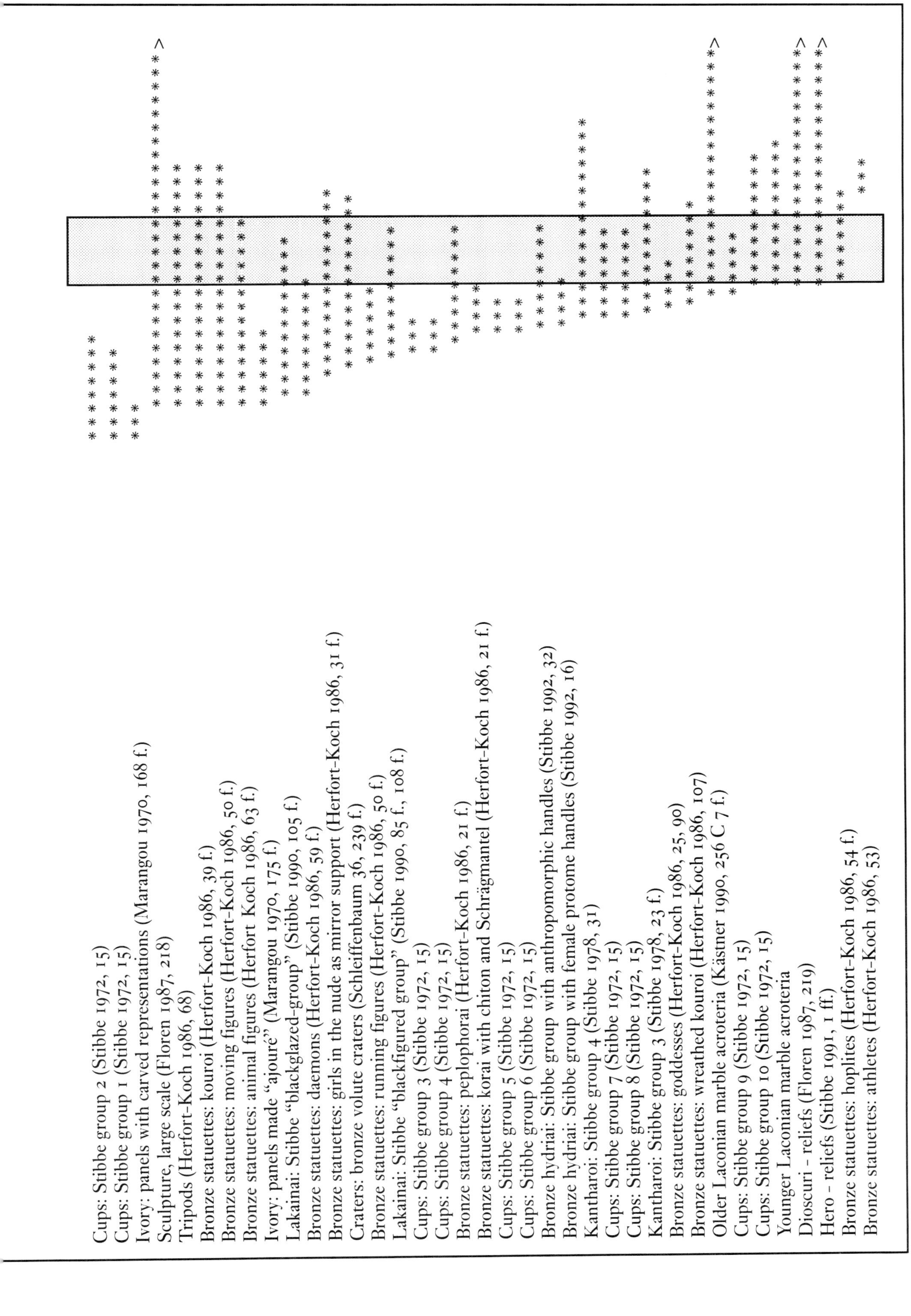
Cups: Stibbe group 2 (Stibbe 1972, 15)
Cups: Stibbe group 1 (Stibbe 1972, 15)
Ivory: panels with carved representations (Marangou 1970, 168 f.)
Sculpture, large scale (Floren 1987, 218)
Tripods (Herfort-Koch 1986, 68)
Bronze statuettes: kouroi (Herfort-Koch 1986, 39 f.)
Bronze statuettes: moving figures (Herfort-Koch 1986, 50 f.)
Bronze statuettes: animal figures (Herfort Koch 1986, 63 f.)
Ivory: panels made "ajouré" (Marangou 1970, 175 f.)
Lakainai: Stibbe "blackglazed-group" (Stibbe 1990, 105 f.)
Bronze statuettes: daemons (Herfort-Koch 1986, 59 f.)
Bronze statuettes: girls in the nude as mirror support (Herfort-Koch 1986, 31 f.)
Craters: bronze volute craters (Schleiffenbaum 36, 239 f.)
Bronze statuettes: running figures (Herfort-Koch 1986, 50 f.)
Lakainai: Stibbe "blackfigured group" (Stibbe 1990, 85 f., 108 f.)
Cups: Stibbe group 3 (Stibbe 1972, 15)
Cups: Stibbe group 4 (Stibbe 1972, 15)
Bronze statuettes: peplophorai (Herfort-Koch 1986, 21 f.)
Bronze statuettes: korai with chiton and Schrägmantel (Herfort-Koch 1986, 21 f.)
Cups: Stibbe group 5 (Stibbe 1972, 15)
Cups: Stibbe group 6 (Stibbe 1972, 15)
Bronze hydriai: Stibbe group with anthropomorphic handles (Stibbe 1992, 32)
Bronze hydriai: Stibbe group with female protome handles (Stibbe 1992, 16)
Kantharoi: Stibbe group 4 (Stibbe 1978, 31)
Cups: Stibbe group 7 (Stibbe 1972, 15)
Cups: Stibbe group 8 (Stibbe 1972, 15)
Kantharoi: Stibbe group 3 (Stibbe 1978, 23 f.)
Bronze statuettes: goddesses (Herfort-Koch 1986, 25, 90)
Bronze statuettes: wreathed kouroi (Herfort-Koch 1986, 107)
Older Laconian marble acroteria (Kästner 1990, 256 C 7 f.)
Cups: Stibbe group 9 (Stibbe 1972, 15)
Cups: Stibbe group 10 (Stibbe 1972, 15)
Younger Laconian marble acroteria
Dioscuri - reliefs (Floren 1987, 219)
Hero - reliefs (Stibbe 1991, 1 ff.)
Bronze statuettes: hoplites (Herfort-Koch 1986, 54 f.)
Bronze statuettes: athletes (Herfort-Koch 1986, 53)

visual art at the beginning of an age of austerity. But the undeniable change in the structure of production was of a far more complex character. If particularly ostentatious works of art were tolerated in the public arena, that does not rule out the stifling of art for personal use. For all the public projects, a resolution of the *Apella* and the agreement of Kings, Ephors and the *gerousia* may be seen as a precondition.

In the first two quarters of the fifth century BC, no new forms were created and the number of existing ones fell dramatically—to seven and then to five.

The change in the fifth century is manifested not only in the selection of the already existing genres, but also in the narrowing range of production. This may reflect the weakening competitiveness of the only half-tolerated *cheirotechnai* of Sparta, a fate from which even the more important Corinthian art could not escape. More significant was the growing decline in clients at Sparta itself. For, if this had not been the case, the losses in production might have been replaced by the import of goods, or artists. On the contrary, Sparta intensified its isolation from the outside world. In any case, the demise of the archaic types does not mean that the use of art in Sparta stopped as well. For a long time research overlooked two factors: artistic production of the fifth century BC in Sparta itself and public votive-offerings. Characteristically enough, Kritias, quoted by Athenaios and Plutarch, speaks about highly skilled centres of production still existing at the end of the fifth century BC, although these are strictly limited to the production of very basic goods. These products existed alongside goods meeting the highest demands, which were made for dedication in sanctuaries. Also in the fifth century Sparta placed important votive-offerings in the great sanctuaries inside and outside Laconia: the tripod commemorating Plataia at Delphi, the two portrait-statues of Pausanias himself by the altar of Athena Chalkioikos in Sparta, two statues of Nike in the sanctuary of Athena Ergane at Sparta dedicated by Pausanias, the statues of the Dedication of Lysander at Delphi made by the greatest sculptors in Greece. Furthermore, there is a great difference between the Spartan choice of public projects and those patronized by other poleis: the very extensive communal projects like those carried out in Athens or Argos, which were characteristic of the Greek polis in the Classical period, are missing at Sparta. In brief, the Spartans used art in completely different ways derived from different traditions. This suggests a variety of motives for the groups of patrons and clients, which may be assigned to two main currents: an aristocratic, luxury-loving tendency and a gradually pervading restrictive attitude to visual art. Spartan art did not die, but it underwent a decisive transition from the first to the second approach.

5

Patterns of bronze dedications at Spartan sanctuaries, *c.* 650–350 BC: towards a quantified database of material and religious investment

Stephen Hodkinson

INTRODUCTION AND BACKGROUND

The aim of this paper is to advocate and describe a new approach to Laconian archaeology which can shed fresh light on important aspects of Spartan society. There is of course a variety of ways in which one can approach the material culture of a society, several of which are well-established in Laconian research: for example, studies of the typology and production of Laconian art, of its iconography, and study of the social function of particular classes of artefact. The study described here, however, adopts a different approach by examining the artefacts from four main Spartan sanctuaries as a record of expenditure and of material and religious investment.

In certain respects the previous neglect of issues of expenditure and investment is surprising, because several earlier studies have attempted to use the evidence of Laconian material culture to document the growth of the austere lifestyle ascribed to Classical Sparta by ancient writers (e.g. Dickins 1908b; Blakeway 1935; Stubbs 1950; Holladay 1977; Fitzhardinge 1980). Indeed, this concern arose precisely out of the finds made earlier this century by British excavations at Artemis Orthia and other Spartan sanctuaries. Logically, issues of Spartiate expenditure and investment, as revealed by patterns of dedications at these sanctuaries, ought to have been at the centre of the debate about Spartan austerity. But instead, from the very start (Dickins 1908b), the debate was deflected towards a discussion of the production of Laconian art and its supposed decline from the late sixth century onwards. I have argued elsewhere (Hodkinson, forthcoming) that this orientation of the debate was, fundamentally, a wrong turn. Since in the Classical period the Spartiates themselves were (with perhaps a few, unimportant exceptions) not directly responsible for craft activity, patterns of Laconian artistic production are a less meaningful test of their austerity than the direct evidence of their expenditure and investment revealed by the material record. But, quite apart from its relevance to this particular debate, the question of how wealth was expended and resources invested by the inhabitants of Laconia in antiquity is surely an important issue with significant implications for many aspects of their society. There is good reason to add this perspective to our repertoire of approaches towards the archaeology of Laconia.

A DATABASE OF BRONZE DEDICATIONS: OBSTACLES TO A QUANTIFIED APPROACH

In this paper I shall describe my attempt to apply this perspective to a specific corpus of archaeological evidence relating to the Spartiate citizen body in the Archaic and Classical periods, the excavated finds from four main Spartan sanctuaries: Artemis Orthia, the Menelaion, the sanctuary of Apollo at Amyklai and the sanctuaries on the Acropolis. Given the paucity of excavated material from Spartan habitation or burial contexts, the sanctuary finds—although not unproblematic in character, as we shall see—form the most coherent body of available archaeological evidence, the product of excavations going back over 100 years, with the potential to inform us about the Spartiates' expenditure and investment of wealth on votive offerings to the gods.[1] Among the range of finds, I chose to focus upon the bronze votives. My selection was influenced by the status of bronze as a relatively precious metal whose votive use indicates a not insignificant investment which,

1. The finds from early Greek and German work at the Amyklaion were reported in *Archaiologike Ephemeris* 1892: 1–26; *Mitteilungen des Deutschen Archäologischen Instituts, Athenische Abteilung* 52, 1927: 1–85. For the original British excavations at Artemis Orthia, the Acropolis and the Menelaion, *Annual of the British School at Athens* 12 (1905/6) –16 (1909/10); Dawkins 1929. Subsequent work in the 1920s, esp. on the Acropolis, appeared in *BSA* 26, (1923/4)–30 (1928/9). For preliminary reports of the more recent Menelaion excavations, Journal of Hellenic Studies, *Archaeological Reports* 23 (1976/77) 24–42; *Lakonikai Spoudai* 2 (1975) 258–69; 3 (1977) 408–16; 8 (1986) 205–16.

nevertheless, came in the form of a variety of offerings, large and small, reflecting a wide range of expenditures.[2]

I should immediately emphasize the obstacles to this enterprise. First, although bronze survives in greater quantities than more expensive metals, the archaeological record of bronze dedications at Spartan sanctuaries, as elsewhere in Greece, is seriously compromised and depleted by several post-depositional factors: the melting down of votives by temple officials, the increasing frequency of plunder from the late Classical period onwards, and the susceptibility of bronze to corrosion and disintegration, especially in damp and humid climatic conditions, such as at Artemis Orthia with its low-lying situation by the flood-prone River Eurotas (Droop 1929: 196). Consequently, the numbers of excavated bronzes are a minimum to be multiplied many times over in any estimation of the original level of bronze dedications. An even greater problem, however, is the differential effect of the above factors upon votives of different types and periods. For example, large objects of sheet metal, such as sizeable vessels, are more easily melted down and corroded than cast objects and have therefore typically suffered greater depletion. (This phenomenon is only partly compensated by finds of the cast handles and ornaments of vessels whose bodies no longer survive.) Conditions have also often been more conducive to the preservation of Archaic than Classical material. At Artemis Orthia the sealed deposit created when the Spartans covered the sanctuary with a layer of sand in the early sixth century enabled earlier votives to escape the worst effects of the site's humidity, whereas the unsealed Classical and later bronzes have suffered much more heavily.

The incomplete and differential survival of the original dedications is not in itself an unusual problem. Those of us who work regularly with ancient written sources, for example, are well-accustomed to the challenges posed by surviving evidence which forms only a small and partial sample of the original literary corpus. The problem is, however, compounded by a second difficulty: the incomplete publication of the excavated finds. The fundamental requirement for a thorough study of expenditure and investment is a complete database of the finds, in order to permit quantification of the numbers of dedications of various types made in different periods. Unfortunately, few of the excavation reports display an interest in quantification of the bronze finds and many of the bronzes remain unpublished.[3] The incomplete publication of the metal finds from Tsountas's 1890 excavations at the Amyklaion has recently been detailed by Calligas (1992), and the record of the early British excavations was little better. Publication of the bronzes from Artemis Orthia (Droop 1907a and 1929; Lamb 1927b), in contrast to some other classes of finds (Dawkins 1929), was confined to selected artefacts and biased towards finds from earlier periods. The bronzes from some years of the 1920s Acropolis excavations received fuller treatment from Winifred Lamb (1927a); but, even so, her coverage was biased towards objects of artistic significance, with other finds mentioned in such generic fashion (for example, 'handles of various types') as to lack statistical value. She did not, moreover, attempt to re-study the bronzes from the earlier Acropolis excavations which had received much less satisfactory coverage (Dickins 1907a: 146–50; 1908a: 145; Woodward 1925c: 266–74). The early reports from the Menelaion excavations (Wace, Thompson and Droop 1909) were similarly inadequate, providing little discussion of individual artefacts or indication of numbers of bronzes.

The published evidence, then, provides only a selective coverage of the finds governed largely by considerations of artistic quality rather than by concern for the assemblage as a whole. To resume the analogy with written evidence, it is as if the original editor of the Aristotelian *Constitution of Athens*, a work discovered on papyrus in 1890, in the same year as Tsountas's excavations at the Amyklaion, had decided to publish only those parts of the text judged to be of literary merit! Ultimately, a comprehensive study of the bronze votives will therefore need to go back beyond the published reports to a re-examination of the finds themselves. An essential preliminary, however, must be to bring some order to the haphazard state of the published evidence, currently scattered over numerous excavation reports, by compiling a systematic database of all the bronzes mentioned (however inadequately) in publications to date. The outcome of this exercise is set out in TABLES 5.1, 5.3a–c and 5.4a–d, where the data is presented in quantitative form, covering the period *c.* 650–*c.* 350 BC. My chronological focus reflects partly the historical period central to my personal research, but partly also the imprecise classification of earlier finds in the excavation reports: typical labels such as 'Geometric' are too vague for the finer chronological specification required. The tables, naturally, bear many marks of the deficiencies of the published reports. The frequent appearance of the 'Ind' and '+' signs, for example, indicates the large number of cases in which reports fail to specify the precise number of artefacts. The reports also often provide either no information

2. Although some sanctuary finds were not votive offerings *sensu stricto* (most notably, utensils and vessels used in cult rituals), such objects were often gifts by worshippers and as such constitute good evidence for private expenditure and religious investment.

3. Spartan excavation reports are of course not the only ones to suffer from these deficiencies; *cf.* Simon 1986, 175 on the varied quality of publication of Ionian sanctuary sites.

TABLE 5.1: **Published bronze finds from Spartan sanctuaries, *c.* 650–*c.* 350**

	Orthia	*Acropolis*	*Menelaion*	*Amyklaion*	*Total*
c. 650–*c.* 600	40+	3	24+	5+	72+
c. 600–*c.* 550	22	7/8	22+	3+	54+
c. 550–*c.* 500	6	15–18	6+	8/9	35+
c. 500–*c.* 450	2	10–14	2+	1/2	15+
c. 450–*c.* 400	1	5–7	Ind	0/1	7+
c. 400–*c.* 350	-	1	-	-	1
Early Archaic	1	-	-	-	1
Archaic	13	-	Ind	5	19+
Late Archaic	-	-	-	3	3
L. III–V and later	-	-	11+	-	11+
DNG	3	74+	3+	115+	195+

Key: DNG = Date Not Given; L. = Laconian
The signs '+' and 'Ind' signify the existence of an indefinite number of artefacts whose limit is not specified in the relevant excavation reports.

or only vague indications concerning the dating of artefacts; hence the large number of objects with unhelpful labels like 'DNG' (Date Not Given) or 'Archaic'. This lack is clearly most serious at the Amyklaion where, as TABLE 5.1 makes clear, fully 80% of the finds are undated.

Does this provisional and incomplete database shed any light on the issues of Spartiate expenditure and religious investment? Following the catalogue of deficiencies rehearsed above, it might be questioned whether the published evidence can be used to any serious effect. But I would argue that even the flawed database currently available can suggest significant hypotheses for future, more comprehensive study. These hypotheses may also serve a heuristic role in demonstrating the academic potential of a more complete database, thus encouraging efforts towards a systematic re-study of the finds. The remainder of this essay will attempt to put some flesh on the bones of these propositions.

THE GROWTH OF AN AUSTERE SOCIETY?

TABLE 5.1 presents the global statistics of published bronze finds from the four main Spartan sanctuaries in the period *c.* 650–*c.* 350 BC, divided into periods of 50 years. TABLES 5.3a–c then provide a more detailed breakdown of the dedication of the most common types of bronze votives (vessels, jewellery, statuettes and figurines) across the range of sanctuaries, while TABLES 5.4a–d examine the distribution of these types sanctuary by sanctuary. What conclusions do the Tables suggest? For a start, they provide unambiguous confirmation that in the period to *c.* 550, and even down to *c.* 500, Spartans expended their resources on a range of metal votive offerings. The published bronze record attests a number of relatively grandiose objects such as vessels, furniture with metal attachments, armour, decorative plaques, as well as more modest statuettes and personal and dress items.

In the period after *c.* 550, as TABLE 5.1 shows, there is a decline in the total number of bronze finds. At first sight this might seem to document the growth of the austere society depicted in the ancient sources; but the picture is in reality more complex. Between *c.* 550 and *c.* 500 bronze finds actually increase on the Acropolis, and possibly also at the Amyklaion. There is also more continuity into the fifth century than might at first be apparent. On the Acropolis dedications maintain their higher levels on into early fifth century. Even in the later fifth century they are still at a level comparable with votives of the early sixth century, and higher than those of the later seventh century. In fact, there is cause to think that the fifth-century figures might be significantly increased. The Acropolis finds include between 40 and 50 bronze bells; but only five of these which bore inscriptions were individually itemised and dated in the excavation reports; the remainder were mentioned only in passing.[4] All the inscribed bells were dated by the excava-

4. The five itemised examples are discussed in *BSA* 24 (1919–21) 118 nos. 66–8; 26 (1923–25) 273–4 no. 7; 30 (1928–30) 252 no. 5; the passing mention of *c.* 40 other bells comes in *BSA* 30 (1928–30) 273.

tors to the fifth century. If similar dates should apply to the other 40 or so (currently included among the category 'Date Not Given'), then the fifth-century Acropolis bronzes would outnumber finds of earlier periods by a considerable margin.

It is only at Artemis Orthia and the Menelaion that the figures suggest a marked decline in bronze votives in the later sixth century. It might be argued that this in itself betokens some degree of austerity, especially since these two shrines have also produced the largest numbers of cheap lead votive figurines (Wace, Thompson and Droop 1909: 127–41; Wace 1929; Cavanagh and Laxton 1984). These leads have been cited as proof of the Spartans' increasing disdain for more precious metals which, it is argued, led them to opt for cheaper votives (Wace 1929: 250). TABLE 5.2 documents the increasing use of lead votives at Artemis Orthia from the later seventh century, rising to a dramatic peak in the sixth century, followed by a decline during the fifth century and later. (The chronological trajectory of the less well published Menelaion leads is apparently similar.) There is a certain overlap in the later sixth century between the decline of bronze votives and the peak of the leads. But the leads began increasing in popularity as early as the later seventh century and the period of their greatest use commenced in the second quarter of the sixth, both developments taking place before the decline in bronze dedications at the sanctuary. Moreover, the leads themselves declined early in the fifth century, in parallel with the further fall in bronze votives, during the period when Spartan society was supposedly becoming more austere. The lead figurines cannot, therefore, support the notion of an overall increase in austerity or explain the decline of bronze dedications at Artemis Orthia or the Menelaion. More germane to this decline is the sharp fall in jewellery and vessel dedications, a phenomenon by no means unique to Sparta, as we shall see below.

In sum, the present evidence indicates divergent trends between different Spartan sanctuaries and offers little material support for an overall growth of a uniquely austere society. This picture of specific change rather than global decline emerges still more clearly from the more detailed breakdown of votive trends provided in TABLES 5.3a–c and TABLES 5.4a–d. This suggests that jewellery and vessels formed the most frequent bronze dedications in the period *c.* 650–*c.* 550 (TABLES 5.4a–d). After *c.* 550 jewellery votives then fall away (TABLE 3b). The bronze vessels also decline after *c.* 550, except on the Acropolis where they continue at an undiminished level into the second half of the sixth century (TABLE 3a). Free-standing statuettes and figurines, on the other hand, increase in number after *c.* 550 and become the most prominent votive, especially on the Acropolis and at the Amyklaion (TABLES 5.3c, 5.4b, and 5.4d).

These changes were not confined to the bronzes. Jewellery motifs among the leads at both Artemis Orthia and the Menelaion declined significantly in numbers of both types and varieties during Leads III–IV (that is lead figurines of types dating *c.* 580–500), subsequently disappearing entirely in the fifth century. At Artemis Orthia the textile motifs, which may represent the items of clothing with which dedications of jewellery were often associated, also cease after the end of Lead II (*c.* 620–580).[5] Similarly, the upward trend of bronze statuettes and figurines finds some parallel among the leads, although at a somewhat earlier date: leads depicting human and animal figures (real or mythical) are very few in Lead I (*c.* 650–620), but increase and exceed jewellery motifs from Lead II (*c.* 620–580) onwards (Wace 1929: 280–1).

TABLES 5.3a–c and TABLES 5.4a–d. also indicate considerable variation in the distribution of various classes of bronze artefact between different sanctuaries. Vessels are found in reasonable numbers at all four sanctuaries. Jewellery votives, however, are much more prominent at Artemis Orthia and the Amyklaion than on the Acropolis. (There are also significant, though unspecified, numbers at the Menelaion.) Statuettes and figurines, in contrast, are most frequent on the Acropolis and quite common at the Amyklaion, but less frequent at Artemis Orthia and the Menelaion. These differences in the distribution and chronology of the various classes of votives are the reason for the divergent votive chronologies of the various sanctuaries evident in TABLE 5.1.

SPARTAN BRONZE DEDICATIONS IN THE WIDER GREEK CONTEXT

If the patterns of bronze dedications at Spartan sanctuaries are not suggestive of the growth of a uniquely austere society, the question follows whether they are indeed distinctive to Sparta. The capacity to pose this question is one of the most valuable advantages of the database since, inadequate as the statistics clearly are, they nonetheless have the merit of enabling us to bring the Spartan material record into relation with the wider Greek world. Quantifying the finds creates an independent basis for comparison with sanctuaries elsewhere, permitting us to go beyond impressionistic judgements which may be over-influenced by assumptions of Spartan uniqueness derived from the literary sources.

In broad terms, the patterns revealed here appear not to be unique, but to conform to general trends in

5. Wace 1929, esp. 279–82; Wace, Thompson and Droop 1909, 127. Wace himself did not recognise the textile motifs as such, terming them 'pendant plaques' and 'decorative plates (pendants?)': 1929: 255–6, 264–5, 270. I owe this point to Lin Foxhall.

TABLE 5.2: **Chronology of lead figurines from the sanctuary of Artemis Orthia**
(after Wace 1929: 251–2, with revised chronology)

	Period	*Number*	*No. per annum*
Lead 0	(? –650)	23	-
Lead I	(650–620)	5719	191
Lead II	(620–580)	9548	239
Lead III–IV	(580–500)	68822	860
Lead V	(500–425)	10617	142
Lead VI	(425–250)	4773	27

TABLE 5.3a: **Published bronze vessel finds**

	Orthia	*Acropolis*	*Menelaion*	*Amyklaion*	*Total*
c. 650–*c*. 600	6+	-	6+	4	16+
c. 600–*c*. 550	8	5	10+	2	25+
c. 550–*c*. 500	1	5/6	2+	1	9+
c. 500–*c*. 450	0/1	0/1	-	-	0–2
c. 450–*c*. 400	0/1	-	-	-	0/1
c. 400–*c*. 350	-	-	-	-	-
DNG or Vague	7	5+	1+	12+	25+

TABLE 5.3b: **Published bronze jewellery finds**

	Orthia	*Acropolis*	*Menelaion*	*Amyklaion*	*Total*
c. 650–*c*. 600	18	3	Ind	-	22+
c. 600–*c*. 550	11	-	Ind	-	12+
c. 550–*c*. 500	1	-	-	-	1
c. 500–*c*. 450	-	-	-	-	-
c. 450–*c*. 400	-	-	-	-	-
c. 400–*c*. 350	-	-	-	-	-
DNG or Vague	1	6	3+	75	85+

TABLE 5.3c: **Published bronze statuette/figurine finds**

	Orthia	*Acropolis*	*Menelaion*	*Amyklaion*	*Total*
c. 650–*c*. 600	1	-	Ind	-	2+
c. 600–*c*. 550	2	2/3	0/1	0/1	4–7
c. 550–*c*. 500	2	7–9	-	6/7	15–18
c. 500–*c*. 450	2	6–8	1	1/2	10–13
c. 450–*c*. 400	1	3/4	-	0/1	4–6
c. 400–*c*. 350	-	1	-	-	1
DNG or Vague	-	9+	1	12+	22+

bronze votive offerings throughout Greece, especially towards the end of the Archaic period. It has long been noted that these years witnessed a significant decline in the quantity of small votives at many Greek sanctuaries, including a marked decrease in bronze dedications (Payne 1940: 93; Tomlinson 1976: 23; Simon 1986: 106; Kyrieleis 1993: 129). Snodgrass (1990a) has argued that this phenomenon reflects major changes in the nature and role of votive offerings resulting from a profound change in religious practice—a further sign that we should not interpret the Spartan patterns in terms of a growth of local austerity. As the relatively small number of statistical case-studies cited in Snodgrass's study shows, there is need for many more systematic, quantitative studies of the nature and precise chronology of the phenomenon. A survey of published reports from a scatter of sites across the Greek world suggests, however, that the timing of the decline in (bronze) votives varies from sanctuary to sanctuary, at some places beginning early in the sixth century, at others not until the fifth. At the sanctuary of Hermes and Aphrodite at Symi Viannou on Crete the bronze plaques decline markedly around 600 (Lembesi 1985), as do other offerings. Indeed, several Cretan sanctuaries—though, note, not all—show a marked decline in votives in the sixth century (Morris, forthcoming). At the harbour sanctuary at Emporio on Chios few bronze finds were dated later than Period IV, which terminated *c.* 600 (Boardman 1967: xii, 205–29, 257). On the acropolis at Lindos on Rhodes the decline seems to commence in the later sixth century, to judge from the absence of bronzes ascribed to the period 525–400 (Blinkenberg 1931). At the shrine of Artemis on Samos votive deposits peak *c.* 550–525 and start to decline thereafter (Tsakos 1980); whereas at the sanctuary of Hera the decline is delayed until the fifth century (Kyrieleis 1993: 129). (Note, again, this example of differences between sanctuaries on the same island.) At Olympia the decline in helmet and jewellery dedications is also under way by the early fifth century (Kunze 1958: 118–51; 1961: 56–137; 1967: 111–83; Philipp 1981: 8–10), though other bronzes continue in force until the onset of a major rupture around 450 (Gauer 1991: 169; *cf.* Rolley 1993: 394–5). At Isthmia the peak of arms and armour dedications comes in the period after *c.* 550, only to be terminated abruptly with the destruction of the Archaic temple of Poseidon around 470 (Jackson 1992: 141–4); and the following period witnesses a comparative paucity of other valuable dedications (Broneer 1959: 339). These examples suggest that Spartan dedications patterns conform to the general Greek norm, not only in the general decline in bronze votives, but also in the variations between different Spartan sanctuaries in the precise timing of that decline.

So much for the general picture. But to what extent do the specific changes in the frequency of different types of votives at Spartan sanctuaries mirror developments elsewhere in Greece? Certainly, the frequency of Spartan early jewellery dedications *c.* 650–550 BC fits in with the general pattern at Archaic sanctuaries elsewhere (Simon 1986: 198). The subsequent decline of jewellery votives also occurs at other sanctuaries. It may be related to changes in style of clothing which included an increasing simplicity in decoration and ornamentation (Bonfante and Jaunzems 1988: 1390–91; *cf.* Herodotus v 87–8); but how closely the sixth-century decline of jewellery at Sparta matches the timing elsewhere is at present unclear. At Olympia the decline is largely a phenomenon of the early fifth century, and even then finger rings remain relatively numerous in the Classical period after a comparatively undistinguished showing in earlier centuries (Philipp 1981: 8–10). Similarly, the extramural sanctuary of Demeter and Persephone at Cyrene witnessed a marked fall in jewellery finds after the Archaic and early Classical periods (Warden 1990: 14, 40). A closer parallel to the Spartan timing comes from the sanctuary of Hera Akraia at Perachora where the numerous seventh-century jewellery finds at the so-called temple of Hera Limenia on the upper, E terrace decline markedly during the sixth century (Payne 1940: 124, 168). Likewise, at the harbour sanctuary at Emporio, as we have seen, the decline in bronze jewellery, as with the other bronze finds, begins in the early part of the same century.

As regards Spartan statuette and figurine dedications, a certain idiosyncrasy appears in the infrequency of dedications at the start of our period, a phenomenon coinciding with a long dearth of local production between the termination of Geometric horse figurines at the start of the seventh century and the emergence of statuette production in the early sixth (Rolley 1982: 39, 76 n.201).[6] After *c.* 550 Spartan trends are more in line with those elsewhere. Many more detailed studies of trends at specific sanctuaries are again urgently needed. At the extramural sanctuary of Demeter and Persephone at Cyrene bronze figurines are said to decline significantly after the Archaic period (Warden 1990: 12), though no precise figures are given. At the Kabeirion in Boiotia stylistic dating of bronze and lead oxen statuettes (Schmaltz 1980) suggested a huge drop from 122 later Archaic dedications period to only six Classical. Subsequent epigraphic dating of the 37 inscribed statuettes from this group, however, suggests a general lowering of dates (22 Archaic, 12 Classical, 3 Hellenistic) and a less sharp decline, focused mainly on the early fifth century (Roesch 1985; *cf.* Rolley 1986b: 387–8).

6. There is, however, a similar trend at Delphi where numbers of freestanding human and animal statuettes decline from over 100 in Geometric times to fewer than 20 in the seventh century (Rolley 1969).

TABLE 5.4a: **Categories of published bronze finds: Artemis Orthia**

	Vessels	*Jewellery*	*Statuettes*	*Other*
c. 650–*c.* 600	6+	18	1	15
c. 600–*c.* 550	8	11	2	1
c. 550–*c.* 500	1	1	2	2
c. 500–*c.* 450	–	2	–	–
c. 450–*c.* 400	–	–	1	–
c. 400–*c.* 350	–	–	–	–
DNG or Vague	7	1	–	9
Total	22+	31	8	27

TABLE 5.4b: **Categories of published bronze finds: Acropolis**

	Vessels	*Jewellery*	*Statuettes*	*Other*
c. 650–*c.* 600	–	3	–	–
c. 600–*c.* 550	5	–	2/3	–
c. 550–*c.* 500	5/6	–	7–9	3
c. 500–*c.* 450	0/1	–	6–8	4/5
c. 450–*c.* 400	–	–	3/4	2/3
c. 400–*c.* 350	–	–	1	1
DNG or Vague	5+	6	9+	54+
Total	15+	9	28+	64+

TABLE 5.4c: **Categories of published bronze finds: Menelaion**

	Vessels	*Jewellery*	*Statuettes*	*Other*
c. 650–*c.* 600	8+	Ind	Ind	14+
c. 600–*c.* 550	11+	Ind	1	9+
c. 550–*c.* 500	2+	1	–	3+
c. 500–*c.* 450	–	–	1	Ind
c. 450–*c.* 400	–	–	–	Ind
c. 400–*c.* 350	–	–	–	–
DNG or Vague	Ind	3+	1	14+
Total	22+	6+	4+	42+

TABLE 5.4d: **Categories of published bronze finds: Amyklaion**

	Vessels	*Jewellery*	*Statuettes*	*Other*
c. 650–*c.* 600	4	–	–	Ind
c. 600–*c.* 550	2	–	0/1	Ind
c. 550–*c.* 500	1	–	6/7	1
c. 500–*c.* 450	–	–	1/2	–
c. 450–*c.* 400	–	–	0/1	–
c. 400–*c.* 350	–	–	–	–
DNG or Vague	12+	75	12+	37+
Total	19+	75	19+	40+

General surveys of Greek bronze statuettes suggest a staggered decline in votives comparable to that in TABLE 5.3c, occurring at some sites in the early fifth century as at the Amyklaion, but at most places in the years after 450 as on the Acropolis (Lamb 1969: 106; Rolley 1986a: 169).

The Spartan decline in bronze vessel dedications raises further issues for future research. At first blush, it is tempting to explain the decline in local terms by connecting it with the end of Laconian bronze vessel production *c.* 530–520 (Rolley 1982: 75–8); but the link is not strong, since (apart from on the Acropolis) the decline in dedications starts earlier, around the middle of the century. So, once again, we must ask whether it was part of more general changes in the role of bronze vessels. Modern discussions of the decline in bronze dedications tend to focus on smaller dedications; but there are indications that larger votives were also affected. At Olympia, vessels reach their peak in the sixth and early fifth centuries, but then share in the general decline of bronze dedications after *c.* 450 (Gauer 1991: 1, 169). More generally, Rolley (1986a: 169) suggests a shift in the period 450–300 BC towards the use of bronze vessels as funerary objects and items of display in private houses. If this is so, one issue requiring particular clarification is whether the decline of bronze vessels as sanctuary offerings is connected with the emergence of the life-size bronze statue during the later sixth and early fifth centuries as the most prestigious dedicatory object (Mattusch 1988: 58–118). At Spartan sanctuaries there is at present no archaeological evidence that statue dedications did replace offerings of vessels. Since very few bronze statues survive from anywhere in the Greek world, their absence from the Spartan material record is unsurprising; but there also seems a lack of evidence for the more durable stone bases on which such statues would once have stood.[7] Literary evidence presents a similar picture to the material record: there are no attested personal statues of athletic or military victors in Sparta itself before that of Euryleonis, possibly in 368 BC (Pausanias 3.15.1). We need further research elsewhere in Greece to determine whether Spartan practice once again simply matches general Greek trends; or whether this is one phenomenon which is peculiar to Sparta, a sign of the desire of the Spartan homoioi to control the display of wealth and status in front of fellow citizens.

CONCLUSIONS AND PROSPECTS

This paper has attempted to demonstrate the value of examining the finds from Spartan sanctuaries as evidence of material and religious investment. Limits of space prevent an examination here of important issues, pertaining especially to the religious aspects of the phenomena in question: most notably, the marked differences in types of votive offerings at the various Spartan sanctuaries and their relation to differences in the needs and status of worshippers at each shrine; and Snodgrass's argument (1990a) that the broad dedicatory trends under discussion reflect a general shift from 'raw' to 'converted' offerings.[8] Critical scrutiny of these topics would demonstrate even more clearly the benefits of a systematic database of finds whose quantitative character raises fresh issues and adds new insights to those derived from purely qualitative studies. In particular, in enabling the Spartan material record to be compared with that of other Greek cities in a more systematic manner than previously possible, the process of quantification has the capacity to highlight wide-ranging questions about both Laconian and broader Greek developments in urgent need of research.

I would argue that the importance of these questions should prompt us to take the process still further, for the present study is merely a toe dipped in the broad and deep ocean of Laconian, let alone Greek, material culture. Within the more limited sphere of Spartan sanctuaries, we need a quantified database of the full range of finds—and over a longer timespan than has been attempted here; for patterns of bronze dedications can supply merely part of a picture which will be more fully intelligible only in the light of patterns of votives in other media.

I am encouraged to find that my perception of this need is no mere personal idiosyncrasy, but is shared by a recent reviewer who has called for a 'comprehensive study of all Archaic Laconian artefacts within the framework of the socio-cultural history of pre-Classical Sparta' (Cartledge 1988: 345; *cf.* now Förtsch 1994). Within my immediate field of enquiry into the sanctuary finds there are, indeed, some promising signs for future. The final publication of the recent Menelaion excavations should provide a more complete coverage of the rich new finds from that site; and we are promised a more extensive publication of older material from the Amyklaion (Calligas 1992: 41). Beyond that, the pressing need is for systematic re-study and publication of the finds from the older British excavations. This would, of course, be no simple or straightforward task. Both the scale of the enterprise and the necessary range of expertise would require a major collaborative venture. But there is now an unprecedented opportunity, with the proposed foundation by the British School of a Sparta Study Centre, for the creation of an institutional framework and local base which could provide coordi-

7. I presume that references to inscribed statuette bases of the fourth or third centuries in preliminary reports of the recent Menelaion excavations (Catling 1977a: 41) refer to somewhat smaller objects.

8. I shall address these issues in a chapter of a planned monograph on Property and Society in Classical Sparta.

nation and support for such an enterprise in a manner which has not hitherto been possible. With the prospect of these various developments, I look forward to the time when an expanded database will permit a more rigorous analysis of the hypotheses and comparisons hazarded in this preliminary study. For the present, however, I hope to have demonstrated the potential value of a quantitative archaeological approach to the issues of Spartiate material and religious investment, and the inherent interest and importance of the questions to which it can give rise.

ACKNOWLEDGEMENTS

I am grateful to Susan Cole, Catherine Morgan, Ian Morris, Robin Osborne, Christopher Simon and Anthony Snodgrass for their advice concerning patterns of votive offerings outside Sparta. The database on which this article is based was constructed during my tenure of a Nuffield Foundation Social Science Research Fellowship, further research during study leave funded by the Humanities Research Board of the British Academy.

6

Exceptional shapes and decorations in Laconian pottery

Conrad M. Stibbe

When discussing exceptional shapes and decorations in Laconian pottery it may be useful to make the following preliminary remarks. Given that Sparta occupies a rather exceptional place in the thiasos of Greek city states in pre-hellenistic times, we might also expect to find some sort of reflection of this special cultural and political status in its minor arts, and in particular in its pottery. As I hope to show, there is no reason to be disappointed about this expectation.

This conviction, however, immediately raises the vexed question of who produced this pottery. Did the Spartan citizens participate, or were the perioikoi alone responsible for its production? In other words: can we view the shapes and decorations of Laconian pottery as representative of the requirements and taste of the ruling class of Spartiatai in the capital, or should we assume that the pots reflect only the predilections and conceptions of the mercenary, provincial people of the perioikoi? Or do we need to consider a third possibility which makes the black-and-white distinctions of the first two options superfluous? This third possibility would be that the production of Laconian pottery was not a privilege of one social class or another, but rather a branch of artistic industry open to all inhabitants of Laconia, whether free, less free or unfree.

I take it that archaic Sparta of the seventh and sixth centuries BC was an open society in which artists of all kinds could freely move and produce what they wanted with no other social restrictions than those which applied to all other aristocratic societies of Greece during those centuries. This implies the possibility that full citizens, including whole families, could engage in the production of pottery, stone-sculpture, ivory-carving, bronze-casting and so on. This further implies that from the shapes and decorations of seventh and sixth century pottery a complete picture of the tastes and preferences of the whole society of free, less free and unfree inhabitants of Sparta and Laconia can be gathered.[1]

Moving now from general background considerations to the more limited ones relating to Laconian pottery, I would first like to explain the title of my lecture. What do I mean by 'exceptional'? To clarify this it would first be useful to establish what is common in Laconian pottery. In terms of shapes, we can distinguish on the one hand those which were successfully exported, such as kraters, aryballoi and cups, and followed, a long way behind, by amphorai, hydriai and oinochoai; and on the other hand shapes which were common on the local market, such as lakainai, skyphoi, kantharoi, cylindrical mugs, small goblets, bell-kraters and other high-walled shapes. In both categories we find exceptional shapes and decorations, though these might be termed 'variants'.

But there is more. A third category comprises shapes and decorations which are not found in the first two categories, and which we can describe as exceptional in the sense that they are unique or almost unique. Surprisingly, some shapes which are common outside Laconia, such as the lekythos with an elongated body or the dinos or the pilgrim bottle or the askos, are exceptional in Laconia and therefore belong to this third category. Moreover, we have quite a number of vase-shapes for which, perhaps by chance of excavation, no parallels are known, either inside or outside Laconia.

As for the decoration, this is a story in itself, on which much study has still to be done, particularly in the field of secondary ornaments.[2] For our purposes today, however, we can state that the ornaments are of less importance, with a few exceptions which will be discussed later, in the appropriate place.

In this paper I will start with a shape which cannot even be called a vase. It is a sort of cylindrical tube, since it lacks a bottom and a mouth (FIG. 6.1a–b). There is no doubt about the measurements because the rims at both ends are well-preserved and from the decorations we can even determine which side is the top and which the bottom. The present example was

1. For more on these problems see P.A. Cartledge, 'Did Spartan citizens ever practise a manual tekhne?', *LCM* 1: 115–119.

2. After the extremely useful study of Laconian iconography by Maria Pipili in 1987, there still remains a series of unsolved problems. In the field of secondary ornaments, such as lotos-palmette compositions, friezes of animals, of pomegranates, of lotos buds etc., as produced by the different Laconian vase-painters, for which the material has been assembled in LV, much research remains to be done.

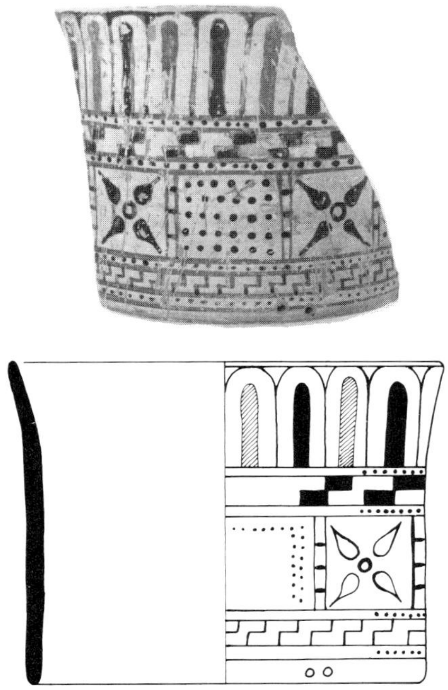

Fig. 6.1 (a) Tube or stand from Sparta; (b) the same, profile drawing (1:2). Sparta, Museum.

found in the sanctuary of Artemis Orthia at Sparta.[3] It is dated in the Laconian II period (*c.* 620–580).[4] The height is 8.3 cm, the diameter 11–10 cm. From the same site we have three other examples of the same shape. The second piece (FIG. 6.2a–b), like the first, is decorated with secondary ornaments of the Laconian II period, but shows an additional gorgoneion in outline technique. This example was about 3 cm higher than the first; this is shown by a fragment of the rim, now lost, on an old photograph.[5] The third piece (FIG. 6.3a–b) is unpublished. It has no paint at all but is instead decorated with moulded ridges. Its height reaches 9.3 cm, its diameter 9.8 cm at the upper rim. The fourth piece (FIG. 6.4a–b), also unpublished, lacks even moulded decoration. The shape is reduced to the mere skeleton of a tube, but its wall is not simply cylindrical: it forms a fine concave curve, and from the thickness of its wall, which becomes thinner higher up, we may conclude how it should stand.

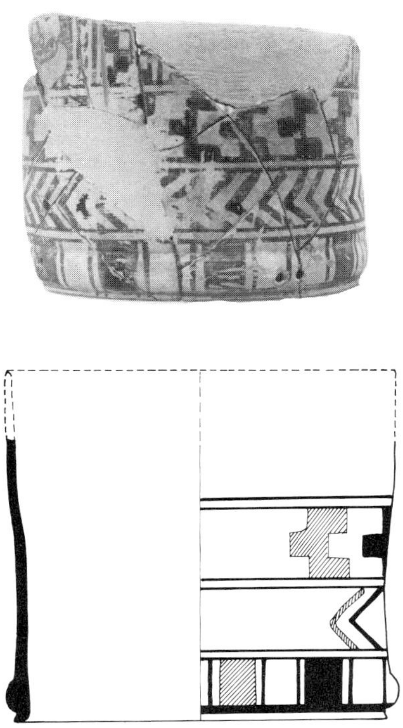

Fig. 6.2 (a) Tube or stand from Sparta; (b) the same, profile drawing (1:2). Sparta, Museum.Museum.

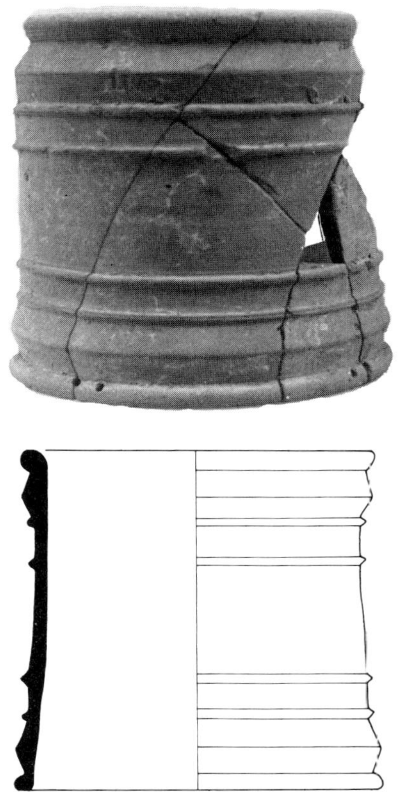

Fig. 6.3 (a) Tube or stand from Sparta; (b) the same, profile drawing (1:2). Sparta, Museum.

Common traits of the four tubes from Artemis Orthia are that they all have a reserved inside and that the preserved or estimated diameters of the lower rims are almost equal (10.0, 9.4, 9.8 and 9.6 cm respectively). Moreover three of them have two holes

3. Dawkins 1929: 80, Fig. 53. Lane 1934: 125.

4. For the decorative patterns see Lane 1934: 124, Fig. 12.

5. Dawkins 1929: 80, Fig. 53 left. *Cf.* Lane 1934: 123, Fig. 11 g (profile drawing).

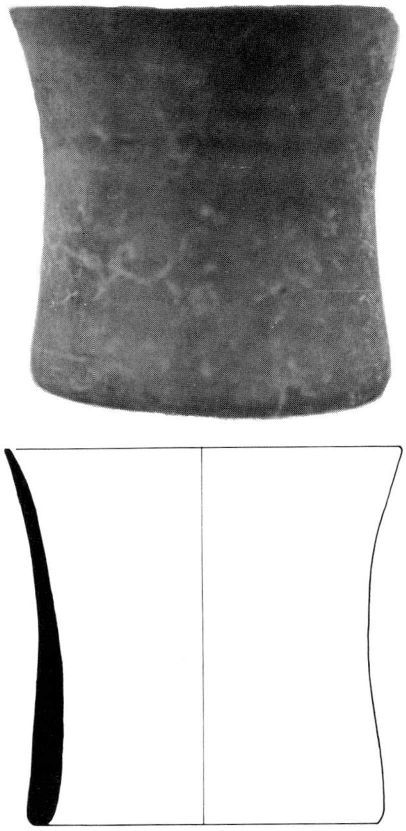

Fig. 6.4 (a) Tube or stand from Sparta; (b) the same, profile drawing (1:2). Sparta, Museum.

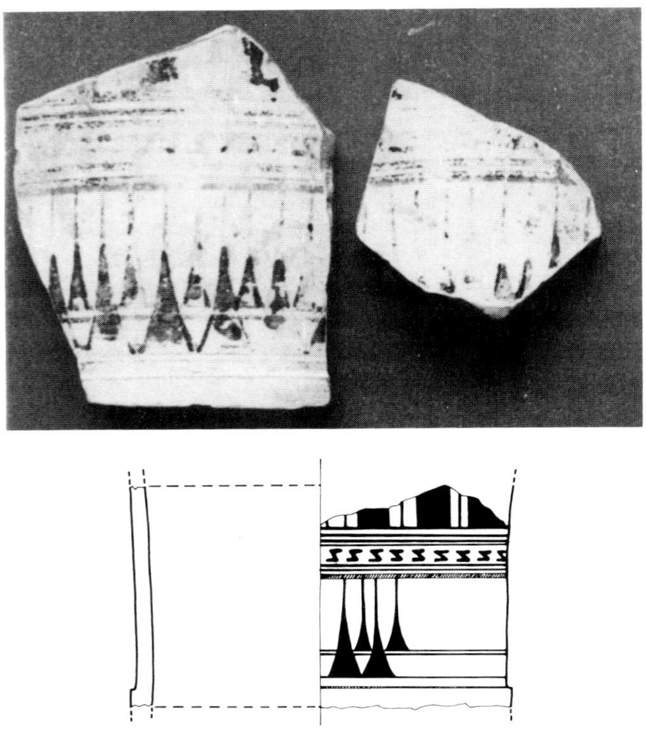

Fig. 6.5 (a) Two fragments of tube or stand from Samos; (b) the same, profile drawing (1:2). Samos (Vathy), Museum.

near the lower rim.[6] With the help of these data it has been possible to identify a fifth tube among the still unpublished Laconian fragments from the Heraion at Samos (FIG. 6.5a–b). Here too the inside is reserved and the lower rim has a diameter of 10.0 cm. The decoration, consisting of standing tongues at the (partly lost) upper rim and rays at the (slightly set off) lower rim, suggests a tube of almost the same dimensions as the four examples from Sparta. The decoration as such seems to be more advanced and a production date in the first half of the sixth century BC would be appropriate.[7]

Now, with five examples at hand, one of which was even exported, we are in a position to try and explain this exceptional shape. When we look for parallels outside Laconia, we are reminded of a black-figured Attic tube of about the same dimensions in the Liebieghausmuseum in Frankfurt (FIG. 6.6).[8] Its height is 12.5 cm. If we are prepared to admit that the

Fig. 6.6 Attic black-figured tube or stand. Frankfurt am Main, Städtische Galerie Liebieghaus, inv. no. 560.

differences, such as the slightly more tapering shape of the wall, the offset rim with four knobs, and the decoration are due to a chronological distance of about one century and to its non-Laconian origin, then we can use the Attic example as an aid to the interpretation of these Laconian tubes. Most striking, of course, is the representation of Charon sitting on

6. These holes can be explained as suspension holes, the tube being a votive object (see *infra*), or for fastening a lid.

7. I thank H. Kienast for the permission to publish this fragment.

8. Eckstein 1969: no. 65.

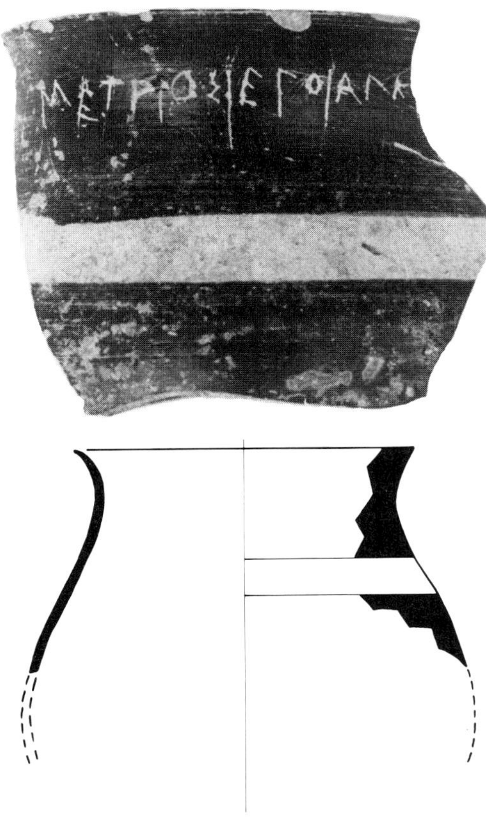

Fig. 6.7 (a) Fragment of olpe with graffito; (b) the same, profile drawing (1:2). Sparta, Museum.

the stern of his boat among the whirling souls of the dead. This lively picture was used by the first owner of the piece, Adolf Furtwängler, to connect the shape with the cult of the dead.[9] This can only have been intended to be a small reproduction in clay, for votive purposes, of the large stone ἐσχάρα, the altar used in hero-worship in particular, examples of which were already known at the time from the Mycenaean period.[10] H.-V. Hermann observed in his dissertation that the version in clay would have a double function: 'Opferröhre und Untersatz für das Grabgefäss', that is to say as a tube for sacrifices and as a stand for the funeral vase.[11] If this is correct, we can surmise that these tubes also served as simple stands without any connection with the cult of the dead. In fact, quite a few Attic stands of this type, decorated in black- and red-figure technique, are known today, and do not seem to have any relation with that cult.[12] The fact that all the Laconian tubes were found in sanctuaries would suggest a non-funerary use.[13] The two holes at the lower rim of three of the four examples from Sparta should perhaps be understood as suspension-holes, which would underline their votive character.

Yet another explanation for the Laconian tubes was offered by Arthur Lane in his fundamental study (1934) of Laconian pottery.[14] He referred to them as 'ornamental poloi', and compared them with some Boeotian pieces;[15] the latter, however, show their polos character more clearly than the Laconian tubes.[16]

In conclusion, then, we must admit it is not easy to arrive at a clear-cut solution for the use of these tubes. I myself prefer the interpretation of a double function as tube for sacrifices and as a stand. The metallic character of the third example from Sparta seems to me to provide an additional argument for the latter function; it suggests the existence of bronze tubes which would be much more suitable for use as stands than the fragile clay examples.

We now turn to a rather puzzling fragment from the Spartan acropolis (FIG.6.7a–b). This has been studied several times for the interesting graffito below its lip,[17] but never for its shape and decoration. The preserved height is only 6.0 cm, and the estimated diameter of its lip turns out to be 9.0 cm. The bulky shape of its body has no parallel among Laconian pots, but it is reminiscent of the Attic round-mouthed olpe.[18] If this comparison is correct, we should fit our fragment with a high-swung handle and a low echinus-ringfoot.

The reserved band, however, argues against this solution: on Laconian pottery, this usually indicates the handle-zone, that is the zone to which the lower attachment of the handle is adjusted.[19] This zone is also found on the Attic black-glazed olpai, but much lower down the belly, where the loop of the handle finishes comfortably. So the handle of our vase may have been of a less elegant, shorter type. The metallic lustre of the glaze is also exceptional in our

9. Furtwängler, 'Charon', *AfRw* VIII 1905: 191ff.

10. *Cf.* Rohde 1927: 35; Oeconomus 1921: 46ff.; Kinch 1914: 26–34. On the eschara in general see J. E. Harrison 1908: 63.

11. H-V. Hermann, *Omphalos* (1959) 53ff.

12. L. Talcott 1936: 68. R. Lullies 1957.

13. Comparable tubes were also found on Crete, in Gournia and Prinias, not in graves, but in sanctuaries; *cf.* S. Wide, *AM* 26, 1901: 247, Pl. XII.

14. Lane 1934: 125.

15. E. Langlotz 1932: no. 67. P. N. Ure, *AA* 1933, 7.

16. *Cf.* E. Simon 1969: 58.

17. Woodward 1930b: 251 no. 2. T. A. Boring 1979: 10f. no. 76, Pl. III.

18. Sparkes and Talcott 1970: 76 with no. 252, dated 550. Among the Laconian shapes there is a certain resemblance to the small oinochoai, which were widely exported (*cf.* Stibbe forthcoming), but there the neck is mostly offset and the mouth has a trefoil shape.

19. See e.g. Pelagatti and Stibbe 1988: 17 fig. 10, 18 figs 12–13, 21 figs. 29–30.

fragment. We would only expect to find this on geometric or hellenistic, and not archaic Laconian, pottery. Since vases with reserved handle-zones usually belong to the archaic period, we should seek for an explanation for this. Perhaps the potter who imitated the Attic shape also imitated the lustre of the Attic black-glazed ware?

The Attic round-mouthed olpe-shape, which we would compare, is found in the Gorgon Painter's workshop and was also made by Amasis.[20] It appears no later than Amasis in figured ware, and the Attic black examples also agree with this. The latter are dated to the middle years of the sixth century.[21] Since the first clear signs of imitation of Attic models by Laconian vase painters start exactly around this time, it would not be at all out of place if an Attic black-glazed shape like the olpe also happened to find an imitator in Laconia. This would also allow us to establish an upper limit for the dating of the inscription.[22] The well-preserved part of this inscription reads ΜΕΤΡΙΟΣ ΕΓΟ, which might indicate a measure or the capacity of the pot,[23] in the same way as such indications are found on an Attic olpe in the Louvre[24] and on an early Laconian mug from Kythera in the British Museum.[25]

That the olpe was not a totally unknown shape in Laconia, is proved by a few black-glazed jugs of small size. One almost complete, unpublished, example was found in the Artemis Orthia sanctuary at Sparta (FIG. 6.8a–b),[26] and three others in Tocra.[27] But even taking together these four examples of the small version, the shape remains exceptional in the Laconian repertoire.[28]

From the olpe we make a jump to the lekythos. Here we must distinguish, again within the archaic period, an elongated and a globular version of the shape. The first, which was popular in Corinth and Athens, did not meet with any success whatsoever in Sparta. In fact we have only one Laconian example

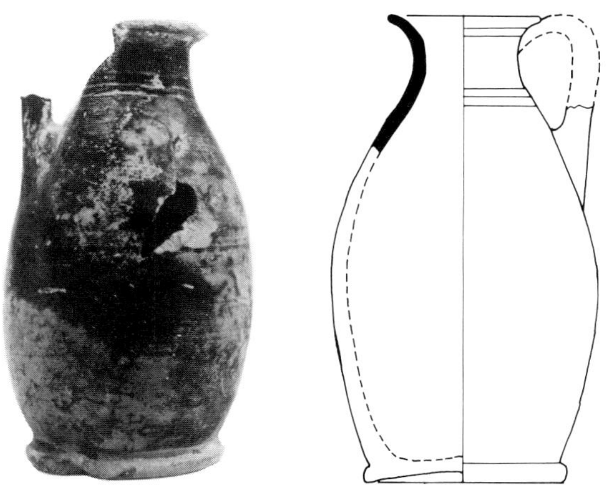

Fig. 6.8 (a) Small olpe from Sparta; (b) the same, profile drawing (1:2). Sparta, Museum.

from Sparta itself, and this did not turn up in one of the known sanctuaries of the town, but rather during a rescue excavation near the bridge over the Eurotas by George Steinhauer in 1972 (FIG. 6.9a–b).[29] In this piece the shape of the mouth is remarkable, being straight and flaring in contrast to the Corinthian Deianeira-type, which has a thickened round rim and a bowl-like shape with a 'drip ring' at the junction of mouth and body.[30] A date around the middle of the sixth century may be appropriate for this piece.[31] There is an earlier stage with a concave mouth, which comes a little closer to the Corinthian model: a black-glazed Laconian lekythos, again with elongated body and a flat base, from Megara Hyblaea (FIG. 6.10a–b); its context includes two Corinthian Deianeira-lekythoi.[32] There

20. Beazley 1956: 9 and 11; later olpai: Beazley 1956: 153 and 446. von Bothmer 1985: 150 no. 31.

21. Sparkes and Talcott 1970: 77, nos 247–253.

22. Woodward 1930b would date the inscription in the early sixth century.

23. *Cf.* Sparkes and Talcott 1970: 2 note 6. Also Boring 1979 is of this opinion; according to him it would indicate 'a middle-sized vessel', followed by the name of its owner, which is partly lost.

24. Louvre F 339, Beazley 1956: 446, 1.

25. Stibbe 1994: 45, 141 no. B9.

26. H. 11.5, Dm. max. 6.3. Three grooves on the neck. Will be published more extensively in Stibbe forthcoming.

27. Boardman and Hayes 1966: 88, 91 no. 971–972, pl. 66 and Boardman and Hayes 1973: 40 no. 2112, pl. 21. John Hayes, in Boardman and Hayes 1966, 88 thought these juglets made after East-Greek models and mentions two parallels in Delos (*Délos* X. 60, pl. 37 D, nos 132–133); in Boardman and Hayes 1973:, 35 he also sees Attic influence. There is a bottom-wall fragment from Cyrene, of which the Laconian origin is uncertain; *cf.* G. P. Schaus 1985: 21f., no. 69, fig. 2.

28. The dating of these juglets is not easy. Comparison with the Attic series of black-glazed juglets of the same shape with disc-foot,would lead to a dating in the fifth cent.; *cf.* Sparkes and Talcott 1970: nos 278–281, pl. 13. The examples from Tocra, however, suggest an earlier date, somewhere in the sixth cent. Laconian imports seem to stop there about the 530s BC (*cf.* Boardman and Hayes 1966: 12 and 170: Deposit III). A parallel (without foot) in Olympia (Gauer 1975: 23, 109, pl. 14, 3 from the well 29 StN, dated to the third quarter of the sixth century) would confirm the earlier dating. *Cf.* also Weber 1983: 148ff.

29. Steinhauer 1972: 242ff., pl. 181.

30. *Cf.* H. Payne 1931: 191, 324. Sparkes and Talcott 1970: 151.

31. This type of mouth comes into fashion with the globular lekythoi around this time; see below and Stibbe forthcoming.

32. Unpublished.

Fig. 6.9 (a) Lekythos with elongated body from Sparta; (b) the same, profile drawing (1:3). Sparta, Museum, inv. no 6451/2.

are a few more, probably Laconian, examples from Tocra and Selinunte, but in most of these the mouth is not preserved, and so they are less useful for comparison.[33]

By contrast, the lekythos with a globular body is well represented and is a much more successful member of the Laconian black-glazed repertoire. The series starts quite early and goes right down through the sixth and fifth centuries BC,as do the Attic parallels.[34] The earliest Laconian example, however, can be dated to the last twenty years of the seventh century (FIG. 6.11).[35] The mouth is rather wide, shallow

Fig. 6.10 (a) Lekythos with elongated body from Megara Hyblaea; (b) the same, profile drawing (1:3). Syracuse, Museo Regionale, inv. no 12005.

and angular. This is a forerunner of the more common mouth-shape of the first half of the sixth century, which is plain and shallow, as a black-glazed fragment from Sparta shows (FIG. 6.12a–b): the diameter of the

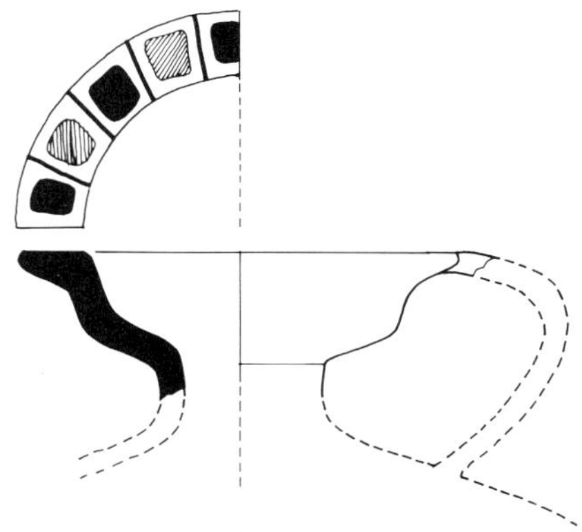

Fig. 6.11 Fragment of the mouth of a lekythos with a globular body from Sparta, profile drawing (1:2). Sparta, Museum.

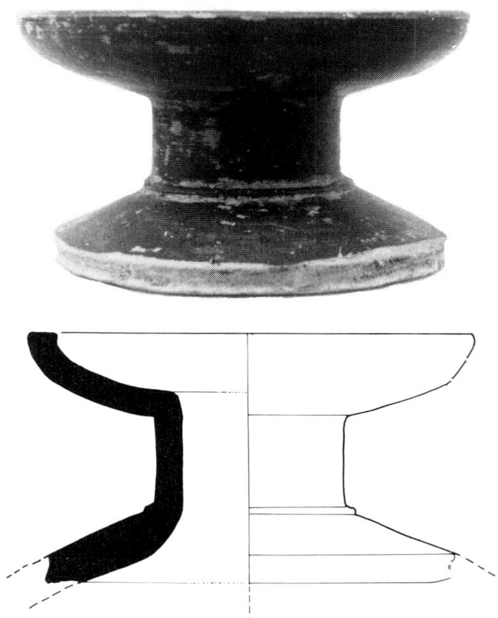

Fig. 6.12 (a) Mouth, neck and shoulder-fragment of a lekythos with globular body from Sparta; (b) the same, profile drawing (1:2). Sparta, Museum.

33. *Cf.* Boardman and Hayes 1966: 90, no. 969, pl. 66. Others are unpublished. A black figure fragment from Olympia, Gauer 1975: 112, pl. 15,4–6, seems to be a local imitation of a Laconian model.

34. *Cf.* Sparkes and Talcott 1970: 151f. nos. 1100–1111.

35. Dawkins 1929: 75 fig. 47 q. The decoration of the upper face of the rim with alternating black and purple squares is common in the Laconian II period (620–580), but should fall early in that period; *cf.* Lane 1934: 123, fig. 11 H; Stibbe 1994:, 240 no. 96, fig. 335.

mouth is 11.8 cm; as a result the maximum diameter of the belly can be estimated at about 30.0 cm, which makes a rather impressive container. The body is broken off exactly where a thick offset collar on the shoulder ends.

A complete Laconian example comes from Megara Hyblaea (FIG. 6.13a–b),[36] but here the shape of the mouth is concave rather than convex. The maximum diameter of the body is 21.0 cm. This remarkable change of mouth shape took place not long before the middle of the sixth century BC.[37]

Both mouth shapes recur in small versions, which we usually call aryballoi. The concave mouth, which is apparently the older, is found with Laconian aryballoi from the first half of the sixth century, as the following intact and very fine example from Kythera in the Ashmolean Museum in Oxford demonstrates (FIG. 6.14a–b).[38] Its height is 10.6 cm and its diameter 9.8 cm.

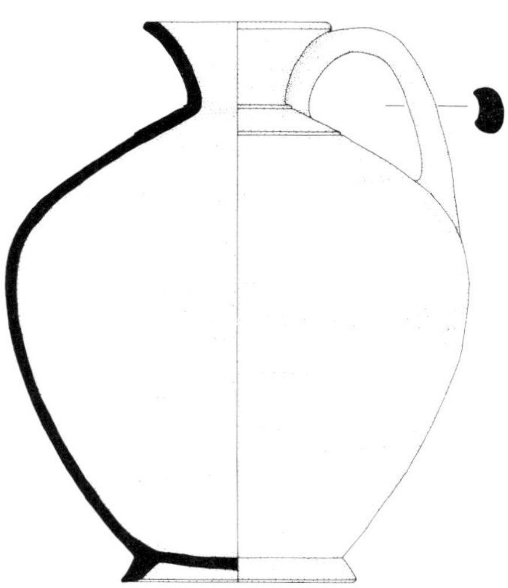

Fig. 6.13 (a) Lekythos with a globular body from Megara Hyblaea; (b) the same, profile drawing (1:4). Syracuse, Museo Regionale.

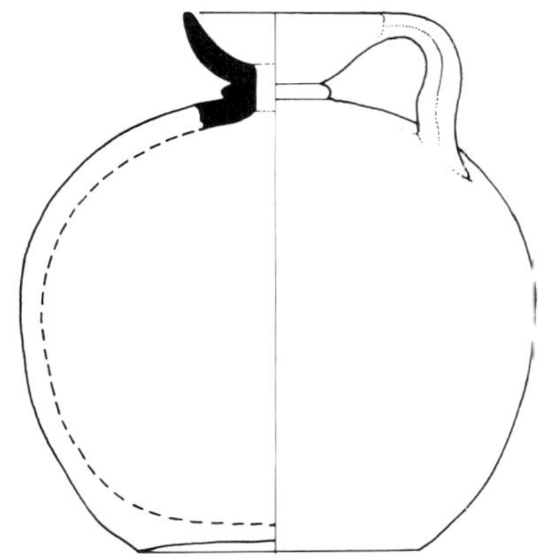

Fig. 6.14 (a) Lekythos-aryballos from Kythera; (b) the same, profile drawing (1:2). Oxford, Ashmolean Museum, inv. no. 1932.674.

Post-archaic developments of the globular lekythos can be illustrated by two examples from the rescue excavations near the bridge at Sparta (FIG. 6.15a–c). These have an average height of 16.0 cm, which is right between the average heights of the archaic globular lekythoi and aryballoi. They should be dated well into the fifth century BC. Apart from the clay and the glaze there is little difference from the contemporary Attic version of the shape.[39]

As I noted earlier, the globular lekythos cannot be reckoned among the exceptional shapes in Laconia, unlike the lekythos with its elongated body. In my forthcoming study of Laconian black-glazed closed shapes I have catalogued 26 globular lekythoi, divided into four groups, whereas the whole corpus of Laconian lekythoi with elongated body consists of only four or five pieces.

36. This is one of a pair: *cf.* P. Pelagatti 1989: 23, 24 fig. 98; 50f. no. 168. Pelagatti and Stibbe 1990: 146 fig. 98; 177 no. 168.

37. *Cf.* Stibbe forthcoming.

38. Ashmolean Museum 1932.674. Unpublished.

39. *Cf.* the Attic parallels in *Hesperia* 22 (1953) 80f. with pl. 31.

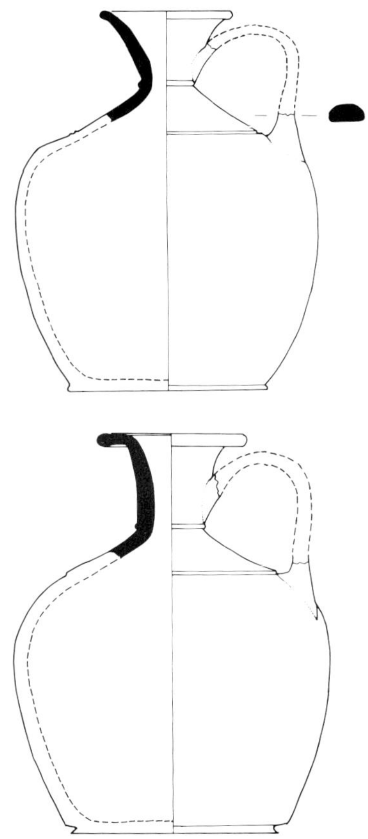

Fig. 6.15 (a) Two fragmentary lekythoi with globular bodies from Sparta; (b and c) the same, profile drawings (1:3). Sparta Museum, inv. nos 6451/1, 6451/3.

I would like to invite you now to look at one of the most exceptional shapes in Laconian pottery we know (FIG. 6.16a–b).[40] All that survives is a fragment of a decorated long neck and the beginning of a body; where the two join there is a plastic fillet. The long neck is decorated in black-figure technique. We can recognise the feet and long robe of a human figure standing to the left between the tails of two upcurling snakes. There is no slip. The long robe of the standing figure seems to be a himation with a carelessly incised fringe; above the fringe there is a horizontal zone between incised lines filled with white dots, now faded.[41] A purple band between black bands adorns the fillet at the join of neck and body.

In its first publication in the Artemis Orthia volume of 1929 (104, Fig. 78 b) there is another fragment, now lost, belonging to the same vase (FIG. 6.16c): this shows part of the neck with a handle-attachment. We can only see parts of the decoration of the head (with a purple braid) and of the left arm and shoulder of the same standing figure.

The two fragments, taken together, present us with two problems: how should we interpret the shape of the vase, and how should we interpret its decoration? In two drawings I have tried to regain as much as possible from the poor remains (FIG. 6.16d–e). Let us start with the shape. The reconstruction, with a globular body and a handle going down to the shoulder, is based on a comparison with a series of long-necked jugs from Olympia, called by Werner Gauer 'Giraffenhalskännchen' (giraffe-necked jugs).[42] These long-necked jugs mostly have a trefoil mouth at which the handle is attached. The bodies are globular and the handle runs down to the shoulder. One of the examples from Olympia (FIG. 6.17), a fragment of the neck like ours, shows not only the same fillet at the join of neck and body, but also a decoration which is clearly influenced by Laconian models. On the shoulder are hanging rays of Laconian type,[43] and on the neck a frieze of stylised pomegranates of a type which we often encounter on Laconian pots of the late seventh and early sixth century BC.[44] The combination of incised and outline details points to a date between 620 and 580.[45] If this is indeed a local

40. Dawkins 1929: 104, fig. 78 b.

41. Clearly indicated in the reconstruction drawing in Dawkins 1929:, fig. 78 b. Some lengthy white dots are also visible on the downpointing slap of the himation in front of the figure.

42. Gauer 1975: 111 with pl. 13.

43. Gauer 1975: 111.

44. Not recognized as such by Gauer 1975: 111. For the type see Lane 1934: 172f.1 fig. 21, 1; 119; 124, fig. 12, 26; Stibbe 1972: 179 no. 3; 181.

45. This is the Laconian II period. *Cf.* Gauer 1975: 111 'Kaum weit über die Mitte des 7. Jahrhunderts hinaufdatieren', that is somewhat earlier than the dating proposed here.

Fig. 6.16 (a–b, above left and centre) Two views of a fragment of a long-necked jug from Sparta; (c, above right) the same, drawing after Dawkins 1929: 104, fig. 78b; (d–e, right and far right) the same, drawing of profile and decoration. Sparta,

imitation of a Laconian prototype, then there must have been quite a long tradition of vessels of this type in Laconia itself. Nothing remains of this tradition except our fragment, which, because of the style of its decoration, should be dated much later, around 500 BC.[46]

A standing human figure between upcurling snakes is not so easy to explain. A similar composition is found on an ivory plaque from the sanctuary of Artemis Orthia (FIG. 6.18), which has been dated in the second quarter of the seventh century BC.[47] The scene, with a standing winged female figure in a long robe between two upcurling snakes (one is lost) holding a bird of prey in one hand, has been convincingly interpreted as a representation of Artemis Orthia herself.[48] On this interpretation, the snakes should be understood here not as symbols of death but of fertility, in line with their general chthonic nature.[49] A well known Laconian multifigured handle of a bronze hydria found in the tomb of a Celtic chieftain at Grächwil near Bern, Switzerland (FIG. 6.19) offers a good parallel: here again we see a winged mistress of animals. The snakes this time extend from behind her head along the rim of the vessel to serve as a base for roaring lions. This hydria has been dated in the first

Fig. 6.17 Fragment of a long-necked jug from Olympia. Olympia, Museum.

46. For the style, which was labelled 'Laconian V' by Droop (Dawkins 1929: 104) see below.

47. Marangou 1969: 22, with fig. 14 (inv. no. 15 503).

48. Marangou 1969: 24 with note 135.

49. Marangou 1969: 24.

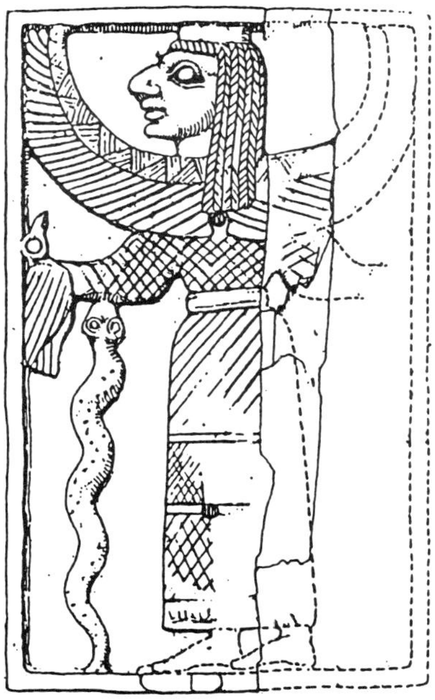

Fig. 6.18 (above) Fragmentary ivory fibula-plaque from Sparta. Athens, National Museum, inv. no. 15 503. Drawing after Dawkins 1929: 207, pl. 93, 2.

Fig. 6.19 (right) Bronze hydria from Grächwil. Bern, Bernisches Historisches Museum. Photograph courtesy of the museum.

quarter of the sixth century BC,[50] still about a century before our neck fragment.

Such representations of the *potnia theron* ceased to be made in the beginning of the sixth century, a fact which is less surprising than their apparent return at the end of the same century in Sparta. The similarity of the motif cannot be denied, even if the representation is only in part preserved. But what we should most probably suspect and expect is that the meaning of the figure between the snakes has changed in the meantime. In the first place, the figure need not be female;[51] secondly, our fragment originated in a period, between *c.*550 and 450 BC, in which the hero-cult in Laconia found its expression in sculpture and vase-painting more than ever before or after.[52] In a recent article I brought together quite a few examples of the chthonic and Dionysiac symbols as they are depicted on Laconian vases of that period. Upcurling snakes before and behind standing or sitting figures in long robes are represented there (FIG. 6.19) as they are on contemporary stone reliefs.[53]

Since the careless style of painting and incision and the unslipped background suggests a dating around 500 BC, our fragment should be seen in this context of the hero-cult. The shape of the vase can be explained in the same way: it revives a model of the seventh century, but is used as jug for libations in contemporary hero-cult. If this is true, we still have to envisage the same problem as with the above-mentioned tubes for libations: how could they have served as votives in the cult of Artemis Orthia, who, as far as we know, had nothing to do with the cult of the dead? Are we perhaps justified in supposing that Orthia, a goddess of fertility, also extended her realm to the chthonic world of the dead, as, in a way, we have already observed when looking at her representation on an ivory-plaque as a winged figure between upcurling snakes? I leave the question open, hoping to obtain an answer from you, my most distinguished readers.

I would like to finish with an oddity, a vase which has twice been published as a Laconian cup,[54] but which on reconsideration turns out to be an Attic C-

50. Stibbe 1992: 20ff., 25, no. G1 with fig. 32.

51. This was already stated by Marangou 1969 222 note 119.

52. *Cf.* C. M. Stibbe, *BaBesch* 66 (1991) 1–44.

53. C. M. Stibbe, *BaBesch* 69 (1994) 77 fig. 1; 78 fig. 4; 82 fig. 12. id., *BaBesch* 66 (1991) 14 fig. 8 ff.

54. K. A. Rhomaios, *Praktika* 1911, 266f. with fig. 8 (graffito). Phaklaris 1990: 175, pl. 77.

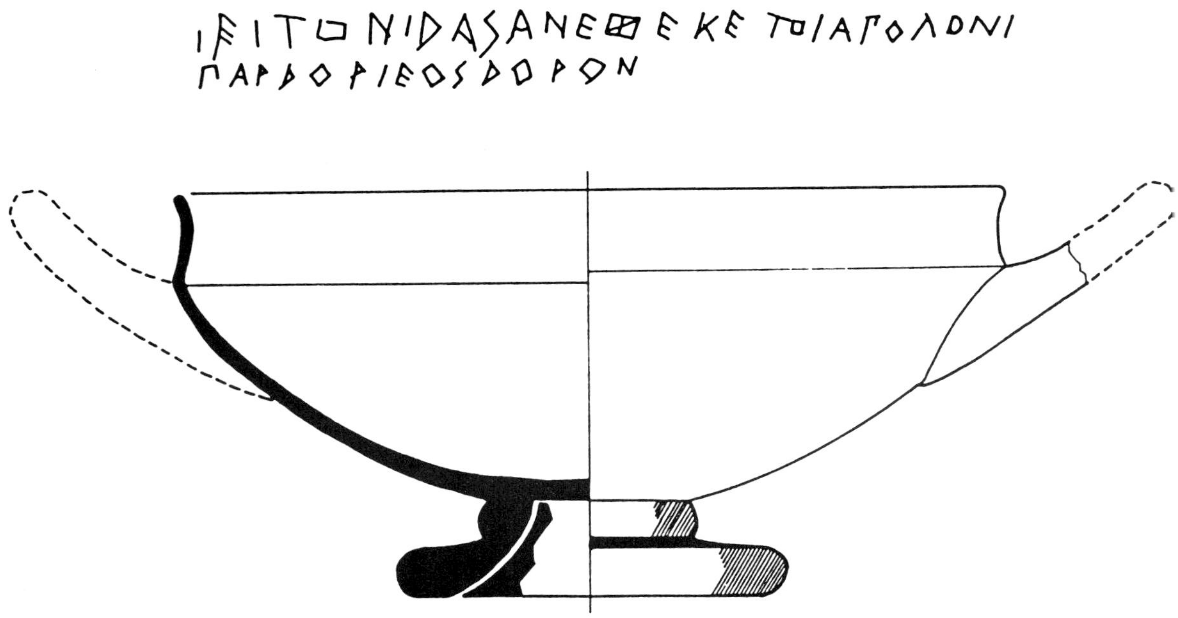

Fig. 6.20 Fragmentary Attic C-cup with graffito, from the sanctuary of Apollo Tyritas in Laconia, profile drawing. Astros, Museum

cup (FIG. 6.20).[55] It was certainly found in a Laconian sanctuary, and it bears a Laconian graffito of much interest. This reads in transcription:

[ΕΥΓ]ΕΙΤΟΝΙΔΑΣ ΑΝΕΘΗΚΕ ΤΩΙ ΑΠΟΛΟΝΙ ΠΑΡ' ΔΟΡΙΕΟΣ ΔΟΡΟΝ

This would mean that a certain Eugeitonidas dedicated the vase to Apollo as a present on behalf of Dorieus. Now, who might be this important personality in whose name an Attic cup was offered to Apollo? Since the Attic cup is well datable around 525 BC,[56] and since there was at the time only one well-known person in Laconia of the name Dorieus, there can be hardly any doubt that we have here stumbled over the unhappy Spartan prince of that name. Before leaving Laconia on his second expedition to the west around 510 BC, he took many precautions to prevent a second failure, as Herodotus tells us (v 43). One of these precautions could have been to send his friends and supporters to the more important sanctuaries to plead for the support of the god of Delphi, whom he had passed over and neglected when he started his first expedition.

I won't go further now into the details of this exciting document. I only wanted to present it to you for further discussion, because it has not attracted the attention it certainly deserves since being excavated in the sanctuary of Apollo Tyritas in eastern Laconia and published for the first time at the beginning of this century.

ACKNOWLEDGEMENTS

I want to thank the following persons and institutions for the permission to study and publish the objects mentioned in this paper: the Managing Committee of the British School at Athens and the Ephoroi G. Steinhauer and T. Spyropoulos (for the material from Sparta and Laconia); H. J. Kienast (Samos); P. C. Bol (Frankfurt am Main); G. Vozza (Syracuse); M. Vickers (Oxford) and K. Herrmann (Olympia).

55. When I studied the cup at the Museum of Astros, where it is kept with inv. no. 78, I discovered that a foot, which was kept in another box and which was separately published by Phaklaris (in his dissertation *Archaia Kynouria*, 1985, p. 148 b, bottom right), joined the body and that it should be an Attic C-cup. The height is 8.0, the diameter of the lip 16.0 cms. It was first published in its more complete state by me in *Hermeneus* 3 (1991) 205–210.

56. Bloesch 1940: 113f. ('Frühgruppe'); Sparkes and Talcott 1970: 91 nos 398–403.

7

Dances, drinks and dedications: the Archaic komos in Laconia

Tyler Jo Smith

Laconian vase-painters include the komos figure and komast scenes in their Archaic repertoire. The komast figure, literally a male 'reveller', is characterized in Corinthian and Athenian iconography by his protruding features and his bottom-slapping dancing gesture (Greifenhagen 1929; Seeberg 1971; Brijder 1983; Brijder 1991). Though he is often called a padded or fat-bellied dancer, we shall see that in Laconia, as elsewhere, this is not always the case. A look at the iconography of the Laconian komos, both in vase-painting and in other media, may help identify not only the role of Sparta in the Archaic iconographic tradition, but also the origin and place of the komast dancer within this tradition. An overview of komos iconography is presented here, keeping in mind both the form and the function of the archaeological evidence. Furthermore, the possible role of komast dancers within the social and religious life of Archaic Sparta is examined.

KOMASTS ON VASES

When speaking about the black-figure technique for decorating pottery, the names Corinth and Athens most readily spring to mind. However, a full black-figure style also flourishes in Laconia, and the local artists of Sparta employ it regularly throughout the sixth century BC. By *c.* 580 the technique of painting human and animal figures in black silhouette, and incising details or adding these in red paint, is firmly established. On the whole, the choice of subjects painted by Laconian artists reflects those of the dominant Corinthian school. It is thought that Laconian vase-painters copy both the subjects and the iconography from Corinthian vases. At the same time, a certain amount of acquaintance with Athenian painting (by the second half of the century), as well as with the iconography of East Greece, are both obvious in the subjects and subsidiary decoration of Laconian vases. The same types of myth and figure scenes chosen by Laconian vase-painters appear frequently in the crafts of other media, namely stone, bronze, lead and bone (Pipili 1987). Many of these objects have been found in the sanctuary of Artemis Orthia, and must be some reflection on the dedication practices of its visitors.

The evidence for the komos in Laconian vase-painting is diverse and plentiful. At least thirty-five known vases display komast scenes (Pipili 1987: 204–210). The cup is the most common shape, but two kraters and one hydria are also represented. The chosen field for figure decoration by Laconian painters is normally the interior of the cup. Though the exterior is often decorated as well, only one cup is known to display a komast scene on its exterior (Stibbe 1972: no. 64, pl. 26; Pipili 1987: 117,179). This scheme of decoration defies the normal practices of Corinth and Athens, and gives the Laconian cups a strongly marked character of their own (Seeberg 1971; Brijder 1983). The archaeological evidence, though fragmentary, does not suggest that any one painter pioneered komos iconography on Laconian vases. Rather, the komos is chosen as a subject by each of the major painters, such as the Arkesilas, Naukratis, Hunt and Rider painters, though it was not a particular favourite of any one of them.

Scholars have been as uncertain about the context of the Laconian komos as they have been about Corinthian and Athenian scenes depicting the same subject. Sparta, however, poses a slightly different set of questions. Although Sparta seems never to have developed dramatic festivals in the Athenian sense, the possibility that these dancers are mimetic entertainers of same description should be considered (Parker 1989: 151). We question also whether the komast scenes present a picture of Spartan dining practices, syssitia, phiditia, or symposia, or if the dancers are mythological or religious in origin (David 1989; Murray 1991). Another possibility exists: the Laconian komoi copy conventional scenes, taken from Archaic stock, and are adjusted to local customs or tastes to create a personalized product.

On a cup attributed to the Allard Pierson Painter by Stibbe (FIG. 7.1), the tondo is dominated by a nude male at a prostyle building, which could be identified as a temple or a fountain (once London Market; Pipili 1987: 118, 208). The pose of this figure suggests that he is a komast dancer. He leans his body back and kicks his left leg forward. He holds up a cup in his left hand in such a way that the vessel, presumably empty, does not inhibit his dancing. With his right hand he clutches, or slaps, his bottom. Although this scene

Fig. 7.1 Laconian cup. Once London market. Photo J. Boardman. 'Komast at a temple or fountain'.

has been connected with the Capture of Silenos, this human reveller is clearly not Silenos or a satyr of any kind (Pipili 1987: 38–9). The Spartan satyr on vases is characterized as a bearded male with a hairy body, a large phallus, and a conspicuously missing tail. If this man is merely a komast, he may have escaped from the symposium to the fountain house to refill the water, needed for mixing the wine. However, a cup seems an inappropriate vessel for the job. On the other hand, if the structure is a temple, and his vessel is a phiale, this might be the scene of a religious event (Greifenhagen 1929: 54; Heath 1988, 182). It should be noted, though, that this painter follows the Rider Painter, who uses architectural settings in scenes showing other subjects (Stibbe 1986).

A connection between the komasts and the myth of the Capture of Silenos exists on another Laconian cup. On the upper frieze of a cup in the Villa Giulia (57231) a tailless satyr is pursued from behind by two men in oriental dress. This scene has been identified as the Capture of Silenos (Brommer 1941). The scene in the lower frieze of the same cup displays several dancing komasts also in oriental dress, accompanied by a standing male figure toting a wineskin. The poses of the dancers relate them to more lightly dressed komasts, but their elaborately decorated garments are thus far unique. It is significant that the human revellers share both the tondo and the dress style with the mythological figures. This second example suits the theory of an East Greek origin for the Capture of Silenos myth nicely.

On a cup attributed to the manner of the Hunt Painter, two males, one bearded and one beardless, are draped in long belted chitons and are dancing on either side of a large standed vessel (Sotheby's 1993: 10). Although this scene is identified as a komos (Pipili 1987: 118, 209h), neither the attire nor the movements of the dancers clearly identifies them as komasts. The vessel in the centre is not a mixing krater of the type seen on many Laconian komos representations (Stibbe 1989: 18–19). Another possibility is that these two dancers are competitors rather than entertainers (Bloesch 1982: 20, no. 7). The large vase between them could be a tripod-cauldron, a prize for the victor in a dancing contest. Cauldrons of this type were standard dedications in sanctuaries, and this dance could have a religious context.

Another vase by the Hunt Painter, a hydria in Rhodes (15373), also allows for a religious interpretation of its komos scene (Stibbe 1972: no. 219, pls. 76–7; Pipili 1987, 118,209c). Here six nude males dance around the shoulder of the vase. Two of these figures hold drinking-horns, and at least three of them hold objects which have been identified as pomegranates. Similarly, on a cup from Tocra (FIG. 7.2) by the same painter, the bottom-slapping hand of a male komast is visible holding a pomegranate (Boardman and Hayes 1966: no. 940). Pipili recognizes the pomegranate as a fertility symbol, and further suggests that dances of this kind probably belonged to the Orthia cult (1987: 73). As a votive object, the pomegranate was dedicated at the sanctuary of Artemis in various forms, including terracotta, bronze, bone, ivory, and lead (Dawkins 1929: e.g. nos. 158, 202, 216, 245 and 257). Perhaps the pomegranate, which had a particular local interest as a votive object, made its way

Fig. 7.2 Laconian cup fragments, Tocra 940. After Boardman and Hayes. 'Komast holding a pomegranate'.

into vase-painting for the same purpose. These dancers perform a religious dance in honour of a local cult (Greifenhagen 1929: 55). However, these two examples are by the same hand, and both were found outside Sparta. We should also recognize that the pomegranate was already a common ornamental motif in Laconian black-figure painting (Lane 1934: 119, 172–3). Its is also carried by female 'worshipper' figures and by komasts on Chian chalices (Lemos 1993: nos. 735, 890, 1552). It may have been a particular favourite of the Hunt Painter, who at least twice includes it as an attribute in human figure scenes.

Plutarch informs us that the helots were obligated to perform vulgar and humiliating songs and dances, and to drink excessive amounts of unmixed wine at the syssitia; under duress the drunken entertainers served as an example of the consequences of intemperance for young Spartan boys (Lycurgus 28; Ducat 1990: 107–27; David 1989: 6; Fischer 1989: 34). Perhaps we see this unique Spartan ritual demonstrated on the exterior of a cup from Artemis Orthia in the manner of the Naukratis Painter (Stibbe 1972: no. 64, pl. 26). Here several beardless human males perform in the presence of bearded males and a hairy, tailless satyr. Lane first identified the komasts in this scene with their unusual capped buttocks and anklets as women (1934: 160). Although he believed that the participants regardless of gender were completely human, he further asserted that this was a representation of some 'orgiastic rite'. He also suggested the possibility that these dancers perform the kordax, which is identified by Theophrastus (The Characters 6) as a grotesque and undignified dance (Schnabel 1910: Simon 1982: 29). The kordax was danced at Elis in honour of Artemis and, interestingly, this cup was dedicated at the Artemis Orthia sanctuary. The possibility of a Dionysian atmosphere should also be considered, as indicated by the presence of the satyr (Greifenhagen 1929: 56; Fitzhardinge 1980: 36; Pipili 1987: 52–4; Parker 1989: 150–1; Stibbe 1992b).

The examples we have looked at thus far have been, for the most part, exceptions from the Laconian stock of figure painted vases. The majority of the iconographic evidence suggests that the Laconian komos occurred either before, during or after the symposium. Lane suggests that the banqueting scenes of the kind found on Laconian vases are typified by hetairai, flute girls and padded dancers. He concludes that these scenes are so like the Corinthian examples that they must have derived from this model. He further points to the flute-girls and hetairai as possible 'artistic material without any allusion to local Spartan institutions' (1934: 158). If Lane believed this to be the case, why did he not consider the padded dancers a similar borrowing? There is no doubt that the komast figure in Laconian art, taken alone, would share many of the features of a Corinthian prototype: often a short chiton, protruding features, the bottom-slapping gesture, attributes of drink and song. However, both komoi and flute-girls were produced in Sparta in other media—namely as lead figurines, a characteristically Spartan votive item. Furthermore, at Sparta, where a school of lyric poetry is thought to have been organized at the time of Terpandar (late seventh century), and where multiple varieties of dance are also attested, it is easy to imagine events which combine food, drink, song and dance (Plutarch Moralia 1134b–c; Hooker 1980: 71–4). Though dining spaces of the type found elsewhere in Greece are absent from the archaeological record at Sparta, Alcman (fr. 19) describes the standard seven couch arrangement as he must have know it from personal experience (Berquist 1990). Spartan citizens may have frowned upon excessive drinking, but banqueting in a communal setting was a well-known part of daily life. In other words, Laconian artists need not to have copied entire scenes directly from Corinthian or Athenian models, and clearly they did not. Everyday life provided all the inspiration necessary.

The representations of komast dancers in a probable sympotic environment occur in several iconographic types. On a cup by the Rider Painter in Würzburg (166), a komast and two pipers entertain at a symposium (Langlotz 1932: 25, no. 166, pl. 28). The male dancer is inside the andron, dancing beside a kline. The composition is symmetrical with one piper standing opposite the dancer, and the kline with the reclining symposiast and second piper are presented in the middle. The painter includes the dancer in the same scene with musicians, kline, and a symposiast perhaps to indicate that all events occur in the same place at the same time.

A similar type of scene is painted more frequently, where the painter divides the symposium from the komos by placing each in a separate frieze. A cup attributed to the Naukratis Painter reveals one of the best known examples of this arrangement where the komos appears below the symposium (Practica di Mare E 1986, from Lavinium; Paribeni 1975: 362–8, Figs. 434–5, pl. 5). The symposium takes place in the upper frieze of the tondo, complete with recliners, a flute-player, attendants, animals, and winged daemons (Lane 1934: 158–9; Pipili 1987: 64–5, 72,n.692). This complicated scene would catch the viewer's attention rather than the diminutive komos frieze below it. In the lower frieze six males dance around a krater, and some hold drinking-horns. Their dance is lively and fun, but apparently separate from the symposium scene above, as well as void of its participants' attention. A composition very close to this is found on the interior of Taranto 20909, a cup now attributed to the Allard Pierson Painter (Pelagatti 1955–6: 36–9, Fig. 37). Again the komos occurs in a separate pictorial space. On this cup, however, the painter has even further distinguished the two events by placing an animal frieze between them.

Another type of scene which suggests a festive or sympotic context are those in which dancers appear either in the presence of musicians or playing music themselves. When the komast himself plays the music it is normally the pipes as on a cup in Leipzig (T 2177) by the Rider Painter (Stibbe 1972: no. 314, pl. 112,1), or on the well known dinos in the Louvre (E662), where the dancer on the right wears padding across his front and phorbia across his cheeks (Stibbe 1972: no. 313, pls. 110–11). A cup in Florence (3879) depicts three komasts wearing ornate chitons and the one in the centre playing a syrinx (Stibbe 1972: no. 227, pl. 80,1). On a cup in the Vatican, attributed to the manner of the Hunt Painter, two beardless, draped dancing males perform on either side of a large kitharode (Guglielmi Collection B9; Stibbe 1972: no. 272, pls. 90,2 and 91). Similar versions of this scene are found on vases by other Laconian painters, such as the Rider Painter (Stibbe 1992b: 145). The image of an oversized kitharode in the presence of komasts is peculiar to Laconian iconography. This large lyre-player performing at the symposium or in the company of human revellers has sometimes been considered the god Apollo or, more recently, the god Dionysos. Pipili disregards the suggestion of padded dancers before a deity as an 'unusual image', stating (and I agree) that we should regard these musicians as ordinary people (1987: 52). It is possible that both the dancers and the musicians are ordinary youths performing in a religious festival in Sparta. The fact that the existence of such scenes is specifically Laconian makes this theory a distinct possibility. While many would choose to consider Dionysos the god of the komos, in Archaic komoi outside Sparta (i.e. at Athens, Corinth, Boeotia, and East Greece) the god of wine never presides. The notable exception to this is a series of vases by the Amasis Painter, where fully human revellers are present in scenes with Dionysos (Henrichs 1987). The identity of the human figures is uncertain, but they appear to be taking the role of satyrs in the works of this particular artist. Their respectable behaviour and sexual restraint perhaps contribute to their short-lived role in this capacity (Carpenter 1986: 88).

A sympotic atmosphere is also implied on scenes where the dancers either hold drinking attributes or dance in the presence of a krater (Lissarrague 1990). The drinking-horn, the most popular drinking attribute on early Athenian black-figure representations of the komos, is not the only preoccupation of Laconian vase-painters. The dancers brandish a variety of shapes: the kantharos (Sparta Museum, Stibbe 1972: no. 244, pl. 85,4) as well as the drinking-horn and the cup (British Museum B3, FIG. 7.3). This variety of drinking attributes may reflect a slight case of painter's preference, but the appearance of the krater certainly does not.

The krater was a popular shape in Laconia, produced in both clay and metal. Painters include the krater in a large number of komos scenes. These vases not only suggest a sympotic atmosphere but also connect the dancers with the mixing or drinking of wine, if not the transporting or stealing of it, tasks often reserved for satyrs. The frequency of the krater in komos scenes, as well as the prevalence of the sympo-

Fig. 7.3 Laconian cup, British Museum B3. Photo British Museum. 'Komasts around a krater'.

sium indicates that Laconian painters are attempting to represent scenes from Spartan social life rather than from local cult ritual (Stibbe 1989: 21). On a cup in Paris by the Hunt Painter, two beardless, nude males dance at one side of a large volute-krater topped with an oinochoe (Cabinet des Médailles 192; Stibbe 1972: no. 228, pl. 80,3). The komasts are solely preoccupied with dance, and do not hold drinking vessels or touch the krater. On the British Museum cup by the Rider Painter (FIG. 7.3) a standing, nude male holds two drinking vessels, a drinking-horn and a cup, while his friend plays the pipes. Although neither male is dancing, these attributes of drink and song identify them as komasts. The male with the cups stands before the dominant krater, which is flanked by two birds. Shortly, he will help himself to some wine or will refill the wine vessels for another dancer or banqueter.

KOMASTS IN OTHER MEDIA

Among the over 100,000 lead figurines dedicated to Artemis Orthia (winged goddesses, warriors, animals, etc.), and among the several thousand from the Menelaion, there are a number of komast figures (Dawkins 1929: 249–84; Wace 1909b: 127–41; Tod and Wace 1906: 228–30). Based on the publications of the lead votives from Laconia, it is difficult to place the komast figures into a dated context, or to number them. The komasts must begin as early as the late seventh century, and continue throughout the sixth century. Wace clearly did not know what to call these grotesque dancers, who slap their bottoms. Often his 'running man', 'satyric type' or 'allied type' male must be a human reveller, comparable to the type depicted on black-figure vases. Wace was himself aware of the similarity between the lead figurines and the types on vases, but he clearly lacked the current terminology (1909b: 130). He recognizes a number of musicians, both male and female, lyre-players and pipers, as well satyrs. By *c.* 500 the musicians, dancers and satyrs seem to fade from the picture, and the popularity of mythological divinities, other than Artemis, increases. However, the Archaic appearance of the lead votives is maintained through all periods.

The lead figurines of komasts are small, only two or three centimetres high. Like the other types in lead, the dancers are moulded on one side, and were never meant to stand upright. Like the revellers on Laconian black-figure vases, the humble lead votive figurines are in full-profile; their stiff and rigid poses convince us of a dancer in motion. Their identity as komast dancers is indisputable. The dancers are all nude males, some have large buttocks, stomachs and/or thighs, and many demonstrate the characteristic bottom-slapping gesture (Hooker 1980: Fig. 36). Some seem to have beards, though these may be Spartan satyrs, often shown without tails. The lyre-players and pipers are no doubt related figures, if not simply themselves komasts, who play musical instruments. From the Menelaion, there is at least one lead figurine of a male, possibly a komast dancer, wearing a kilt (Wace 1909b: Fig. 10, 32). Komasts wearing kilts are known from Fikellura vases, thought to be produced in Miletus during the sixth century (Cook 1992). Komasts in eastern costume are not unknown

Fig. 7.4 Bronze figurine, recliner, British Museum 1954-10-18-1. Photo British Museum.

in Sparta, as we have seen on a vase in the Villa Giulia previously discussed.

A bronze statuette from Corfu stands 11.8 centimetres high and represents a male figure (Corfu Museum 1602; Dontas 1969). The male wears a partial beard and faces frontally. Although he does not slap his bottom in the usual manner, his kneeling-running pose, decorated kilt, and most importantly his drinking-horn associate him with komast figures on vases (Dontas 1969: 40–4). The style of the figure is Archaic, and it was discovered in the burnt destruction levels of the Archaic sanctuary at 'Mon Repos' (Dontas 1969: 39–40). The statuette is worked on all sides. The flat plates attached to each foot, with holes at both the front and the back, indicate that the statuette was once attached to the rim of a bronze vessel, perhaps a large tripod-cauldron, a standard shape for an elaborate dedication (Dontas 1969: 40–6).

Dontas attributes the bronze komast to Laconian craftsmanship on the basis of style (1969: 47–8), though he distinguishes this dancer from the painted Laconian versions by his non-padded costume. As we have seen, the komast dancers of Laconia are rarely padded, and often appear as nude males with oversized anatomical features. The Ionian costume of this dancer turns our attention east, and recalls also the single lead figurine of a dancer in similar dress.

Connected with the Corfu bronze are a series of Laconian bronze ornamental statuettes, also thought to be from tripods or kraters, produced during the second half of the sixth century and early in the fifth. The statuette of a naked male carrying a hydria was found in southern Laconia, and stands 8.5 centimetres high (Athens NM 7614; Fitzhardinge 1980: Fig. 126). Though Beazley suggests that the male is a craftsman, perhaps a potter or bronzesmith, the figure can just as easily be considered a komast (Beazley 1946: 7). We have seen that komasts are often nude, and seem to be responsible for the carrying and mixing of wine, in addition to the drinking of it. Also related to vase imagery is a bronze banqueter in the British Museum (1954-10-18-1; FIG. 7.4), a bearded, reclining male holding a drinking cup. Satyrs in running, dancing or reclining poses were also produced in Laconia, such as the small frontal figure from the Acropolis at Sparta (3245; Pipili 1987: no. 187, Fig. 100), or the satyr from Amyklai (Athens NM 7544; Fitzhardinge 1980: Fig. 149), who poses similarly to the komast from Corfu.

A large bronze volute krater from Sicily, now in the National Archaeological Museum at Syracuse (23123), displays a komast scene (Hitzl 1982: no. 7, pl. 8–10; Stibbe 1989: 62–3). The fragmentary krater comes from Monte San Mauro, near Caltagirone, and it is completely restored. It stands over 52 centimetres high, and has a diameter of 37 centimetres. Though it is described as 'primitive', if not 'provincial' (possibly a local imitation), it is the oldest known bronze volute krater (Payne 1931: 218; Karouzou 1955: 195). The krater was dated by Orsi to the second 1/4 of the fifth century (1910: 812–3), but it is now considered a work of the early sixth century (Stibbe 1989: 62–3). At least thirteen male figures are incised around the neck of the vase on one side. The opposite side is decorated with centaurs. Three of the males are draped in a long garment and play the auloi. These three are spaced evenly along the frieze with one on each end and another in the centre. The other figures are nude, dancing males, some of whom have beards. Several of them slap their buttocks, or kick their legs high in the air toward the dancer in front of them. Humphry

Payne saw a 'distinctly Corinthian style' in these engraved dancers, more on the basis of attitudes than costume (1931: 218). Though the krater is identified as Laconian work, there is nothing in the execution of the dancers and musicians that can be regarded as particular to Laconia. Even the komast figures which decorate the shoulder of a better known Laconian black-figure vase from Sicily, attributed to the Hunt Painter, bear little resemblance to these basic incised dancers on bronze (Stibbe 1990). This is the only known example of a komast scene incised on a bronze vessel from Archaic Greece.

CONCLUSIONS

Komast figures and komos scenes produced in Laconia take a variety of forms: black-figure vases, lead figurines, bronze statuettes, and a bronze krater. Outside Laconia, the Archaic komast figure decorates black-figure vases, and is very rarely seen in other media. The black-figure vases of Laconia seem to indicate that komast dancers participated in events connected with banqueting, drinking and music. We also noticed that many of the vases hinted, if only slightly, at a religious event. Accompanying this evidence are lead figurines in the form of komasts, serving a strictly votive purpose, along with bronze tripod attachments, and incised dancers, decorating grander dedicatory objects.

Archaic Sparta presents the first and only instance of the komast figure employed for religious or dedicatory purposes. Taken as a whole, the archaeological evidence may say something about the Artemis Orthia cult and the events (i.e. banqueting, dancing, contests) connected with it (Pipili 1987: 74–5). This study of Spartan komoi also demonstrates the way in which the komast figure, or a style of dancing, may have been inspired from elsewhere (i.e. Corinth), yet was transformed or considered suitable for local needs. There is no need to overemphasize the importance of the komast dancer as a votive object—particularly in lead—or the other subjects represented (e.g. the sphinx, centaurs, and gorgons) should also be considered to have special significance at Sparta. Rather, these are Archaic mythical images, standard on vases and in other media throughout the sixth century. Similarly, we must view the komast as part of a bigger picture of Archaic Greek iconography—an image which spread on black-figure vases to all the major centres of production, Corinth, Athens, Boeotia, East Greece, and in Sparta found its way into other media.

ACKNOWLEDGMENTS

I wish to thank Professor J. Boardman, Dr O. Murray, Dr M. Pipili, M. Vickers, and Dr S. Walker for their help at various stages in the preparation of this paper.

8

Archaic Laconian vase-painting: some iconographic considerations

Maria Pipili

INTRODUCTION

When, some years ago, the Hamburg Museum acquired a new Laconian cup (Hamburg 1983.281: Hornbostel 1984; Pipili 1987: 10–11, no. 22a, fig. 15), another puzzling scene came to be added to the long series of unexplained representations on sixth-century Laconian vases. The cup shows on its interior a richly dressed figure with an unusual hair-do who is attacking men and youths well wrapped in their himatia which also cover their heads. Two are fleeing to the right, two more lie dead on the ground. The cup is by the Hunt Painter, one of the leading black-figure Laconian vase-painters, and can be dated to the years around 550 BC. Many names have been given to the hero shown on this vase: the late Hans Jucker, taking into account the fact that the man's face might once have been painted white, thought of Talos, the brazen giant who killed the foreigners who landed on Crete; Erika Simon thought that the victims were participating at a symposium when attacked because of the fact that they are in pairs of a man and a youth each and because of their dresses, and suggested Aigisthos killing Agamemnon and his companions after their return from Troy.[1] We could also think of a story of local Laconian interest: Herakles killing Hippokoon and his sons in order to restore Hippokoon's wronged half-brother Tyndareus to the throne (Pipili 1987: 11), a scene which was to be depicted later in the century on the Amyklai Throne (Paus. iii 18 11). There can be other suggestions (Steuben 1991: 341), but we shall not insist on this cup here. If we mention it at all, it is because it is a very good example of the puzzling character of much of archaic Laconian iconography. There are several such nameless figures in Laconian vase-painting which have no close parallel on other vases: for example, the man holding a lion by the leash on a cup in Rhodes (Rhodes 10711: Stibbe 1972: no. 190; Pipili 1987: 24–5, no. 77, fig. 35), the hero attacking a snake on the much reproduced cup in Paris (Louvre E 669: Stibbe 1972: no. 303, pl. 107, 1; Pipili 1987: 50–1, no. 141, fig. 77) and on a replica from Gravisca (Boitani 1990: 35, no. 18, fig. 33), the struggling pair—a man in a short chiton grasping an elderly figure in a long dress by the neck in the presence of another man—on a cup in Athens (Athens NM 13910: Stibbe 1972: no. 103; Pipili 1987: 31–3, no. 88, fig. 46), the youth between two winged horses on a cup in the British Museum (London B2: Stibbe 1972: no. 96; Pipili 1987: 37–8, no. 96, fig. 52).

Alongside these unique scenes there are mythical scenes which do belong to the common archaic iconographic repertoire and yet are treated in a way which does not follow the standard Corinthian or Attic schemes: for example, the original Herakles and the Amazons on a cup by the Arkesilas Painter in Rome (Stibbe 1972: no. 193; Pipili 1987: 5–7, no. 14, fig. 9), where Herakles is not fighting against an Amazon, as usual, but is shown chasing two terrified creatures who flee without offering any resistence, a rare scheme used also on some Tyrrhenian amphorae; or Bellerophon and the Chimaera on a cup by the Boreads Painter which entered the Getty Museum not many years ago (Getty Mus. 85.AE.121: Pipili 1987: 19, no. 57, fig. 29; Stibbe 1991), where Bellerophon is not riding his winged horse but is shown in a kneeling-running pose between Pegasos and the Chimaera who rear over him. And there is also one particular Laconian artist, the Rider Painter, who used elements from different scenes to build up new ones without making it clear what exactly he was depicting: the Achilles lying in wait for Troilos in front of a low prostyle building (a sanctuary or a fountain), a scene treated several times by him (Zancani Montuoro 1954; Pipili 1987: 27–30, nos. 84–6), is very close to the warrior attacking a snake on the Louvre cup that we have already mentioned (in both scenes there is a snake coiled around the column, one or more birds on the roof, and on the Louvre cup the exergue is occupied by a hare, an animal found under Troilos' horse on one of the Rider Painter's versions of the myth); and the Silenus being captured at the fountain on a fragment from Samos in Berlin (Berlin WS 4: Stibbe 1972: no. 292; Pipili 1987: 39, no. 98, fig. 53) is turned into a komast dancing before a fountain on a cup once on the London Market (Pipili 1987: 39, 75, no. 208, fig. 107)—a work not by the Rider Painter himself, however, as we would have thought at first sight, but by a close imitator, the Allard Pierson Painter, as

1 Jucker's and Simon's interpretations are cited by Hornbostel 1984: 148–9.

Conrad Stibbe has shown (Stibbe 1986). We cannot be certain if these unexplained scenes are totally different subjects or if they are merely careless, summarized renderings of the other recognisable stories.

Besides the many unexplained mythological scenes on Laconian vases, there is another large category of puzzling scenes which, I think, present more interest and which will be the subject of this paper. These are scenes which seem to have both an everyday life and a religious character; they are typically Laconian and have provoked much discussion as to their real meaning: symposia attended by small winged daemons, komasts surrounding an imposing musician, a single rider surrounded by the same winged creatures which appear at the symposia. It is mainly because of such scenes rather than the mythological ones that adjectives like 'unorthodox', 'eccentric', 'original' have been used for Laconian vase iconography as a whole. Of course, symposia, komoi, riding, were everyday activities, and as such were, together with hunting and fighting, favourite scenes on black-figure Corinthian and Attic vases. But many of the Laconian scenes have elements which put them apart from the other archaic vases and have often been given a religious meaning.

Of the five major Laconian vase-painters exhaustively studied by Stibbe in his fundamental *Lakonische Vasenmaler des sechsten Jahrhunderts v. Chr.*(Stibbe 1972), it is the Naukratis Painter, the one generally credited with the introduction of the small winged daemons in Laconian art, who seems to have been most fond of such scenes. FIG. 8.1 shows a graphic representation of the number of vases with myth scenes (shaded bars) as compared to vases with these 'other' scenes (open bars) for each of the five major Laconian vase-painters. The 'other' scenes are images of gods on their own, and scenes of symposia, komoi and riding, not only those which can be given a religious meaning but all such scenes. The data used is from Stibbe's catalogue. As we see, the Naukratis Painter, with two myth scenes and sixteen of the 'other' scenes (six images of gods on their own and ten symposia, komos scenes and riders), clearly favoured such non-myth scenes more than the other artists. What I should like to show here is that the Naukratis Painter, being one of the earliest Laconian vase-painters, and one who did not imitate others but was on the contrary widely imitated, was probably the one who introduced most of these compositions in Laconian art giving to Laconian iconography much of its character. If we wish to understand these scenes more fully, we should examine them as a whole and also as part of this artist's work.

THE NAUKRATIS PAINTER

General characteristics

Named by Arthur Lane in his comprehensive study of Laconian pottery (Lane 1934) after the well-known cup from Naukratis in the British Museum showing a goddess surrounded by winged daemons (London B 4: Stibbe 1972: no. 23; Pipili 1987: 41–2, no. 101, fig. 54) (FIG. 8.5), the Naukratis Painter was until recently the least esteemed of the Laconian vase-painters. Brian Shefton called his work 'unenterprising' (Shefton 1954: 303), and for Paola Pelagatti he is 'the least talented of Laconian vase-painters, certainly not very original' (Pelagatti 1955–56: 27). These opinions, when expressed, were to some extent justifiable since very few works by this artist were known at the time. It was only after the appearance of Stibbe's monograph in 1972, in which many more pieces by the painter were published, most coming from the Samian Heraion, that we were able to assess fully this painter's worth. Stibbe listed some 60 vases by the Naukratis Painter (Stibbe 1972: 269–72), while in Shefton's 1954 article only 22 pieces were mentioned (Shefton 1954:

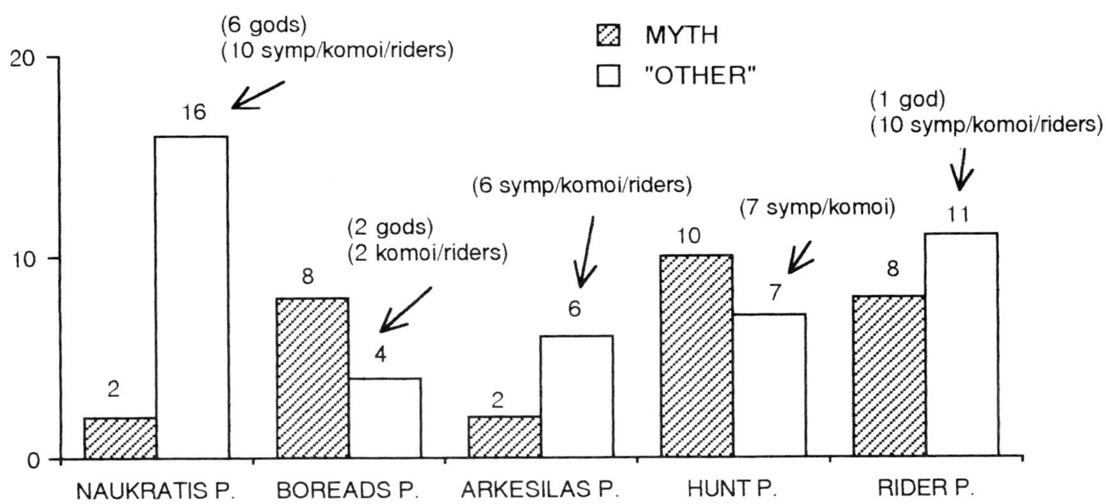

Fig. 8.1 Bar chart of the five major Laconian vase-painters showing numbers of vases with mythical (shaded) and non-mythical scenes (open)

303–4). Stibbe's work is, therefore, essential for our knowledge of the painter, who emerges there as a high quality artist both in miniature work and in large scale, and with a very good feeling for secondary ornament. Stibbe showed that the Naukratis Painter had a relatively long career (from 575 to 550 BC), compared to the other early black-figure Laconian vase-painter, the Boreads Painter, who started at about the same time but did not work for more than a decade. He was also widely imitated, not only by minor artists who painted in his manner until the last decades of the sixth century BC, but also by the three other major painters, particularly the Arkesilas Painter at his beginnings and the Rider Painter, while the Boreads Painter influenced only the Arkesilas Painter. The Naukratis Painter also produced a wide range of shapes, not just cups as the Boreads Painter, and his works were found both in Laconia and abroad, while the Boreads Painter is not represented in Sparta at all. Stibbe showed the painter's artistic merit as far as style of drawing, potting and influences are concerned; his iconographic remarks, however, are necessarily brief and randomly expressed in the discussion of certain vases only. I should like to emphasize here the Naukratis Painter's subject-matter and iconographic renderings and hope to show that he was also a most interesting and inventive vase-painter from an iconographic point of view, perhaps more so than any other of his Laconian colleagues.

Corinthian influences

As one of the earliest black-figure artists in Laconia, using a technique obviously taken from Corinth, it is no surprise that in his early works the Naukratis Painter shows strong Corinthian influence in his liking for animal friezes on the exterior of his cups, as well as in the use of emblematic daemonic figures on their interiors (there are five cups of his with a winged Boread [Pipili 1987: 64–5, figs. 91–2; 117, nos. 170–4] very close to the Corinthian ones, a fragmentary cup with a Gorgon [Pipili 1987: 16–17, no. 41, fig. 24], and a whole cup with a sphinx [Stibbe 1972: no. 7, pl. 4, 1]). This liking for Corinthian emblematic figures on the interior of cups is also met in the work of the other early painter, the Boreads Painter, who otherwise shows few Corinthian elements and no animal friezes in the Corinthian manner. These daemonic figures decorating the tondi of the Laconian cups continue to the latter part of the sixth century (see, e.g., the Chimaera cup in Heidelberg, dated *c.* 530 BC: Stibbe 1972: no. 352, pl. 128, 1; Pipili 1987: 19–20, no. 58, fig. 30), something natural since such figures fitted well in the round space of the tondo, much better than a narrative composition.

Also from Corinth the Naukratis Painter may have taken his liking for symposia, komoi, fights and cavalcades. Was he a Corinthian himself? On a fragment found in Cyrene and discussed by Gerald Schaus (Schaus 1979) (FIG. 8.17) next to an enthroned goddess holding a wreath who was probably approached by one or more persons, a composition to which we shall return, there is part of an inscription—the only inscription by the Naukratis Painter—with a three-stroke iota, a letter unknown to the Laconian script, but belonging to the Corinthian one. This type of iota appears also in the Theran-Cyrenaic script, and Schaus suggested that the artist might be a Cyrenean working in Sparta, using this as a further argument for the existence of particularly close ties between Sparta and Cyrene in the archaic period. We shall return to this fragment and to the inscription later.

East Greek influences

Apart from its early corinthianizing features, the Naukratis Painter's work has also a very strong East Greek character. This character has not been given much attention, and it is the Boreads Painter who is usually thought to have borrowed East Greek motifs and to have been imitated in the East—he has even been thought to have arrived from Ionia. But the East Greek elements in the Naukratis Painter's work are unmistakable:[2]

a) Together with the Boreads Painter he seems to have introduced the exergue under the main scene; an early example of his is a cup in the Louvre with a sphinx in the tondo and a fish in the exergue (Louvre E 664: Stibbe 1972: no. 7, pl. 4, 1). This division of the interior into a main scene and an exergue was obviously copied from East Greek plates dating from the late seventh and early sixth centuries BC (see, e.g., Walter-Karydi 1973: nos. 1070, 1121, pls. 133, 136).

b) Another arrangement of the interior decoration of his vases is also met on Ionian cups: a concentric frieze running round a central medallion, as, for example, on his symposium cup in the Louvre (Louvre E 667: Stibbe 1972: no. 13, pl. 6, 1; Pipili 1987: 71 ff., no. 194, fig. 103) (FIG. 8.6) or on a fragmentary cup from Egypt (Alexandria 9362+9390: Venit 1985: 395, no. 4, pl. 42, 1). The Boreads Painter also used often such concentric friezes for rows of dancing komasts, riders, hare-hunt, etc.[3]

---

2 In a recent article Brian Shefton aptly supports the view that 'the intensive current of influence flowing both ways across the Aegean between Samos and Laconia in the decade or so before the middle of the sixth century . . . is particularly tied to the person of the Naukratis Painter' (Shefton 1989: 63).

3 Stibbe 1972: no. 121, pl. 40, 3 (hounds chasing hare); no. 141, pl. 45, 1 (komos); no. 146 (riders); no. 148 (hounds chasing fox). For a very similar East Greek frieze see the hare-hunt on a Samian cup from the Heraion dated *c.* 550 BC : Kyrieleis 1981: 46, fig. 33.

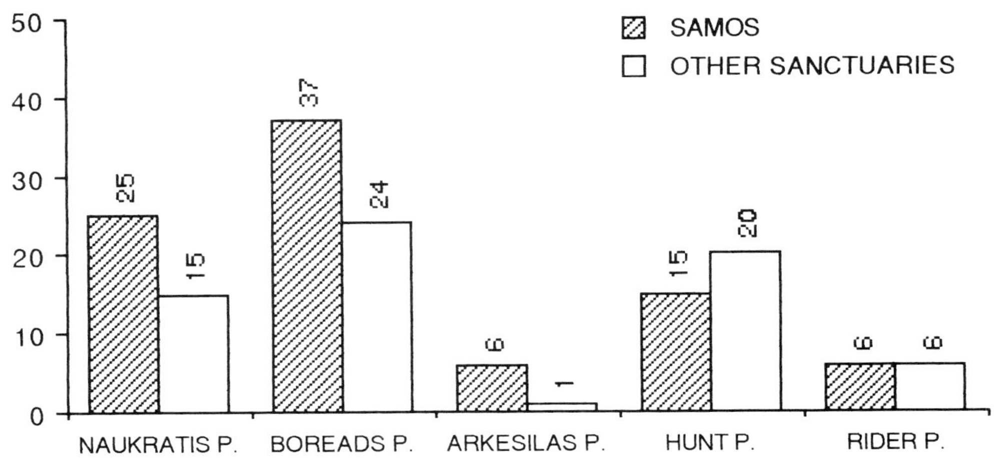

Fig.8.2 Bar chart of the five major Laconian vase-painters showing the numbers of their vases from the Samian Heraion (shaded) compared with those from all other sanctuaries (open)

c) The characteristic high-stemmed Laconian cup, probably an invention of the Naukratis Painter (Stibbe 1972: 68) since the earliest such vase is his Zeus cup in Taranto dated around 570 BC (Taranto I.G. 4988: Stibbe 1972: no. 8, pl. 4, 4 and p. 20, fig. 5), may also have been introduced in Laconian art under eastern influence and have been maintained because of its popularity with overseas markets.[4]

d) The exterior of the sphinx cup in the Louvre already mentioned is clearly imitating Ionian cups (Stibbe 1972: 49–50).

e) Two cups by the Naukratis Painter, one from Samos, very fragmentary and now partly lost (Samos K 1188: Stibbe 1972: no. 10, pl. 5, 4), the other from Italy (Stibbe 1972: no. 11, pl. 5, 5), show palmettes of the Ionian type with separate leaves.

f) Finally, the rich floral friezes decorating the internal lip of many of the Naukratis Painter's cups, something imitated by the Arkesilas Painter and the Rider Painter on works which obviously copy works of the Naukratis Painter, are very close to the rich floral friezes on some Ionian Little-Master cups: an interesting parallel, published recently by Brian Shefton, is in Osborne House on the Isle of Wight (Shefton 1989: 58–9, figs. 12 c, e). Here, as in many other cases, the current of influence seems to have flown the other way: the East Greek painter probably imitated the decoration of the Laconian cups. The Naukratis Painter was, therefore, well acquainted with East Greek and more particularly Samian vases, since clay analysis has now shown that the Ionian Little-Master cups must have been made on Samos (Shefton 1989: 44 with n. 4), and was, in turn, imitated by his Samian colleagues.

Sparta and Samos

It is well-known that Sparta was in close contact with the eastern world, and particularly with the island of Samos, already from the seventh century BC. There is much eastern material and East Greek influence in the votives from the Artemis Orthia sanctuary at that time, and it is generally thought that these came to Sparta through Samos. The famous 'special relationship' between Sparta and Samos (Cartledge 1982) becomes particularly obvious from the late seventh century when Laconian pottery starts being exported to Samos in quantities. The great sanctuary of Hera, patron deity of Samos, is the second site after Sparta herself to have yielded such a great amount of sixth-century Laconian vases. These vases belong especially to the years 570 to 550 BC. About 540 BC the tyranny of Polykrates marked a break in the close relations between Sparta and Samos and a swing by the Samians towards Athens. As a result, Laconian pottery becomes less common on Samos from that time until about 525 BC when commercial relations between the two states stop altogether. It was in 524 BC that the Spartans attempted to overthrow Polykrates and restore some aristocratic Samian exiles to power.

The Naukratis Painter, like his contemporaries, the Boreads Painter and the Arkesilas Painter, worked at the time of the big export of Laconian vases to Samos. Most of these painters' vases have actually been found on Samos, and in FIG. 8.2 we have a graphic representation of the number of vases found in the Samian Heraion (shaded bars) as opposed to vases found in all other sanctuaries (open bars) for each of the five main

4 That the high stem was popular in the East from an early period is indicated by the stemmed dishes dating from the mid-seventh to the mid-sixth century BC (Walter-Karydi 1973: 10), as well as by some other related shapes (ibid. pl. 23, no. 265).

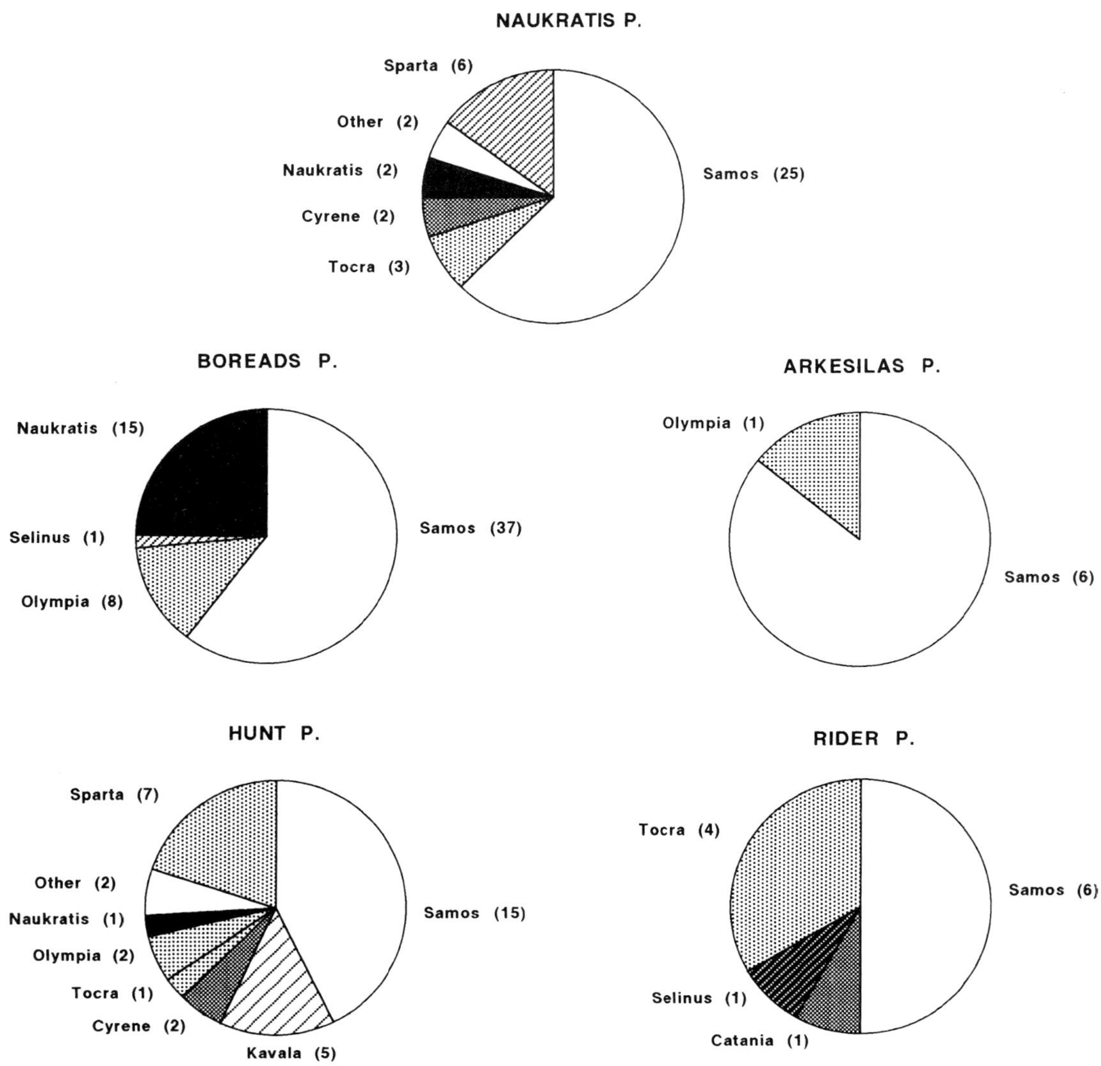

Fig.8.3 Pie charts showing sanctuaries where Laconian vases have been found

Laconian vase-painters (the data is again from Stibbe's catalogue). For the three painters who worked until about 550 BC the vases from Samos outnumber by far those found in other sanctuaries. The Hunt Painter who worked also in the second part of the century, until about 530 BC, had his vases directed to other areas. The pie-diagrams in FIG. 8.3 show in detail the sanctuaries where Laconian vases were found. Apart from the Samian Heraion, Laconian vases were dedicated at the sanctuaries of Demeter and Kore at Tocra and Cyrene, the various sanctuaries of the emporia at Naukratis, the sanctuary of Olympia, and, of course, the local Laconian sanctuaries, mainly those of Artemis Orthia and of Athena on the Spartan Acropolis. That these Spartan sanctuaries are not represented here very well is due to the fact that the works of the main black-figure painters were mostly exported. We should note here that most Laconian vases come from sanctuaries; in FIG. 8.4 we have a graphic representation of the number of vases found in sanctuaries (light-shaded bars) as opposed to vases found in graves (dark-shaded bars) for each of the five main Laconian vase-painters (the data is again from Stibbe's catalogue).[5]

ICONOGRAPHIC THEMES

So, the Naukratis Painter's vases were clearly directed to Samos more than to any other sanctuary. It is natural to think, therefore, that the East Greek elements in the shape and decoration of his vases must have

5 Since 1972, when Stibbe's book appeared, more Laconian vases have been published, a great number of them from sanctuaries (Cyrene: Schaus 1978 and 1985; Naukratis: Venit 1985; Gravisca: Boitani 1990). Unpublished still, among others, are most of the Laconian vases from Olympia (some appear in Stibbe's catalogue), vases from Bassae, from the temple of Artemis on Samos (see below n. 14), and from the sanctuary of Parthenos at Kavala.

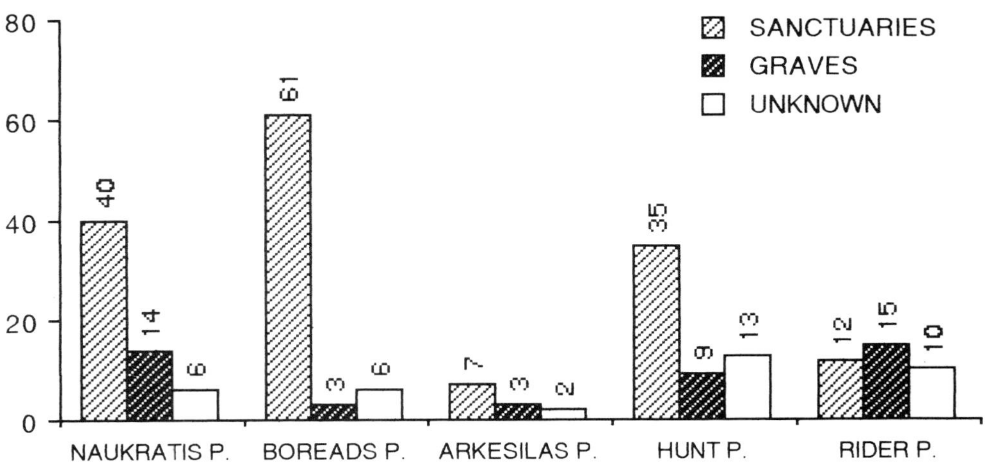

Fig.8.4 Bar chart of the five major Laconian vase-painters showing the numbers of their vases from sanctuaries (light shading) and cemeteries (dark shading)

been due to the artist's attempt to make his vases popular with that clientèle. We may think here of the Athenian potter Nikosthenes who imitated Etruscan wares and used East Greek features which were popular in Etruria because his vases were directed there. Were the Naukratis Painter's choice of subject-matter and iconographic renderings also directed by the needs of export?

The Nature Goddess

We mentioned earlier the painter's liking for daemonic beings of the Corinthian type for the interior of his cups. These creatures fitted well into the central tondo and were an appropriate decoration for this field. Of his other scenes, there are two possible mythical scenes on which we shall not insist. Then, we have six images of a deity alone, outside any narrative context. Most famous of these is the goddess on his name-vase in the British Museum already mentioned, dated about 565–560 BC (FIG. 8.5). The vase is sadly very damaged, and we can only see the goddess' feet in outline and part of her long dress and hair. She held branches and was surrounded by birds and winged daemons, some bearded, some not. The cup was found at Naukratis and was very probably dedicated there by Samians (in fact, most of the Laconian vases found at Naukratis must have been brought in by the Samians who had founded sanctuaries there and kept trade connections with the area). That the vase was originally intended for Samos is strengthened by the fact that two other cups (and perhaps also a third), very fragmentary, by the same artist which seem to preserve part of the same composition come from Samos itself. One (Samos K 1229: Stibbe 1972: no. 25b, pl. 13, 1; Pipili 1987: 41 ff., no. 102, fig. 55) (FIG. 8.6) shows two winged daemons very similar to those on the Naukratis cup and disposed in the tondo in the same way; the other (Stibbe 1972: no. 24, pl. 12, 2; Pipili 1987: 41 ff., no. 103, fig. 56) (FIG. 8.7) preserves part of the impressive plant held by the goddess, a bird, and the head of a small figure which looks to the right. This fragment also preserves something from the lost part of the Naukratis cup: the end of a volute which probably sprang from the goddess' head, an ornament which appears often on Laconian vases, particularly on works by the Naukratis Painter. The Naukratis goddess has been called Cyrene by those early scholars who regarded the Laconian vases as Cyrenaican. She has also been called Persephone surrounded by the souls of the dead, or Aphrodite surrounded by Erotes.[6] I have accepted elsewhere Lane's and Shefton's interpretation of the figure as Artemis Orthia (Lane 1934: 165–7; Shefton 1954: 303, no. 3), and have suggested that to the dedicator she might have been identified with the Samian Hera, since both goddesses had the same character as deities who favoured growth and fertility of plants, animals and humans, and would thus be appropriately shown with a plant in hand (Pipili 1987: 42). Tradition says that Hera was born under an osier tree on the banks of the river Imbrasos and this association of the goddess with the tree and vegetation in general makes her very close to the Laconian goddess Orthia whose sanctuary was likewise situated in a low marshy place by the banks of a river, the Spartan Eurotas. The small winged daemons would then be symbols of fertility and vegetation, daemons of nature who accompany the Great Goddess. The other three images of gods by the Naukratis Painter come from graves: the earliest, a seated Zeus and his eagle, was found in Taranto (Taranto I.G. 4988: Stibbe 1972: no. 8, pl. 4, 3; Pipili 1987: 46 ff., no. 129); two more come from Etruscan tombs—another version, of much higher quality, of the seated Zeus and his eagle (here facing right) in the

6 For the various interpretations, Pipili 1987: 41–2 with nn. 417–24.

Fig. 8.5 (above) *Cup by the Naukratis Painter. London, British Museum B 4.*

Fig. 8.6 (left) *Cup fragments by the Naukratis Painter. Samos K 1229.*

Fig. 8.7 (below) *Cup fragments by the Naukratis Painter. Samos.*

Louvre (Louvre E 668: Stibbe 1972: no. 31, pl. 15, 3; Pipili 1987: 46 ff., no. 130, fig. 69), and a Poseidon riding his hippokamp—a beautiful work found not many years ago at Cerveteri (Cerveteri 90287: Stibbe 1972: no. 35; Pipili 1987: 49–50, no. 135, fig. 73).

Small winged daemons

The small winged daemons surrounding the Naukratis goddess appear also on some other scenes on Laconian vases and seem to have been introduced by the Naukratis Painter. These daemons are perhaps one of the most interesting features of Laconian vase-iconography. They are totally unknown in Corinth, and in Athens they appear as Erotes only at the very end of the sixth century.[7] The only area where we find early examples of such winged creatures is East Greece. A Fikellura cup from the Samian Heraion dated around the mid-sixth century has a row of such

Fig.8.8 Fikellura cup frr. From the Samian Heraion. Photo DAI Athens, neg. no. Samos 1997.

winged daemons in a frieze surrounding the tondo which is decorated with a Gorgoneion (Walter-Karydi 1973: no. 335, pl. 40; Shefton 1989: 69, fig. 20b) (FIG. 8.8), and on a Chian chalice fragment from Naukratis in Cambridge, dated around 575–560 BC, the winged boots of a similar daemon who flew to the right are preserved above a siren turned left (Lemos 1991: no. 1461, pl. 193; p. 157, fig. 88) (FIG. 8.9). These works have sometimes been regarded as copying Laconian works (Stibbe 1972: 46, n. 1), but the influence probably went the other way round (*cf.* Schaus 1986: 275; Hermary 1986: 934). East Greek art seems to have favoured winged creatures of the 'Eros' type from an early period. An Ionian plastic vase of the second quarter of the sixth century has the form of an Eros riding a dolphin (Hermary 1986: 869, no. 178), and

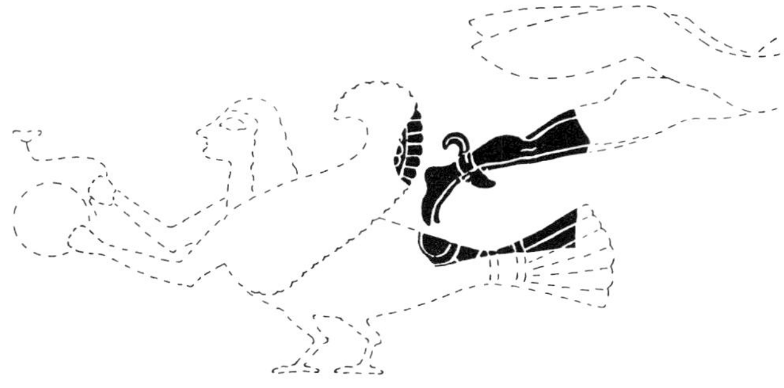

Fig.8.9 Chian chalice fr. Cambridge (from Lemos 1991, fig. 88).

after the middle of the century there are eastern gems, Clazomenian sarcophagi and even a Caeretan hydria with similar creatures. The Naukratis Painter, who introduced these daemons in Laconian art along with many other eastern motifs, may have used an eastern iconographic type for vases intended to be exported to Samos, as were the three cups with the Great Goddess. It has been suggested that the presence in Sparta of Ionian poets like Alkman who praised Eros may have contributed to these images (Hermary 1986: 934), but I do not know if the Laconian winged creatures are meant as Erotes. I prefer to call them 'daemons' in general, sprites of some kind, who probably help to give a higher religious status to the scene in which they appear.

Symposia

Another type of scene of the Naukratis Painter showing winged daemons are the symposia. On his well-known cup in the Louvre (Louvre E 667: Stibbe 1972: no. 13, pl. 6, 1; Pipili 1987: 71 ff., no. 194, fig. 103) (FIG. 8.10), dated around 565 BC, two such small creatures and two sirens fly over five male diners holding florals and wreaths. They are naked and lack their winged boots. The other cup was found rather recently at Lavinium (Pratica di Mare E 1986: Stibbe 1972: no. 19; Pipili 1987: 71 ff., no. 195) and shows two reclining men and three flying daemons who do not seem to be holding anything. Neither of these symposia by the Naukratis Painter was found on Samos, but the fact that on the Louvre cup the symposiasts recline on the ground in the oriental way,[8] as well as the presence of winged daemons which we have seen as borrowed from eastern art, make us believe that this type of composition was originally intended for export to Samos. This is strengthened by the fact that

---

7 For the iconography of Eros see Hermary 1986 with the earlier bibliography.

8 For oriental elements in the Laconian symposia see Fehr 1971: 44.

Fig. 8.10 Symposium cup by the Naukratis Painter. Paris, Louvre E 667.

from the Samian Heraion comes a very interesting cup by the Arkesilas Painter (Samos K 1203, K 1541, K 2402 and Berlin 478x, 460x: Stibbe 1972: no. 191, pl. 58; Pipili 1987: 71 ff., no. 196, figs. 104–104a) (FIG. 8.11a–b) which is so close to the Naukratis Painter that it certainly copies a work by him. The style of drawing is very similar to that of the Naukratis Painter, and so is the rich floral frieze decorating the interior of the rim, and the type of the winged daemons. The cup is unfortunately very fragmentary, with the fragments split between Samos and Berlin, but we can detect some basic elements of the composition: the meal here is held in the open air next to a building and a tree, and there are also women flute-players accompanying the symposiasts. As on the Naukratis Painter's Louvre cup, the diners recline on the ground in the oriental way, and there is another eastern element—the woman's headdress, an oriental mitra. A third, very fragmentary symposium with a winged daemon, comes from Samos again and is by the Hunt Painter (Samos K 2073: Stibbe 1972: no. 215, pl. 71, 3; Pipili 1987: 71 ff., no. 197). I have explained elsewhere these meals as cult-meals in honour of Artemis Orthia and the eastern elements in them as due to Alkman's presence in Sparta—Alkman, who had composed songs in honour of Orthia (Pipili 1987: 73–4). But no such vase has been found in Sparta. The Arkesilas Painter's vase was dedicated to the Samian Hera and so might have been his prototypes by the Naukratis Painter, so it is more likely that the Laconian painters depicted cult-meals in honour of Hera.[9] These cult-meals must have been a very important occasion in the life of Samos, and we may note here a series of contemporary Attic cups by the KX Painter from the Heraion decorated with rich symposia with men and women,[10] which indicate that there was probably a demand for such vases used and dedicated during those celebrations.

The Lyre-Player

We know that the festival of the Heraia also included musical and athletic contests. An interesting composition which I think had its origin in the Naukratis Painter, although no such whole work by him has been

9 In her review of Pipili 1987, J. Carter rightly stresses the fact that no symposium scene has been found in Laconia, and suggests that the Arkesilas Painter's cup shows "life on Samos, women in Eastern caps banqueting with men, as the Arkesilas Painter imagined it" (Carter 1989: 475).

10 Beazley 1956: 26, nos. 27–28, and at least four more cups some of which were presented by J. Brijder at the International Conference 'Athenian Potters and Painters' (American School of Classical Studies at Athens, December 1994). A full publication of the Attic black-figure vases from the Samian Heraion is being prepared by B. Kreuzer and will appear in the *Samos* series.

Fig. 8.11 Cup fragments by the Arkesilas Painter from the Samian Heraion
(a) Berlin, Staatl. Museen 478x.
(b) Samos K 12c3, K 1541, K 2402 and Berlin 460x, 478x (from Pipili 1987, fig.104, after Stibbe 1972, pl. 58).

preserved, is that of a musician standing among dancing komasts. One is a cup in Florence, badly preserved, in the manner of the Naukratis Painter, which probably copies a work by the master (Florence 3882: Stibbe 1972: no. 71; Pipili 1987: 51–2, no. 205a). Three other such works are by the Rider Painter—two come from Samos and are very fragmentary: one has a musician standing in the middle, a cock on his lyre, and komasts of various sizes dancing on either side (Samos K 2522: Stibbe 1972: no. 293, pl. 98; Pipili 1987: no. 205d); from the other only the feet of the musician and of two of the komasts are preserved (Samos K 1960: Stibbe 1972: no. 315, pl. 112, 4; Pipili 1987: no. 205e); the third appeared recently on the Basel Market (Stibbe 1992) (FIG. 8.12) and is the most interesting of all. It is very well preserved, an early work of the Rider Painter, of a period during which he was influenced by the Naukratis Painter. This composition shows clearly that the prototype was a work by the Naukratis Painter: the whole design is very close to that of the Naukratis cup—a huge central figure in a long dress (a goddess there—a musician here) surrounded by small creatures (winged daemons there—komasts here). The interior of the rim is decorated with a rich floral frieze in the Naukratis Painter's manner. A small fragment by the Naukratis Painter in Naples has a komast placed in the tondo in the same way (Stibbe 1972: no. 15, pl. 7, 3) (FIG. 8.13), so it is possible that it belonged to a similar scene.[11] The Hunt Painter also produced this kind of composition: we have a small fragment by him from Samos (Stibbe 1972: no. 247, pl. 86, 3; Pipili 1987: no. 205b); and there is also a work in his manner in the Vatican with

11 Compare especially the Rider Painter's cup from Samos (Samos K 2522: Stibbe 1972: no. 293, pl. 98) where three komasts dance to the left away from the musician who stands to the right in the middle of the tondo, or the cup in the Vatican (Stibbe 1972: no. 272, pl. 90, 2).

Fig. 8.12 Cup fragments by the Rider Painter. Once Basel Market (from Stibbe 1992, pl. 25, 1).

a more proportionate musician in comparison to the dancers (Stibbe 1972: no. 272, pl. 90, 2; Pipili 1987: no. 205c). The huge figure of the musician, especially in the Rider Painter's works, and his similarity to the Naukratis goddess could lead to the assumption that we have a god here too. Stibbe saw Dionysos (Stibbe 1992), others Apollo (*cf.* the works cited by Pipili 1987: 51, nn. 505–6; Stibbe 1992: 141, n. 11). But there are difficulties with both interpretations: how easily can we accept a Dionysos with a lyre? or Apollo among komasts? I believe that this scene, like the symposia, should be associated with a real-life cult celebration. Since most such scenes come from Samos, this might be a musician playing at the Heraia.

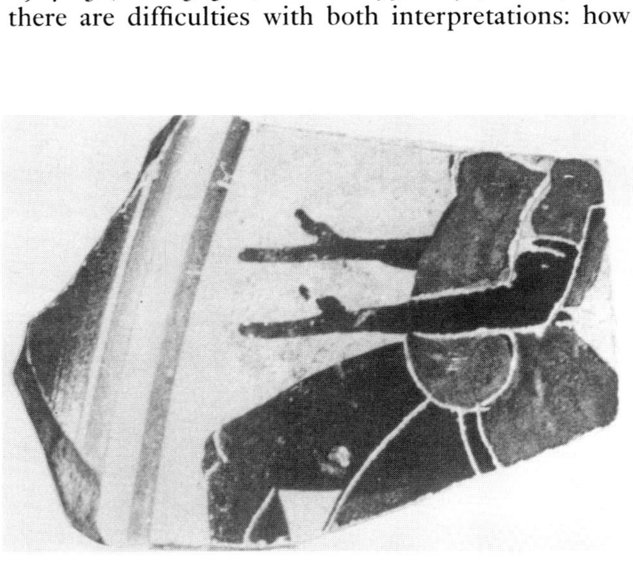

Fig. 8.13 Fragment by the Rider Painter. Naples (from Stibbe 1972, pl. 7, 3).

The Rider

Let us now come to the enigmatic rider. Three cups by the Rider Painter, one in St. Petersburg, another in the British Museum and a third in the Louvre, works of the period 550–540 BC, show a single youthful rider accompanied by winged daemons. The St. Petersburg cup (St. Petersburg 183: Stibbe 1974: pl. 5, 1; Pipili 1987: 76, no. 213) has a winged daemon flying behind the rider, carrying in both hands what look like cups; on the London cup (London B 1: Stibbe 1972: no. 306, pl. 108, 1; Pipili 1987: no. 214, fig. 108) (FIG. 8.14) there is a daemon at exactly the same place, here holding wreaths; on the Louvre cup (Louvre E 665: Stibbe 1972: no. 307, pl. 108, 4; Pipili 1987: no. 215, fig. 109) (FIG. 8.15) the daemon runs in front of the horses with extended arms. The daemons are very similar to those by the Naukratis Painter, with the wings growing from their chests as in his works, and this makes us suspect that in this case, too, the prototype was a work by this artist. Moreover, the St. Petersburg cup is very close in style of drawing to works by the Naukratis Painter and has a rich floral frieze in this painter's manner on the inside of the rim. A small fragment by

Fig. 8.14 Cup by the Rider Painter. London, British Museum B 1.

Fig. 8.15 Cup by the Rider Painter. Paris, Louvre E 665.

the Naukratis Painter from the Samian Heraion (Stibbe 1972: no. 48, pl. 23, 2) has preserved part of a large horse's head, and Stibbe rightly suggested (Stibbe 1972: 20, nn. 12–15) that this might be part of the prototype for the Rider Painter's cups, since the head is so large that it can only belong to a single horse covering the inside of the cup. So, although none of the Rider Painter's cups comes from Samos, the prototype for the scene probably did, and I am inclined to connect this scene also with celebrations in honour of Hera—perhaps a victorious athlete in the goddess' festival; or a young aristocrat participating in a procession at the same festival. A common element in all three cups are the many water-birds which probably indicate the setting as a marshy place.

So, it seems that the Naukratis Painter produced many works intended for a specific market, that of Samos, and for the needs of a particular cult, that of Hera. Hence the eastern elements in his work and the choice of his themes. Of course, some of the works to which we have given a religious meaning are not from Samos (the Nature Goddess, for instance, comes from Naukratis), but these are few and might have been exported elsewhere by Samian merchants. The scenes created by the Naukratis Painter for cult purposes seem to have been imitated by other Laconian artists who were influenced by the early master. One of them, the Rider Painter, presumably copied mechanically the rider, or the musician, on vases which were not intended mainly for the Samian Heraion neither for some other sanctuary, but were made in a period when the export to Samos had declined and most Laconian vases found their way to Etruscan graves.

Gods and worshippers

Let us finally come to a type of scene on Laconian vases which has a clearly votive character, much more so than the works that we have seen: that of a seated god or gods approached by worshippers (Pipili 1987: 60–3). The earliest such scenes are by the Boreads Painter who seems to have favoured the composition. We have an unpublished fragmentary cup from Olympia with a seated male figure approached by others, another from Gravisca, a third from Cyrene and a fragmentary cup from Naukratis in the British Museum known for a long time (Pipili 1987: nos. 157–60). On this cup there were probably more figures behind the one preserved, as on the Olympia cup. The composiition is not new to Laconian art. It appears on stone and clay reliefs dedicated to gods or heroes. But for vases it is something not common, and it is an odd choice for the interior of cups where the restricted space does not allow the representation of many figures in a row. Religious processions with worshippers holding offerings do appear, however, on some East Greek vases; see, for example, the figures on some fragmentary Chian chalices of the Grand Style from Naukratis: a man with a lotus-flower, or a woman with pomegranates quite similar to the youth on the Boreads Painter's vase (Lemos 1991: nos. 704, 735, pls. 92, 96, and p. 100, fig. 54) (FIG. 8.16). The Chian works are contemporary to the Boreads Painter's vases, dated in the years 570–560 BC.

Until recently we knew no such vase by the Naukratis Painter. We now know that he also pro-

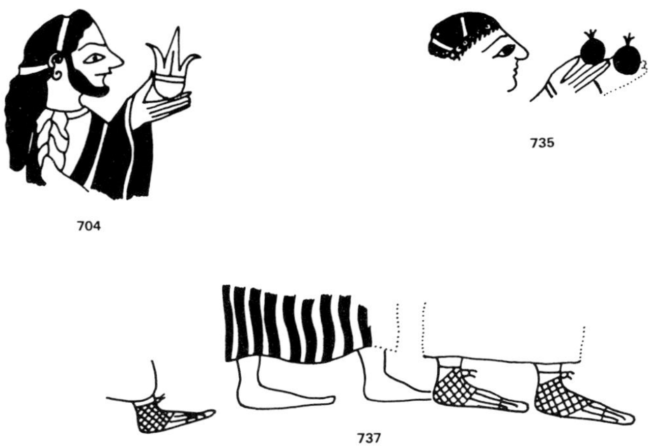

Fig. 8.16 Chian chalice fragments. London, British Museum 1888.6-1.483, 1.508, 1.513 (from Lemos 1991, fig. 54).

Fig. 8.17 Fragment by the Naukratis Painter, with part of an inscription. Cyrene 71-659 (from Schaus 1979, pl. 16).

duced vases of this type: we mentioned earlier his inscribed fragment from Cyrene (FIG. 8.17). The seated figure here is female since her naked flesh is in outline (probably Demeter or Kore since the piece was dedicated to their sanctuary), but the inscription presents some problems. It is part of a name—but what name? A possibility is that we have an artist's signature, something not met elsewhere in Laconian. If it is not the Naukratis Painter's name, then is it the name of the figure standing before the goddess? As the inscription was written before the firing, we would have here a clear case of a special commission, where the dedicator would have dictated to the painter the name to be written on the cup. But there are difficulties with this explanation, too, so the question must remain open. Another work by the Naukratis Painter which may have shown a seated deity, a goddess—presumably Hera since the vase comes from the Samian Heraion—is a fragmentary krater in Samos and Berlin dated *c.* 570–565 BC (Samos K 1445 and Berlin Sa 138, 462, 479x: Stibbe 1972: no. 37, pl. 19; Pipili 1987: no. 202) (FIG. 8.18). The bird on the figure's seat indicates a deity. The figure was in association with a symposium, as there are more fragments with klinai and tables, so, was this a cult-meal in the goddess' honour? The horse behind the goddess' seat probably belonged to an adjacent different scene.[12] Votive cups of this type have been found only in sanctuaries, so we should

12 Another such figure in association with a symposium is on a late fragment from the Artemis Orthia sanctuary, a work in the manner of the Hunt Painter: Stibbe 1972: no. 278, pl. 92, 3; Pipili 1987: no. 166.

Fig. 8.18 Krater (?) fragments by the Rider Painter. Samos K 1445.

assume that they were special commissions made for dedication. The Naukratis Painter who favoured religious scenes and who also painted the seated Zeus may well have introduced the type. Anyway, such cups continue to the end of the sixth century and most are in the Naukratis Painter's manner. A late example comes from Samos, one of the rare vases exported to the island in the years around 525 BC (Samos K 1428: Stibbe 1972: no. 102; Pipili 1987: 61 ff., no. 164, fig. 89; most of the fragments are now lost). A kitharode stands before the seated goddess, probably Hera since the cup comes from the Heraion. It is possible that we have a worshipper before the goddess, unless this is Apollo in conversation with Hera, as on a cup in Kassel Zeus and Hermes face each other (Kassel T 354: Stibbe 1972: no. 353, pl. 128, 2; Pipili 1987: 47–8, no. 132, fig. 71). On a contemporary cup from Olympia a small figure stood before the seated divine pair (Olympia K 1293: Stibbe 1972: no. 101; Pipili 1987: 61 ff., no. 163, fig. 88); and on another unpublished cup from Olympia dating from the late 520s we have again Zeus and Hera and more figures standing opposite them (Olympia K 2101: Pipili 1987: 61 ff., no. 165). Most of the late vases found their way to Olympia and to the local Laconian market. In a debased black-figure style, dating from the early fifth century BC, are votive cups dedicated to Zeus/Agamemnon and Alexandra/Kassandra who had their sanctuary near Amyklai.[13] But we shall not end with these degenerate works which are but a distant echo of the earlier Laconian votive cups. Let us return to Samos from where we began.

SOME OTHER LACONIAN VOTIVE WARES: THE CASE OF THE SAMIAN ARTEMISION

In 1979 an important chance discovery was made by the local ephoreia near the ancient town of Samos, just outside the city-walls. A rich votive deposit full of good black-figure vases was discovered and, as many of the fragments had inscriptions naming Artemis, the excavator, K. Tsakos, rightly connected the deposit with the sanctuary of Artemis mentioned by Herodotus (iii 48) as the place where the 300 hostage Corcyrian youths, who were being sent by the Corinthian tyrant Periander to Sardis to serve as eunuchs, took refuge.[14] The sanctuary was probably destroyed in the late sixth century, either during the Spartan expedition against Polykrates in 524 BC, or in the events following Polykrates' fall in 522 BC. Among the Laconian vases found in the deposit, there are vases of a rather rare shape—Stibbe calls it a calyx-crater (Stibbe 1994: 55); Lane, a chalice on a high foot (Lane 1934: 146). There are three quite well preserved examples (FIGS. 8.19–21), one preserving its high foot, and fragments of more. Until now we knew of only one whole such example, from the Samian necropolis, with no figure decoration, dating from about 550 BC (Boehlau 1898: 125–6, pl. 10, 7). From the Samian cemetary we also have a contemporary Samian example (Boehlau 1898: pl. 6, 1; Walter-Karydi 1973: pl. 36, no. 502), but it is not clear if the Samians imitated the Laconian shape or vice-versa. Lane draws attention to early forms of this shape from Laconia dating from the first half of the seventh century (Lane 1934: 110).

Whatever its origin, it is clear that this type of vase was a ritual one, probably associated with the Artemis cult—and we can think here of the krateriskoi dedicated at other sanctuaries of the goddess, especially that of Brauron, and of the early Laconian forms of the shape just mentioned from the Orthia sanctuary, an Artemis sanctuary again. Also, the scenes decorating these vases are certainly associated with cult. On one vase we have a procession of riders, an old man leaning on his staff, and more figures in a row, as well as a seated figure (FIG. 8.19), on another a procession of men with flute-players among them (FIG. 8.20), on a third a procession of riders and women with drawn himatia in conversation (FIG. 8.21). With these vases we seem to have another case of Laconian vases made especially for dedication. The shape is a very special one and the date of the vases rather late—the decade 530–520 BC, when Laconian vases were not normally exported to Samos—so, it is very probable that we have here special commissions for the Artemis sanctuary. The cycle which had started with the impressive works by the Naukratis Painter on Samos seems to close with this no less impressive series of votive wares.

---

13 Some of these cups are illustrated in Stibbe 1972: pl. 132, 7; Stibbe 1976: pl. 5, 1. On one vase a warrior stands before the seated god; on another the god is seated holding a kantharos as on many stone and clay reliefs.

14 On the find, Tsakos 1980; *cf.* also, *A. Delt.* 35 (1980) B2: 460–4; *BCH* 107 (1983) 817; *AR* 1982–83: 50–1.

Fig. 8.19 (above) *'Calyx krater' from the Sanctuary of Artemis, Samos. Samos 3959.*
Fig. 8.20 (above right) *'Calyx krater' from the Sanctuary of Artemis, Samos. Samos 3960.*
Fig. 8.21 (lower right) *'Calyx krater' from the Sanctuary of Artemis, Samos. Samos 4006.*

CONCLUSION

To conclude: it is not the mythical scenes that are the most interesting in Laconian vase-painting, but the many other scenes probably associated with cult that we have seen. When considered outside their find-spots, these scenes might make no sense at all and might be totally misunderstood, but, when brought into association with the sanctuaries where they were dedicated, and with the artist who created the compositions, they become much more clear. It would seem that archaic Sparta with its religious tendencies responded more than other centres to the special demand for particular scenes or shapes at particular sites during the sixth century. Special commissions for sanctuaries seems to have been a flourishing industry for Laconian vase-painters. And in this, the Naukratis Painter had certainly led the way.

ACKNOWLEDGEMENTS

I should like to thank Dr. Susan Walker for kindly inviting me to deliver this paper as part of the Colloquium on Ancient Sparta, as well as the Institute of Classical Studies and its Director, Professor Richard Sorabji, for subsidising it. Also, Mr. K. Tsakos for allowing me to illustrate the calyx-craters from the Artemis sanctuary on Samos, and Drs. C. M. Stibbe and A. A. Lemos for providing me with photographs and slides and allowing me to use some of them here.

9

The Ancient Theatre at Sparta

G. B. Waywell, J. J. Wilkes and S. E. C. Walker

I THE FIRST DORIC PHASE OF SPARTA'S THEATRE

G. B. Waywell

The Ancient Theatre at Sparta, which is situated on the slopes of the Acropolis hill below the sanctuary of Athena Chalkioikos, has been a famous landmark since the eighteenth century, being one of the few buildings mentioned by Pausanias in his tour of Sparta in the second century AD whose location is known for certain (Dickins 1906b; Waywell and Wilkes 1994: 429). It was partly dug by the British School at Athens in the period 1906–1928, mainly under the direction of A. M. Woodward (Woodward 1925a, 1926a, 1927a, 1928a, 1930a); and then, following supplementary work by the Greek archaeologists Christou and Steinhauer in the 1960s and 70s (Christou 1960a, 1960b, 1962), excavations were resumed by the British School at Athens in 1992–5 under the direction of Geoffrey Waywell and John Wilkes, the aim being to seek fresh evidence for the architectural appearance, date of construction and later history of the theatre (Waywell and Wilkes 1995). In the course of this work a completely new survey of extant remains was undertaken by Nigel Fradgley, trenches were put down in key areas of the orchestra and cavea, and a catalogue of extant architectural blocks including many from the stage-building was compiled by Susan Walker (FIGS. 9. 1–2).

Fig. 9.1 Sparta theatre. General view from NE.

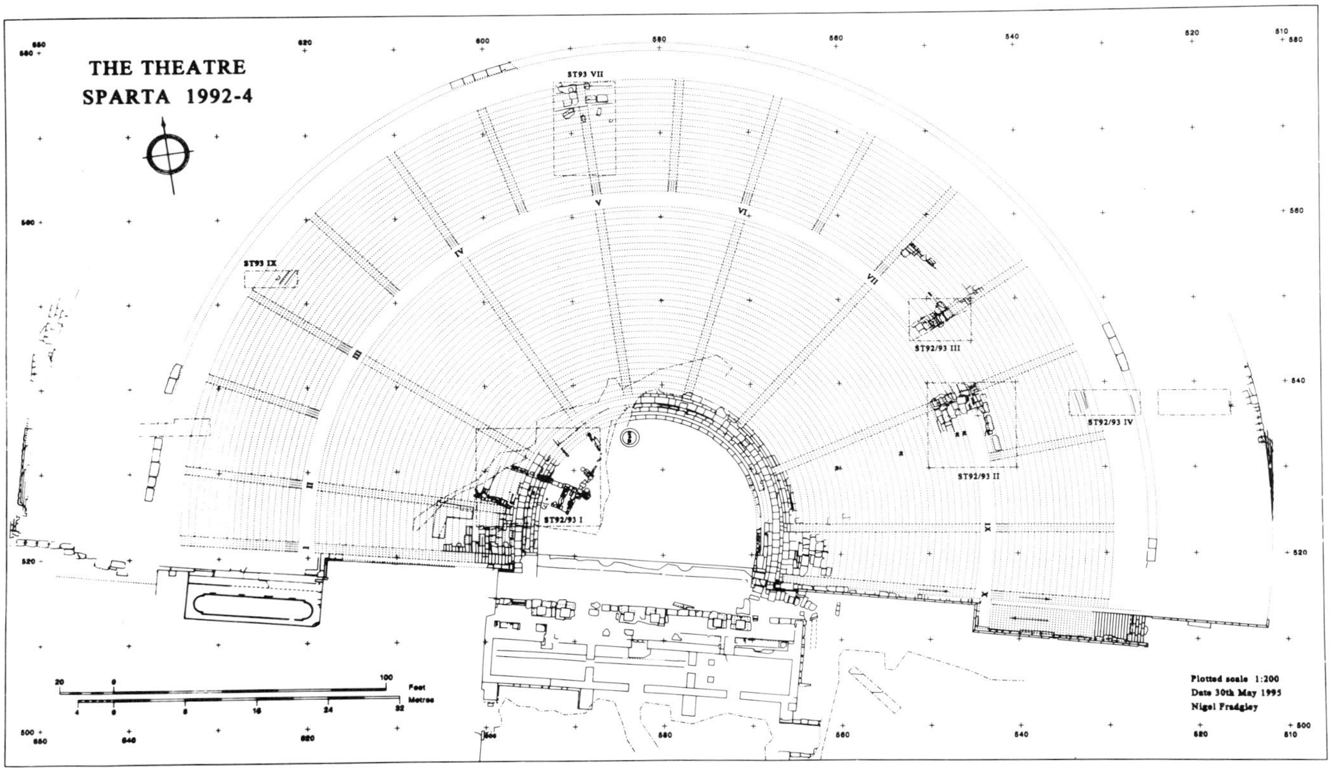

Fig. 9.2 (above) *Sparta theatre. Reconstructed plan by N. Fradgley.*

Fig. 9.3 (left) *Sparta theatre. Eastern retaining wall for cavea.*

Fig. 9.4 (below left) *Sparta theatre. Eastern parodos and staircase.*

Our excavations in the SW area of the orchestra revealed the lower parts of staircases II and III, and confirmed Woodward's findings that while the front seats of honour, the walkway behind it, and two or three rows of benches above, are fairly well preserved with their marble *in situ*, the remainder of the theatre was severely damaged in the middle Byzantine period (9th-13th centuries) when most of the marble seating and some of the poros foundations were removed for building purposes.

The reconstructed plan of the theatre as suggested by De Jong in 1925 was found to be correct in the lower part, although we discovered new evidence for the dimensions of the diazoma, the upper cavea and the upper walkway (Woodward 1925a: pl.14; Waywell and Wilkes 1995). Sparta's theatre can be seen to have been a handsome, marble-faced construction, close in size to the great Classical Greek theatres at Megalopolis and Epidauros, and following in their traditions of design, although clearly much later in date, belonging without doubt to the late first century BC (whether the earlier theatre at Sparta, recorded since 465 BC, was on this site is still not known). Fine outer retaining walls, of cushioned ashlar masonry with drafted margins, late Hellenistic in style, and set

147 m apart, support the extended semicircle of the cavea (FIG. 9. 3). This is 114 m in diameter (compared with Epidauros' 117 m), and is marked by a wall of poros ashlars resting on concrete foundations. The orchestra, 25.52 m in diameter, was fronted by a detached stage-building, separated from the cavea by open parodoi. The marble-faced retaining wall of the E parodos, which came to be inscribed with the names of Spartan officials in the later 1st–2nd centuries AD, is interrupted by an open staircase that rose by 55 steps to the central gangway (diazoma) that divided the cavea into lower and upper parts (FIGS. 9.4 and 9.2). Remains of the foundations of the diazoma, with fragments of its marble paving surviving in position, were revealed in trench II on the E cavea, and these enabled its original width to be calculated as *c.* 1.80 m. (FIG. 9. 5). Below it were ten radial staircases; while above it there were seventeen, as intermediate stairways were placed between main staircases II–IX in the upper cavea. This plan conforms quite closely to that of the Greek theatre as defined by Vitruvius in his *De Architectura* (v 7), writing *c.* 30 BC (Knell 1991; Isler 1989; Sear 1990; Gros 1994a). There were probably 31 rows of seats in the lower cavea, including the front seats of honour with high backs, and 17 in the upper cavea, making 48 altogether. This arrangement has similarities in many points of detail with the Megalopolis theatre which seems to have provided the design inspiration for Sparta (Buckler 1986).

Important dating evidence for the theatre's construction came from trench IV, located in the upper E cavea between the inner and outer radial walls of the cavea, where large amounts of pottery fragments were recovered from the mud-brick that forms the artificial make-up of the cavea at this point. Successive layers of this mud-brick were excavated to a depth of two metres, to a point below the concrete foundations for the inner and outer radial walls which were set within the mud-brick in curious fashion. The pottery, which was added to the mud-brick as sharp aggregate, is uniformly late Hellenistic in date, *c.* 100–50 BC, and includes relief bowl fragments of 'Megarian' type (FIG. 9.6) (Hayes 1995). This pottery, taken with the style of the theatre and its architecture, strongly suggests a construction date in the late first century BC.

Fig. 9.5 (above) *Sparta theatre. Remains of foundations of diazoma on E cavea.*

Fig. 9.6 (below) *Sherds of relief pottery from construction layer of E cavea.*

A likely time is the period immediately after the battle of Actium, *c.* 30–20 BC, when C. Julius Eurykles was ruler of Sparta, which now received highly-favoured status having supported Octavian-Augustus at Actium (Cartledge and Spawforth 1989).

Two aspects of the theatre's architecture deserve to be highlighted. One is the unusual mixed building technique employed, which involves the combination of layered mud-brick and rubble-concrete as foundations for a theatre of traditional stone and marble construction. This makes Sparta's theatre of some interest in the transition from Greek to Roman building practice in Greece.

Fig. 9.7 (above) *Sparta theatre. Upper staircase V with seat-blocks of upper rows 15–17 in position on left.*

Fig. 9.8 (left) *Doric columns from upper colonnade of Sparta theatre; beside them, spiral fluted columns possibly from facade of Flavian stage-building.*

Fig. 9.9 (below) *Sparta theatre. Dividing wall between central and W rooms of Flavian stage-building, showing fragments of Doric architecture from first stage-building built into foundations.*

The other important feature is the Doric appearance of the theatre in its original late Hellenistic phase, as expressed in the Doric upper colonnade and in the Doric order of the original stage-building. Evidence for the upper colonnade was found in trench VII beside staircase V (FIG. 9.7). Here blocks from uppermost rows 15–17 survive in place, resting on a spread of mortar which was supported by a curving radial wall of concrete-bonded stones which ran below row 14. Traces of a column setting on the topmost block, *c.* 60 cm in diameter, suggest that a colonnade of Doric columns surrounded the walkway at the top of the cavea. Doric column shafts of Pentelic marble found in the orchestra in 1924 are of the correct dimensions to have stood here (FIG. 9.8). The overall height of the colonnade would have been about the same as the width of the walkway, *c.* 4.80 m. Colonnades at the top of theatres are often thought to be a Roman feature. One occurred at the top of the Theatre of Pompey in Rome, built *c.* 62–55 BC, but this was considered in its day to be a Greek theatre modelled on the theatre at Mytilene on Lesbos, where it is not yet known whether such a feature occurred (Bieber 1961: 181–2; Beacham 1991: 157–63; Sear 1993; Gros 1994a: 74). Given the evidence from Sparta, we may cautiously suppose that an upper colonnade was a phenomenon of the late Hellenistic Greek theatre, from which it was borrowed for Roman theatre design. A study of the architectural remains of the stage building of Sparta theatre, carried out in the course of the 1994–1995 seasons, supported Woodward's observations that the elements of a Doric

Fig. 9.10 (right) *Detail of Doric architecture in foundations of SE corner of W room of stage-building, showing section of column and fragment of Doric capital*

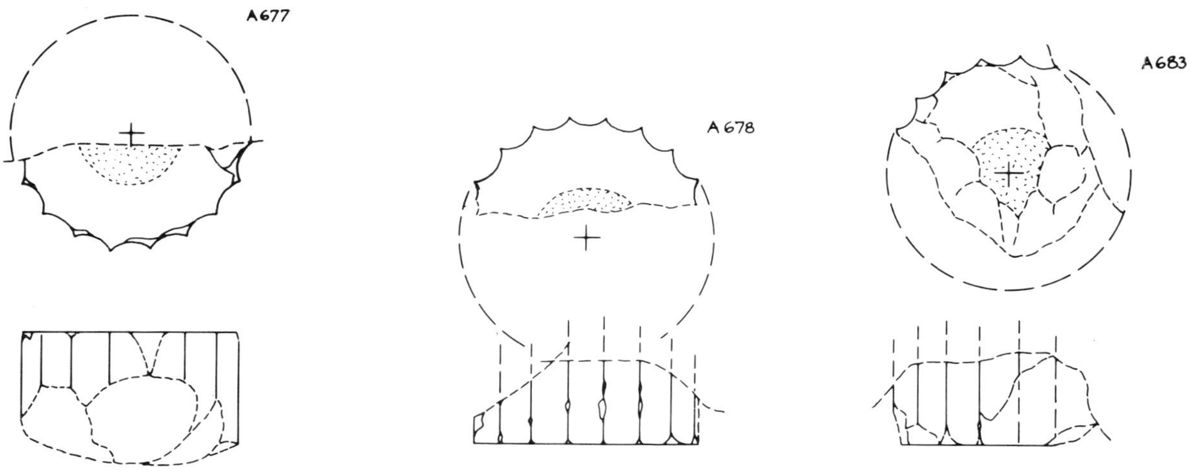

Fig. 9.11 (below) *Fragments of Doric columns A677, A678 and A683, built into foundations of stage-building. Drawn by N. Sunter. Scale c. 1:20.*

Fig. 9.12 (bottom) *Part of Doric capital built into foundations of S wall of stage-building. cf. Fig. 9.10. Drawn by N. Sunter. Scale c. 1:20.*

colonnaded structure, associated with the earliest phase of the theatre, were deliberately smashed into small pieces, which were incorporated within the foundations and fabric of the walls of the three rooms forming the later stage building (FIGS. 9.9–10) (Woodward 1930a: 159). These fragments are of a different (slightly larger) scale to the Doric of the upper

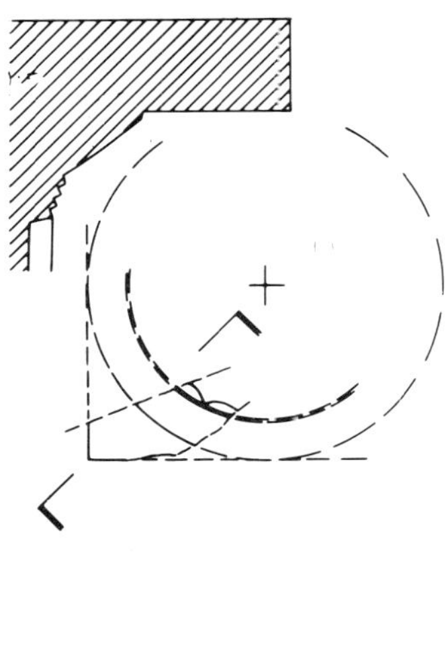

colonnade and must have belonged to some part of the stage-building. The question of where they may have been placed is a complex one to which there is at present no certain answer. The lower column shafts which survive are too large to have stood on the two lines of poros foundations called C–C and CC–CC by Woodward (discussed below in Part II by John Wilkes). I will confine myself to observations on the nature and style of the architecture.

Fragments have been identified of almost all parts of the Doric order, which is elegantly carved in Laconian marble. Several fragmentary lower columns (A677, A678, A683, FIG. 9.11) give a lower diameter of *c.* 64–65 cm and allow the reconstruction of an order *c.* 5.60 m in height, assuming Vitruvian proportions. Other significant elements identified include a capital block with necking-rings, echinus and abacus (FIGS. 9.10 and 9.12); architrave blocks (A790, A791, A722, FIG. 9.13); a triglyph (A767, FIG. 9.14) and plain metopes (A804, A805); and—most importantly—two different varieties of cornice and sima. One sima is of

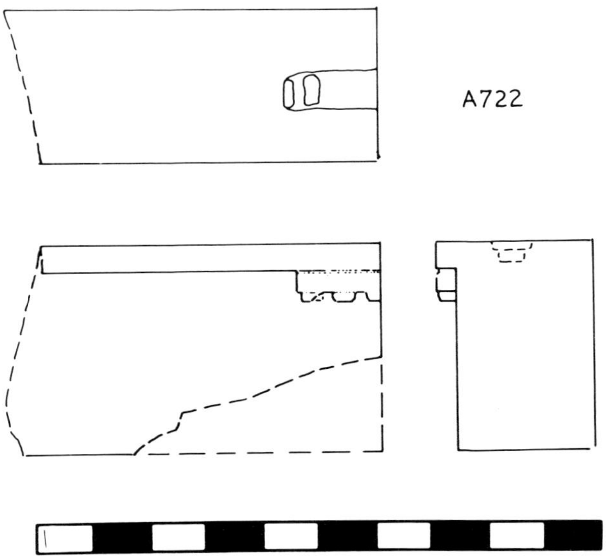

Fig. 9.13 Fragment of Doric architrave, A722. Drawn by N. Sunter. The scale is divided in 10 cm sections.

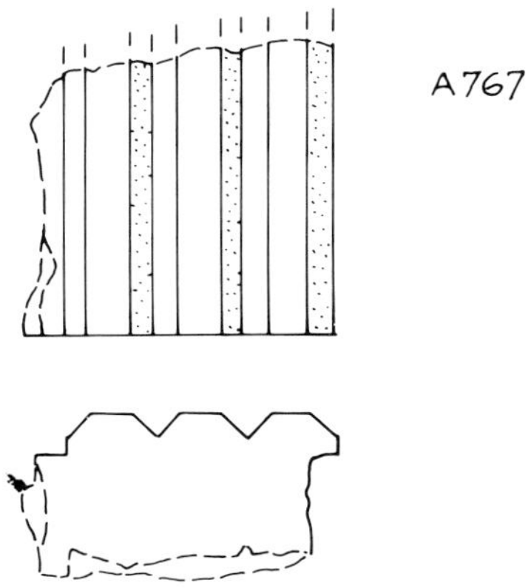

Fig. 9.14 Fragment of Doric triglyph, A767. Drawn by N. Sunter.

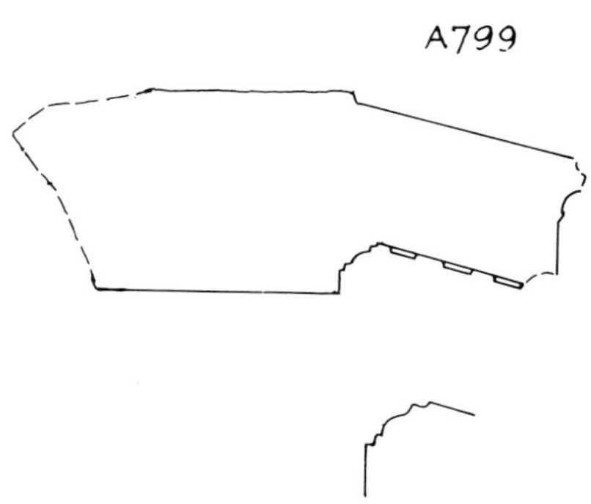

Fig. 9.15 Fragment of Doric sima, A799, with enlarged detail of soffit moulding. Drawn by N. Sunter.

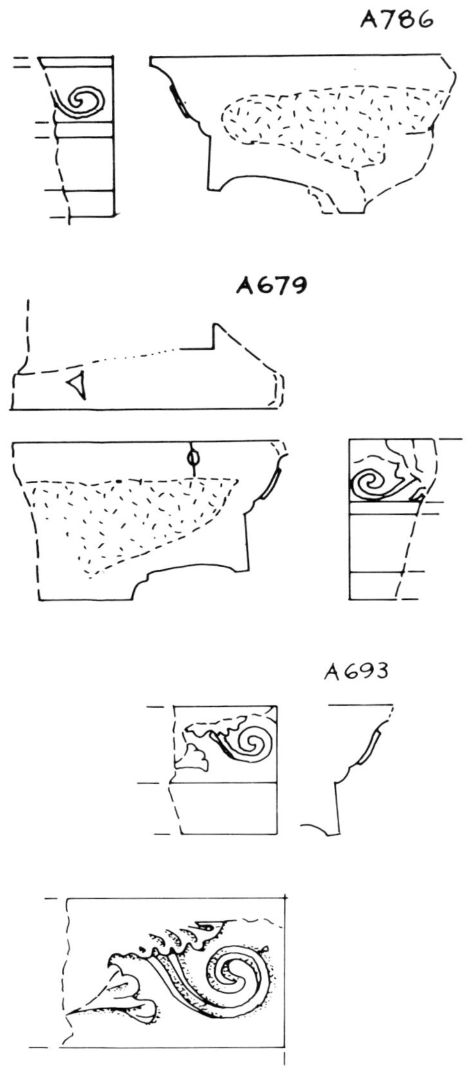

Fig. 9.16 Three fragments of Corinthianising sima, A786 (above top), *A679* (above centre), *and A693* (above), *with enlarged detail. Drawn by N. Sunter.*

standard Doric type, with downward canted soffit decorated with mutules and guttae (A799, A800, A806, A793, A796, A802, FIG. 9.15). The other is a Corinthianising sima decorated with a design of acanthus leaves and tendrils (A693, A786, A797, A679, A798, FIG. 9.16). Comparable simas have been found at Corinth, belonging to Temple E of Augustan date, and Temple F of Tiberian date, so confirming the attribution of these fragments to the original stage-structure at Sparta (Scranton 1951). The existence of the two types of sima suggests either that there were two storeys to the structure, or else it faced in two different directions inwards and outwards from the theatre. That the former interpretation of two storeys may be correct is tentatively supported by surviving fragments of smaller Doric shafts, which may have belonged to an upper order that supported the Corinthian sima. A fine marble antefix with palmette

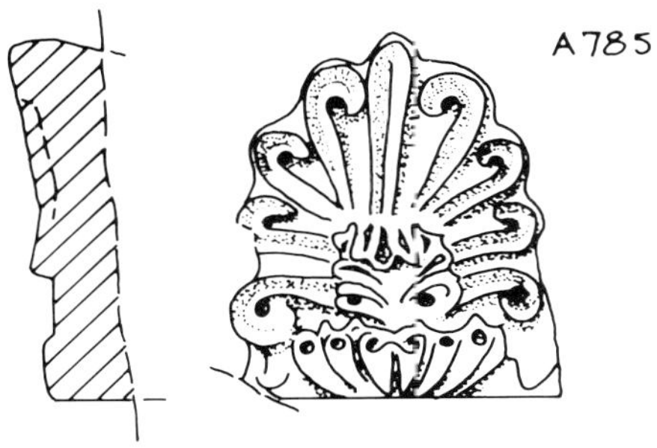

Fig. 9.17 Marble palmette antefix built into foundations of W wall of stage-building. Drawn by N. Sunter.

decoration (A785, FIG. 9.17), which survives built into the foundations of the west wall of the stage-building, would have decorated the roof-line.

If it is true that the two lines of poros foundation blocks C–C and CC–CC carried the track of a rolling stage platform (see below, Part II by John Wilkes), any permanent Doric-columned stage-building must have been set beyond it to the north. This would mean that the Doric façade would have been aligned just in front of where the stage-wall of the later Flavian building was constructed, so separating the original moving-stage more distinctly from the orchestra than in the later Roman phase, and in keeping with normal Hellenistic Greek theatre design. No certain traces of the foundations for such a Doric façade have been observed beneath the projecting stage of the later building, although it is possible that they once continued the line of the north wall of the skanotheke building located by Bulle within the west parodos (Bulle 1937:10–11). Further investigation and study needs to be carried out on this aspect of the original theatre (FIG. 9.18).

From all this the conclusion is that the theatre at Sparta is basically of late Greek rather than Roman type, and that it represents a grandiose recreation of the fine Classical Greek theatre design, utilising up-to-date features of construction techniques, and stressing in its appearance the Dorian heritage of Sparta under Eurykles. In addition its stage arrangements may have originally incorporated state of the art machinery of the kind developed in the prestigious temporary theatres of metropolitan Rome in the first century BC.

II THE FIRST STAGE OF SPARTA'S THEATRE: RECENT OBSERVATIONS

J. J. Wilkes

The British School excavations of 1992–94 confirmed an earlier conclusion that the marble cavea of Sparta's theatre is of one build and dates from the last decades of the first century BC, most likely from the period (*c.* 30–20 BC) when Sparta was ruled by the dynast Julius Eurykles, who enjoyed for much of his life the favour of the emperor Augustus (Waywell and Wilkes 1995). In 1995 the focus of attention of the excavators shifted to the remains of the stage-building, revealed by A. M. Woodward in the excavations of 1925–26 to consist of a complex tangle of structures dating from the four centuries of the theatre's existence, subsequently overlain by many houses of the medieval town (Woodward 1925a, 1926a).

Leaving on one side the possibilities suggested by the short stretch of limestone footings located within the area of the stage but aligned 11 degrees from the principal east-west axis of the theatre, we can accept Woodward's conclusion that the surviving remains of the first stage structure consist of two parallel lines of roughly dressed limestone blocks set 5.25 m apart and which originally ran across the entire stage-area (his designations C–C for the front [north] line and CC–CC for the rear [south] line continue in use). The single courses of blocks, which had been neither clamped nor mortared, are set directly upon a natural soil of orange gravel and clay. At the east end of the stage-area the two lines may have terminated with a cross-line that was later incorporated in the plinth course of the east wall of the later stage-building (this is how it appears on the published plan of De Jong (FIG. 9.18), although no reference to it is made in Woodward's account of the excavations, nor do the remains at present visible give any support for the existence of this cross-line belonging to the first phase). At the west side of the stage-area it was established that the rear line of blocks continued into the west parodos beyond the side wall of the later stage-building, aligned more or less with the western limit of the orchestra. Here Woodward's excavations in 1927 revealed the marble-lined pool of a later Roman fountain (*nymphaeum*), constructed largely of re-used bricks bearing the stamp *skanotheke*, indicating that they had originally been manufactured to build the scenery store which had occupied the site in the first century AD (Woodward 1930a: 226–31). With a width of *c.* 0.5 m, the blocks which make up the two lines (C–C and CC–CC) are too narrow and appear too ill-founded to have supported any major structure such as the marble façade or stoa in the Doric order, whose shattered remains form the footings of the Flavian stage-building (the Doric construction is described by G. B. Waywell in Part I of this report, above, and the Flavian stage-building by S. E. C. Walker in Part III, below).

As Woodward noted, the only evidence for what had rested on these two lines consists of the two conjoining blocks of conglomerate stone set upon the front line (C–C) at the west end of the stage area (FIGS. 9.19–23). The correspondence of the clamp sockets and the alignment of the half-rounded channels cut into the top surfaces of the stones indicate that the blocks are almost beyond doubt still in their original positions. The upper surfaces of both blocks have

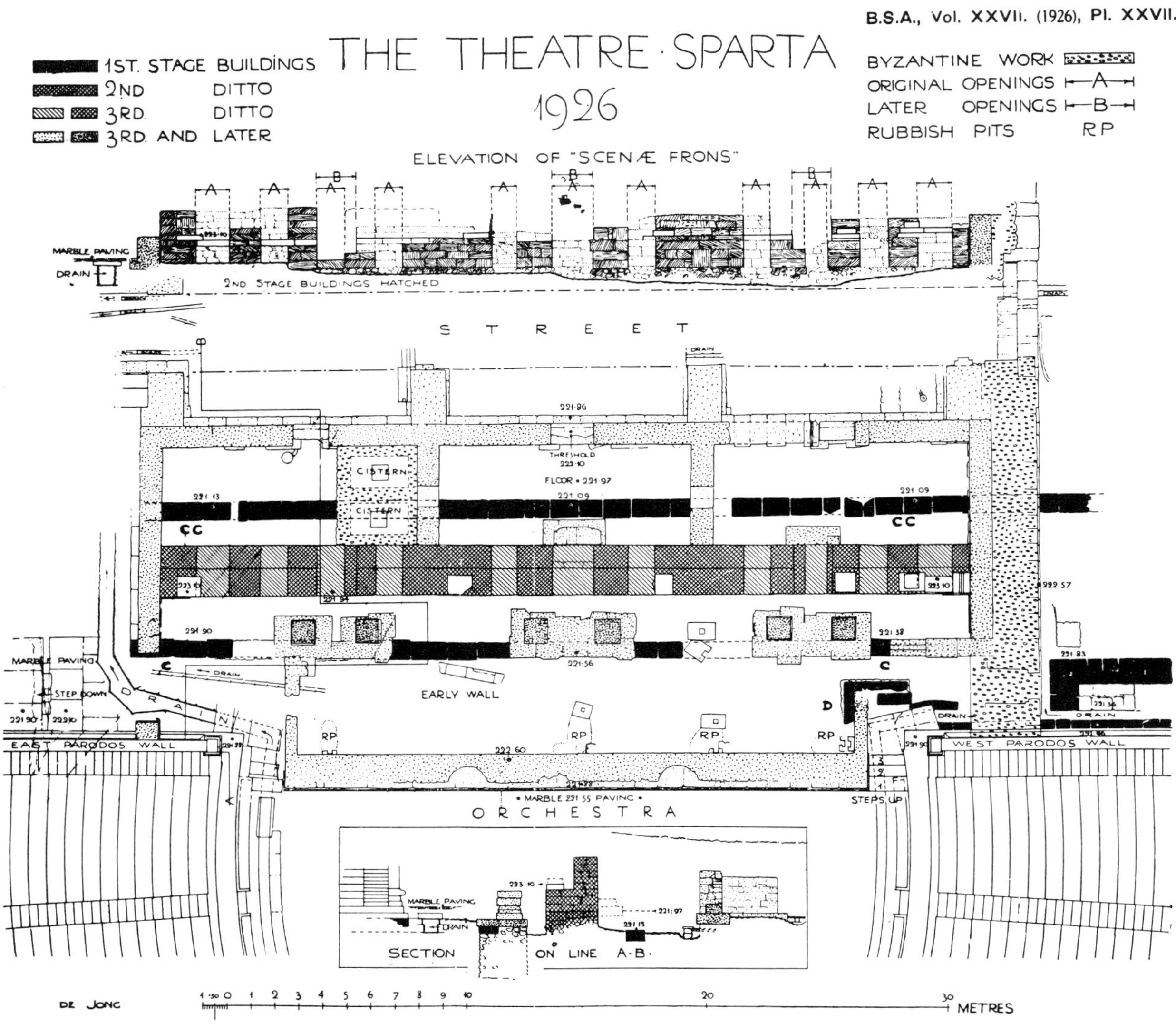

Fig. 9.18 Plan of stage-building of Sparta theatre by P. de Jong, 1926.

been worn smooth, and close inspection in different lights makes it hard to escape the conclusion that the condition of the top surfaces and of the channels results from a heavy mass being rolled to and fro over them. Woodward preferred to interpret the blocks as rainwater channels moved to their present position for later re-use (see Appendix, below).

Although much of the front line (C–C) has been removed by the construction of three massive piers, with foundation rafts of mortared cobbles nearly two metres deep, which supported the projecting porches of the columned façade of the later stage-building, there exists towards the east end, just beyond the easternmost pier, a fragment of another channelled block on the same alignment and at the same height as those at the west end, which also appears to be *in situ* (FIG. 9.24). This is to be distinguished from the channelled blocks on the same line further to the east which belong to a later rebuild consisting of mortared blocks resting on footings of mortared rubble.

In 1927 the remains were inspected by the distinguished German archaeologist Wilhelm Dörpfeld. He informed Woodward that he believed the channelled blocks to represent evidence for a 'rolling stage', citing the term *scaena ductilis* used by Servius, the late Roman commentator on Vergil (see Appendix, below). Woodward, however, still adhered to his original belief that the channels were for rainwater, a view in which he was supported by the American archaeologist Oscar Broneer. A few years after Dörpfeld's pronouncement, Heinrich Bulle published his hypothesis that the early stages of the theatres at Sparta and Megalopolis had rested on iron-clad rollers, on which they could be moved sideways between the orchestra and the *skanotheke* in the adjacent parodos (Bulle 1928). In Autumn 1935 Bulle, aided by the technician Wolfgang Weyhe, had made a fresh record of the visible remains at Sparta theatre and had carried out new soundings on the presumed location of the *skanotheke* in the west parodos. Bulle's monograph, published in

Fig. 9.19 (left) *Sparta theatre, W end of stage area. Wall C–C with two channelled blocks in place.*

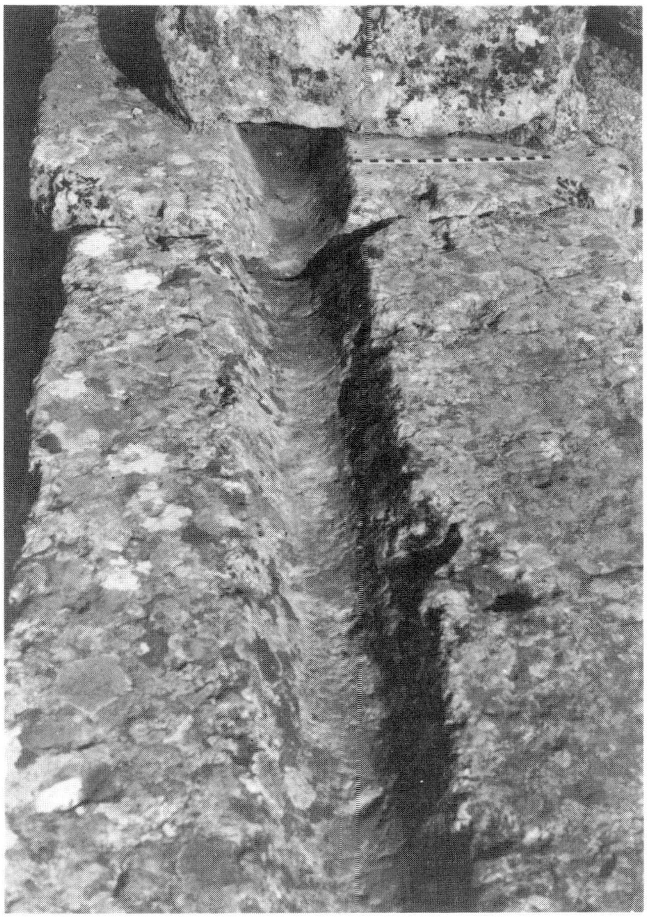

Fig. 9.20 (below left) *Detail of channelled blocks in Fig. 9.19.*

Fig. 9.21 (below) *Detail of channelled blocks in Figs. 9.19–20, showing alignment of channel and clamp cuttings.*

1937, set out in detail the evidence for the moving stage at Sparta (FIG. 9.25). In addition to the blocks excavated and recorded by Woodward, Bulle located and recorded more than three dozen channelled blocks of conglomerate stone, most of which were re-used in the rear wall of the Flavian stage-building. A sounding by Bulle at the east side of the later Roman *nymphaeum* revealed a channelled block that was apparently *in situ* on the line of the front row of blocks (C–C), but unfortunately the line of the rear row (CC–CC) lay beyond the limit of Woodward's excavation of the *nymphaeum* and could not be investigated by Bulle. At an intermediate point Bulle located another channelled block, which he judged to be *in situ* and from which he inferred that there had been a third row of channelled blocks on a middle line (CCC), although no trace of such a third line has yet been recognised in the excavated area of the stage.

So matters rested until 1986, when Caroline Buckler published a paper entitled 'The myth of the moveable skenai', in which she sought to refute Bulle's thesis for rolling stages in the theatres at Sparta and Megalopolis (Buckler 1986). Buckler pointed out several weaknesses in the detail of Bulle's presentation, while expressing support for the view of Woodward and Broneer, that the most likely explanation for the

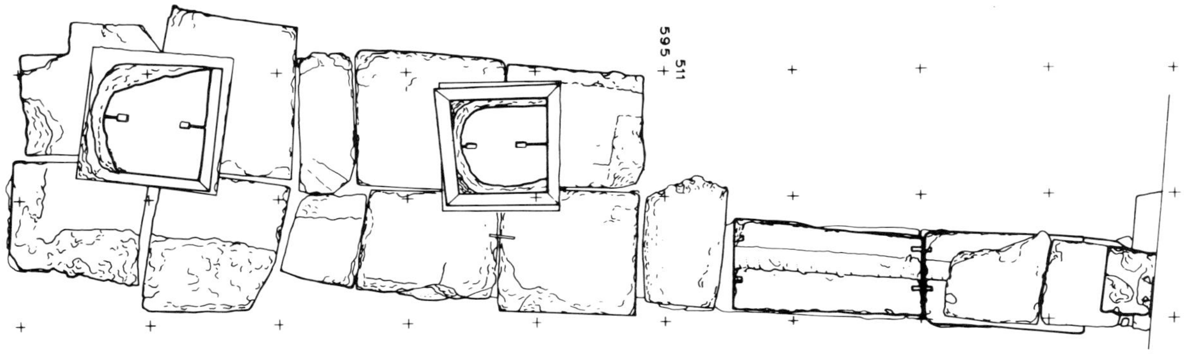

Fig. 9.22 (above) *Sparta theatre,* W *stage area. Detail of plan of* W *pier and wall C–C with channelled blocks in position. Drawn by Anne Hooton, 1995. The grid squares represent 1m.*

Fig. 9.23 (below) *Detail of Fig. 9.22, showing wall C–C and channelled blocks.*

Fig. 9.24 (bottom) *Sparta theatre,* E *end of stage area. Channelled block in position immediately to the* E *of the easternmost porch.*

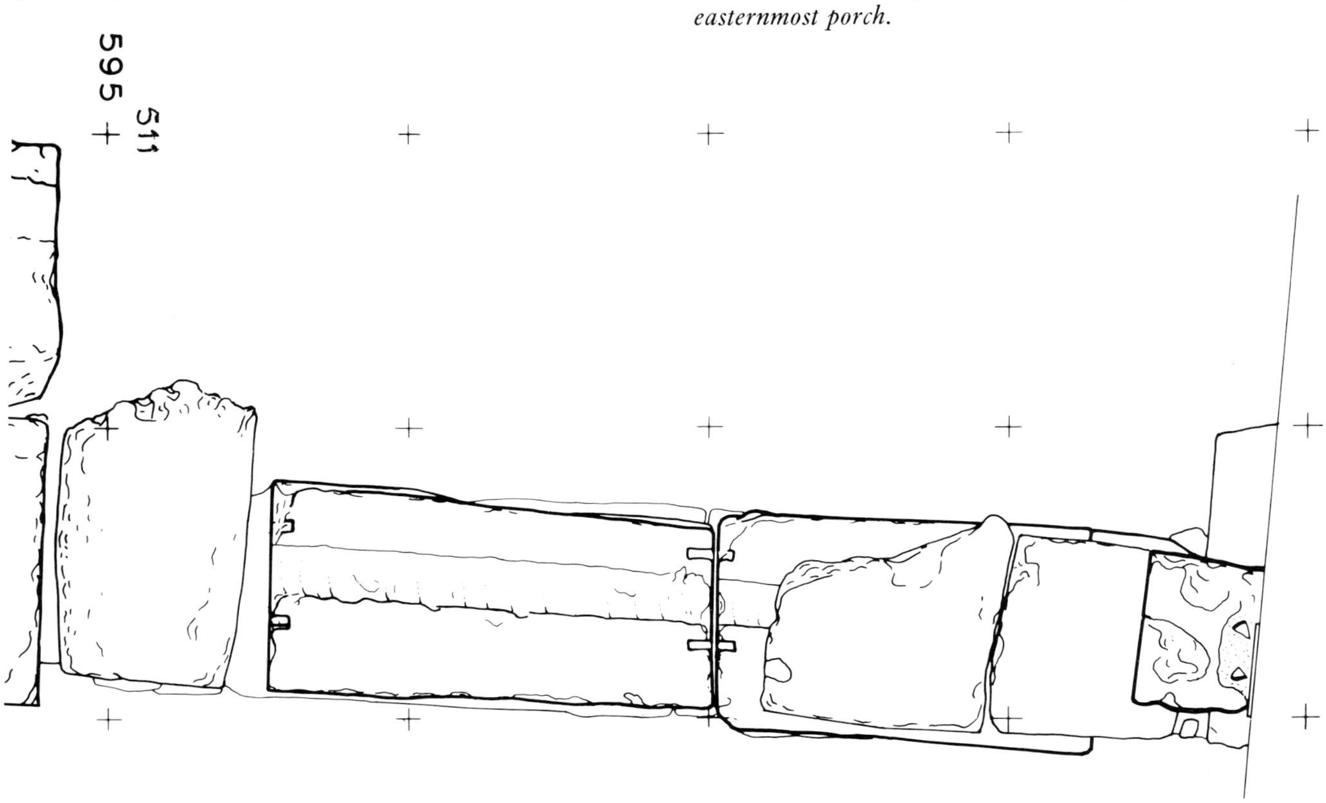

channels was rain gutters. Buckler also maintained, following Woodward's judgement, that the easternmost blocks on the front line were original and *in situ*, and that the difference in level between these and the two channelled blocks at the west end ruled out the possibility of any rolling stage. The 1995 excavations have established, however, that these easternmost blocks in fact belong to a later mortared rebuild and are not *in situ*, whereas a single block at the east which is *in situ* is at the same level as the two western blocks (as indicated above). The evidence on the ground, as recently re-examined, tends therefore to support the hypothesis of Bulle rather than its refutation by Buckler.

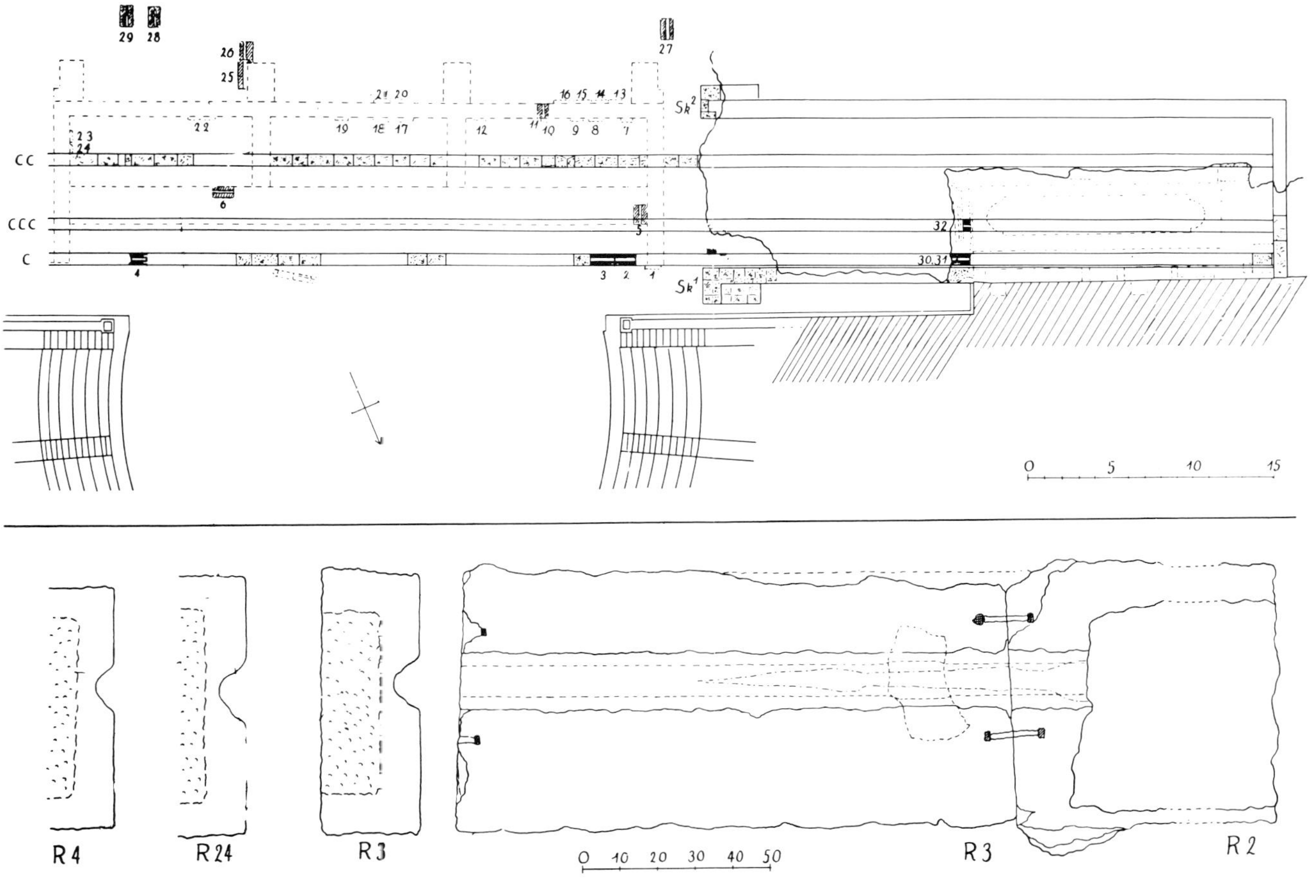

Fig. 9.25 (top) *hypothetical reconstruction by H. Bulle of the foundations and channelled blocks for a moving stage at Sparta theatre;* (above) *scale drawings of channelled blocks numbered by him as 2, 3, 4 and 24.*

The results obtained in 1995 may be summarised as follows:

1. The lines of limestone blocks (C–C and CC–CC) are too narrow and too ill-founded to have supported permanent architecture of any significance.
2. The three channelled blocks of conglomerate stone, two at the west and one at the east, which rest on the limestone blocks of the front line (C–C), are *in situ*.
3. The smoothed upper surfaces of the conglomerate blocks and the rounded channels within them are consonant with wear caused by a heavy rolling structure passing over them.
4. The criticisms of Buckler do not accord with the evidence on the ground, and the hypothesis of some form of rolling stage construction in the first phase of Sparta's theatre should be reinstated and further investigated.
5. The conclusions outlined above, taken with the uncertain record of Bulle's soundings, suggest that the question is likely to be resolved only by further excavation in the area of the west parodos.

APPENDIX

Woodward's accounts of the remains of the first stage.

1925a: 148–9: '(The) wall is only one block wide and consists of a footings-course of roughly-dressed limestone, *c.* 16 cm high, on which rests a course of hard conglomerate, which is dressed smooth, and indeed takes a high polish. On the upper surface, along the central axis of the block, runs a narrow semicircular sinking 16 cm wide and 7.5 cm deep. The foundation rests on yellow gravelly earth, which looks like undisturbed ground, at a level of .30 m below the Orchestra-paving'.

1926a: 190–1 (describing the work of the 1926 season): 'But we still lack data for the reconstruction of this building and have no fresh clues to the interpretation of the puzzling channelled blocks built into the west end of the north wall. If they were for rain-water, and therefore intended to carry off the drippings from a roof or possibly a colonnade, they cannot be in their original position, for there seems to have been no building from which rain could drip, at this date. They might very well, on this theory, be a later addition, to carry off rainfall from a later structure than the wall . . . On the other hand, if they are essentially part of the original fabric of the wall, they must have served some technical purpose in connection with performances at the theatre, which is quite consistent with our inference that the skenotheke lay to the west of the stage.'

(footnote 1 on p. 192): 'Professor Dörpfeld, who paid a visit to the site in 1927, tells me he believes that they represent the *scaena ductilis* (*cf.* Serv. *ap. Verg. Georgics* iii. 24*; Dörpfeld-Reisch, *Griech. Theater* p. 138; D(aremberg)-S(aglio) s.v. Machina p.1468), and that in the early imperial period there was no raised stage in the Sparta theatre. With all deference to an interpretation offered by so great an authority, I am still disposed to believe that these are merely rain-water channellings!'.

**'scaena autem quae fiebat, aut versilis erat aut ductilis: versilis tunc erat, cum subito tota machinis quibusdam convertebatur et aliam picturae faciem ostendebat; ductilis tunc, cum tractis tabulatis hac atque illac species picturae nudabatur interior'*.

III THE CORINTHIAN PHASE OF SPARTA'S THEATRE

S. E. C. Walker

In the study season of 1995, considerable progress was made in understanding the Corinthian phase of the stage-building of Sparta's theatre. This paper offers a brief account of the present state of knowledge, and an outline of outstanding problems.

The stage-building was carefully studied by Woodward, who received excellent advice from Edmund Wiegand on the dates of the column capitals (Woodward 1930a: 178–83). However, Woodward was eventually defeated in interpreting the phasing and appearance in elevation of the stage building by the number and variety of the architectural elements surviving on the site. To avoid similar difficulties, it is presumed here that a logical system of construction must have pertained at the time the theatre was built and, despite the undoubted incidence of re-use of building material, in subsequent periods of its use. The form in elevation of the original building may, at least in part, be recovered from the surviving remains: to find it, effort must be concentrated on the elements that do form a coherent pattern and join each other; no attempt has been made to devise a reconstruction that uses every element now on the site. The outstanding problems must then be identified, described, and an attempt made to solve them.

For some time it has seemed likely that Woodward was mistaken in assigning the inscribed epistyle *IG* V 1 691 to a colonnade beside the theatre or portal across the east parodos, of which no trace was then or is now visible on the ground (Woodward 1930a: 202, 209). The coincidence in date (AD 78) of the text, which describes the gift of an unspecified structure (of which the epistyle formed a part) to the city of the Lacedaemonians by the emperor Vespasian, with the starting dates of the inscriptions on the east parodos wall recording the careers of local worthies (Cartledge and Spawforth 1989: 105), and with the apparent dates of some of the architectural elements lying on the site of the stage building, was too great to ignore. The transformation of the stage-building, Sparta receiving from the emperor a Roman type of stage in place of the Hellenistic building described above by Geoffrey Waywell and John Wilkes, surely coincided with the fall of the Euryclid dynasty under Nero and the consequent political transformation of Sparta from a kind of independent fiefdom within the Roman Empire to a more normal Roman provincial town,

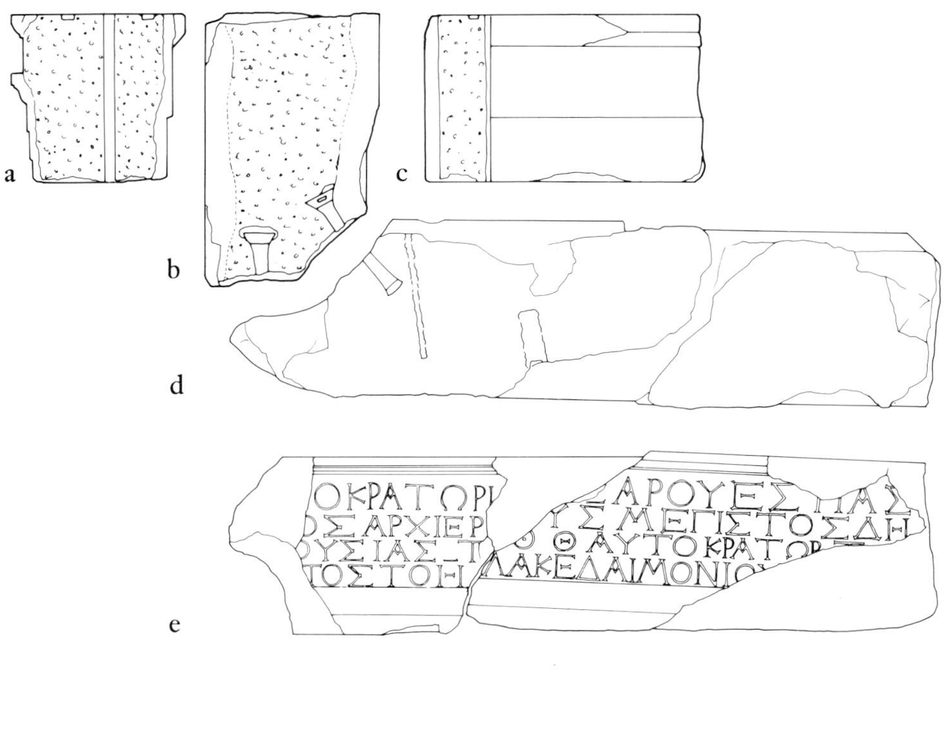

Fig. 9.26 (a)–(c) Section, top view, and interior elevation of A618; a short block from the entablature of the lower order, showing (b, d) how such a block might join A757 (= IG V 1 691); the inscribed epistyle (e). Drawings by G. B. Waywell, inked by S. Bird. Scale 1:25.

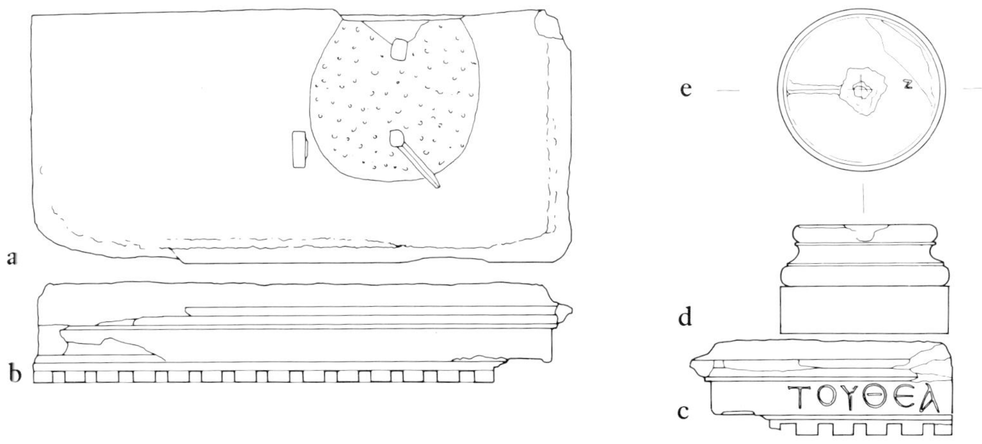

Fig. 9.27 Inscribed cornice block from the E *end of the lower order: (a) top view with cutting for circular plinth; (b) side elevation; (c) inscribed front elevation, with (d, e) column base on a circular plinth. Drawings by G. B. Waywell (a)–(c) and S. Bird (d)–(e). Scale 1:25.*

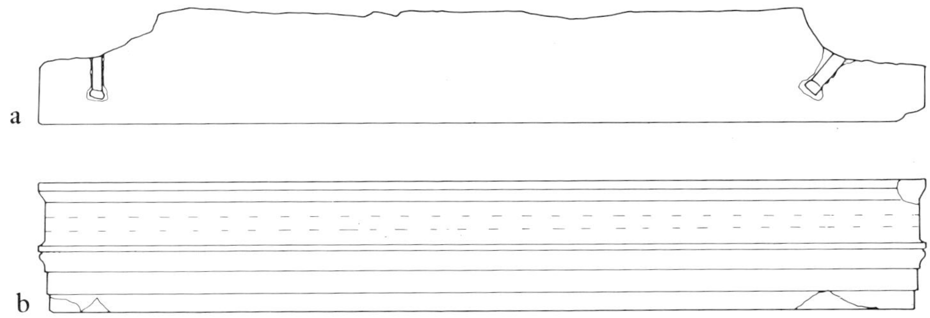

Fig. 9.28 (a) Upper view and (b) front elevation of epistyle and frieze block from the W *end of the upper order, with (a) mitred ends with angled dowel cuttings (compare Fig. 9.26d). Drawings by G. B. Waywell, inked by S. Bird. Scale 1:25.*

Fig. 9.29 Sparta theatre, W *end of stage area. Epistyle blocks fallen from* W *end of scaenae frons.*

albeit with peculiar magistracies and customs redolent of Sparta's extraordinary past (Cartledge and Spawforth 1989: 97–104). The imperial endowment fits well with what is known of the better studied theatres of Italy and the western provinces, most of them built in the first century AD, and as much a mark of Roman political and cultural domination as the buildings of fora, temples to the Capitoline triad and the imperial cult, aqueducts and baths (Gros 1994b).

It was, then, very satisfactory to discover in the 1995 season that the finished appearance of the inscribed epistyle block could indeed be matched with a short epistyle (A619), and that the mitred end and associated system of dowelling surviving on the upper surface at the left end of the block was evidently intended to join it at right angles to a short block of similar form (compare A618, FIG. 9.26), thereby demonstrating that the inscribed epistyle must have

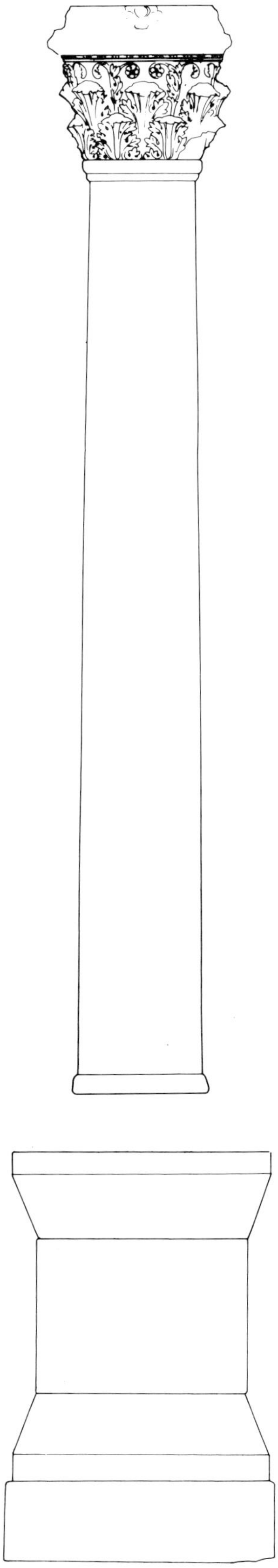

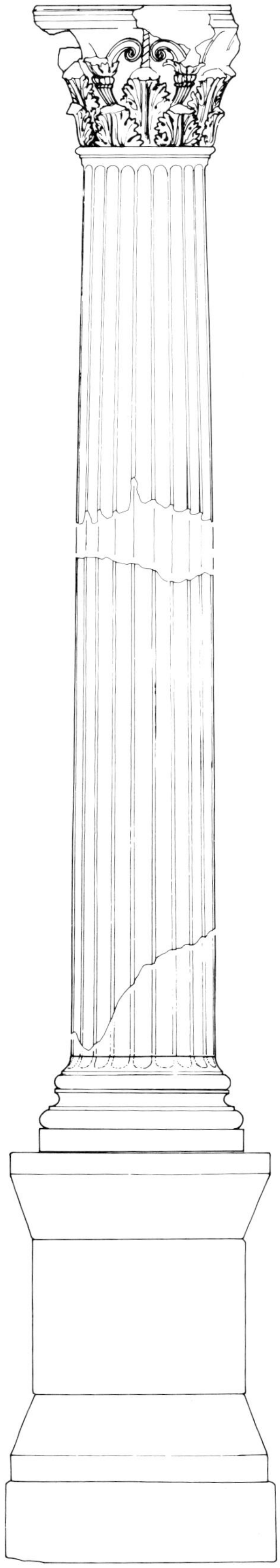

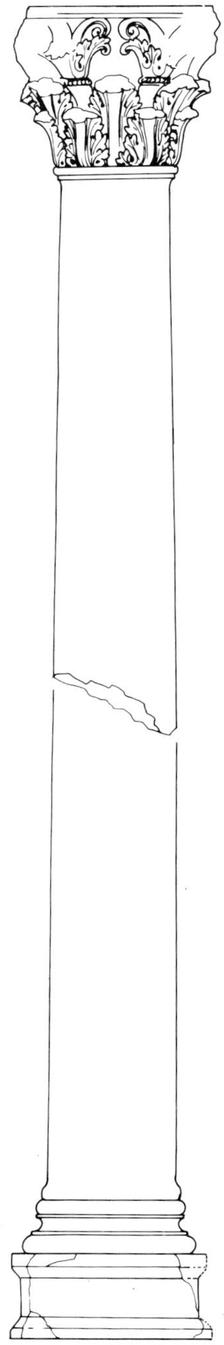

Fig. 9.30 (far left) *Reconstruction of flanking pier of scaenae frons surmounted by granite column and marble composite capital. Drawn by S. Bird.*

Fig. 9.31 (left) *Reconstructed central pier with column base on plinth surmounted by fluted shaft and Corinthian capital of Pentelic marble. Drawn by S. Bird.*

Fig. 9.32 (above) *Reconstructed column from lower order of stage wall, with square plinth and white marble base supporting unfluted column shaft of Laconian marble and Corinthian capital. Drawn by S. Bird.*

Fig. 9.33 (right) *Reconstructed column from upper order of stage wall, with circular plinth and base supporting unfluted shaft of Laconian marble and Pergamene capital. Drawn by S. Bird.*

been part of the projecting columnar façade set upon the piers in front of the stage building. To show the text to best advantage, it may have spanned the central intercolumniation of the lower order, though the block was found beyond the west wall of the stage-building (Woodward 1930a: 201).

It was also realised that the cornice blocks cut with circular depressions in the front of their upper surfaces, believed by Woodward to support bases for statues (Woodward 1926a: 207), were originally set on these epistyles, the cuttings holding circular plinths supporting the upper order, of which one example survives of appropriate dimensions, though the surviving cuttings are a mismatch (A535, FIG. 9.27). It is likely that a complete plain epistyle with mitred ends (A684, FIG. 9.28), which now lies in front of the west end of the stage-building (FIG. 9.19), spanned the western intercolumniation of the upper order. Indeed, it appears that much of the western end of the *scaenae frons* lies today near to where it fell in late antiquity (FIG. 9.29).

A new proposed reconstruction employs the piers still partially intact in front of the stage, which would have been level, when the original crowning moulding was in place, with a terrace cut in the front of the stage wall, on which stood marble plinths supporting a free-standing order to which the projecting columns were attached by the aforementioned short epistyles. This is a much simpler proposition than that offered by Woodward, who associated the piers with a later raising of the level of the *scaenae frons* (Woodward 1926a: 195–8, 204). It is not without its difficulties, but in principle must be correct.

Such an arrangement offers three pairs of projecting columns, and a row of twelve columns along the stage wall. To the objection that the order does not reach the ends of the stage wall (and it should be pointed out that the plinth now sitting at the extreme east end of the wall is not *in situ*), it may be observed that the columnar façade was evidently related not to the rooms of the stage-building behind it but to the ends of the cavea in front (FIG. 9.18). Of the projecting columns, it may be surmised that the two flanking pairs were of similar, and the central pair of different, form. From the findspots carefully noted by Woodward (1925a: 146), four shafts of Troad granite (of which A 301, 320 are complete) would be well placed on the flanking piers, and would neatly fit fine composite capitals of Laconian marble, of which three survive on the site (A 154, 289, 598, FIG. 9.30). The central piers would then be occupied by fluted shafts of Pentelic marble, surmounted by Corinthian capitals of Pentelic marble of outstanding quality (A 151, FIG. 9.31). Along the stage wall were unfluted shafts of Laconian marble (A 302, 309), with Corinthian capitals (A 140, 668) and white marble bases (A 148) set on rectangular plinths (FIG. 9.32). These last capitals have rounded sepals matching in form the *acanthus mollis* used in the smaller Pergamene capitals (A 141, 143, 146–7) which surely adorned part, at least, of the upper order. These were set on unfluted shafts of Laconian marble (FIG. 9.33); it is not out of the question that spirally fluted shafts (A 303, 307, FIG. 9.8) were used for the central part of the upper order (Woodward 1925a: 146, fig. 11; 1930a: fig. 13).

Such details, and the date of the upper order, need more study. It is possible that the upper order was restored later, perhaps at the turn of the second and third centuries AD, and that at the same time the buttresses were added to the south wall of the stage building to strengthen the structure (Woodward 1926a: 302). There is also a difficulty in interpreting the construction of the front wall of the stage-building, of notably poorer superstructure than the side and south walls of the rooms. Most likely it was a secondary phase of the Flavian stage-building; like the other walls, it rests on foundations of the deliberately demolished Doric elements of the colonnade associated with the Augustan theatre, the location of which remains uncertain.

Another problem arises in the assignation of bases to the orders set on the piers (FIGS. 9.30–3). Three bases survive, all set on plinths evidently intended to fit the piers. Two of the bases (A 625, 626) are of equal height, and one of these (A 626) has an additional collar which would fit the lower end of a fluted column shaft of the sort proposed for the central projecting order (FIG. 9.31). Like the upper surfaces of the other two bases, the collar is fitted with double dowel sockets, and it is assumed that the lower end of the fluted Pentelic shaft, apparently not surviving on site, had matching cuttings. One of the other bases (A152) is of lesser height; given that the two Pentelic shafts might be assigned to the other surviving bases, this third base might have been intended for one of the granite shafts. However, as it stands, the base is too large for the shaft, and the shaft has only a single dowel hole in its base. It is tempting to postulate here an error in the original commissioning of the architectural elements: there was no difficulty with the bases and shafts of the central order, which were both supplied from the Pentelic quarries near Athens, but the granite shafts ordered from the Troad did not fit the bases sent to Sparta from Athens.

10

Roman mosaics from Sparta

Anastasia Panayotopoulou

Recent excavations that are due to the expansion of the contemporary city have brought to light a number of mosaics. This paper aims at presenting the evolution of the mosaicist's art in Sparta: the characteristic features of each period, the geometric patterns and figurative scenes and the particularities of the local workshop.

There are surprisingly few publications on Spartan mosaics. Most of the available information comes from preliminary reports published in the periodicals of either the Greek Archaeological Service or the British School at Athens. The Hellenistic mosaic representing a Triton remains the best published (Salz-mann 1982: 40–169). Some mosaics have appeared in Chrysanthos Christou's article 'The mosaics of Sparta' which was published in the 1968 calendar of the Ionian and Popular Bank of Greece. Other mosaics have also appeared in Chrysanthos Christou's archaeological guide *Ancient Sparta* (1960). Several Spartan mosaics appear in two articles, which remain essential for the study of Greek mosaics: 'Catalogue of Roman Mosaics with Human Figures in Greece' by Yota Assimakopoulou-Atzaka (Assimakopoulou-Atzaka 1973) and that by Elizabeth Waywell 'Roman Mosaics in Greece' (Waywell 1979). The early Christian mosaics are examined in the respective volume of the corpus by Yota Assimakopoulou-Atzaka (Assimakopoulou-Atzaka 1987).

During the excavations in plots of the modern city, as well as the neighbouring village of Magoula, there have been discovered to date 137 mosaic pavements in 98 sites. These sites cover a large sector of the contemporary city. The boundaries of this sector comprise Lycourgou Street to the S and Chamaretou Street to the E (there is only one site further E, near the Eurotas river: Demakopoulou 1967, 202), and the slopes of the acropolis, including the hill itself, to the N. The sites appear denser in the area from the SW of the acropolis to the borders of Magoula.

Mosaics usually covered the floors of rooms in luxurious houses, baths, or public buildings. In houses they were used to decorate triclinia, corridors, yards and atria (Spyropoulos 1980: 136, pl. 47b). They also decorated the apsidal rooms of private or public buildings. The only example of wall mosaic found in Sparta covers a niche discovered in the Alikakos plot (Steinhauer 1975: 74–6).

The usual technique is *tessellatum*. Recent excavations have also brought to light Hellenistic pebble mosaics.

The material used was either marble or stone from the nearby quarries. Sometimes the natural colours of tesserae did not satisfy the mosaicists. Thus, they created tesserae of glass paste which they used mostly for bright black, olive green, dark or light blue, crimson, orange, or tesserae of faience for olive-green. Human faces were rendered in great detail by using smaller tesserae than those used for the bodies, cut not only in squares but also in other shapes to define better the details of the face. For geometric motifs, they used tesserae much larger than those used for figures.

From the Hellenistic period mosaics begin to decorate the floors of Sparta. The well-known mosaic representing Triton surrounded by other marine creatures and Dionysiac scenes, together with a recently discovered mosaic with a naturalistic scene of a feline attacking a bull are dated to this period.[1]

A series of mosaics, very simple in their composition and motifs, as well as in the colours used, is dated to the first century AD. Their surface is decorated with large and very simple geometric motifs. The tesserae, because of their shape and size, look more like rough fragments of stone (FIG. 10.1).

During the second century AD and the first decades of the third, Spartans made more frequent use of mosaics as floor decoration. Their composition remains simple: one or two geometric borders around the background of the mosaic, which is also decorated with geometric motifs, without much variation in the motifs or in the colours (Steinhauer 1973–4: 283–5, fig.1). In addition to white, which is mostly used to cover the background of the pavement, two or three other colours are also used: black, red, green, without any colour tone variations, to compose the geo-

1. Vrakopoulou-Vretakou plot, Dioskouron Street. The mosaic is unpublished and all information, as well as the permission to publish it, is due to the excavator, E. Kourinou.

metric motifs. Until now we know of only one example with figured decoration (Demakopoulou 1965: 173–4, pl. 155c).

The production of mosaics increased markedly in Sparta during the third century and especially in the second half of that century, possibly due to the prosperity that the city enjoyed at that time. The invasion of the Heruli in AD 267 appears not to have interrupted the mosaicists' production.

At the beginning of the fourth century the production of mosaics continued, but with more schematic figures and with large 'brush-strokes' of the same colour, without sophisticated colour tone variations, as before, and lacking a good sense of proportion (Assimakopoulou-Atzaka 1973: no 64, pl. 29a). The figures later become even more schematic ending, in the second half of the century as sketches (FIG. 10.2).

The production of mosaics declined dramatically during the fourth century but had an important revival in the early Christian period. However, the mosaicists did not stop work completely even in the years when production was reduced. The example in Philippopoulos plot supports this observation. This fourth-century pavement continued in use into the sixth century with several repairs and alterations. An entire section of the geometric decoration was replaced by two panels depicting aquatic birds and, when in the course of another such repair they wanted to represent a fish, they tried to incorporate it within the geometric design (Assimakopoulou-Atzaka 1987: pl.159b). A small fragment of mosaic of the fifth or sixth century, found in that same plot, is an indication of later production (Assimakopoulou-Atzaka 1987: no. 49).

As far as the organisation of the pavements' surface is concerned, we should note that from the first century AD up to the beginning of the third it is actually very simple. An all-over carpet covered the floor, with one or two geometric borders surrounding the background, the latter usually decorated with geometric motifs as well (Steinhauer 1973–4: 283–5, fig. 1).

Fig. 10.1 Lyberakos plot, detail of the mosaic (photo A. Panayotopoulou).

This arrangement was embellished, during the third century, by the use of more geometric borders surrounding the background (Christou 1960: fig. 8), or by adding four rectangular panels, mostly with geometric decoration, around an all-over carpet design. These panels are wider than the borders but they are used in the same way. In most cases they are of the same width (FIG. 10.3). In other cases, however, the width is different; there are two narrow panels on the long sides of the room, bordering the all-over carpet, and the panels on the shorter sides are wider (Nicholls 1950: fig. 14). There is only one case where these bordering panels were decorated with figurative decoration.[2]

Concerning the decorative patterns of the mosaic pavements, we note that floral motifs were not commonly used by mosaicists during the Roman period. They would rarely cover a whole panel, being usually laurel or ivy leaves restricted to borders (FIG. 10.4). Sometimes they occupied the margin between the all-over carpet design and the walls of the room (FIG. 10.2).

On the other hand geometric motifs are very common. More than half of the mosaic floors that have come to light in Sparta have only geometric decoration.

For the decoration of the background of an all-over carpet tangential eight-lozenged stars were used (Christou 1964b: pl. 138b), also intersecting circles (Demakopoulou 1965: pl. 153a), a grid of decorated bands (Kourinou 1985: pl. 32a), an orthogonal pattern of meander with swastikas and squares (FIG. 10.4), tangential octagons and squares (Steinhauer 1973: fig. 5) and intersecting octagons (Demakopoulou 1965: pl. 155c).

Different circular compositions appear as well. There are simple circles decorated with figurative scenes inscribed into a square; the pattern known as the 'vault design' (Christou 1964b: pl. 138a), composed of a circle inscribed in a square and divided in four equal trapezoidal panels, which appears in Greek mosaics for the first time (FIG. 10.3); and the composition of an inscribed circle with a central medallion, and divided into many trapezoidal sections (FIG. 10.2).

The panels were decorated with tangential eight-lozenged stars, four-pointed stars, an imbrication pattern, guilloche mat, (FIG. 10.5), tangential hexagons forming six-pointed stars, wheels of *peltae*, a grid of a simple line of tesserae, a chessboard pattern

2. Chatzis plot, Leonidou Street. Unpublished.

Fig. 10.2 (left) *Alikakos plot, the pavement of the apsidal room (photo E' Ephorate).*

Fig. 10.3 (below) *Paraskevopoulou plot, the Medusa pavement (photo E' Ephorate).*

Fig. 10.4 (opposite) *Mazis plot, general view of the pavement (photo E' Ephorate).*

of tangentially poised squares, and a chessboard pattern of tangential lozenges (Spyropoulos 1980: fig. 2).

Some compositions are unique, as for example the oblique grid, in each case with a stylized four-petalled flower, which decorates the background of the big panel where the 'Toilet of Venus' is depicted (FIG. 10.6).

Sometimes familiar and rather common geometric patterns, as for example, the eight-lozenged stars are treated in a different way (FIG. 10.3).

The colours used for the geometric decoration of those pavements dated to the third and the beginning of the fourth century are always the same: black, red, green, yellow, grey and white, the last usually reserved for the background.

We have observed that, up to the beginning of the third century, mosaic pavements were decorated mostly with geometric motifs. In contrast, during the third century, and especially in its second half, the mosaicists decorated pavements with figurative scenes. In the choice of pictorial themes one can observe a preference for a limited repertory of the usual iconographical cycles, which were common to the rest of the Roman world in mosaics of the same period. Certain scenes are depicted in few examples while others do not appear at all.

Scenes connected with music, poetry and the theatre were popular. The Muses were depicted two at a time in four square panels in a pavement found in the W of the city (Spyropoulos 1980: 142–3). In the central panel of the same pavement the ninth Muse is presented together with Apollo. The pavement has been seriously damaged, so we can only identify Ourania with Kalliope, Thaleia with Melpomene, the lyre of Erato or Terpsichore and the double flute of Euterpe.

From the representation of the nine Muses in another mosaic floor, only Kalliope and Ourania have been preserved. In square panels of the same pavement the poets Alkman, Anakreon, Alkaios and Sappho are represented (Christou 1964b: pl. 138c and 139).

The scene of Orpheus charming the beasts with his music has been found twice in Spartan mosaics. In the best known mosaic Orpheus plays his lyre seated among the animals depicted in superposed rows (Waywell 1979: fig. 42). In the second mosaic the animals are turned to him, attracted by his music,and the whole scene is set against a rich background.[3]

3. Papadimitriou and Nikoletos plots, Herakleidon Street. This mosaic, as the previous one, is unpublished. I owe many thanks to the excavator G. Steinhauer for the information and the permission to publish them.

Fig. 10.5 Chatzakos plot, general view of the pavement (photo E' Ephorate)

Six theatre masks are represented in a row at the N section of a border surrounding the central panel of a pavement (FIG. 10.4). The Three Graces decorated a square panel (Spyropoulos 1980: pl. 48b).

Scenes inspired by the world of gods or demi-gods are also often depicted. In the central panel of one such pavement Dionysos, seated in a diphros, offers a phiale to a comic actor who bends to drink (Demakopoulou 1965: pl. 154b–c). Exactly the same scene is represented in one of the panels decorating the atrium, which was found in a plot very close to the previous one, just S of the acropolis (Spyropoulos 1980: 136–9).[4]

In the scene of the 'Toilet of Venus' (Panayotopoulou 1989: 74–5) represented in the centre of another pavement, the goddess stands in the middle surrounded by four Cupids who are helping her to dress and put on her jewellery. This scene is rare in Greek and East Mediterranean mosaics but very common in North African mosaics, where marine Venus is usually represented.

Another pictorial cycle is inspired by the gods' love affairs. We have the representation of the rape of Ganymede by Zeus in the form of an eagle (Spyropoulos 1983: 90, 92) and in another mosaic the rape of Europa by Zeus in the form of a bull (Waywell 1979: fig. 46).

Pairs of gods or demi-gods decorate the square panels of a pavement found to the S of the acropolis (Spyropoulos 1980: 136–9). Ares, having left aside his weapons, rests in the arms of Aphrodite. Eros and Psyche are kissing. Ariadne is represented sleeping on the shore of Naxos. There is also Daphne's metamorphosis into a laurel, to enable her to escape from Apollo.

From the world of the chthonic gods comes the figure of Medusa depicted in five pavements, a rather high proportion considering the total number of mosaics with figurative scenes. Only three other subjects, namely Orpheus charming the beasts, the Nine Muses and Dionysos offering a drink to an actor, are repeated more than once.

The Gorgoneion is represented at the centre of two pavements , with the rest of the decoration subsidiary to it. The earliest example of such a Gorgoneion was found in the Paraskevopoulou plot (FIG. 10.3). The central medallion of a large circle, inscribed in a square, is decorated with a Gorgoneion surrounded by a border of particoloured scales, representing thus a variation on the motif of a shield with imbrication pattern and a Gorgoneion in the centre. On the second pavement, which came to light in Haghiou Nikonos Street in front of the Alexopoulos plot (Christou 1964b: pl. 137a, 138a–b), a Gorgoneion is represented in the centre of a 'vault design' pavement facing those entering the room.

In the third example the Gorgoneion had a secondary position. It is depicted in a rectangular panel

4. In the central panel of a mosaic excavated recently at Valioti plot, in Thermopylon Street, is depicted the same scene, slightly differentiated. The information is due to the excavator Y. Efstathiou.

among scrolls of acanthus, which appear to have grown from the same root (FIG. 10.4).

The pavement found in the Chatzakos plot (FIG. 10.5) offers us a completely different representation of Medusa: the beheading of Medusa, at present a unique scene in the repertory of mosaics (Panayotopoulou 1994: 376, 378). The scene appears to relate the myth exactly as it is told by Apollodorus. The figure of Perseus, holding his sickle in his right hand, dominates the scene; he beheads Medusa who is kneeling before him. The hero is aided by the goddess Athena, who holds up her shield so he can see Medusa's reflection in it and avoid her petrifying glance. Behind Medusa's head Pegasus can be seen. The figures are also identified by the inscriptions written above or under them. The female figure with the inscription ΛΙΒΥΗ is probably the personification of the country where, according to ancient writers, the scene took place. The two female heads represented at Medusa's side are probably her sisters, the Gorgons.

There are fewer examples of scenes inspired by Homer's epics, the forces of nature and everyday life. The scene of Achilles (Assimakopoulou-Atzaka 1973: pl. 29a) being discovered by Ulysses in the king's court at Skyros, even though he is wearing women's clothing, is shown on a pavement found at the centre of town. The return of Briseis to Agamemnon, accompanied by Patroclus and Talthybius is depicted on another pavement (Christou 1964b: 137–8).

Personifications of the Sun, Day, Night and the Moon decorate square panels of a pavement (Christou 1964b: pl. 140). In another the figures of the Sun and the Moon also emblazon the centre of a large circle inscribed in a square. In the remainder of the circle the Zodiac cycle appears and in each corner, between the circle and the square, a Wind (FIG. 10.2).

Two other mosaics give scenes inspired by everyday life, such as a hunt and the return with the prey (Christou 1964b: 138–41).

Scenes inspired by the marine world were also popular. In a large rectangular panel three Nereids are depicted riding sea monsters.[5] In other rectangular panels of the same pavement there are cupids playing with dolphins, fish in superposed rows and shell-fish. A mythical marine creature seems to have been depicted in a panel of another pavement, although there were some problems in identifying it due to the mosaic's bad state of preservation.[6] Two superposed lines of fish decorate three sides of a border, continuing the series of masks that I have already described (FIG. 10.4). Fish also decorate the background of a pavement covering one room of a bath complex (Demakopoulou 1967: 202). In another mosaic floor two dolphins confronting each other are represented within the four semicircles surrounding the central medallion with a Medusa head, while a fish decorates the curve-sided squares (Christou 1964b: pl. 138a). Two dolphins appear in the central panel of a pavement decorating a bath (Demakopoulou 1965: pl. 155c).

Fig. 10.6 Pergantis plot, detail of the geometric decoration (photo A. Panayotopoulou).

The representation of animals is less common. Free standing animals are not often shown except in cases where they are an element of the scene, as when Orpheus charms the beasts or in the 'Toilet of Venus' where a pigeon, the goddess' symbol, is depicted above a half-open case where her jewellery is kept. There are also a few examples of animals confronting each other. In a panel of the pavement that was excavated in front of Alexopoulos' house, two panthers are standing one on each side of a vase (Christou 1964b: pl. 137b).

The mosaicist would sometimes inscribe the names of the depicted figures to ensure their identification. Evidence of this appears in the beheading of Medusa (FIG. 10.5), the Homeric scene of the return of Briseis or the representation of poets and Muses (Christou 1964b: 138–41).

In studying the Spartan mosaics, we observe some distinctive features in contrast with those found in the rest of the Greek world or the Roman empire. Such features include the arrangement of four panels

5. See note no 2.

6. Stavros Pergantis plot, Kyprou Street. Unpublished.

around an all-over carpet design, the new rendition of familiar geometric patterns, the amazingly diverse and multi-coloured geometric motifs, originality in the choice of the figurative scenes and the imaginative representation of well-known mythical scenes. All these oblige us to conclude that a local workshop was active in Sparta during the third century, and especially in the second half of the century. The mosaicists of this workshop were able to create new motifs based on the tradition of their art. On the figural scenes they used the copy books with patterns but they varied them, inspired by literature. They had the ability to exploit all the potential that their primary materials could offer. Although they followed the artistic expression of their time, some of the figurative scenes they created are unique in mosaic art. Embellishing familiar compositions with new elements, they expressed their artistic erudition. They evoke the paintings of Pompeii and through them give us a notion of what great art of the Classical period was like.

AKNOWLEDGMENTS

I would like to express my gratitude to my colleagues Katie Demakopoulou, Georgios Steinhauer, Theodoros Spyropoulos, Zissis Bonias, Eleni Kourinou and Yanna Tsirigoti, who kindly gave me permission to publish mosaics they have discovered in Sparta and encouraged me during my studies. This study is the subject of my doctoral thesis in progress at the University Paris X-Nanterre.

11

A Roman portrait from Monemvasia of the early second century AD

Anna Vasiliki Karapanayiotou-Oikonomopoulou

The portrait head published here was found by chance in the storeroom of a private house in the Kastro of Monemvasia. It is inventoried as no. 11668 in the Museum of Sparta, where it was handed in by employees of the 5th Ephorate of Byzantine Antiquities.

DESCRIPTION

The head (FIG. 11.1), which has a sturdy neck and a stone tenon for insertion into the torso, depicts a mature bearded man looking slightly upwards and to the right, a deviation from the strict frontal pose. It is carved from a fine-grained white marble, probably Pentelic, and has a yellowish patina. The figure it came from was life-sized: the maximum preserved height of the whole sculpture is 42 cm and of the head 25 cm. It is not well preserved: the nose is broken, the regions of the eyebrows, the left eye and the lips are abraded and the whole face is slightly chipped. The head was carefully finished and only very faint traces of the rasp are visible behind the lobe of the left ear. The drill was used sparingly for the earholes and inner corners of the eyes.

The shape of the head is characterized by the strongly curved occiput and the elongated face, which is roughly pentagonal with the upper parts of the cheeks accentuated. The upper part of the rather high forehead is covered with long thick falciform locks, falling forwards from the crown of the head, and arranged in two clusters of unequal width, which divide over the inner part of the left eye with the larger, tripartite, cluster on the left, and the smaller one on the right. In both profile views (FIGS. 11.2–3) the locks spread forwards from the top of the head and stop abruptly at the ears; one lock hangs separately over the temple. On the nape of the neck (FIG. 11.4 seen in back view), there are two more bands of crescent-shaped locks running in opposite directions; these are intertwined and crowned with four concentric locks in the form of a rosette. On the crown of the head the hair is coarsely rendered. The rendering of the hair above the forehead and at the back is, in general, plastic and detailed. The treatment of the hair in the profile views, however, is schematic and flat, with the details indicated by shallow incision. The ears are large and well-shaped, and integral with the head. The lower part of the forehead (FIG. 11.1) has a long horizontal furrow and a prominent frontal bone. The arched eyebrows turn down at the sides.

The man's large eyes (FIG. 11.1) immediately draw the viewer's attention. Starting with the better preserved right eye, the upper lids are heavy and fleshy and descend abruptly, covering the outer corners of the lower lids. The eyeballs are large and slightly convex with the corners of the eyes accentuated, the tear ducts indicated and the crescentic folds incised. The free edges of the lower lids are rendered with a thick double line, and there are bags beneath the eyes, indications of middle-age.

The features of the lower part of the face are clearly visible in spite of the damage: a small tightly closed mouth with slightly down-turned corners; above the right corner, small shallow incisions are just visible indicating a vestigial moustache, which has not been preserved because of damage in this area. Below the mouth is a deep groove and prominent chin.

The face was bearded. From the temples small spiral curls in light relief, outlining the cheeks, descend as far as the angle of the jaw, leaving the chin and mouth bare. Below the jaw the curls stop suddenly at the level of the throat. Here too, as with the hair on the head, the part of the beard on the right side is thick and evenly arranged, while that on the left is unkempt with flame-like curls.

The head has a barely perceptible upward tilt to the right. Another feature is the marked prominence of the Adam's apple and the line tracing the throat.

DATE

In spite of its poor state of preservation, there is plenty of evidence for its date. The arrangement of the hair on the brow carefully reproduces a favourite design in portraits of Augustus (this is the most widely distributed portrait-type of Augustus, the Prima Porta type, which was probably developed in 27 BC. (See most recently Boschung 1993: 38–50, 64–5, 139–95 [cat. nos. 64–217]).

The special attention paid by the sculptor to the treatment of the eye region shows that this work postdates the classicism of the Julio-Claudian (Kleiner 1992: 161–3) and already presupposes the realism characteristic of the Flavian period (Kleiner 1992:

Fig. 11.1 Sparta Museum no. 11668, front view

Fig. 11.2 Sparta Museum no. 11668, right profile view

202–3). A more general date after the middle of the first century AD is supported by a comparison with the head of the emperor Domitian, reworked from a portrait of Nero, and now in the National Archaeological Museum of Athens (Cat. no. 345), which is directly derived from an imperial type created in Rome at the time of his assumption of power in AD 81. The type persisted until the assassination of the emperor in AD 96 (Kavvadias 1890–92: 247 no. 345; Daltrop, Hausmann and Wegner 1966: 37–8, 97, pl. 32 c–d; Bergmann-Zanker 1981: 365–6; Datsouli-Stavridi 1985: 37–8 no. 345, pls. 32–3). If, however, the shape of the face and the expression are examined more closely, it can be seen that the features of the Laconian head are very different from those of the Domitian at Athens: note the squarish, bulky outline of the head, and the plump, fleshy skin with the double chin.

In the noble but distant air conveyed by the Monemvasia head, and its severe expression, amplified by the small, tightly-closed mouth, the influence of the iconography of the emperor Trajan (AD 98–117) is clearly apparent (Gross 1940; Balty 1977/1978; Jucker 1984; Fittschen-Zanker 1985: 39–43 nos. 39–44, pls. 41–8).

The oval outline of the face with its elongated section from the eyes downwards is characteristic of all the iconographical types of that emperor. The particular arrangement of the hair on the brow corresponds to a type of Trajan dated to AD 103/104 (the Paris 1250/Mariemont type, so-called from the museums in which the chief examples are exhibited: Balty 1977/78; Jucker 1984: 39–41; Fittschen-Zanker 1985: 40–1, no. 41, pls. 44–5). Even though in the arrangement of the hair on the brow our head adopts elements from earlier portrait-types of Trajan, other facial features and particularly the imprint of the marks of old age in the region of the eyes are closer to a later type of the emperor, known as the "Opferbildnistypus" (Gross 1940: 105–111; Jucker 1984: 47–51; Fittschen-Zanker 1985: 43, pl. 48). Related details, such as the shape of the eyebrows, the heavy upper eyelids, the imperceptible crow's-feet at the outer corners of the eyes, the bags under the eyes, the thin, closed mouth and the arrangement of the hair at the sides and in back view, which are combined with a more general similarity in the outline of the face and tilt of the head, point to a date clearly after AD 112, when this image of the emperor was created. Our suggestion of a date for the portrait after 112 is fur-

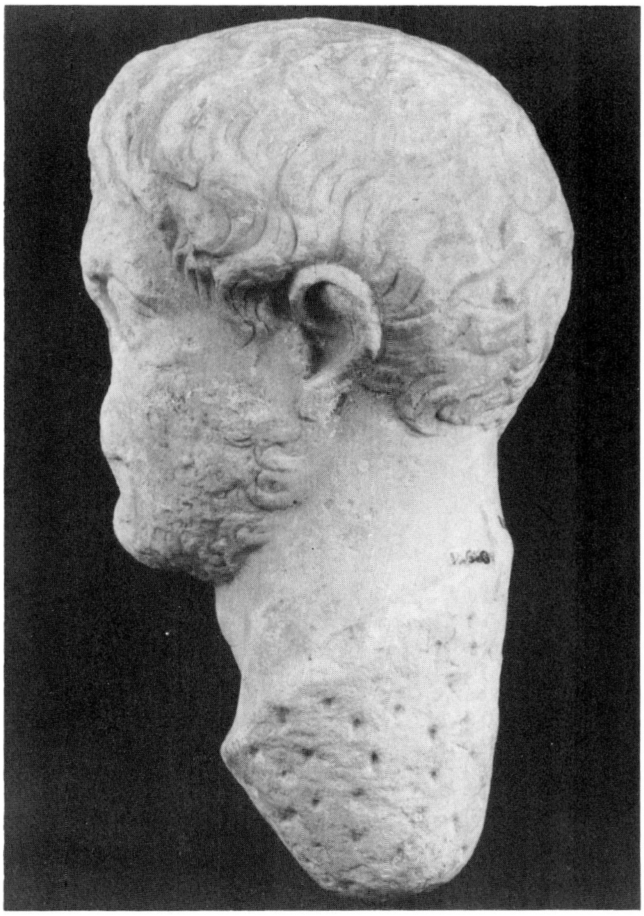

Fig. 11.3 Sparta Museum no. 11668, left profile view

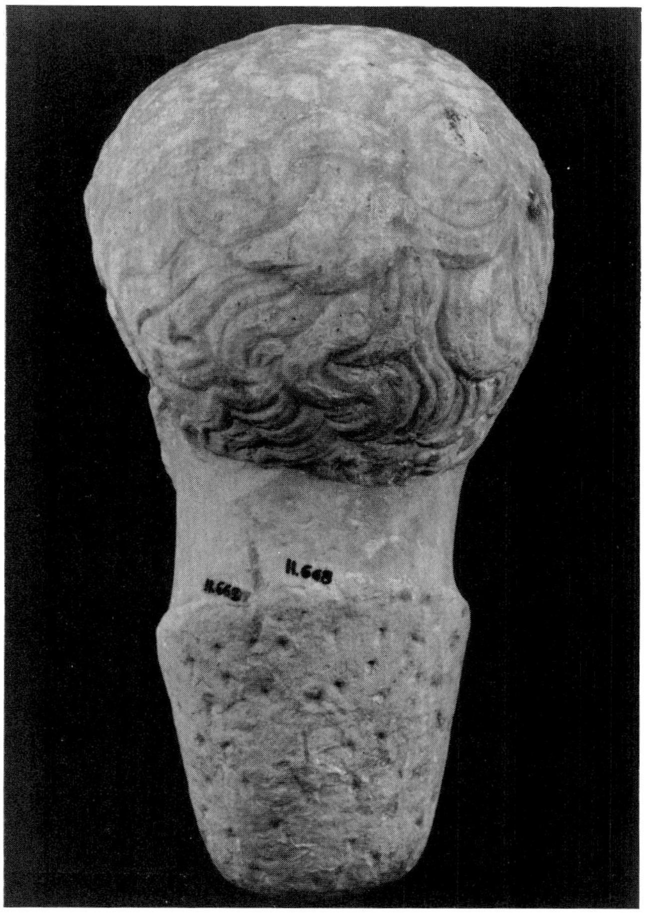

Fig. 11.4 Sparta Museum no. 11668, back view

ther strengthened by its close stylistic relationship to certain figures in the relief decorationon Trajan's Arch at Benevento, a work dated with certainty to AD 114 (Hassel 1966; Rotili 1972; Fittschen 1972; Evers 1994: 56–8); these are, specifically, two portraits in which some scholars have recognized the future emperor Hadrian (Wegner 1956: 31–2, 55, 64, pl. 1 a, b; Bracker 1968: 77–8, figs. 3, 8; Bonano 1976: 83–4, 88–9, figs. 159, 168; Evers 1994: 56–8).

A comparison with types of Hadrian makes it possible to offer a firmer suggestion for a closer chronological attribution of the Monemvasia portrait. In fact, even though in its hair arrangement and facial features our head exhibits traits of the Trajanic period, a more detailed comparison in terms of the outline of the face and the modelling of the flesh with an early type of Hadrian could well argue in favour of a close connection of the sculpture with second century production; this is a type known as *Rollockenfrisur*, probably created in AD 119 and very popular in Greece (Wegner 1956: 13–1;. Fittschen 1984; Fittschen-Zanker 1985: 49–51 no. 49, pls. 54–5; Evers 1994: 233–40). The more even outline of the face, oval rather than elongated, together with the subtle heightening of the upper part of the cheeks, the softer modelling of the flesh with its gentle transitions, the avoidance of mobility of the flesh and of hard characteristics, and the generally tranquil mood, are sufficient evidence for dating the work to the end of the first or beginning of the second century AD. One final comment concerns the presence of the beard in the sculpture. It is well known that Hadrian was the first emperor to be portrayed with a beard, but in the case of ordinary personal portraits in the Roman period, men never abandoned the custom of having themselves depicted wearing a beard; hence this distinctive feature of the Monemvasia head does not by itself constitute a safe criterion for the date (*cf.* recently on this subject Cain 1993: 100). Especially in Greece, and more particularly at Athens, Philopappos is shown with a beard in the relief decoration of his monumental tomb, a work dated to AD 114 (Kleiner 1983; 1986; 1992: 233–5. Compare also Cain 1993: 139 no. 18 for an unpublished portrait of a young man from Eleusis dating to the late Flavian period).

ATTRIBUTION TO A WORKSHOP

As regards the provenance of the sculpture, the appearance of the marble, consistent with Pentelic, initially suggests that it came from an Attic workshop.

This is also supported by its close relationship to other contemporary Attic works.

To start with, let us cite two over life-sized heads of the emperor Trajan, one in the Piraeus Museum: no. 276 (Carducci 1933; Gross 1940: 74, 101–102, 130 no. 54, pl. 27 b; Balty 1977/1978: 59 no. 67); and the other in the Ancient Agora Museum, no. S 347 (Shear 1933: 308, fig. 17, 309 [identified as Claudius]; 1935: 411–13, figs. 35–6; Harrison 1953: 27–8 no. 17, pl. 12 [identified as a priest]; Vermeule 1968: 387–388 no. 4; Balty 1977/1978: 55 no. 3). In the case of the Agora head in particular, in spite of the difference in size, it can be seen that the relationship is more than just chronological. The treatment of the eye region is just the same (we may point out here the special manner in which the inner corners of the eyes are rendered, which is characteristic of Attic early second century AD portraits; *cf.* Harrison 1953: 27 no. 17); and, although the arrangement of the hair above the forehead is different, the finishing technique is the same: the locks above the brow are rendered more plastically, are differentiated from each other and terminate in fine tips, unlike the side views, in which the continuous wavy locks are more simply rendered. In both cases the head is supported on a long, sturdy neck, is slightly tilted up and turned to the right, and the throat and forehead are wrinkled. Lastly, a cold, distant expression together with a classicizing spirit characterizes both works. Close similarities are also presented by the over life-size head of the emperor Hadrian in the Piraeus Museum no. 1197, which is attributed to the type *Rollockenfrisur* (Kallipolitis 1964: 69, pl. 66b; Zoridis 1982: 153–4 no. 8, fig. 16). Here the close correspondence in the shape of the face as well as the execution of the beard strengthens the suggestion of an early Hadrianic date.

The association of the head with the workshop in question is confirmed by a comparison with a group of personal portraits from Attica in the National Archaeological Museum at Athens dating to the early Hadrianic period; they are the works with the following inventory numbers: 372 (Kavvadias 1890–92: 253 no. 372; Hekler 1921–24: 178 fig. 62; Stern 1975: 131–2; Datsouli-Stavridis 1985: 53–4 no. 372, pl. 57), 342 (Kavvadias 1890–92: 246 no. 342; Datsouli-Stavridis 1985, 54-55 no. 342) and 3085 (a portrait from a grave relief: Kourouniotes, K., 1911: 252, 253 figs. 21–2; Hekler 1921-1924: 200–201 fig. 71; Stern 1975: 67–8; Datsouli-Stavridis 1985: 55–6 no. 3085, pls. 59–60). It is worth pointing out here the similarity in the rendering of the hair; in every case incision is the sole method used by the artist: deeper incision to differentiate the locks and shallower ones for the detail. The particular rendition of the hair above the brow occurs not only in the portraits 372 and 3085, but also on the Cosmete 416 in the National Archaeological Museum (Kavvadias 1890–92: 265 no. 416; Graindor 1915: 311 no. 6, fig. 13; Hekler 1921–24: 177, 178 fig. 61; Lattanzi 1968: 38–9. pl. 6 a, b; Stern 1975: 52, 68, 135–6, 141, 145, 154; Datsouli-Stavridis 1985: 94–5 no. 416, pls. 139–40 a–g; Meyer 1991: 227 pl. 139, 2). In the case of the last one, if we except the more classicizing spirit in the rendering of the face on the Cosmete, the relationship both in the treatment of the hair in all views and of the beard is striking.

IDENTITY OF THE PORTRAIT

In answer to the interesting basic question of whom the Monemvasia head depicts, we will try to use the direct and indirect evidence afforded by the work.

From what we have said above, the quality of the workmanship and the type of marble would appear to eliminate a Laconian origin and attribute the head more probably to an Attic workshop or, less probably, to a local one following Athenian models.[1] We therefore have to do with a competent craftsman, very likely Athenian, who seems to have known and been influenced by the more recent trends in metropolitan portrait art, as represented in the imperial iconography and the figures on Trajan's Arch at Benevento.

As to the original site where the portrait was exhibited, we may presume that the head and statue were erected in one of the Laconian cities, in the region around Monemvasia, which flourished in Roman times and would have belonged to the Eleutherolaconian League (RE 5.2 (1903) 2353 sv Eleutherolakones (Brandis); Kennell 1985: 24–30; Cartledge and Spawforth 1989: 101, 113, 114, 138, 139, 149, 150, 173–4). At some point, in unknown circumstances, the sculpture was taken to the Kastro. This hypothesis is supported by the following: from time to time other fine sculptures and works have been found in the Kastro and the sea around it which have been regarded as Laconian works.[2] Moreover, as we

1. The following may be cited as indicative: a. the sculpture no. 6702 in the Sparta Museum which was fished up from the sea in the Monemvasia area; b. a half-finished male head from a statuette picked up in the Kastro in 1971 (Sparta Museum inv. no. 6462); and c. part of a Roman inscription discovered in 1980 in the church of Ayia Sophia in the Kastro, which probably came from neighbouring Epidauros Limera: Hasluck 1908: 178–9; *IG* V 1 933.

2. For portraits of the Roman period from Laconia, see the appended catalogue in Datsouli-Stavridis 1987. For the sources of Laconian marble, see, recently, Cartledge and Spawforth 1989, 169, 171.The likelihood that the work was made locally can be ruled out, if one considers the Laconian workshop which made trapezophora: these were no more than imitations of their Attic counterparts, and the standard of their workmanship hardly surpassed that of a manual labourer; on this subject, see Stephanidou-Tiveriou 1993: 178–81. A final answer to the question cannot be given, since no analytical study has been made of the numerous surviving Laconian sculptures.

know from written sources and archaeological evidence, the medieval town of Monemvasia (RE 15. 2 (1932) 1858 no. 3 sv Minoa (Fiehn). Xanalatou-Dergalin, Kouloglou-Pervolaraki 1976) was built at the end of the sixth century AD by the inhabitants of neighbouring Epidauros Limera, a known centre of the Eleutherolaconian League.[3]

The epigraphic evidence recording the erection of statues in different cities in Laconia during the Roman period gives further impetus to the question of the identity of the person portrayed. From the inscriptions we learn that those honoured with a statue were usually members of a closed aristocracy, centred in Sparta, and who belonged to distinguished families which had received privileges and honours from the Roman conquerors. Their social supremacy was founded on their economic prosperity and the properties they owned in different parts of Laconia (for the aristocratic families in Roman Sparta: Spawforth 1985, 191–258; Cartledge and Spawforth 1989, 160–5). The statue was commissioned either by the population of a whole city—in the case of the Eleutherolaconian League—or by a member of the family of the person honoured (for statues given by Laconian cities in honour of an individual, see Spawforth 1985: 200, 205 n. 43, 208–9; and inscriptions recording Eleutherolaconian cities which honoured individuals for their services: *IG* V. I. 931. 954, 955, 957, 958, 959, 1177, 1243, 1246, 1248. For statues erected by the person's family, see Spawforth 1985: 192 n. 3). Moreover, marble was an expensive material and only a city or a rich family could meet the cost of commissioning a marble statue (for the prices of statues, sarcophagi and other works of sculpture under the Roman Empire, see Pensabene 1983: 55–63; Stephanidou-Tiveriou 1993: 214 n. 46).

All the above evidence leads us to an admittedly bold but not entirely unfounded theory about the identity of the subject portrayed by our head. Could we perhaps recognize in the face of this noble yet cold man the person of Gaius Julius Eurycles Herculanus, the last important descendent of the great Euryclid dynasty, one of the dominant families in Sparta and Laconia during the Roman period [Gaius Julius Eurycles Herculanus sv Vibullius Pius: RE x 1(1917) 580–5 no. 221 (A. Groag); PIR^2 I. 302; Spawforth 1978: 249–60; 1980: 204 n. 7; Kennell 1985: 58, 64–5; Cartledge and Spawforth 1989: 110–12, 193–4)? The founder of the dynasty was the ancestor with the same name as Herculanus, Gaius Julius Eurycles, who was the governor of Sparta in the Augustan period (Bowerstock 1961: 112–18; Kennell 1985: 35–44; Steinhauer 1988; Cartledge and Spawforth 1989: 97–104). This is not an arbitrary suggestion, but is based on the following evidence pointing to the theory that the Gaius Julius Eurycles Herculanus, who was born soon after AD 72 and died in AD 137/137, is the person portrayed:

a) There is epigraphic testimony to the development of special connections between Herculanus and the Eleutherolaconian cities, which awarded him the honorary title of protector or benefactor of the city, and certain of them, for example Asopos and Gytheion, put up a statue to him (*IG* V, 1 971, 1172; *cf.* Kennell 1985: 29 n.26). At Asopos, indeed, his statue was erected beside that of his ancestor and namesake.

b) Herculanus was the first Greek together with Herodes Atticus to be admitted to the Roman Senate. As a consequence he was resident in Rome at around the end of Trajan's reign and would have come into contact with and been influenced by all the artistic movements current in the Roman capital as well as the latest trends in the art of portraiture. As we said above, the Monemvasia head had clearly been subject to influences from early second century Imperial iconography.

c) It has been shown, on the basis of epigraphic evidence, that Herculanus was related to the deposed king of Commagene, Philopappos, for whom the monumental tomb at Athens was built (Spawforth 1978). Herculanus' close family ties with Philopappos would thus explain why the same workshop as that employed by the Eastern monarch was also commissioned to make the statue of the Laconian aristocrat. The influence of the Roman tradition on the Attic workshop is apparent both in the decoration of the tomb and in the portrait (for the Philopappos Monument see above).

d) The particular arrangement of the hair above the brow recalls, as we have seen, a popular type of the Julio-Claudian period which was established by Augustus (see reference on p. 119); the reappearance of the motif later on in the iconography of Trajan—in the type Paris 1250/Mariemont—has been thought to have been deliberately devised in order to associate the new emperor with his glorious predecessor (see above, p. 120). This conscious imitation of a motif which indirectly harks back to the time in which the distinguished founder of the Euryclid dynasty lived is also to be expected in the case of the portraits of Herculanus. All the conduct of the last representative of the dynasty was based on the principles and works of his famous ancestor.

---

3. For Monemvasia's special importance in the Byzantine period, see Armstrong, Cavanagh, Shipley 1992, 302–3 n. 31). For Epidauros Limera, see the recent communication by my colleague E. Zavvou in the Proceedings of the 5th International Congress of Peloponnesian Studies (in press).

Even, however, if the work published here is not a portrait of this distinguished early second century Spartan aristocrat, it must at least depict a Laconian nobleman who was a contemporary of Herculanus.

ACKNOWLEDGMENTS

The sculpture was found in the course of tidying up and cleaning the storeroom of the Zoumboulaki house in the Kastro of Monemvasia. It was handed over together with a Byzantine coat of arms by the owner, Mr Traïforos, to the custodian of antiquities of the 5th Ephorate of Byzantine Antiquities, Mr Skangos, who in his turn brought it to the Sparta Museum. I wish first of all to thank the Ephor of Antiquities, Dr Theodore Spyropoulos, for granting permission to publish the material, and my fellow archaeologist, Mrs S. Raftopoulou, for making it available to me. I am also indebted to Professor K. Fittschen, Professor E. Harrison, Dr S. Walker and Professor G. Waywell for our discussions on particular questions of the chronology of Roman portraits. I also wish to thank the conservator of our Ephorate, Mr D. Koukoutsis, for his observations on technical aspects of the sculpture. Lastly, I am most grateful to Professor G. Kokkorou-Alevra, who read the text of the communication and made many useful comments. The photographs were taken by my colleague, Dr V. von Eickstedt, whom I warmly thank. The present study, in the Greek version, was included in the Proceedings of the 5th International Congress of Peloponnesian Studies which was held at Nafplio in September 1995 (in the press).

12

New finds from Sparta

Stella Raftopoulou

Archaeological activity at Sparta has been sparse, allowing therefore the well known claim of Thucydides (i 10), that the buildings at Sparta did not have the monumental character of the Athenian counterparts to burden Spartan studies. Sparta has never enjoyed the extensive excavations that took part elsewhere in Greece. A simple statistical analysis of the historical and archaeological bibliography on Laconia clearly shows how great the divide is between the archaeological record and the textual evidence. All the same, Laconian archaeology impressively illustrates many aspects of local history; more specifically, some objects can illuminate Spartan society. Nevertheless, hardly ever is material evidence used to complement research conducted on any social, political or military aspect (see Förtsch, this volume).

The 5th Ephorate for Prehistoric and Classical Antiquities of Sparta has been conducting urgent rescue excavations on private plots within the modern city for the past 35 years. This activity has uncovered fragments of the lower city, with different phases covering a long period from Protogeometric to Middle Byzantine. Here I shall describe finds and conclusions of rescue excavations within the modern city during 1991–95, the period I spent as Epimeletria of Antiquities at Sparta.[1]

At Sparta, there are no impressive objects; occasionally unique and important stray finds are encountered in modern houses and yards. But real interpretative value is borne by objects found in meaningful contexts in our excavations, and of course the ancient ruins themselves. Although we cannot plan our digs in the direction we would like to, we constantly record everything in the hope that some day we shall manage to collect all information in a complete survey of the ancient city. Such a comprehensive study may eventually lead us to the most desired aim, the study of the evolution of the town plan of Sparta, with its peculiar and locally specific process of gradual urbanisation, leading to the urban topography of the Roman period.

I PUBLIC BUILDINGS

When working in the lower city of Sparta, the most surprising observation is the lack of large structures and grand buildings. Except for the baths, some of which have always been visible,[2] and some other uncovered in excavations,[3] the only buildings of public character are Christian basilicas dated from the fifth century AD onwards.[4] Recently a fifth basilica was located and partly excavated, S of the Tomb of Leonidas [SITE 1] (FIG. 12.1).[5] Another public building must have been the peculiar trefoil-shaped structure partly excavated by the British School in 1905. It has been recently rediscovered, but was not found in a well preserved condition [SITE 2] (FIGS. 12.2–3).[6] Most

1. Years in parenthesis refer to the particular year an excavation took place, and a number after the initials bb refers to the official number of modern building blocks of Sparta.

2. Visible above ground were the baths at modern Triakosion St. (plot Dipla, bb 127): K. Demakopoulou, Deltion 20 B (1965) 173-174 and Deltion 21 B (1966) 155-59. The later phase that presumably belongs to a Byzantine monastery has been studied by Ch. Bouras, Ephemeris 1982, 99-112. Baths of Arapissa: A. J. B. Wace "The Roman Baths (Arapissa)", BSA 12 (1905-6) 407-414; O. Palagia, "Seven pilasters of Herakles from Sparta" in S. Walker-A. Cameron (eds), The Greek Renaissance in the Roman Empire (1990) 187-192; M. Torelli, "Da Sparta a Villa Adriana: le terme dell' Arapissa, il gimnasio del Platanistas e il Teatro Maritimo" Stips votiva, Festschrift Stibbe (1992) 225-232. For a survey of the antiquities visible in the early 19th c. and recorded by the French Expedition (E. Blouet, L'Expédition Scientifique de Morée, II (1824) see G. Steinhauer, Deltion 28 B (1973) 170.

3. Baths have been uncovered in the plot of the 2nd Primary School: G. Steinhauer, Deltion 28 (1973) 170 (visible in the 19th c.), and at the Karras plot, bb 102, Th. Spyropoulos, Deltion 36 B (1981) 121.

4. 1. Basilica at the Hill: A. Delivorias, Deltion 24 B (1969) 138; 2. Basilica at Kirkiris plot: G. Steinhauer, Deltion 29 B (1973-4) 287-9; 3. Basilica at Varvitsiotis plot: K. Demakopoulou, Deltion 20 B (1965), 175; 4. Basilica at Kleombrotou St.: A. Delivorias, Deltion 24 B (1969) 135-7 (part of the cemetery); G. Steinhauer, Deltion 28 B (1973) 168-170 (part of an apse with mosaic pavement) and E. Bakourou, Deltion 47 A (1992) forthcoming.

5. Asimakopoulos plot (1992), bb 16, and Agidos St., west of this plot: Deltion 47 B (1992) forthcoming.

6. Found at Agidos St., east of bb 8: G. Dickins, "Topographical Conclusions", BSA 1905-6, 435.

Fig. 12.1 (left) *Mosaic of the Basilica at Asimakopoulos plot and Agidos St. Detail from the trench at Agidos St. [SITE 1].*

Fig. 12.2 (below left) *Public building at Agidos St. [SITE 2].*

Fig. 12.3 (below) *Ground plan of the building at Agidos St. [SITE 2] as uncovered in 1995.*

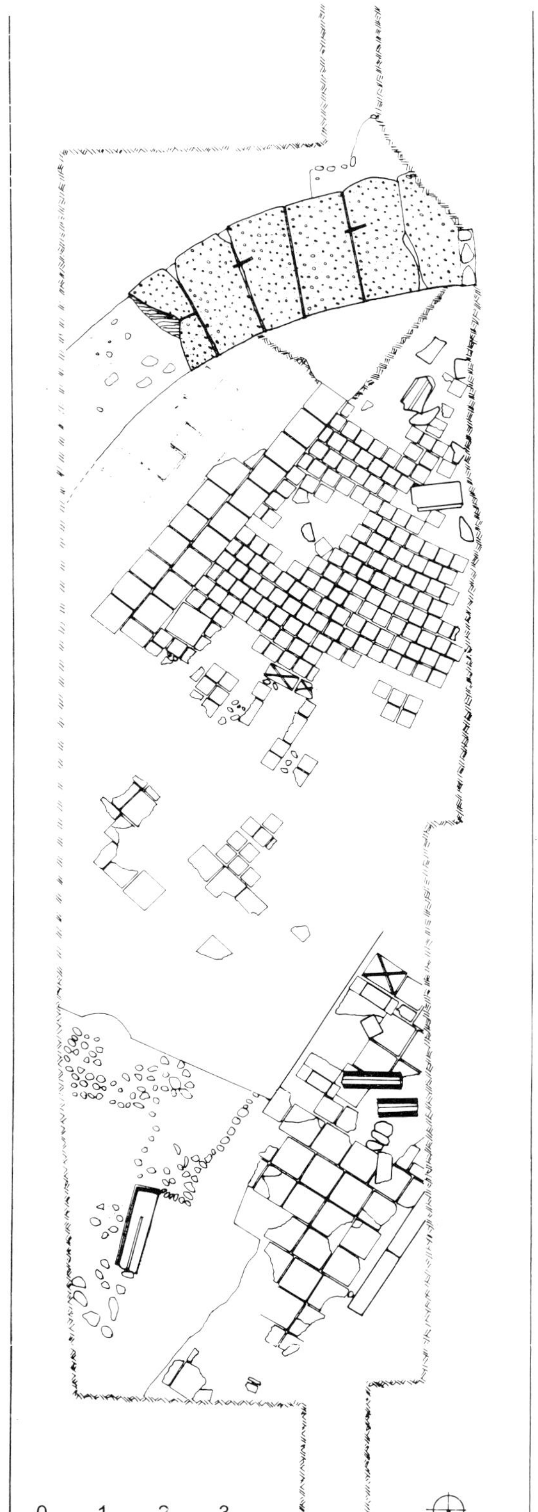

of its large blocks come from Roman structures, but the layout as seen today must be of much later date, perhaps well into the Byzantine era. This absolute lack of public buildings among the domestic *insulae*, however untypical of Roman cities, suggests that all of them were gathered on the low hill of the Acropolis.[7] Pausanias, who visited Sparta after the regular town plan was applied, describes buildings that housed public institutions together with several sanctuaries within the city itself, all of which might have been comparatively humble structures. The many *Heroa* he saw may well have been the Hellenistic monumental tombs that belonged to a fairly systematically organised cemetery on the lowland between the hills, which clearly antedates the institution of the Roman town-plan (*see infra*).

II SANCTUARIES

No architectural remains of sanctuaries have been found in recent years, and such a find is not expected. What remains of the places of cult at Sparta is usually the large deposits of characteristic votive offerings: miniature vases and terracotta plaques. A small deposit of miniature *lakainai* and kantharoid vases with the occasional lead wreath has been found at the S flank of the Acropolis [SITE 3],[8] though a large deposit of figurines and plaques has been excavated in the E part of the city, in the area of the ancient *kome* of Limnai, some 200 metres NW of the Sanctuary of Artemis Orthia [SITE 4].[9] Another small cult place has been excavated S of Toumbano, on the N side of the hill [SITE 5]. This must be related to a small archaic and classical cemetery, with a two-storey simple tomb, where some sort of worship was offered, and should therefore be considered a *heroon*.[10] The actual context of another deposit with figurines and plaques is not clear, but the presence of moulds points to a workshop, rather than to the shrine itself [SITE 6].[11] This of course poses many more intriguing questions about manufacturing activity in Laconia and the presence of *perioikoi* within Sparta and the *politike chora*.

III DOMESTIC ARCHITECTURE

Domestic remains at Sparta were found through the whole area that we excavated, but unfortunately, they are so fragmentary that it is not possible to make out the plans of the houses. It is clear though, that in Classical and Hellenistic times there was no regular town-plan, just like Athens, Argos, Eretria and all other mainland archaic cities. At Sparta the first attempt at regularisation dates to the Roman Imperial period. Hellenistic layers are quite rich, but even those are destroyed by later building activity. Mosaic pavements and the occasional wall painting [SITE 7] (FIG. 12.4)[12] remain the most solid evidence of domestic architecture available to date.

Fig. 12.4 Wall painting at Gitiadas St. [SITE 7].

All the mosaics uncovered at Sparta till now, even of Hellenistic date, have been tessellated ones. Recently we found the first pebble mosaic, dating to the third century BC [SITE 8].[13] It has been only partially cleaned and therefore its size and shape are unknown: it consists of a series of concentric simple bands, a composition which is typical of pebble mosaics elsewhere in Greece. One of the outer bands is decorated with wave pattern made of black pebbles, though one of the central bands had stylized vegetal decoration. However, it is not possible to reconstruct the plan of the house (FIG. 12.5).

Roman houses in Sparta were large, impressive mansions, urban *domus* in every sense. They sometimes became large complexes with gardens and private baths. They can be divided in two different chronological groups; the earlier ones are dated to the

7. Mercantile activity has been detected in the area north of the trefoil structure in rescue excavations that took part in the past. There may be an urban market, but the architectural remains uncovered are not explicit enough for restoring any building. Possible site of the Makellon?: cf Varro, De Lingua Latina V, 146.

8. Polychronakos field. For another votive deposit SW of part of the Acropolis, at Bilidas field, see Th. Spyropoulos, Deltion 37 B (1982) 112.

9. This deposit, found at Stauffert St., between bb 97 and 98, is currently under study by my colleague Chr. Flouris, who is preparing a PhD thesis on this subject for the University of Naples.

10. Zaimis plot, bb 117 A: see infra.

11. Theodoropoulos-Liokaftos plot, bb 120 A: Deltion 47 B (1992) forthcoming.

12. This Hellenistic wall-painting was found at Gitiadas St., south of bb 104. There are further wall-paintings that should be dated to the Roman period.

13. Triakosion St., south of bb 113.

Fig. 12.5 (above left) *Pebble mosaic at Triakosion St. [SITE 8].*

Fig. 12.6 (left) *Detail of the mosaic at Triakosion St. [SITE 9].*

Fig. 12.7 (opposite above) *Mosaic at Agidos St., [SITE 10].*

Fig. 12.8 (opposite) *Mosaic at Herakleidon St. [SITE 11].*

first-second century AD, just after the foundation of the Roman city and the establishment of a regular town-plan, but most of the mosaics excavated in the past four years belong to a local workshop, (currently studied by Anastasia Panayotopoulou, cf. her paper in this volume) and are dated to the second half of the third and the beginning of the fourth century AD. External walls were built of stones and strong mortar, but, because we have not located any staircases, it seems likely that there was no upper floor; houses could expand at ground level, as there was plenty of land available within the area of the new town-plan for the city. Internal walls were of mudbrick, sometimes decorated with wallpaintings or even marble revetment. The general layout of these *domus* and their average size remain unknown. Polychrome mosaic decoration is usual in reception rooms, but sometimes there are further tessellated pavements within the same house.

A fragmentary mosaic, which presumably decorated a secondary room of the *domus*, has been found in the N part of the modern city [SITE 9] (FIG. 12.6).[14] The central panel has not been preserved, but the marble revetment on the walls points to the presence of water: it might have been a courtyard. This floor has a panel with tangent *peltae*, and two symmetrical side panels with a polychrome chessboard pattern, together with particolour scales. The central part, now lost, is surrounded by a guilloche mat. On the plot just S of this spot, an important mosaic was uncovered several years ago, but it dates to the fourth century AD, and although may belong to the same structure, it is not clear whether both pavements were in use at the same time.[15]

The richest decoration was always reserved for the *triclinium*, a room where symposia took place. *Triclinia* are distinguished by the characteristic layout of the pavement, related to its function, and the arrangement of couches. There is a centrepiece with complicated decorative and figural representations, surrounded by a frame of decorative patterns.

A most impressive mosaic belongs to a *triclinium* and bears a grid with geometric patterns surrounding

---

14. Triakosion St., between bb 126-136.

15. Alikakos plot (bb 1”6): G. Steinhauer, Deltion 30 B (1975) 74-76. The room with the mosaic of the zodiac circle has an apse and a built-in fountain.

Fig. 12.9 (left) *Mosaic at Lycourgou St. [SITE 12].*

Fig. 12.10 (below) *Plan of the atrium at Lycourgou St. [SITE 12].*

a magnificent representation of Dionysus Nimbeatus[16] [SITE 10] (FIG. 12.7). This central grid is framed by a garland of laurel leaves and rectangular panels decorated with tangent four- and eight-pointed stars. The figurative centrepiece of Dionysus with a Satyr and a half-naked Maenad must depend on a Hellenistic painting, as the representation is an artistic comment on human nature: the dark, manly body of the Satyr contrasts vividly with the soft, bright appearance of the god, and the feminine elegance of the Maenad. The aesthetic quality of the average Spartan mosaic is not impressive, so that examples like this one, despite the occasional clumsy details, are to be warmly welcomed. Next to this room another mosaic with geometric decoration has been partly cleared. It presumably belongs to the same *domus*, although the room seems too big for a courtyard and no *impluvium* has been found.

Another richly decorated *triclinium* has been excavated some 100 metres N of the previous one, near the so-called tomb of Leonidas. Interestingly enough this has another Dionysiac subject as centrepiece [SITE 11] (FIG. 12.8). Judging from the scarcity of the subject among Spartan mosaics, and the vicinity of the two mansions, the respective *domus* owners might have been rivals. These mosaics also indicate how important private patronage must have been in the competitive society of Roman Sparta, and the degree this (and its implicit social conflict) influenced the local workshop. Moreover, this pavement derives directly from an earlier, somewhat larger and rather more complicated floor that was excavated at Korone, now kept in the Museum of Kalamata.[17] The central panel, in 'vault design', bears a circular roundel with the representation of Drunken Dionysus supported by a Satyr, and accompanied by a Maenad and a goat. Other compartments of the 'vault design' are decorated with wild cats and kantharoi. The whole central panel is surrounded by a zone of rectangular and square panels decorated with theatrical masks, pairs of birds, various table animals, a roast pig, fish and fruit. The frame consists of geometric patterns: tangent four- and eight-pointed stars.

Atria decorated with mosaic pavements are not unusual at Sparta. They are characterised by the shallow pool in the centre, and sometimes by marble revetment on the walls. They seem to have occupied a position at the periphery of the layout of the urban *domus*. As there are no water containers under the courtyard, these houses must be considered 'compluviate', althought the basins are usually called *impluvia*.

Under Lycourgou St., just N of the central square of the modern city, have been found parts of two mosaic pavements [SITE 12] (FIGS. 12.9–10).[18] The one uncovered in its entirety covers the floor of an atrium, badly damaged by modern public works. It has, quite appropriately, a frieze of sea animals and fish around

Fig. 12.11 Mosaic at Dorieon St. [SITE 13].

the central pool. The rest of the decoration consists of intersecting circles that form saltires and a zone decorated with a vegetal scroll. The second mosaic was partially excavated and might have belonged to a *triclinium*. These are the most southerly mosaics discovered to date, and it therefore seems that this large *domus* stood near the limit of the Roman town-grid.

The *impluvium* of another, quite large atrium was reveted with marble slabs, while the mosaic is rather simple, with intersecting circles and a four-strand guilloche [SITE 13] (FIG. 12.11).[19] Both the NW and SW walls that have been cleared are very strong structures and must have been the external walls, implying that this was the edge of the *domus*: here too the courtyard was not centrally placed within the house. On the NE side of the atrium, a series of large slabs has been

16. Found at Agidos Str. between bb 9 and 16.

17. M. N. Valmin, The Swedish Messenia Expedition III (1938) 469-75.

18. Found at Lycourgou St., south of bb 37.

19. Dorieon St., between bb 118 and 120.

Fig. 12.12 (left) *Plan of the mosaic garden at Chamaretou St.* [*SITE 14*]

Fig. 12.13 (below left) *Mosaic at Chamaretou St.* [*SITE 14*]

uncovered, showing the side of the *triclinium* or an *exedra*, although nothing was found in the trial trenches dug there.

In another case, a room decorated with mosaics had a unique and most unusual layout with a quite original decoration [SITE 14] (FIGS. 12.12–13).[20] It was found partly destroyed, so it is not easy to deduce its position within the *domus*, although there is negative evidence that this too was near the edge of the building. Nevertheless, it is clear that this courtyard, instead of serving as an atrium, had been converted into a miniature garden. The layout of a channel with cut-away corners occurs in some other large gardens found at

20 . Chamaretou St., between bb 41 and 46.

Sparta and elsewhere. However, the owner here presumably tried to substitute luxury for size, covering all the room with mosaics. In the centre of the room covered with intersecting circles there is an octagonal raised structure decorated with a polychrome guilloche mat, dolphins and sea-monsters surrounded by a flower-bed and a low wall, which forms an irregular octagon with concave corners. The quadrants formed by the cut-away corners are decorated with gorgoneia. It is possible that at the centre of the elevated octagon there was a small water fountain.

Parts of several ancient gardens have been excavated in modern plots. A larger, presumably public garden was found SE of the Baths,[21] and might have been the garden of the baths themselves [SITE 15]. It was walled, decorated with low tower-like structures, bearing small shallow quatrefoil basins, which were furnished with water from spouts above the wall and which conducted this water eventually to a large water channel running all along the wall.

Numismatic evidence shows that some of these Roman buildings were in use throughout the fourth century AD. All the late mosaic pavements were covered with a characteristic fill of red earth, which presumably came from the demolition of the walls, with a small amount of pottery, and only some of the tiles from the roof above the pavement. This suggests, I would think, desertion of the building and gradual destruction.

IV TOMBS AND BURIAL CUSTOMS

Tombs and burial customs have always been considered an important part of our understanding of ancient Greek beliefs about death and the afterlife. Nowadays they are increasingly used to argue about both religious practice and social structure. Sparta, however, forms a conspicious gap in the available evidence of Greek funerary customs. Although there is some textual evidence,[22] actual finds do not corroborate or contradict the texts. Very few graves have been excavated at Sparta, and as they are not always published, the number of known examples is surprisingly low. It is possible that burial practices in the area are not archaeologically detectable, or rather, may not be easily detectable. Over the past four years (1991–95) a series of burials have been excavated, enriching considerably our knowledge regarding Spartan customs. Still, the number of cases is very small to allow for comments about social differentiation.

The earliest known burials are a series in which the body lay in a contracted position, found in the area of Limnai, where most of the early finds seem to concentrate. The body is carefully placed, with a stone as pillow, and other smaller stones around the body, laid in the shape of an arc [SITE 16] (FIG. 12.14). There are four of them known, all of them found on natural bedrock and covered by layers rich in Protogeometric pottery. Three of these tombs were found together,

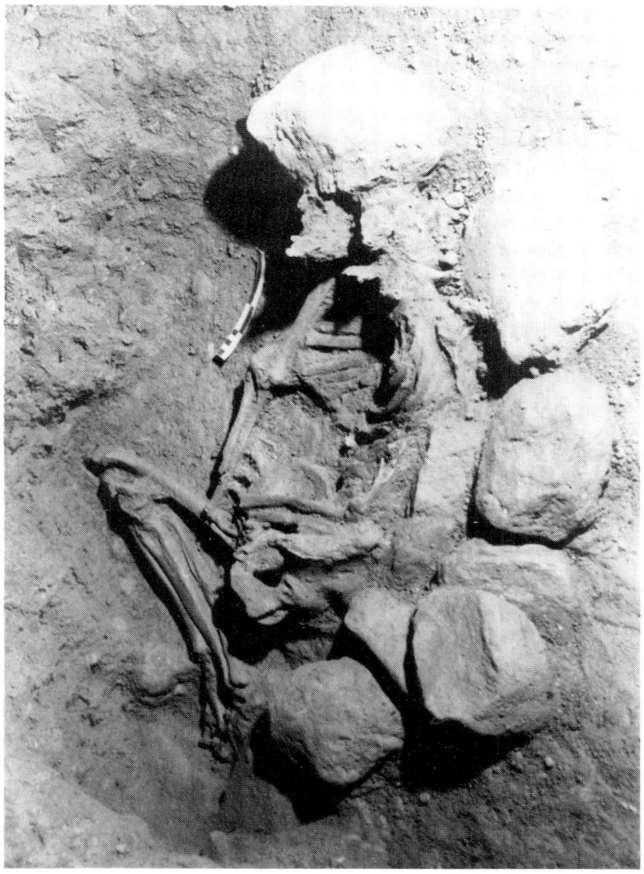

Fig. 12.14 Burial in contracted position [SITE 16].

and must have formed a small family cemetery, for between them stray bones were found as well, belonging presumably to a secondary burial.[23]

To the late Geometric period belong two *pithos* burials with rich metal offerings. A male burial with iron weapons (a sword and daggers) and bronze ornaments was found at Limnai[24] [SITE 17] (FIG. 12.15), though a similar female burial was excavated S of the Acropolis, bearing a large number of bronze cylinders and spiral rings, that might have been used as hair ornaments [SITE 18] (FIG. 12.16). No skeletal remains were recovered, nor was there any sign of fire, so we can plausibly infer that these burials were inhumations.[25] *Pithos* burials went on, as is shown by the

21. Found at Triakosion St., between bb 126 and 136.

22. For a comprehensive survey of the testimonia see P. Cartledge, Agesilaos (1987) 331-343.

23. Another contracted burial has been found near the bank of Evrotas: G. Steinhauer, Deltion 27 B (1972) 245.

24. Another pithos burial has been found at the above mentioned trench, near the bank of Evrotas: G. Steinhauer, Deltion 27 B (1972) 244.

25. See Acts of the 5th International Congress for the Peloponnese (Nafplion 1995), forthcoming.

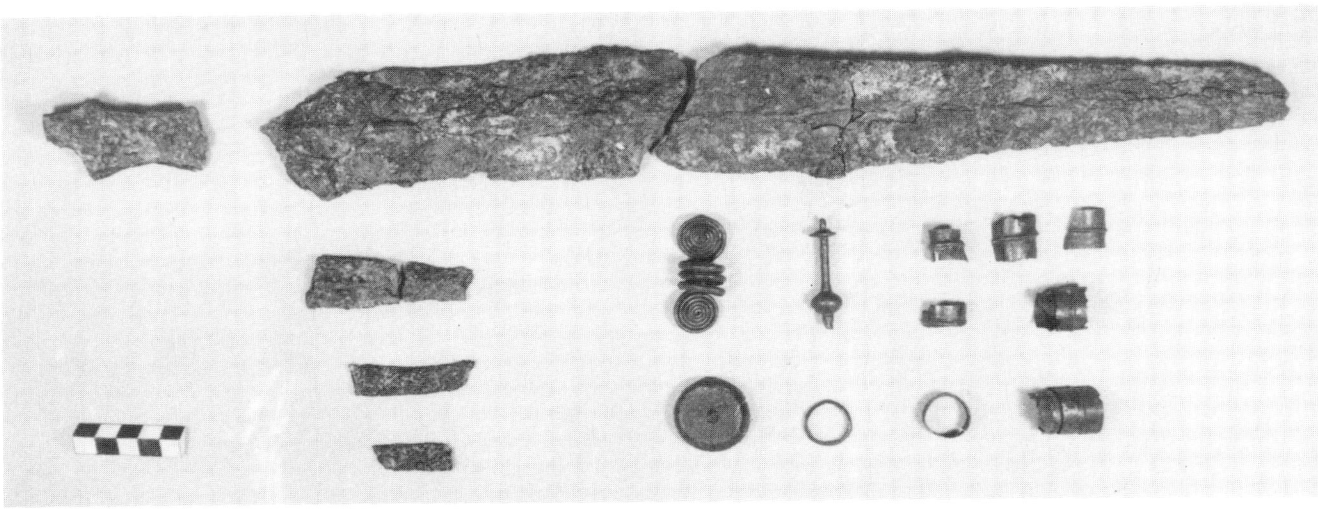

Fig. 12.15 (top) *Burial offerings of Orthias Artemidos St. [SITE 17].*

Fig. 12.16 (above) *Pithos burial at Leonidou St. [SITE 18].*

Fig. 12.17 (above right) *Marble door of monumental tomb.*

presence of the well known archaic relief *pithoi* that have been found bearing decoration on the side visible above ground only.[26]

Typical of Sparta are two-storey tombs, the lower part of which was used for the primary burial and the upper for gathering the bones of earlier burials together with the old offerings. This type of tomb explains the impression Pausanias gained when wandering around, that the city of Sparta was full of *heroa*. Two-storey tombs continued into Hellenistic times, and to this period belong a few monumental tombs of white marble. These were decorated with doors of the type known from Macedonian tombs, imitating real wooden doors and usually made of *rosso antico*, with the characteristic details of bosses and handles rendered in relief (FIG. 12.17).[27]

To the archaic period, and more specifically the first decades of the sixth century BC, belongs a simple two-storey tomb, which later became apparently the SITE of some sort of worship.[28] This cemetery, located near a ravine and at the lower slopes of the Hill, continued in use until the Roman period [SITE 5]. The archaic tomb stood above ground, with an opening uphill on the S side. There were extensive works around it, in an attempt to control water that went

26. Ch. Christou, Deltion 19 A (1964) 123-163.

27. For a fine Macedonian example of such a door see K. Sismanidis, Athens Annals of Archaeology 15 (1982) 275-9.

28. Zaimis plot (1993), bb 117A.

down the hill, towards the ravine. A large channel seems to have been built in late classical times; immediately around the tomb a system of channels made of narrow 'laconian' roof tiles, led rain water away (FIG. 12.18). On one of these tiles a large offering had been deposited: twenty-two complete laconian vases were carefully deposited, after being intentionally pierced, actually 'cancelled', in order not to be used again. The vases comprise one *oenochoe*, five *lakainai*, two cups, seven deep plates, one shallow dish, one baby-feeder, and four salt bowls (FIG. 12.19). It presumably consists of the service used at a funerary symposium for seven, in honour of the dead, and it was ritually deposited next to his tomb. This important pottery group was preserved because at some point after the deposition, the course of the S channel changed, leading water directly to the ravine and the street that run along it.

In the same cemetery, a group of simple burials without offerings was found, covered with fill of late

Fig. 12.18 (above) *Two-storey tomb of Zaimis St. [SITE 5].*

Fig. 12.19 (right) *The Laconian archaic vases offered at the Heroon.*

Fig. 12.20 (below) *Burial receptacle in the shape of a Krater [SITE 21].*

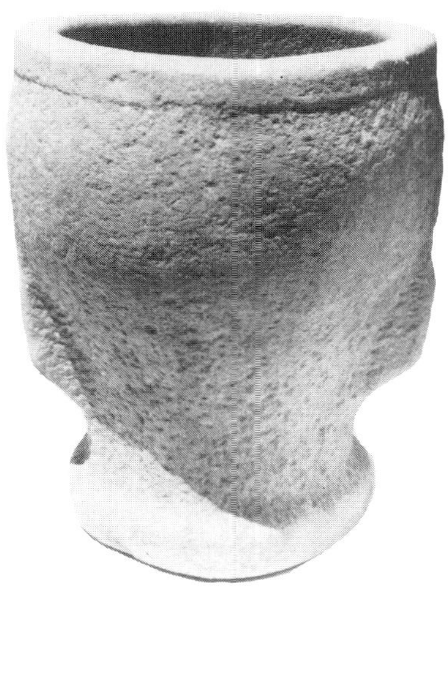

fifth-early fourth century BC. This layer can be used only as a *terminus ante quem* for the burials, and the lack of offerings deprives us of any more reliable and specific dating. In the law code of Lycourgos there is an explicit phrase that prohibits named funerary monuments, showing that at the end of the archaic period there must have been no monumental burial structures. Tomb-stones and monuments are always erected in order to commemorate the dead and preserve the memory of the individual, by demonstrating at the same time the wealth and importance of his family to the passers-by. At Sparta, however, there is a marked desire to allow no individualisation either of citizens (*homoioi*), or of the dead. Although there is no direct evidence, it is reasonable to consider that during the period of the Lycurgan so-called 'austerity', burials always took place within the city. Some of these tombs were excavated in 1907 by the British School, and were recently rediscovered [SITE 19].[29] Another two were excavated in the same area, and one of them was found unlooted. This did not have a burial in the lower chamber, but preserved a rich group of plain hellenistic pottery on the upper floor [SITE 20].[30]

Krater-like stone receptacles are found at Sparta containing burials (FIG. 12.20). Whether they stood above ground or not is not certain. In one case found *in situ*, an upturned Doric capital was used as a lid, a solution which could not be considered elegant enough to be conspicious [SITE 21]. In the krater was placed a lead pyxis containing the ashes of the deceased. Simpler urns with lids are found together with the kraters. Funerary reliefs with figurative representations and inscriptions, quite typical elsewhere in Greece, are very unusual at Sparta. We have recovered only a few of them, in a fragmentary state; we should keep, however, in mind the possibility that the *anthemia* reliefs had funerary use.[31]

In the Roman period, when the city was properly laid out, the first systematic cemeteries appear outside the town, although there is still the occasional individual and isolated burial *intra muros*. The South Cemetery, recently found at the SW part of the modern town, beside the river Magoulitsa [SITE 22] (FIG. 12.21), was in use from the second century BC to the fifth century AD.[32] It is hoped that a detailed study of the Hellenistic pottery will give us reliable chronological clues for the construction of the fortification wall, as there are no domestic finds in the area. The Cemetery follows the bank of Magoulitsa (Knakion) and has been partly uncovered for a total length of more than 500 m. Most of the tombs are simple, built of bricks and *opus caementicium*. There are some graves made in simple oval depressions dug in the bedrock, covered with tiles. There are a few tombs dug in the ground and plastered with clay, which may belong to the earliest use of the area, but unfortunately there were no offerings to date them. The most important tombs in these cemeteries are two built free-standing burial chambers, probably small family *mausolea*. The larger one, which stood on a small eminence of the natural bedrock, has eight or nine cist graves, built in the wall of the structure and presumably covered with arches, with the shape of typical there were no individual burials in the city and the dead were deposited at the Apothetai, the well known Kaiadas and other caves with precipices on mount Taygetos.

In the area around the tomb of Leonidas an extensive Hellenistic cemetery is under excavation. It presumably predates the institution of the Roman grid, and its tombs were found enclosed among later domestic structures, giving the impression that *arcosolia*. There is a second family tomb, smaller in size, with six tombs underground and three larger ones at the sides of the structures. This was decorated with marble slabs and bore inscriptions, which must have been placed on the facade of the building, or inside the tomb, on the visible side of the tomb. The Northern Cemetery located near the third river of the area, Mousga, has tombs that date to the Roman period (second and third century AD), and have preserved most interestingly wall paintings with the representation of Apollo Lykeios and the Muses.[33] Two isolated family tombs, larger than the above mentioned, containing marble sarcophagi, have been found on the periphery of Sparta, perhaps near or within the family estate.[34]

Funerary customs at Sparta seem to have been quite regular, with some local peculiarities, like the use of stone kraters and the *anthemia* reliefs; these show the expected regional differentiation. There is a sense of continuity, especially in the tradition of two-storey tombs, from the Archaic to Hellenistic periods, despite the possible 'austerity' gap in Classical times.The most intriguing feature is the refusal to commemorate the dead by name, although veneration and worship of the ancestors is textually attested and confirmed by our finds. In Roman times, Sparta became a typical provincial city, so that burial customs conform to the norm of the average town within the Empire, to the extent that we cannot distinguish Sparta from many other cities of the Empire.

Finally, we can conclude, in the light of recent excavations, that the earlier settlement of Classical Sparta was in the area E of the Acropolis, which was later called Limnai, where rich Protogeometric and Geometric layers, together with parts of the respective cemeteries have been excavated. In the Geometric period the settlement expanded to the S of the

29. The tombs excavated by the British School in 1907 (A. J. B. Wace-G. Dickins "The Tombs" BSA 1907-8, 155-168) were relocated at bb 124, Orphanos plot. From such a tomb comes a fragment bearing an inscription, published by G. Steinhauer, "An Illyrian Mercenary in Sparta under Nabis" in J. Motyka-Sanders (ed) Philolakon, Lakonian studies presented to Hector Catling (1992) 239-245.

30. Triakosion St., near the corner with Agidos St., bb 125.

31. H. Moebius, Die ornamente der griechischen Grabstelen klassischer und nachklassischer Zeit (1968) 74-79; A. Delivorias, in Palagia and Coulson (eds) Sculpture from Arcadia and Laconia (1992), 205-216.

32. Mavridis plot (1994-5), bb 146.

33. A. Adamantiou, Praktika 1931, 91-96; idem, Praktika 1934, 123-128.

34. Tomb at Magoula: Th. Spyropoulos, Deltion 38 B (1983) 94; tomb at Aphissou: Ch. Christou, Praktika 1963, 130-6.

Fig. 12.21 Plan of the Roman South Cemetery at Mavridis Plot [SITE 22].

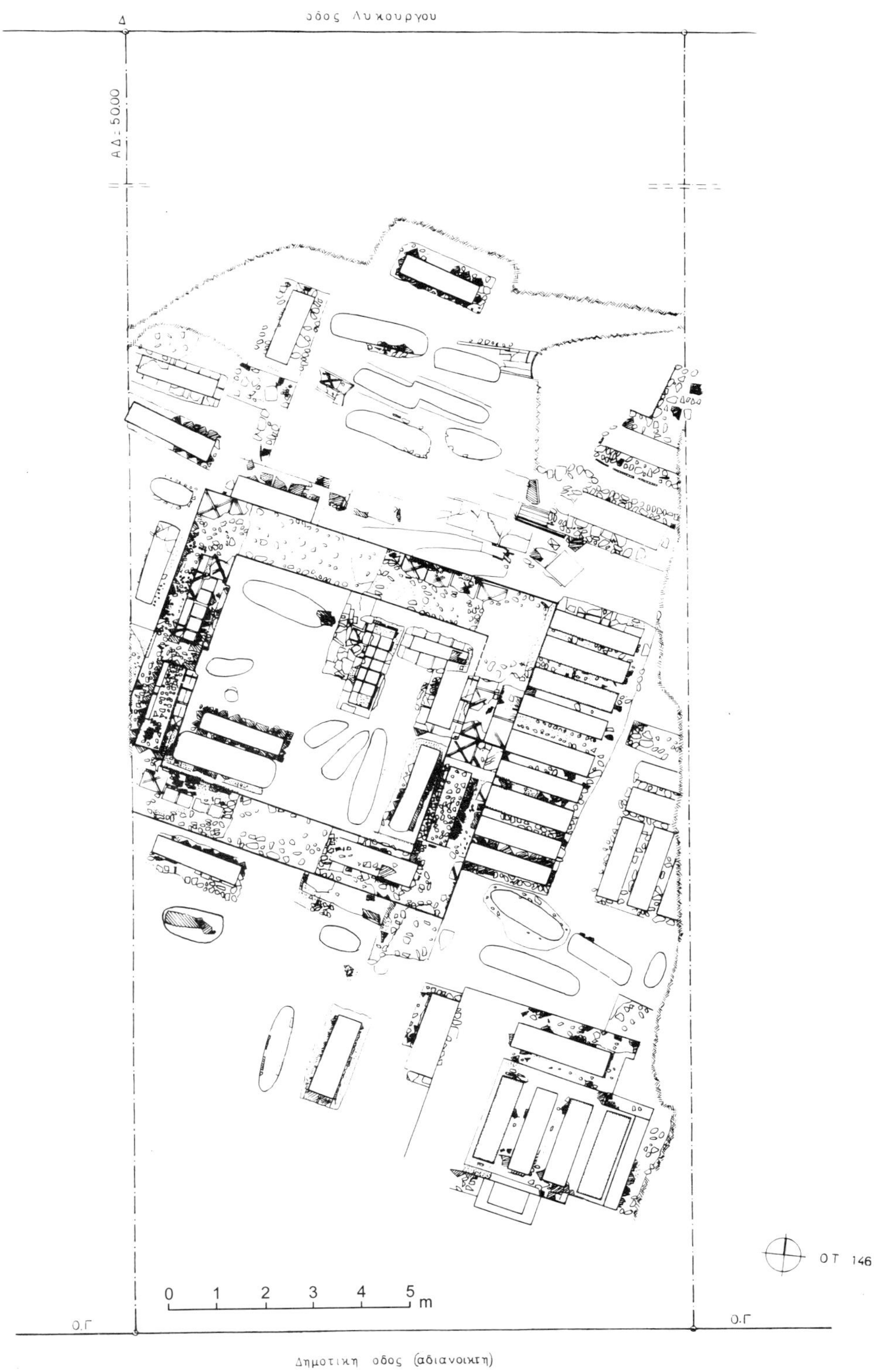

Acropolis, where an important lady was buried in a large *pithos*. Finds from the archaic period are scattered all over the N part of the modern city, though there are very few well dated classical finds. From the Hellenistic period date a series of burials concentrated in small cemeteries, though contemporary domestic layers come from most of the inhabited area including all the hills. The Roman city was a large and prosperous one, with public buildings gathered on the hill of the Acropolis, a regular grid town-plan to the SW of them and in the neighbourhood of Limnai, where villas and factories followed the earlier irregular layout. Roman cemeteries were large and fairly systematically organised outside of the Hellenistic and, by that time, disused fortification wall (FIGS. 12.22–23).

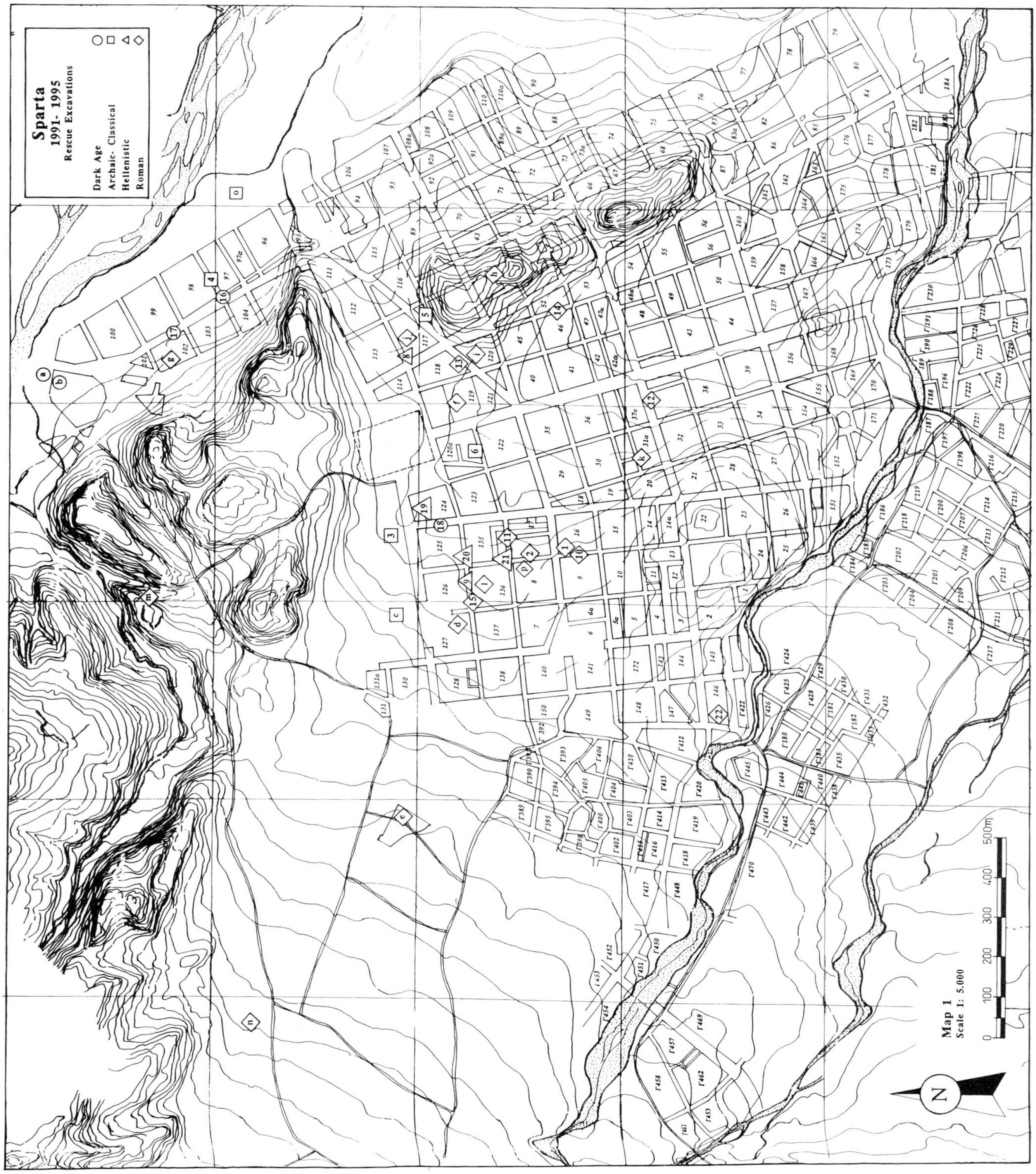

Fig. 12.22 Map of the area enclosed in the Hellenistic circuit wall of Sparta, together with the ancient sites, the modern building blocks and street network.

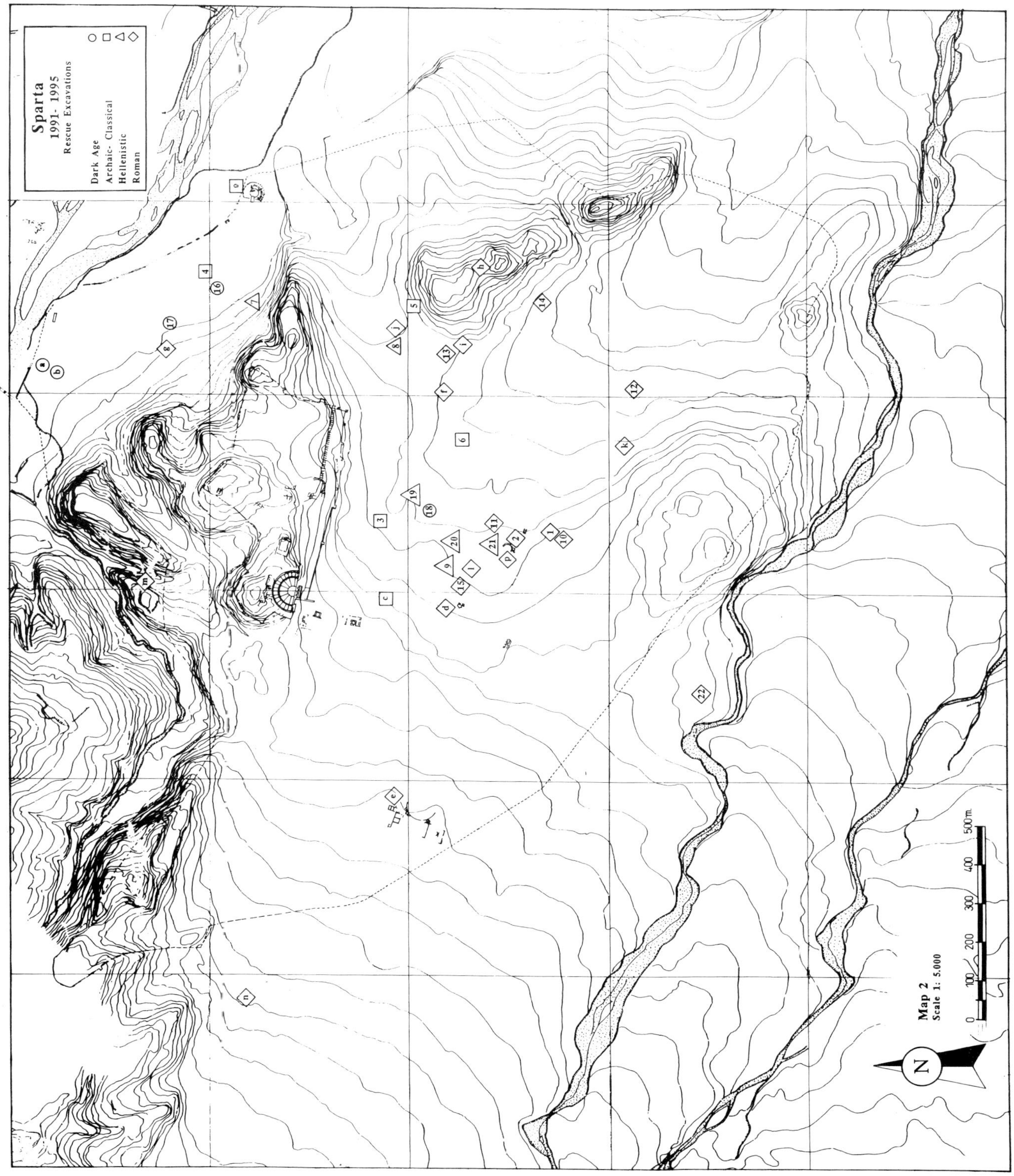

Fig. 12.23 Map of the area enclosed in the Hellenistic circuit wall of Sparta, together with the ancient sites marked by date.

130 years have passed since the pioneer of the Greek Archaeological Service Panagiotis Stamatakis, a Laconian by birth, was sent to Sparta to gather the first finds that formed the nucleus of the local Archaeological Museum,[35] and some 90 years since the British School started excavating different sites at Sparta. Nevertheless, the confidence expressed in 1906 by G. Dickins[36] that the BSA's 'future' excavations would solve the controversial questions of Spartan topography has not yet been justified. There is a lot of work ahead, both on the Acropolis and in the lower city, and the collaboration of many scholars[37], and of different specialists is necessary to manage the task.

ACKNOWLEDGMENTS

I should thank several people for supporting me during that period and advising me about the antiquities at Sparta. Most of the colleagues that worked there before me were most helpful, but I should particularly aknowledge Dr G. Steinhauer, A. Panagiotopoulou and E. Kourinou, who always answered my questions, however stupid they sounded. They all three taught me a lot. The mistakes and misunderstandings that remain are mine. I must also thank T. G. Spyropoulos, present Director of the 5th Ephorate for Prehistoric and Classical Antiquities, for the years of truly unforgettable experiences that he has bestowed upon all who have passed through the Ephoreia of Sparti.

---

35. B. Ch. Petrakos, Lakonikai Spoudai 11, Festschrift Vagiakakos (1992) 642-50; G.S. Korres, Epistimoniki Epetiris Filosofikis Scholis Panepistimiou Athinon (1992-1995) 495-508.

36. G. Dickins, "Topographical Conclusions", BSA 1905-6, 431-439.

37. The former Ephor of Sparta, Dr G. Steinhauer, is currently preparing a study on the Roman town-plan, while E. Kourinou is reading for a PhD at the University of Athens with the subject of the urban topography of Sparta.

13

Diversity in a Greek landscape: the Laconia Survey and Rural Sites Project

C. B. Mee and W. G. Cavanagh

INTRODUCTION

The important excavations at Sparta and other major centres of Laconia such as Mistra, Geraki, the Menelaion, Ayios Stephanos and Pellanes, have been illustrated and underlined in the papers presented at this conference. It is our purpose, however, to focus attention on the more modest archaeology of the Laconian countryside. Laconia was and is an agricultural province, and whilst, particularly in the Classical, Roman Imperial and Palaeologue periods, resources from without helped transform the cities, nevertheless the relationship of city and surrounding countryside is important for our understanding of the economy and history of both capital and province.

THE TRADITION OF ARCHAEOLOGICAL SURVEY IN LACONIA

The results of the Laconia Survey are now available in detail (Cavanagh *et al.* 1996) and it is not our purpose to recapitulate the Survey's findings here. Rather we wish to place the project within a broader strategy of investigation and say something of the Laconia Rural Sites Project which has grown out of the initial survey. Indeed a major advantage of the British School at Athens' historic connection with Sparta and Laconia has been the long perspective in research, allowing us to shape a strategy informed by tradition as well as responsive to advances in scholarship.

Of course the study of Laconia's topography goes back to the origins of Greek archaeology with a long line of research stretching from Cyriac of Ancona (Sabbadini 1910; Ashmole 1959), in the fifteenth century, through Fourmont (Omont 1902), Leake (1830, 1846; Wagstaff 1992), l'Expédition Scientifique de Morée (Blouet 1833, Boblaye, 1836), via Tsountas and Soteriadis (1910, 1911), Bölte (1929) to our colleagues in the Archaeological Service and Foreign Schools today, and this is to select almost at random from the constellation of international scholars who have worked on Laconia. An honourable place in this tradition can be claimed by the British School's early pioneers, preceding (Loring 1895) and following hard on Mackenzie's 'strikingly modern' exploration of Melos (Mackenzie 1897, quotation from Cherry 1994, 91): Dickins (1906c), Forster (1904a, 1907), Hasluck (Hasluck 1908), Hondius (1921), Ormerod (1910), Scutt (1913, 1914), Traquair (1906, 1907), Wace and Hasluck (1908, 1909), Woodward (1907), followed before and after World War II by the important surveys of Cook and Nicholls (1950), and by Waterhouse (Waterhouse 1956) and Hope Simpson (Waterhouse and Hope Simpson 1960, 1961; Hope Simpson 1966).

BACKGROUND TO THE RURAL SITES PROJECT—THE LACONIA SURVEY

One of the striking results of the 'first wave' (Cherry 1994) of archaeological survey in Greece has been the recognition not simply of alternating phases of settlement dispersion and settlement nucleation, so much as of fundamentally differing patterns of occupation in the various phases during the millennia investigated. In the Laconia Survey we can point to the absence of settlement in the Early and Middle Neolithic—there is no parallel in the survey area to match the important neolithic settlement at Kouphovouno (Renard 1989) on the other side of the Evrotas. It has recently been argued that spring-fed agriculture is a key to our understanding of the location of neolithic sites in Greece (van Andel and Runnels 1987; van Andel, Zangger and Demitrack 1990; van Andel and Runnels 1995), but there is certainly still much to be learnt before we can claim fully to understand the processes. In this case surely the next step will involve the excavation of a major Middle Neolithic site in southern Greece.

Not until the Late to Final Neolithic does there occur a colonisation of the LS area, but an unexpected one: the sites are located on or close to rather barren limestone outcrops, no neolithic site has been found in the area of richer agricultural land in the survey area. This is surely to be linked with the colonisation of the smaller Aegean islands (Cherry 1990) and the exploitation of caves, such a marked feature of the LN and FN in southern Greece (Diamant 1974; Phelps 1975; Halstead 1996; Sampson 1992).

In contrast the Early Bronze Age, and more specifically EH II, is marked by a much denser occupation,

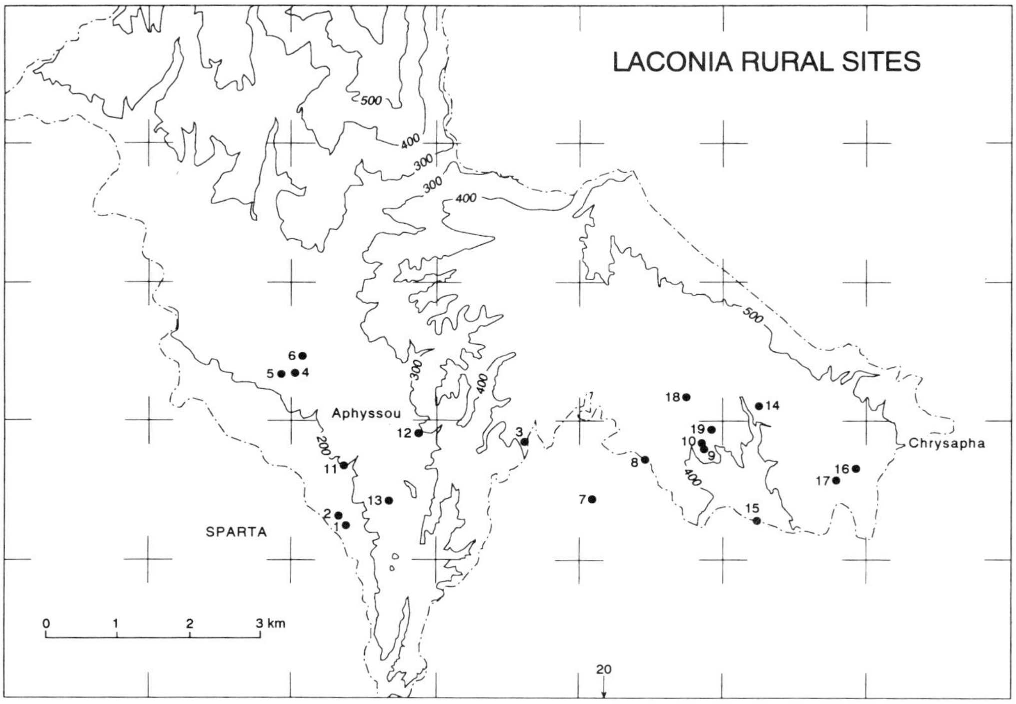

Fig. 13.1 Map of the S *sector of the LS area showing the twenty sites selected for the Laconia Rural Sites Project.*

especially in the more southerly tracts of the LS area (some of the sites in what are now the bad-lands E of the cliffs above Aphyssou, an area that may well have suffered serious erosion, no doubt during or at the end of the Early Bronze Age, as has been documented in other parts of Greece—see, for example, the discussion in James *et al.* 1994). In this period markedly different patterns of historical development and of settlement are being recognised in various parts of Greece thanks to recent surveys. The striking contrast between Keos, which shows effectively one EC II settlement dominating the N part of the island, and Melos with a scatter of small, dispersed, short-lived farmsteads, has recently been emphasised (Cherry *et al.* 1991 esp. 217–32). A comparable diversity is emerging from surveys on the mainland of Greece: the slow growth of settlement in the Southern Argolid through EH I and EH II might be contrasted with the sudden spurt in the LS area in EH II, also reported from the Nemea survey (Cherry *et al.* 1988: 175). Both regions differ from the sparsity of EH sites reported from Boeotia and the Attic/Boeotian border.

The Middle and Late Bronze Ages witnessed another re-mapping of settlement: the major site of the Menelaion dominates a distribution of sites which is very different from that of the previous millennium. The prominence of the Menelaion, set high on its ridge above the Evrotas, is echoed in the setting of second-order sites likewise positioned on ridges with precipitous cliffs; though other secondary sites sit lower in the more fertile valleys and basins. Once established, many of these sites persist for hundreds of years, reflecting a relative stability which is unexpected given the fundamental structural changes that these centuries saw (Cavanagh 1995).

After the gulf of the Greek Dark Age a new organisation slowly emerges. Initially we observe this not through the Dark Age farmsteads like that at Nichoria (McDonald *et al.* 1983), though contemporary villages existed across the Evrotas at Amyklai and Sparta, but through the cult sites of the Menelaion and Zeus Messapeus (Catling 1990). It is not until the sixth century that clear signs of the occupation of the landscape appear in the LS data, and by the fifth century BC the LS area shows that density of small sites which is so much a feature of the landscape witnessed through intensive survey elsewhere in Greece (Snodgrass 1987: 117–9; Bintliff and Snodgrass 1988; Cherry *et al.* 1991: 327–47; Jameson *et al.* 1995). The LS findings indicate that Sparta was evidently not immune to the general economic transformation which affected many other Classical states: another blow to the view that Classical Sparta was subject to an economic primitivism which isolated it from general trends. These observations take on even greater significance in the light of early results from the very important Pylos Regional Archaeological Project which suggest that this pattern of highly dispersed settlement in the Classical period is not to be found in Messenia. Something of the variety of sites from LS can be summarised: small towns such as Palaiogoulas (LS A118 probably the perioikic polis of Sellasia), the fort at Ayios Konstantinos (LS B111), sanctuaries such as that at Phagia (LS U3002), quarries (e.g. LS D50, E49), bridges (e.g. LS H46), cemeteries (e.g. LS A120). Nevertheless these are, to a degree, special cases, and the majority of sites have been characterised as small farmsteads or rural dwellings.

After a climax in the Classical–Early Hellenistic phases, the survey data witness a marked decline in the Late Hellenistic and Roman periods. No doubt the political history of Sparta had its effect: neither the fort at Ayios Konstantinos nor the town at Palaiogoulas survived into the first century BC ; it is not fanciful to see their desertion as a consequence of the Battle of Sellasia, and of Sparta's decline as an independent state. In the Roman period Palaiogoulas seems to have been replaced by two modest farmsteads (LS A100 and A101); indeed the area around is not richly endowed with agricultural land, and the nearest modern villages are some distance away. In the occupation of both village and fort we can see a statement of the Spartan state's strategic concerns; with her military might uprooted, both wither away.

At the same time the trend to fewer sites in the Late Hellenistic and Early Roman periods has been demonstrated elsewhere in Greece (the evidence is assembled in Alcock 1993: Chapter 2) we must seek an explanation in terms that are wider than Sparta's own political history. The sparsity of sites in the countryside must be real, but so unexpected that archaeologists have felt a nagging worry that there may be some contributory factor of a purely archaeological nature that we cannot properly explain (again see the discussion in Alcock 1993: esp. 49—55). Of Northern Keos 'it is worth stressing that closely datable pottery is especially rare in the Late Hellenistic and Early Roman periods (second century BC to third century AD).' (Cherry *et al.* 1991: 330). In the later Roman period small farmsteads once more fill the Greek countryside, though the LS area shows a less dense settlement than many other areas of Greece. These findings were unexpected and a closer examination of some of these small Roman sites is merited.

THE EVIDENCE OF SURFACE SURVEY

These comments are brief and superficial. Our intention is merely to advert to the issues of interpretation raised by survey evidence. Up to now this evidence has rested overwhelmingly on sherd densities and distributions, artefact typology and dating analysis; these tools have been used to estimate site size, site function and the period of occupation. Other types of evidence including geo-chemical (Bintliff *et al.* 1990; Buck *et al.* 1988; Cavanagh *et al.* 1988) and geophysical (Gaffney and Gaffney 1986; Papamarinopoulos, Jones and Gagalis 1990) have been used in combination with the artefact data, and part of our intention, in the Laconia Rural Sites Project has been further to explore these methods.

These data form the basis for our distribution maps, and are interpreted within a context of landscape history and historical ecology (Rackham 1983), to be understood in terms of our prior knowledge of the historical development of Laconia. Surface survey cannot claim the precision given to excavation through stratigraphy, large samples, precise context and environmental evidence, but its imprecision is balanced by gains from the regional scale of reference, the large numbers of sites sampled and the long time perspective.

RURAL SITES

Archaeological surveys have identified hundreds of rural sites in Greece. It is assumed that most were farmsteads (Cherry *et al.* 1991: 336–7; Jameson *et al.* 1994: 249–50; Snodgrass 1990: 125–6), but can we be certain that these sites were in fact occupied and were not simply shelters or storehouses? Were they occupied continuously or only when the agricultural cycle made residence in the countryside more convenient? Were they occupied by their owners, by tenants or by slaves (see inter alios Alcock 1993: 60–2; Alcock *et al.* 1994: 163; Cavanagh 1991: 113–4; Osborne 1992: 25; Snodgrass 1987: 117–8)?

Literary and Epigraphic Evidence

Texts and inscriptions provide some evidence for the function of rural sites in the Classical, Hellenistic and Roman periods. Greek writers were of course more interested in the city than the country. Statements about rural settlement only appear occasionally and can be ambiguous or even contradictory, as Osborne (1985: 119) has pointed out. Nevertheless, Roy (1996: 115–6) believes that Euripides' Electra and Menander's Dyskolos prove that there were isolated farmsteads in the countryside which were owned by free peasants. Yet we should not underestimate the degree of control which the rich will have exerted on the rural economy. Osborne (1992: 24) calculates that '7.5% or so of the population owned 30% of the cultivated land' in Attica, while Foxhall (1992: 157) reckons that 9% of the citizens controlled or owned 50% of the productive land.

It seems unlikely that Athens was atypical. Men of high status leased the temple estates on Delos, Rheneia and Mykonos in the Hellenistic period (Osborne 1985: 125). Since the leases officially ran for ten years but might be held for shorter periods, Osborne (1985: 125–6) does not believe that the lessees would have taken up residence but the slaves who constituted the labour force might have been based on these estates. For the Roman period, Foxhall (1990: 108–11) argues that rural sites identified as farms may have been leased by tenants. From the legal texts collected in the *Digest* it would appear that the landlord might provide expensive items of equipment—such as olive and wine presses, olive crushers, grain mills and pithoi—while the tenant supplied the

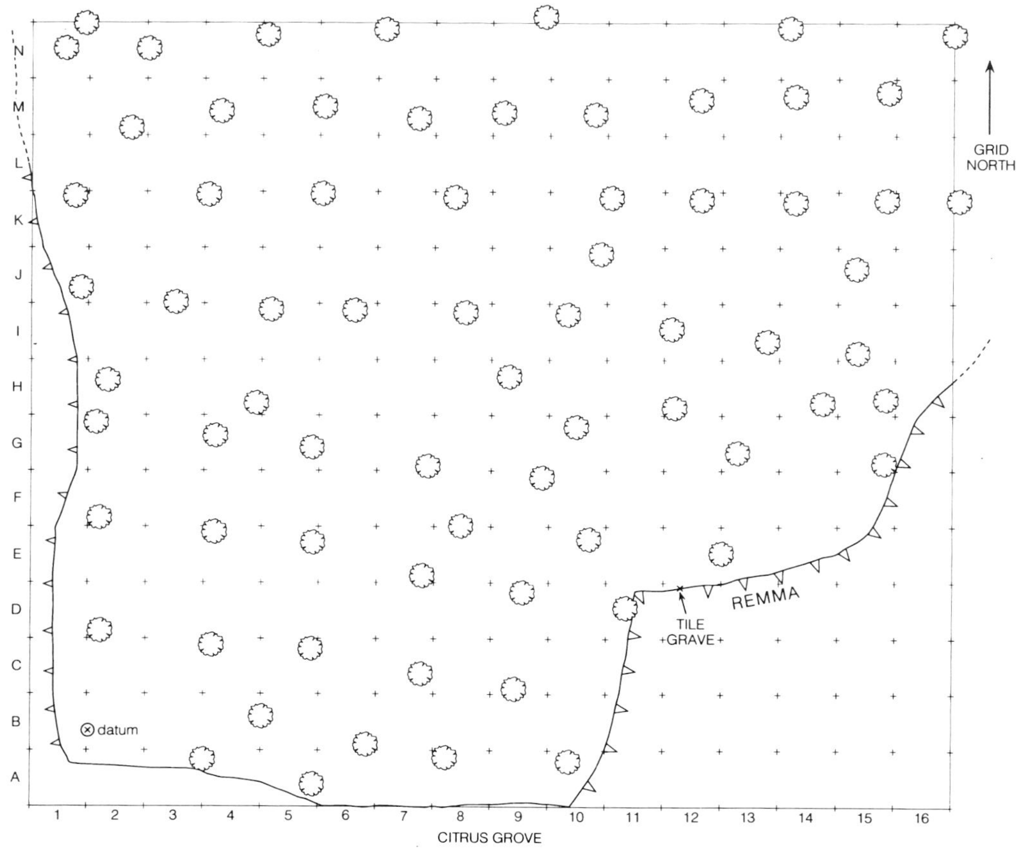

Fig. 13.2 Plan of site LP 1.

ephemera. Whether the lack of fine pottery on sites should be taken as an indication of the status of the occupants (Foxhall 1990: 109) is a moot point (Alcock 1993: 108–9). Nevertheless, it is clear that the presence of equipment which would have represented a major capital investment need not imply owner-occupiers.

Ethnographic Evidence

Whitelaw (1991 and 1994) has undertaken a detailed analysis of recent rural settlement and land use in NW Keos, based on documentary and statistical data, interviews and study of the field systems and structures. He concludes that there is a 'significant distinction between full farms, and limited activity locations and structures'—that is the *spitakia* used as storehouses, animal shelters and winepresses—'the limited function, dispersed facilities are usually the focus of a limited range of activities, leaving a limited and potentially distinctive range of debris, and also usually limited in terms of frequency and duration of use, leading to only minor accumulations of debris, usually below the recovery threshold of most surface surveys' (Whitelaw 1994: 169). He does not believe that a distinction can be made between those farmhouses which were occupied on a seasonal basis and those which were the main residence of the family concerned (Whitelaw 1991: 416–7 and 1994: 168–9).

Most of the rural structures on Keos were built in the later 19th and early 20th centuries, apparently as a result of land reforms in the period after the Greek War of Independence. The estates owned by the archons and monasteries were redistributed amongst the peasants who had farmed the land as share-croppers (Whitelaw 1991: 428–9 and 1994, 164–5). Formerly these peasants had commuted from the Chora but they must have felt that it would be beneficial if they had a base in the countryside and so in time settlement on Keos became less nucleated and more dispersed. 'Individual control over land and agricultural produce appears to have provided an increased incentive for capital and labour investment, which in turn facilitated more efficient exploitation of the landscape' (Whitelaw 1994: 164). Ownership spurred investment but it should be noted that the partible inheritance system had been modified on Keos so that land could be kept in consolidated blocks and not split up (Whitelaw 1991: 429).

Land Tenure and Rural Residence in Antiquity

In an economic system dependent on agriculture, the practice of partible inheritance, in which sons receive an equal share of the property, might seem irrational since farms should become progressively fragmented (Lane Fox 1985). However, as Forbes (1976: 240–7; 1989: 90–1) has demonstrated in his study of the Methana peninsula, scattered plots of land can minimise the risk of crop failure and may offer scope for diversification if they cover different ecological niches. There is some evidence that land was held in discrete plots in the Mycenaean period (Mee and Cavanagh 1990: 230) and Osborne (1987: 37–40) is sure that this was also the case in Classical Greece, even amongst the elite. It might be argued that rural residence would not make much sense unless the blocks of land were contiguous (Alcock *et al.* 1994: 147–8). But as Forbes (1995: 336–7) points out, rural sites on Methana were often situated at the interface between fertile soils and rocky slopes. It seems likely that the better land was used for the cultivation of cereals and olives while sheep and goats would have been pastured on the steep slopes. Even if these sites represent 'the nodal exploitation centres . . . of the estates of the wealthy' (Forbes 1995: 333) rather than farms which were owned by peasants, it is clear that their location would be energy efficient in mixed arable-pastoral agricultural regimes, whether intensive or extensive (Halstead 1987: 83).

It is not only the least effort principle which determines where individuals will live. As Osborne (1987: 54) has observed, 'social structure, economic factors, and political institutions react to and interact with the pattern and organization of settlement'. Nucleated settlement promotes integration and the development of communal ties and obligations which provide at least an illusion of security and other benefits (Alcock 1993: 105–7). Those who were resident in the country, whether through choice or necessity, would have had less political power than their urban compatriots.

We can assume that most Greeks lived in the city. It is reckoned that rural sites accounted for just 5% of the population of the southern Argolid in the Classical-Hellenistic period (Jameson *et al.* 1994: 553). The figure proposed for Boeotia is 25–30% (Bintliff 1991) and 25% for Keos (Cherry *et al.* 1991: 337), although Whitelaw (1994: 171–4) believes that this is an underestimate. Nevertheless, settlement in Greece could be classified as more or less nucleated, rather than nucleated or dispersed (Alcock 1993: 61).

LACONIA RURAL SITES PROJECT

The aim of this project has been to investigate the surface characteristics of rural sites as rigorously as possible and thereby resolve, or at least define, some of the questions about their function. In the first phase of the project in 1992, we revisited approximately sixty of the sites identified by the Laconia Survey. These were single period sites, most of which covered less than 2500 m^2. We then selected 20 which seemed suitable for intensive survey and analysis (FIG. 13.1). The range of periods represented is: Early Helladic (2), Middle/Late Helladic (2), Archaic (1), Classical (4), Hellenistic (3), Roman (6) and Byzantine (2). Twelve of the sites were examined in the summer of 1993, eight in 1994 and there was a study season in 1995.

The procedure adopted on each of the sites was as follows. A five-metre grid of squares was laid out across the whole of the site. The members of the survey team, spaced at 5 metre intervals, counted the number of artefacts and recorded surface visibility along transects which crossed the site and its periphery. This enabled us to identify peaks in artefact density and to decide how we would sample the site. Then every artefact was collected from each of the squares. Tile was sorted by type of decoration and thickness, the different categories were weighed and recorded, and the tile was discarded on site. Sherds, stone artefacts and other finds were taken back to our base to be cleaned, marked, drawn and recorded on our database for which we have used the SIR Relational DBMS. This enables us to generate density maps for the different types of artefact on each site so that we can see whether there is a correlation in, for instance, the distribution of sherd and tile.

In order to identify possible sub-surface features, Neil Brodie undertook a geophysical survey of every site. A Geoscan FM36 Fluxgate Gradiometer was used to detect local variations in the magnetic field. Readings were taken at 1 metre intervals in a series of 20 metre grids. Soil resistivity was measured on a Geoscan RM15 Resistance Meter with a twin probe array. The high temperatures did affect the instruments and the fact that the soil was so dry impeded the use of the resistivity meter in our second season. However, we took advantage of the much wetter conditions in the spring of 1995 to complete the programme of geophysical prospection, except for one site which had in fact been cut off by floods. The results are still being processed but Neil Brodie has identified features on over half of the sites.

The third element in our integrated analysis of each site has involved detailed soil studies under the direction of Peter James, assisted by Jamie Merrick. They have assessed the likely impact of past soil erosion and deposition, and soils have been sampled for analysis of selected elements and mineral magnetic properties. The aim of the analyses is to determine any spatial relationships between soil properties and artefacts, and to consider whether the present soil properties may reflect past human activities associated with each site. Soil samples were taken at a depth of 20 cm from the centre of each grid square or from the boundaries between grid lines. A note was made of the soil texture and colour, consistency, stone and root content, and the number of artefacts in the topsoil was recorded. In each of the grid squares sampled, the gradient and aspect of slope, surface soil characteristics, vegetation and soil cover were also measured. The elements chosen for analysis were phosphorus (P)

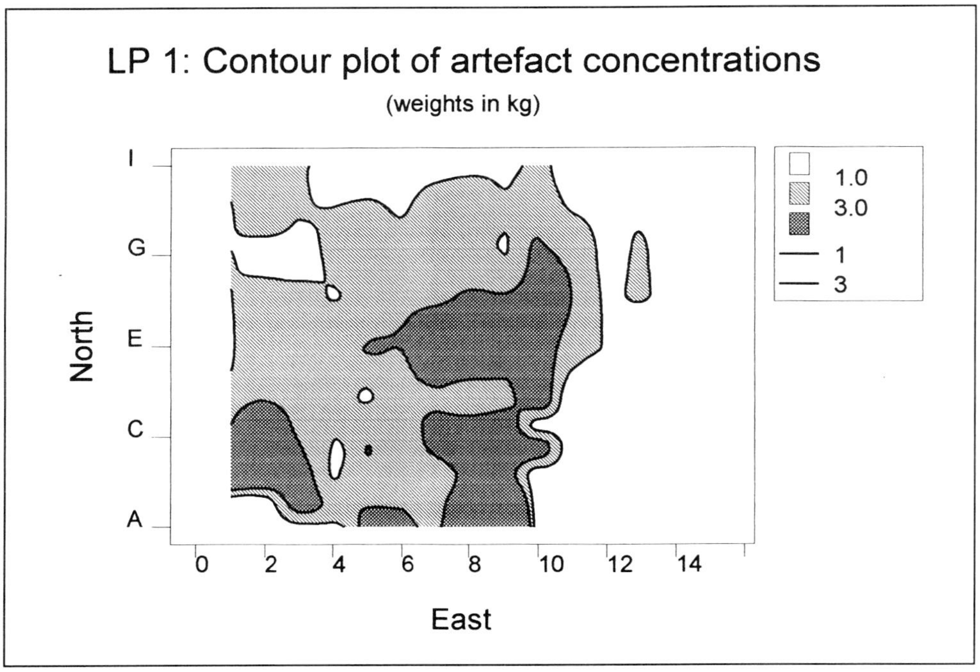

Fig. 13.3 Artefact densities on site LP 1

and four trace metals, lead (Pb), copper (Cu), zinc (Zn) and nickel (Ni). These, and a number of other elements, have been shown to occur in archaeological soils in the Old and New worlds at concentrations above those off-site. P, Pb, Cu and Zn are associated with archaeological sites in Greece (Bintliff *et al.* 1990; Buck *et al.* 1988; James *et al.* 1997). Ni was chosen for analysis as an element which does not have any obvious link with pre-industrial human activity. The total amount of each element was determined by nitric and perchloric acid digestion and atomic absorption spectrophotometry. Low frequency magnetic susceptibility (χ^{lf}) (Thompson and Oldfield 1986) has been measured in the laboratory and along selected transects in the field by 'F probe' at 20 cm depth and on the ground surface. A comprehensive range of soil magnetic properties will be measured for some of the sites.

It is through the integration of these different approaches that we hope to understand how these rural sites functioned. As the analysis of the data is still in progress this is obviously not the moment for definitive statements, but we can offer some comments based on the results from LP1.

LRSP Site 1

The site (FIG. 13.2) is in an olive grove, just E of the Eurotas. We sampled 99 squares *in toto* and so this was one of the largest sites surveyed. There is a Roman tile grave exposed in the remma which cuts across the E side of the site.

Artefact density peaks at three points (FIG. 13.3). Square A10 stands out in a cluster which also includes A9, B9–10 and C9–10. B2–4 and C3 represent a second cluster, while the third occupies squares E8–11 and F9–11. It was in these clusters that the highest numbers of sherds were recorded, so there is a close, if not exact, correlation between the pottery and tile distributions. The roof tile was unpainted and weighed 181.85 kg. At 36 kg of tile per square meter of roof, a figure which we have calculated from complete tiles, this would have covered approximately 5.1 m^2. There were also 47.85 kilos of brick and floor tile, concentrated in squares B2, B10, C3, C10 and E8.

A high proportion of the pottery from LP1, possibly as much as 90%, is closed. There were pithos sherds, especially in the squares defined as clusters 1 and 3, a range of amphorai, also jars, jugs and a lid.

Fig. 13.4 Follis of the Emperor Maurice Tiberius found on LP 1.

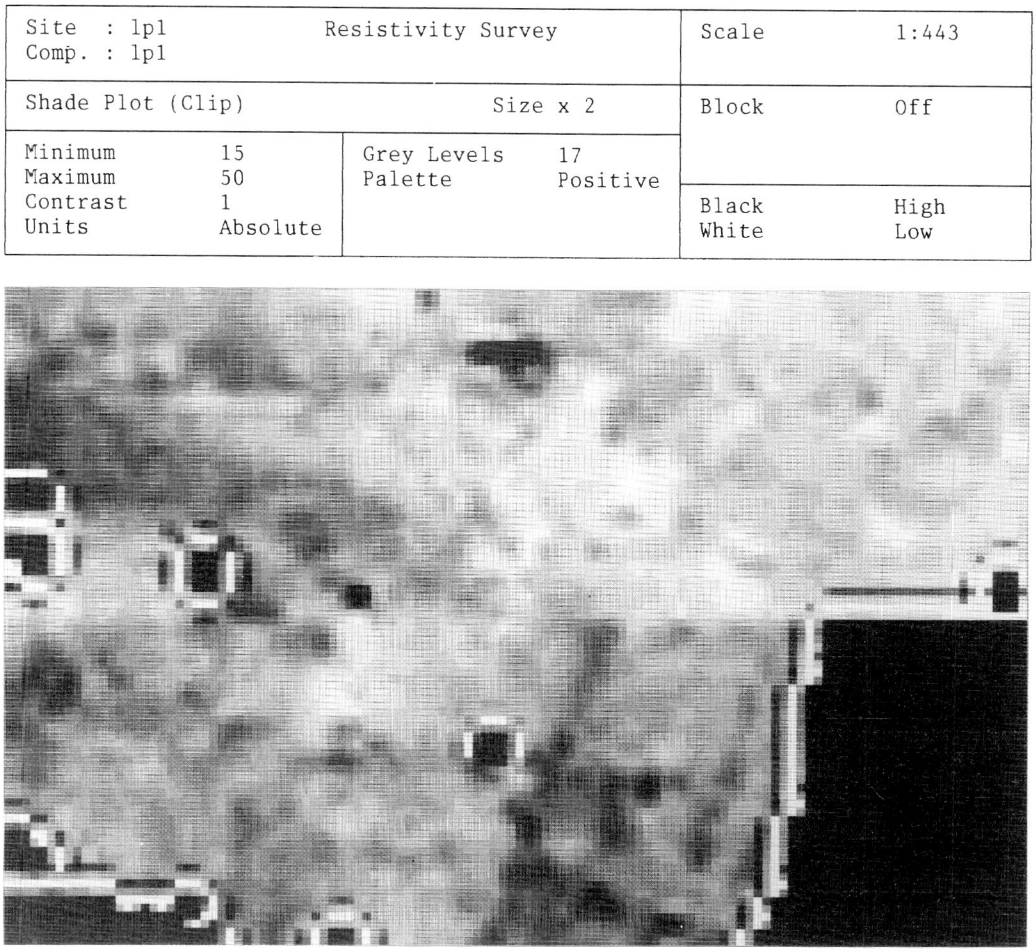

Fig. 13.5 Results of the geophysical survey on site LP 1.

Open shapes include bowls, basins and dishes. A number of sherds preserve traces of BG decoration and a Hellenistic date is likely but not certain. Most of the pottery should be Roman or Late Roman and there were also nine Medieval sherds. A bronze coin, which was in square D9, has been identified by Roger Bland as a follis of the emperor Maurice Tiberius which was struck in AD 590/591 (FIG. 13.4).

Geophysical prospection on LP1 indicated a large magnetic anomaly in squares A8 and A9, which continues into square A10 and covers an area of about 50 square metres (FIG. 13.5). The maximum intensity recorded was in excess of 100nT and suggests the presence of a fired structure, such as an oven or kiln. There is a linear magnetic anomaly traversing the site from square H2 to square D10, which is also visible as a diffuse, high resistance feature. This may mark the path of an old wall or track.

The soil studies revealed that the number of artefacts in the topsoil, although not correlating closely with the surface artefacts, were concentrated in the same areas of the site, in the SW and SE corners of the grid. This suggestion of the 'reliability' of the ground surface artefacts as an archaeological indicator is supported by the geomorphological stability of the river terrace upon which LP1 is situated. Its age is probably late Pleistocene or Early Holocene (~10,000 years), its surface slopes at less than 2°, and the remma to the E, although having cut laterally into the site, is part of a large and mainly stable gully system draining the E side of the Eurotas valley which probably developed prior to AD 500. Thus despite some lateral fluvial erosion, the site has been at little risk from soil erosion and the remma is likely to have protected it from deposition of sediment from the valley-side slope to the E.

The spatial patterns of total P, Pb, Cu Zn and of χ^{lf} show relatively high values in the S part of the grid where densities of tile and sherd are highest. The spatial association is particularly marked for P, Cu and χ^{lf} which highlight the two centres defined by the artefacts. However, also relatively high in the soil of these areas are amounts of clay and organic matter, two important controls on concentrations of the four elements and on χ^{lf}. It is possible that the soil conditions had been modified by those who used the site. The clay might have been brought in when floors were being laid, while the organic matter could derive from mud-bricks.

It would seem that there were two, or possibly three, structures on LP1, which were certainly in use in the Roman/Late Roman period. The lack of domestic pottery and the high proportion of storage vessels suggest that this was not primarily a residential site but a complex of storehouses. The magnetic anomaly may indicate associated 'industrial' activity and this will be investigated further as we continue our analysis of the data.

CONCLUSIONS

The sites which we selected had seemed to us to be similar in character if not date. In fact we have been struck by the differences which intensive investigation can reveal. We will certainly be able to refine our interpretation of the function of these sites once we can combine the results of the artefact analysis, geophysical prospection and soil studies. Nevertheless, it is clear that on a number of these rural sites, and not just in Laconia, what you see is what you get. The entire site is in the topsoil. Excavation would therefore be pointless and the methods which we have developed on our project may be the only option if investigation of these sites is being considered.

ACKNOWLEDGMENTS

The Laconia Rural Sites Survey was carried out under a permit issued by the Greek Ministry of Culture and we are most grateful to the Director of Antiquities, Dr. Y. Tzedakis, and to Dr. T. Spyropoulos, Dr. S Raphtopoulou and colleagues of the Ephoria for Arkadia and Laconia. We wish to thank the director and staff of the British School at Athens for their advice and assistance. Generous grants in support of the project have been made by the British School at Athens, the British Academy, the University of Liverpool and the University of Nottingham. We are also most grateful to Dr Neil Brodie and Peter James for supplying us with data and information on the geo-physical and geo-chemical aspects.

14

Geoarchaeological studies of the Spartan acropolis and Evrotas valley: some preliminary conclusions

Keith Wilkinson

INTRODUCTION

Despite a long history of the archaeological study of Sparta and the Evrotas Valley, comparatively little attention has been focused upon off-site sedimentological sequences, which could provide data to reconstruct past archaeological landscapes. It is true that the Evrotas Valley was included within Bintliff's (1977) survey of later Holocene 'Younger Fill' deposition in Greece, but much of his research was based either on accounts of previous archaeological excavations, or the study of chance exposures within irrigation ditches and other such features. It is also true that the Laconia Survey of the 1980s included the mapping of contemporary soils and also the examination of sequences exposed by agricultural activities (Cavanagh *et al.* 1996 and forthcoming). However, the Laconia Survey area did not extend into the Evrotas Valley (except very slightly, to the N of Sparta), and therefore did not include the complex Pliocene–Holocene fluvial sequences dominating the valley S of the town. Thus at present very little is known of the sedimentation regime that operated in Sparta and the Evrotas Valley even within the most recent geological time span (i.e. the Holocene, 10,000 BP–present), while on current data it is impossible to separate many Pliocene sediments from those accumulating in the Pleistocene. This situation is unfortunate as the detailed archaeological findings from Sparta's acropolis hill, the Menelaion, Amyklai and Mistras cannot be set within a known contemporary landscape. Instead actualistic assumptions have been made (i.e. what exists now also existed in the past: Stoddart 1986), or otherwise the Bintliff model and its associated chronology has been used uncritically. Even the inability to separate Pleistocene from Pliocene sediments has implications for studying the Palaeolithic period in the area, and it is no surprise that few remains of this period have been found, especially within the centre of the valley.

One of the major problems caused by the present lack of knowledge of sediment accumulation is the pattern of site distribution within the Evrotas Valley. For example, why are the majority of sites found on hillocks or slight rises above the rest of the valley? Is it because that is their 'real' distribution, i.e. the remaining part of the valley was unoccupied, and was too valuable as agricultural land to be used for habitation? Or, is it because former sites in the valley have become covered by thick sequences of later sediments and are therefore invisible? Alternatively, have the sites simply been removed by later erosive processes? Until a detailed model illustrating how sediment accumulation within the valley took place and linked to a chronology reconstructed from the use of absolute dating techniques (e.g. C^{14} and the Lumin-escence series of techniques), can be formulated, it is not possible even to begin answering these questions.

In order to provide such a model, a programme of geoarchaeological investigation was begun by the author in 1995. This initially involved the detailed study of a single archaeological site, that would provide a test bed for a suite of techniques commonly used in Northern Europe, but rarely used in the Mediterranean region. The site selected was the Roman Theatre at Sparta, the architectural development of which was then a subject of study by Professors Wilkes (UCL) and Waywell (KCL), and Dr. Walker (British Museum). Subsequently, in 1996, a start was made on a wider survey of longer time scale sequences within the Evrotas Valley adjacent to Sparta. This paper provides a preliminary synthesis of the survey work, and a more detailed account of the application of select sedimentological techniques to two strata types within the theatre.

GEOLOGICAL STRATA OF SPARTA AND THE EVROTAS VALLEY

The geology of the Evrotas Valley has been the subject of several studies, and a reasonably accurate picture can be built up of the sequence stratigraphy of features that project above the valley floor, including the acropolis hill (FIG. 14.1). However, because of the lack of exposures, and the absence of reliable borehole data, little is known of either the nature or chronology of deposition in the base of the valley itself.

Depositional history

The Evrotas Valley is a giant tectonic trough formed prior to the Pliocene. The process is still ongoing and is causing the Parnon and Taygetos massifs to rise

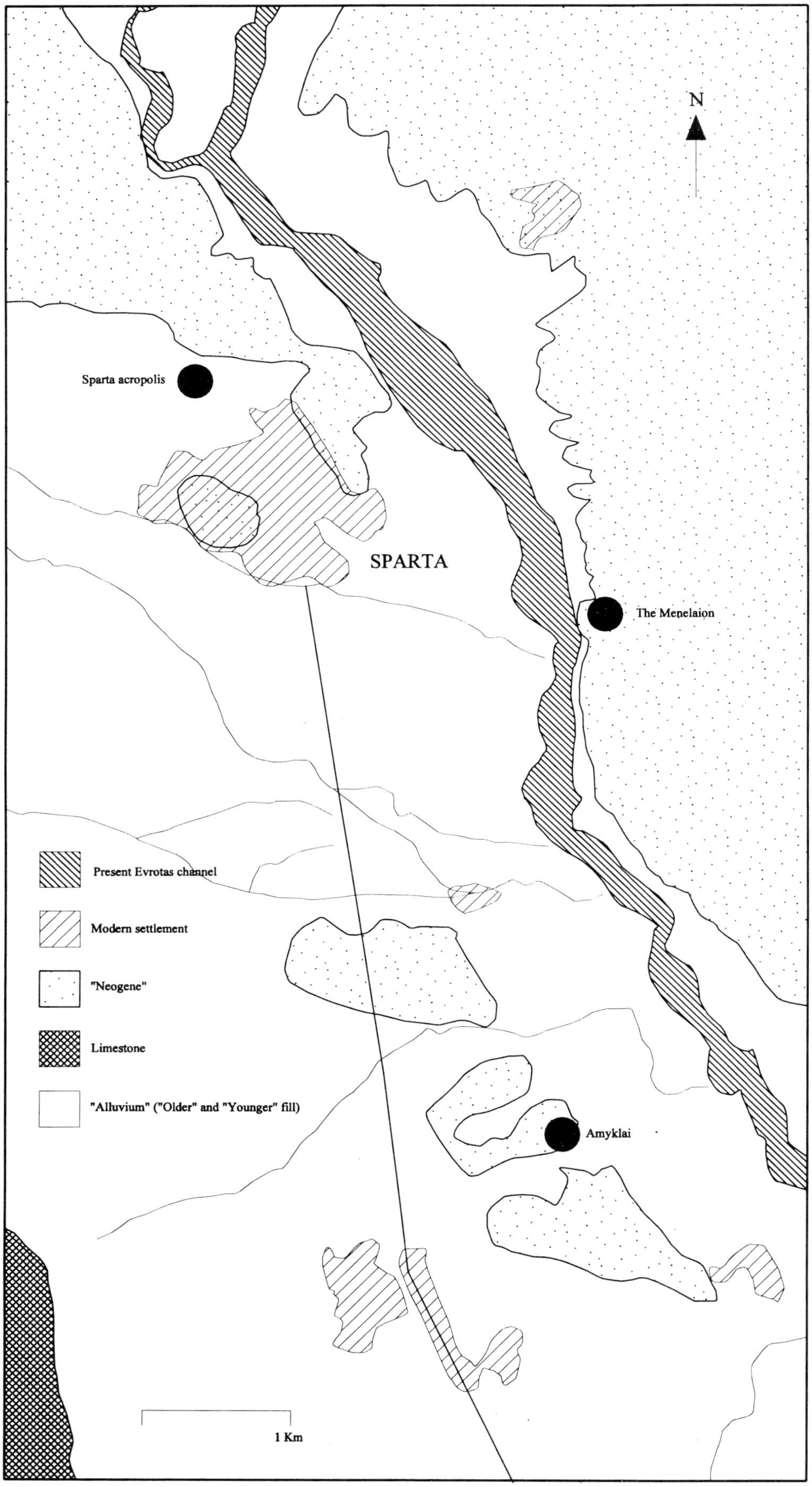

Fig. 14.1 The geology of the Evrotas valley.

while the valley floor falls (Philippson 1959). This has caused erosion of the valley sides, leading to the accumulation of poorly sorted colluvial material in the valley. During the Pliocene there was a marine transgression causing widespread deposition of distinctive bedded gravels, mudstones and sands—which can be seen today in the massive sections below the Menelaion. A subsequent regression during the later Pliocene led to several phases of fan formation, a series of deposits that are collectively known as the 'Neogene' (a particularly unfortunate term as it is also used as a time division (epoch) for a stage of the Tertiary). These alluvial deposits are probably not true fans (*sensu* Collinson 1986), but are fluvial rhythmites deposited in a riverine environment by a proto-Evrotas. Examples of such deposits can be seen in sections in the central ridge to the N of Sparta town and the acropolis hill.

At the very end of the Pliocene and during the subsequent Pleistocene, erosion of the Neogene took place as three phases of glacis formation (van Berghem and Fiselier forthcoming). The latter two phases (glacis d'accumulation) caused the formation from re-deposited Neogene of the hillocks in the Evrotas Valley, such as that on which the site of Amyklai stands. These features have been correlated with Bintliff's (1977) 'Older Fill', or red beds, by van Berghem and Fiselier (forthcoming). During the later Pleistocene and in the subsequent Holocene, the hillocks and elements of the central ridge were dissected by fluvial processes relating to the river Evrotas and its tributaries. For example, it is likely that in the later Pleistocene the acropolis hill became detached from the remaining part of the central ridge by action of the Mousga Torrent. A former channel of the torrent was noted some 10 m higher and 50 m E of its present course during survey work carried out in 1996. At present the date of this palaeochannel is unknown, although it is hoped that Optically Stimulated Luminescence (OSL) determinations carried out in 1998 on the channel sediments will resolve the chronological problems.

During the last two millennia, further alluvial and colluvial deposition has taken place in the Evrotas Valley. The exact mechanism by which this has occurred has been the subject of intense debate. Climatic change, and in particular rainfall variation is thought to be the major contributing factor by Bintliff (1975; 1977). He noted that ceramics found within the few exposures of this 'Younger Fill' (*sensu* Vita Finzi 1969) known in the Evrotas Valley are all of similar age, indicating synchronous deposition that could only have taken place by processes operating at a regional level, and therefore could only have been caused by climate change. However, this thesis has been countered by Wagstaff (1981) who questioned Bintliff's chronology and in turn suggested that the deposition was as a direct result of erosion caused by forest clearance and agriculture. 'Younger Fill' deposits are found throughout the lower lying parts of the valley, but are absent from the 'Older Fill' hillocks and the Neogene ridge, including both the town of Sparta and the acropolis hill. No thick sequences of 'Younger Fill' have been located as much of the Evrotas valley is under cultivation and therefore no sections have been available for study.

With this picture of the recent geological history of the Evrotas Valley it can clearly be seen that sediments within the valley ultimately have one of only two sources. Firstly, if encountered at the edge of the valley, they could derive from the pre-Pliocene limestones of the Parnon or Taygetos ranges, but otherwise are of Pliocene marine and/or Neogene parent material. Since the later Pliocene the Evrotas Valley has been a closed system with little external sediment entering it, but instead material has been eroded and re-deposited. For example fluvial gravels of the 'Older Fill' at Amyklai are composed of re-worked Neogene conglomerates. Therefore all soils and sediments (including archaeological deposits) in the Evrotas Valley will have common characteristics to the *in situ* Neogene. If these latter properties can be determined and filtered out, the differences from undisturbed Neogene sediments can be used in interpreting how a particular deposit formed. Hence the apparent concentration on the study of geological deposits in this text.

Sedimentology of the Neogene - 'Older fill'

Samples taken from various Neogene and 'Older Fill' sections during fieldwork in 1995 and 1996 have been studied using particle size analysis, magnetic susceptibility measurement, and calcium carbonate equivalent, as well as detailed field description. The analytical techniques used have, in all cases, followed those of Gale and Hoare (1991). Although both the survey and laboratory analysis of these deposits is so far limited, a few general conclusions can be reached as to typical sediment structures and properties of *in situ* Neogene. Major deviations from these will in most cases be indicative of re-deposition, either as a result of Quaternary fluvial or Holocene archaeological activity. Further laboratory analysis—including the use of geochemical and mineralogical techniques as well as further analysis of the type already mentioned—and survey, will be able to define many sedimentological properties of the Neogene quantitatively rather than qualitatively as at present. This should allow firmer conclusions to be made as to how, and by what mechanism re-deposition has occurred and what role humans have played in this process.

The Neogene as found in the Evrotas valley typically comprises a series of distinctive facies, consisting of coarsening upward sequences of clay/silt and fine sand interspersed with thin beds of mixed granular clasts and coarse sands. Massively bedded gravels

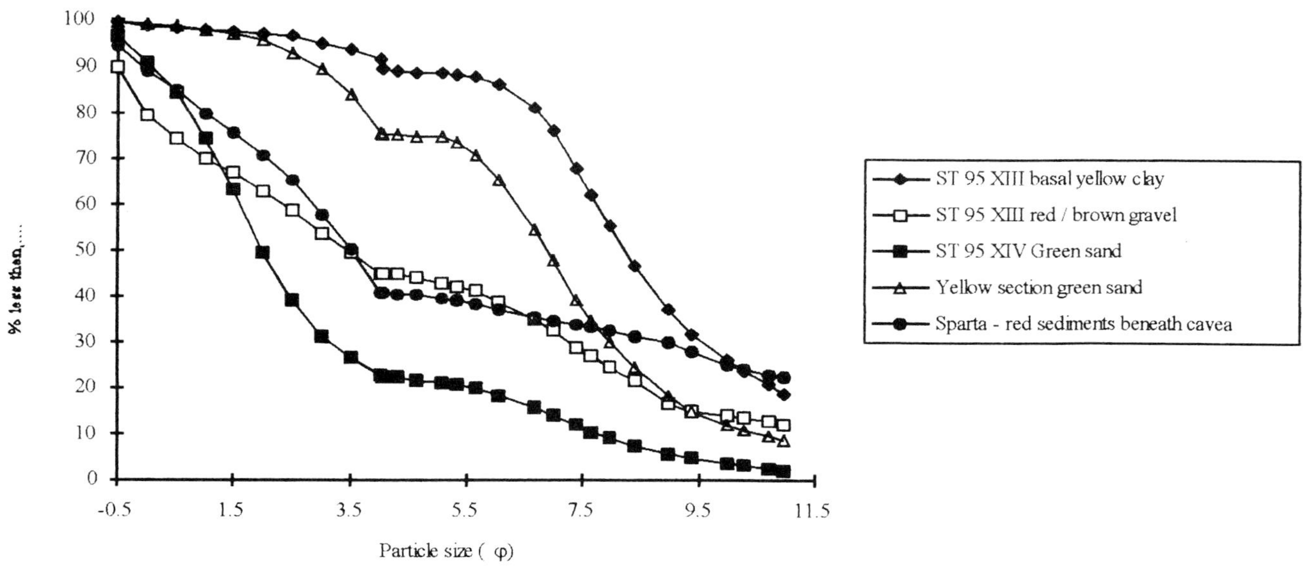

Fig. 14.2 Particle size analysis of select sediments from the theatre plotted against Pliocene data.

occur less frequently, usually with erosional contacts to surrounding sediments. Clasts within these gravels are of an extremely limited lithological range and are almost always rounded or well rounded. These observations indicate that source material of every conceivable particle size exists within the Evrotas Valley. However, most Neogene facies, being either fluvial or marine, are of well sorted sediments (with the exception of some of the gravels), as can be seen for example in material labelled as being from the 'yellow section' in FIG. 14.2. Sediments composed of fine sand, silt and clay also commonly exhibit size trend variations with depth. Magnetic susceptibility measurements from Neogene (FIG. 14.3) indicate that χ^{lf} values (low frequency magnetic susceptibility) are always less than 20 10^{-8} m^3 kg^{-1} and χ^{fd} values (percentage frequency difference between low and high frequency readings) less than 6%. This is in marked contrast to Holocene archaeological and pedological material.

THE DEPOSITIONAL HISTORY OF SEDIMENTS INFILLING SPARTA'S THEATRE 'BOWL'

Prior to the 1995 study season comparatively little was known of the theatre's setting in relation to local geomorphological features, geological and other pre-Roman strata. Indeed a particularly important outstanding question to be addressed was the degree to which areas of the hillside been removed during the theatre's construction in order to modify the pre-existing geomorphology to fit the builders' plans. In the field seasons 1992–3 effort had been concentrated on excavating through thick Byzantine sequences in the orchestra and cavea to reveal the theatre's seating plan. In only two of the nine trenches excavated during this time had deposits below the seating been revealed (Trenches ST92/93 IV and V—both of which were located in the outer E cavea adjacent to the retaining wall), and then only because of the absence of seating blocks in this particular location (Waywell and Wilkes 1995). The presence of re-deposited sediments containing Late Hellenistic ceramics in these locations (Hayes 1995) indicated that the ground in this area had needed raising. However, when investigations were extended to the orchestra during 1995 and 1996, observation was possible of deposits underlying, and hence pre-dating the stage buildings. As part of this campaign a series of samples was taken for sedimentological analysis, to determine whether the deposits below the stage represented *in situ* geological strata, or had been deliberately placed there by the theatre builders. From this initial problem a further series of questions could then be addressed:

i. From which geological formation did the sediments originate?
ii. How did their properties compare to those of sediments previously studied and dated to the Byzantine period (Wilkinson 1993)?
iii. If *in situ* how old are they?

The analysis would also provide background data in the study of the sedimentology of excavated Byzantine deposits.

Deposits post-dating the theatre were studied in detail during 1992–3 in Trench ST92/93 I (Wilkinson, unpublished data). The mode of formation of those deposits, which filled stone structures post-dating the tenth century, is relatively easy to determine on morphological grounds alone. These deposits are formed, it seems, from material eroding from further up slope, combined with deliberately (re)deposited ('dumped') occupation debris, and industrial waste from metalworking activities (Powell 1995). However, below the earliest stone structure was a *c.* 1.5 m sequence of poorly sorted green sediments dating to between the eighth and the late tenth centuries (Sanders 1995), and these were thought to relate either to pooling of water in the orchestra (Woodward 1925a; 1926a; 1927a), or to erosion and diagenesis (Wilkinson 1993). Studies during 1995 and 1996 have provided further details of the mechanism by which they formed.

Sediments pre-dating the theatre

In 1994 and 1995 a series of trenches was excavated through the stage buildings of the theatre. Below the earliest theatre structure in ST95 XIII and XIV, a series of apparently well stratified sands, silt/clays and gravels was noted (FIG. 14.4). Sands of a distinct greenish colour were found as laminae and fine layers, up to 4cm thick, within silt/clay deposits. However, there were no signs of trends in sorting within the silt/clays themselves. The appearance of the sands and silt/clays is, superficially, very similar to Neogene sediments exposed in sections between the village of Karavas and the Sparta–Tripolis road. But the bedding patterns, sorting properties, relationships to, and properties of the gravels are at variance, indicating a different depositional history. The gravels are sub-angular with a finer-grained matrix of a reddish colour, and are separated from the silt/clays below by a sharp, irregular (and hence erosional) boundary, perhaps indicating a substantial time gap between their deposition. No corresponding deposits have been noted in any Neogene section, but similar sediments were found in 1996 in the town of Sparta, for example on the Odos Ep. Vrestenis where a more recent date of formation is suggested (Wilkinson unpublished data). The sequence of deposits beneath the stage buildings, into which two slots had been cut by the theatre builders, are likely to be alluvial deposits of the 'Older Fill' in the case of the fine grained sediments and hence date to the (?later) Pliocene/Pleistocene, indicating the presence of a river close to the acropolis hill at this period. The red gravels could be from a similar source and have later undergone diagenesis/sub-aerial weathering to develop the red coloration (as is the case with *terra rossa* soils in the region). But they are more likely to be the remnants of a true *terra rossa* (see below). The morphology of these deposits and their relationships to the stage buildings indicate that the sediments had been greatly truncated by construction of the theatre.

Samples from the deposits were taken for sedimentological analysis to provide background data for the interpretation of archaeological sediments overlying the cavea and orchestra, to determine their origin and mode of deposition. They were also taken to compare with *in situ* Neogene deposits from the Karavas-Sparta road, to see what common properties existed ('yellow section green sand' on FIG. 14.2). Analysis is still ongoing, but the results of particle size analysis are presented in FIG. 14.2 and of magnetic susceptibility in FIG. 14.3. These indicate that the particle size properties are quite different, with material from below the stage buildings in general being a great deal finer than the 'yellow section green sand', which is actually predominately of silt size material. The coarsest sediments are green sands from ST 95 XIV, whose distribution compares well with that of the 'green layer' in the Stoa (Wilkinson 1993). The finest deposit is the 'basal yellow clay' found in ST 95 XIII, and into which foundation slots have been cut. This material would have been ideal for the placing of a large structure, such as the stage building, so long as it

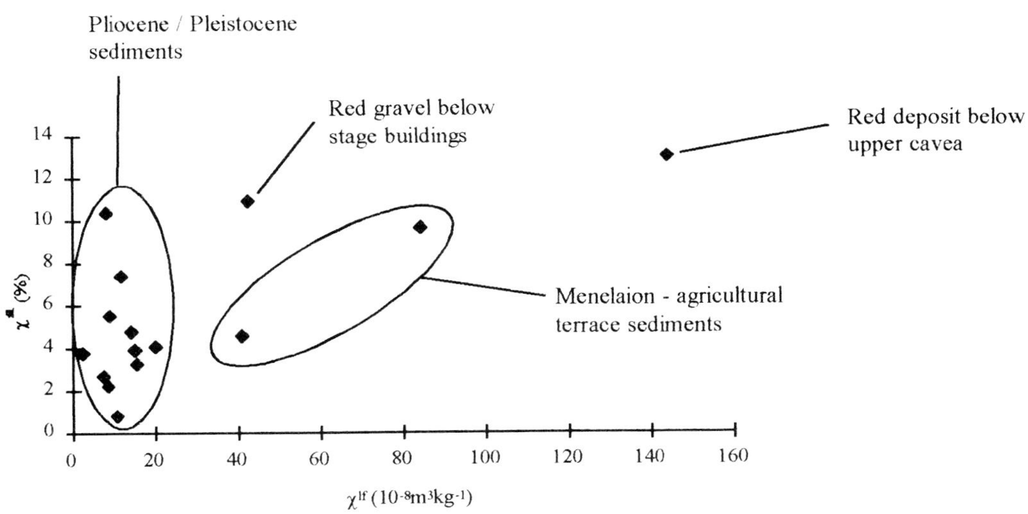

Fig. 14.3 The magnetic susceptibility of sediments from the Evrotas valley.

Fig. 14.4 Red gravel and underlying yellow silt clays; Sparta theatre, stage buildings

remained sufficiently sealed by other deposits not to dry out and shrink, in which case the foundations would have become unstable. It is notable that at the time of sampling, during a particularly hot summer, the yellow clay had a 30% moisture content—far greater than any other deposit the author has ever sampled in the Sparta area. It is of course possible that the theatre builders specifically targeted this deposit in which to locate their foundations.

The plot of χ^{lf} (low frequency magnetic susceptibility) against χ^{fd} (percentage frequency difference between low and high frequency readings), demonstrates that sediments on the acropolis—with the exception of the yellow silt/clays beneath the stage buildings—can be separated from Neogene/Older Fill sediments as both χ^{lf} and χ^{fd} are substantially higher. These high readings are characteristic of soils (Oldfield *et al.* 1985). Indeed, both the magnetic and particle size properties of the red gravel beneath the stage buildings are akin to sediments underlying the upper cavea (see below). The differences can be explained away as factors of redeposition (of material below the cavea), and the absence of upper soil horizons through truncation (in the material below the stage buildings).

Fills underlying the theatre in the upper E cavea have been interpreted as deliberately deposited here to increase ground levels prior to placing seat blocks (Waywell and Wilkes 1995). Deposits of a similar appearance are also found beneath stone structures relating to the theatre, adjacent to the underground reservoir immediately to the N. The sediments are of a bright red colour and are poorly sorted, containing angular clast as well as ceramic material of Hellenistic date. These would appear to have been taken from source material quite different from either the 'Older Fill', as found beneath the stage buildings, or Neogene strata (which are all well sorted and distinctively yellow or green). But, as indicated above, they probably equate with the red gravel found in the orchestra. Both would have an origin in a pre-existing *terra rossa* soil, that had developed on the acropolis hill prior to widespread disturbance during the Roman period. Such soils are known to have an antiquity in the order of thousands or even tens of thousands of years, and as the red coloration is a product of time-dependant weathering, the intensity has even been used as a relative dating technique (Hurst 1977). If there was indeed a *terra rossa* soil on the acropolis prior to the construction of the theatre, its presence would argue for only slight erosion before the Roman period and therefore the absence of intense pre-Roman agriculture on the acropolis hill. *Terra rossa* soils are now largely absent from the Sparta area, as agricultural activity since the Roman period has caused their erosion.

Post-Roman sediments in the theatre: the 'green layer'

A variety of deposits overlies the Roman theatre structure, but in this text only a single stratum is considered—a 1.5 m thick green deposit (context 5217 (Powell 1995))—henceforth termed the 'green layer', overlying the orchestra and inner W cavea. Similar deposits were noted in the stoa during excavations in 1989 (Wilkinson 1993; Waywell and Wilkes 1994). Many questions can be posed of the green layer in the theatre: how, for example, did it form? What caused the distinct green coloration? From where did the sediment derive? What does its presence indicate about usage of the theatre in the eighth–tenth centuries? And why are there so many bones in it? To try and provide answers to these, a detailed sampling and exhaustive excavation policy was implemented. As analytical work is still continuing the account below provides some preliminary thoughts.

The base of the deposit rested in part on the stone seats of the theatre and, elsewhere, on a yellow clay, of superficially similar appearance to that found below the stage building and described above. The top of the green layer was in turn marked by an area of burning, including burnt stake holes, that possibly once defined an enclosure (Powell 1995). In other areas, sections through the deposit revealed that it was homogenous. Nevertheless, its formation appears to have been gradual on the basis of the ceramic chronology, which shows a pattern of increasingly older pottery with depth (Sanders 1995). That such a statement could be made at all is possible only because of the method of investigation, which was through excavation in 10 cm spits rather than removing the whole context under a single label. Twenty litre samples were taken from each spit for flotation processing to examine artefact and biological variation with depth. Animal bones were recovered in great numbers, and many appeared copper stained, leading to suggestions that the green colour of the sediments was due to leaching of copper from the debris of a nearby Roman temple roof. However, despite occurring over a period of perhaps two centuries, deposition does not appear to have been continuous, for magnetic susceptibility profiles show an episode of magnetic enhancement half way through the sequence (Wilkinson 1997). This magnetic signature is probably indicative of soil formation, suggesting that for a time deposition ceased. There is no structural material within the deposit to suggest the presence of buildings during accumulation, and therefore it would seem that during the eighth–tenth centuries the area was not used for habitation. However, the stake holes may indicate that stock enclosures were in place by the tenth century.

Interpretation of how the 'green layer' formed has, as stated above, been a cause for debate. The idea that the green colour is a direct result of waterlogging must now be dismissed as particle size analysis indicates that the sediments are poorly sorted, which would be unlikely if they were gradually settling out from suspension. Thus the sediments are likely to be colluvial, i.e. accumulating as a result of hill slope processes, or deliberately deposited by man, but in either case originating as a result of activity on the rim of the cavea. These activities were no doubt associated with occupation, explaining the widespread presence of the animal bones, broken ceramics, and charcoal. Indeed, it would seem that during this period the theatre acted as a giant rubbish disposal facility, as phosphate readings from the green layer, although at present only carried out qualitatively, are higher than for any other sediment excavated on the site. These data probably suggest that the bones were not clean of flesh when disposed of. It is hoped that a planned micromorphological study will help to address these questions.

The coloration of the deposits is probably a product of source material. As stated above, Neogene sediments are commonly of either a green or, more often, a yellow colour. Therefore it would seem that during the eighth–tenth centuries outcrops of Neogene, or more likely 'Older Fill' sands existed beyond the rim of the cavea, and it was their erosion that provided much of the material forming the green layer. Particle size analysis of the 'green layer' in the Stoa indicates that its size distribution is virtually identical with that of the Green sand found below the stage building (Wilkinson 1993), and which, as stated above, is likely to be part of an 'Older Fill' formation. At present no similar analyses have been carried out from the green layer in the theatre.

CONCLUSIONS

This paper has presented a preliminary view of recent geomorphological survey work carried out within the Evrotas Valley and provided more detailed geoarchaeological data relating to deposition within a single archaeological feature, the Roman Theatre at Sparta. The latter demonstrate that, when a combination of sedimentological techniques is used together with detailed archaeological recording of the sampled stratigraphy, a relatively detailed picture can be built up of sedimentation patterns. Indeed it is probably true to say that the mechanism by which the 'green layer' accumulated in the theatre could not have been reconstructed without the use of such geoarchaeological techniques. The data also demonstrate that, although the majority of deposits (both archaeological and 'natural' [*sic*]) consist of the same Neogene parent material, they can easily be differentiated on the basis of field morphology and other sedimentological criteria.

Although these findings are encouraging, they are applicable only to sedimentation on a macro-scale, i.e.

that of a single site. The survey data are, of course, more relevant at a wider scale, but the major gap in knowledge still remains that of (geologically) recent accumulation/erosion regimes at the meso-scale, i.e. that of the Evrotas Valley as a whole. The mechanism by which the Evrotas Valley has evolved to its present form is relatively well understood for the periods predating the Pleistocene, but, because of the absence of exposures, landscape developments in the Pleistocene and Holocene have had to be reconstructed using data from other geographical areas. This period spans the entire time of man's occupation of the valley and thus the absence of data is particularly unfortunate, as landscape evolution cannot be reconstructed with certainty for any but the most recent archaeological periods. It is nevertheless likely that a considerable depth of Holocene/Pleistocene sediments exist, but they are deeply stratified in the central part of the valley (the 'alluvium' of FIG. 14.1), and have not been exposed because most of the land in this area is given over to olive cultivation. Modern occupation (e.g. the town of Sparta) is more often situated on hillocks of redeposited Neogene and, although the settlement pattern of the archaeological past seems to mirror this pattern, it may well be that former sites on the valley floor are simply too deeply buried by later sediments to be found using conventional archaeological techniques. It is thus of vital importance in interpreting the archaeology of the Evrotas Valley that the Pleistocene/Holocene valley deposits are studied so that models can be put forward for how human- and climate-induced change occurred. Study of such sequences would also allow the chronological framework of sedimentation proposed by Bintliff (1977) to be tested. Unfortunately in the absence of major engineering work or quarrying to produce the necessary sections, only bore hole studies will be able to produce such stratigraphies. In 1993 such a study will commence which it is hoped will enable the questions highlighted in this paper to be addressed, and if not answered then at least subjected to more informed debate.

ACKNOWLEDGEMENTS

I extend my thanks to Professors John Wilkes and Geoffrey Waywell and Drs Susan Walker and Elizabeth Waywell for help and encouragement during excavations on the Sparta acropolis; to Jane Sidell for help in sampling and discussion of the results, and to Nick Branch, Jerry Lee, Mark Lane and Professor Frank Chambers for helping with laboratory facilities. Laboratory analysis was undertaken at the Centre for Environmental Change and Quaternary Research, Cheltenham and Gloucester College of Higher Education, and the Department of Geography, Royal Holloway College, University of London. I also thank Dr Bill Cavanagh for his helpful comments on an earlier draft of this paper.

15

Byzantine Mistra—Sparta in the mind

Donald M. Nicol

The Byzantines were never archaeologists in the modern sense of the word. They would have thought it odd to go digging up the soil to uncover the past. They had no antiquarian curiosity in Greece as a country. They did not go hunting for the site of Delphi or Dodona, of Thebes or Eleusis. At Athens in the middle ages the remains of the pagan, classical past were better preserved than they are now and put to useful purposes. The Archbishop of Athens at the turn of the twelfth century, Michael Choniates, was proud of the splendours of the Parthenon. It was after all his cathedral and a shrine of Christian pilgrimage, for all its rather incongruous sculptural adornment. The Athenians of his day were surrounded by palpable reminders of a pre-Christian past of the Greek-speaking people, the Hellenes; and they were accustomed to use the word Hellene to mean pagan. At Sparta, on the other hand there was little left to see, as Thucydides had predicted and Ovid had observed. Even the name of its city and its bishopric had been changed from Sparta to Lakedaimonia. As such it ranked rather low down in the list of metropolitan cities of the Peloponnese; and it was more celebrated for its miracle-working saint Nikon, who had called the Slavs to Christianity and repentance in the tenth century, than it was for its ancient Spartan warriors and lawgivers.

The Byzantines of the middle ages whether in Greece or in Asia Minor were used to living among ruins of a past which few of them knew anything about. They had no scruples about dismantling and recycling the well-dressed blocks of those ruins for the construction of churches, walls or fountains. What has been called 'the sentiment of place' meant little to them, unless the place were associated with a Christian religious festival or the life and deeds of a saint. Pilgrimage was their form of tourism. They did not experience the romantic pleasure of ruins. What attracted pilgrims to the Parthenon in Byzantine times was not its architectural and sculptural beauty, nor its evocation of a more glorious past of Athens. They were drawn there by the holy relics and thaumaturgic icons contained inside it. Likewise tourists flocked to Sparta or Lakedaimonia not to rub shoulders with the shades of Lykourgos or Leonidas but to sniff the odour of sanctity of the great St Nikon who had died there about AD 998.

Mistra did not then exist. Mistra owed its origins to the catastrophe of the Fourth Crusade, when the western soldiers of Christ conquered and sacked Constantinople in 1204 and set about the dismemberment and colonisation of Greece and the rest of the Byzantine Empire. It was a descendant of one of those crusaders, William of Villehardouin, who built the first castle on top of the hill of Mistra overlooking the plain of Sparta. Mistra is too often romanticised as a Frankish fortress advertising and defending the ideals of western chivalry in an alien land. William of Villehardouin regarded that land as his own. He spoke some Greek. He married a Greek princess, Anna, daughter of the Byzantine Despot of Epiros, Michael II. Some of the romantic aura surrounding the French or Frankish occupation of Mistra stems from this fact. For as early as the sixteenth century it was suggested that the marriage of William to Anna was the medieval equivalent of the tale of Menelaus and Helen, for Mistra was surely Sparta. The fancy was enshrined in Goethe's Faust. It is certain that it would have been lost on the Villehardouin family. For William knew nothing about ancient Sparta. He and his French knights called Sparta Lakedaimonia, but since they found this hard to pronounce they gallicised it into La Crémonie. William liked the place and held his court there. His castle on the hill at Mistra was built to defend the plain of La Crémonie against the predatory Slav tribes who infested Mount Taygetos. It was completed in 1249.

The age of Mistra or of Lakedaimonia as a French or Frankish settlement lasted not much more than ten years. William of Villehardouin was defeated in battle and taken prisoner by the Byzantine Emperor's army in 1259. Not until 1262 was he allowed to return to his principality in the Peloponnese, and then on condition of surrendering his castle at Mistra as well as those at Monemvasia and Mani. It was from this moment that Mistra became the Byzantine capital of the Peloponnese, governed by officials sent out from Constantinople and garrisoned by Byzantine troops. The Greek-speaking population of Lakedaimonia or La Crémonie packed their bags and gravitated towards the new town now being built on the slope of the hill at Mistra. The ancient city of Sparta was soon deserted. It did not come to life again until the nineteenth century. Mistra became the administrative, military, urban and ecclesiastical centre of the Byzantine province of the Peloponnese; and as time went on, and the French and Italian colonists gave up the struggle, Mistra developed into one of the most secure, successful and important outposts of a Byzantine Empire that was in other respects in decline. In 1349 the Emperor John VI Cantacuzene, whose father had served as governor at Mistra, delegated his own son Manuel to take it over the with the exalted title of Despot, which ranked second only to that of Emperor. Manuel Cantacuzene, as Imperial Viceroy, governed the province with considerable success until he died there in 1380. The Despotate of the Peloponnese or the Morea, as it had come to be called, then passed to the care of the family of Palaiologos, the reigning dynasty in Constantinople, whose members provided the succeeding Despots at Mistra until it was conquered by the Turks in 1460.

Manuel Cantacuzene built the church of St Sophia high up on the hillside at Mistra looking down on the Palace of the Despots. Its name of St Sophia or the Holy Wisdom emphasised the fact that Mistra was meant to be a microcosm of the city of Constantinople. And so it became, especially during the last century of its Byzantine existence. In that age, between the years 1350 and 1450, Constantinople experienced a remarkable re-awakening of interest in ancient Greek scholarship, literature and philosophy. It has been called, perhaps rather optimistically, the last Byzantine Renaissance. Mistra, the microcosm of Constantinople, was to become its second home. For, as the lights began to go out in Constantinople, blockaded and isolated as it was by the Turks, scholars, artists and monks flocked west across the sea to the relative peace, quiet and security of the city of Mistra. The scholars brought their libraries with them. Scriptoria were established and patronised by the Despots. Among their products were manuscripts of Plutarch's Lives copied at Mistra in 1362; of Herodotus in 1372; of Aristotle, Isocrates and Arrian in 1441; and of the Hellenika of Xenophon in 1456. When the end came and the Turks walked into Mistra in 1460, many of the Greek scholars fled to the remaining Venetian colonies in the islands or to Italy, taking their manuscripts with them. Demetrios Trivolis, who called himself 'a Peloponnesian from Sparta', copied a manuscript of Plato's Timaeus in Corfu in 1462, and of the Enneads of Plotinus in Crete in 1465.

The stars among their intellectual elite of Mistra in the Pentekontaetia of its cultural history were Isidore, who was to become Bishop of Kiev and then a Cardinal of the Roman church; Bessarion, Bishop of Nicaea, who also settled in Italy and was made a Roman cardinal. Bessarion took all his library with him and left his manuscripts to the Library of St Mark's in Venice. The Italians called him 'Latinorum graecissimus, Graecorum latinissimus'. Another was George Scholarios, later as the monk Gennadios to become the first Patriarch of Constantinople under the Ottomans after 1453. The greatest and most original of them all was George Gemistos Plethon. All these men had in some sense 'Sparta in the mind'. They were aware that Mistra was close to the site of Ancient Sparta, even though they did not feel impelled to go down with spades to explore its ruins. To most of these neo-Hellenists of Mistra the word 'Hellene' was still uncomfortably associated with 'pagan' or pre-Christian. The odd man out among them was George Gemistos Plethon, whose learning they all respected and admired. For Plethon Hellenism was the life-blood of the Greek-speaking people; and Mistra in the centre of the Peloponnese was the focal point from which it could and should be revived. As a devoted Platonist he based his political ideas on the Republic; and he shared Plato's predilection for Sparta over Athens. He lived for nearly fifty years at Mistra and died there in 1452; and Sparta, on whose remains he looked down, was often in his mind. He had an exaggerated estimation of the ethnic purity of the Hellenes who lived in the Peloponnese in his time. He claimed that it was a country which had always been inhabited by the same Greek stock, unsullied by the admixture of any other race. He must have known that this was nonsense. His contemporary, Mazaris, who wrote a satirical work about a visit to Hades, enumerated seven distinct racial types among the people of the Peloponnese in the fifteenth century. Herodotus had been the first to put the number at seven; therefore it had to stand, although his seven were quite different from those listed by Mazaris.

Plethon had more reverence for Lykourgos than for St Nikon. He evolved elaborate schemes for the reform of Peloponnesian society and advocated them in prolix and detailed addresses to the Despots of Mistra and the Emperor in Constantinople. He developed the fantasy that while Constantinople was the New Rome, Mistra could become the New Sparta. In Plethon's version of the history of Greece Athens is not mentioned. He was gratified that Herodotus had inferred that the Athenians were not birthright Hellenes like the Spartans. His preference was for Sparta and other similarly authoritarian regimes. He was not alone among the Byzantines in holding that monarchy was the ideal form of government. But the kind of constitution that Plethon recommended for his New Sparta would have produced a very unpleasant version of military dictatorship quite possibly reinforced by some 'ethnic cleansing' to uphold the Hellenic purity of his Lakedaimonians. The Despots of Mistra and the Emperors of Constantinople listened patiently to the great man's advice and rewarded him for his pains. They were perhaps wise not to act upon his proposals.

Plethon was in the end condemned by the Church, for his Platonism ultimately got the better of his Christianity; and he renounced his ancestral faith in favour of a bizarre amalgam of pantheistic Hellenism, Neoplatonism, Zoroastrianism and other oddities. The anathema on his final work was pronounced by his former friend at Mistra, the Patriarch Gennadios Scholarios. It made sure that St Nikon of Lakedaimonia had triumphed over the new Lykourgos of Sparta. Plethon's name and his dangerous ideas were obliterated in the post-Byzantine Greek world in which Christian Orthodoxy, not pagan Hellenism, fortified the humiliated people under centuries of Muslim domination. It was in the burgeoning world of humanist scholarship in Renaissance Italy that Plethon was to be most highly esteemed. The Italians had welcomed him at Florence where he spent some time in 1438 and where he lectured to the incipient Platonic Academy. It was the Italians who sought him out at Mistra when he was in his declining years. Among them was one who had ancient Sparta in his sights as well as in his mind. He was Ciriaco of Ancona, the antiquarian, humanist and indefatigable traveller.

Ciriaco has been called the first classical archaeologist. Not that he wielded a spade; but he was the first learned traveller on Greek soil systematically to locate and identify the sites and ruins of antiquity, to record inscriptions and to collect manuscripts. On two of his prolonged visits to the Peloponnese he met and stayed with Gemistos Plethon whom he described as 'the most brilliant and influential philosopher among the Platonists'. His second visit to Mistra was in 1447–8, and on this occasion he met the Despot Constantine Palaiologos who was shortly to be invested, if not crowned at Mistra as the Emperor of Constantinople. It was a poignant meeting, for Constantine XI was the Byzantine Emperor. He was killed fighting the Turks at the walls of his capital five years later. But Ciriaco's interest was not so much in the fate of the Byzantine Empire, nor in what was for him the modern city of Mistra. He had come there to see and to explore the vestiges of ancient Sparta which were of little concern to his scholarly friend Plethon; and while he was at Mistra, in February 1448, Ciriaco composed an ode to Sparta in which he mused upon its past glories and its fallen fortune, now as he rather rudely put it, sunk to 'the little measure of the town of Mistra under Constantine' ('Mysithra sub Constantino'). For him Sparta was still 'in the mind'; but it was more tangible, more than a disembodied political and philosophical abstraction. His poem, written in Italian, was put into Greek probably by Plethon himself. It celebrated not Lakedaimonia, nor Mistra, but 'the famous Laconian city of Sparta, the glory of Greece and example to all the world'.

When he was back in Italy, Ciriaco called on Sigismondo Malatesta, the eccentric and extravagant Prince of Rimini. Sigismondo had admired Gemistos Plethon from afar, although they never met; and it was he who led an expedition to the Peloponnese in 1464, four years after Mistra had fallen to the Turks. There he found the grave of the great man. He had the corpse disinterred and carried it back to Rimini to rest in glory in the wall of his flagrantly pagan temple, the Tempio Malatestiano; and there the tomb of Plethon is still to be seen with its inscription entitling him as 'the Prince of Philosophers in his time'. Plethon had died condemned by his church and without much honour in his own country. It was Renaissance Italy that welcomed him, trailing his clouds of Platonic and Spartan glory.

The last of the Byzantine historians, some of whom were writing after the collapse of their Empire and the capture of Mistra by the Ottoman Turks, quite regularly give Mistra the name of Sparta. This was no more than a literary affectation, an archaising gesture which they made without wondering what it implied. It was on a par with the Byzantine literary convention of calling the Turks 'the Persians' or the Serbians 'the Triballi'. The Emperor Manuel II, whose brother Theodore was Despot at Mistra for twenty-five years, composed an immense funeral oration on him in 1409. In this he consistently refers to Mistra as Sparta, though again without giving the matter much thought. He knew that it was not really Sparta. He compares the many virtues and talents of his late brother with those of numerous heroes and warriors of Greek antiquity. but the only local hero with whom he can identify him was Agesilaos of Sparta—which shows at least the Emperor had read his Plutarch.

Sparta then was an archaising name for Mistra. No one, however, not even Gemistos Plethon, believed or claimed that they were the same place. No Byzantine writer would have agreed with the learned M de Pouqueville who, about 1800, declared that, while the ancient city of Sparta was little more than a name, yet 'it is evident that the modern town of Mistra is built upon its ruins'. The Byzantines knew better than that. To them Mistra was a real and lively place. Sparta was a historical fact or a political and philosophical abstraction; and it never occurred to Byzantine scholars to climb down and investigate its mortal remains. Better let it stay in the mind.

Bibliography

Adamantiou, A., 1931. 'Ανασκαφὴ Σπάρτης' *PAE* 1931: 91–6.

Adamantiou, A., 1934. 'Ανασκαφὴ Σπάρτης' *PAE* 1934: 123–8.

Alcock, S. E., 1993. *Graecia Capta: The Landscapes of Roman Greece.* Cambridge.

Alcock, S. E., J. F. Cherry and J. L. Davis, 1994. 'Intensive survey, agricultural practice and the classical landscape of Greece' in I. Morris (ed.) *Classical Greece: ancient histories and modern archaeologies*: 137–70. Cambridge.

Alcock, S. E. and R. Osborne (eds), 1994. *Placing the Gods. Sanctuaries and Sacred Space in Ancient Greece.* Oxford.

Andrewes, A., 1954. *Probouleusis. Sparta's contribution to the Technique of Government.* Oxford.

Andronikos, M., 1968. 'Totenkult' Chapter W of F. Matz and H.-G. Buchholz (eds) *Archaeologia Homerica.* Göttingen.

Arafat, K. W., 1996. *Pausanias' Greece. Ancient Artists and Roman Rulers.* Cambridge.

Armstrong, P., W. G. Cavanagh and G. Shipley, 1992. 'Crossing the river: routes and bridges in Laconia' *BSA* 87: 293–310.

Ashmole, B., 1959. 'Cyriac of Ancona' *Proceedings of the British Academy* 45: 25–41.

Assimakopoulou-Atzaka, Y., 1973. 'Κατάλογος ρωμαϊκών ψηφιδωτών δαπέδων με ανθρώπινες μορφές στον Ελληνικό χώρο' *Ελληνικά* 26: 216–50.

Assimakopoulou-Atzaka, Y., 1987. *Σύνταγμα των παλαιοχριστιανικών ψηφιδωτών δαπέδων της Ελλάδος II. Πελοπόννησος-Στερεά Ελλάδα.* Κέντρο Βυζαντινών Ερευνών. Thessaloniki.

Badian, E. (ed.), 1966. *Ancient Society and Institutions. Festschrift for V. Ehrenberg.* Oxford.

Bakourou, E., forthcoming. *A. Delt.* 47 A [1992]

Balty, J.-C., 1977–78. 'Un nouveau portrait de Trajan' *Cahiers Mariemont* 8–9: 45–62.

Beacham, R. C., 1991. *The Roman Theatre and its Audience.* London.

Beazley, J. D., 1946. 'Potter and Painter in Ancient Athens' *Proceedings of the British Academy* 30: 5–43.

Beazley, J. D., 1956. *Attic Black-figure Vasepainters.* Oxford.

Bergmann, M., and P. Zanker, 1981. 'Damnatio memoriae. Umgearbeitet Nero- und Domitiansporträts. Zur Ikonographie der flavischen Kaiser und des Nerva' *Jahrbuch des deutschen Archäologischen Instituts* 96: 317–412.

Bergquist, B., 1990. 'Sympotic Space: a Functional Aspect of Greek Dining-rooms' in O. Murray (ed.) *Sympotica: a Symposium on the Symposion*: 37–65. Oxford.

Bieber, M., 1961. *The History of the Greek and Roman Theater.* Princeton.

Bintliff, J. L., 1975. 'Mediterranean alluviation: new evidence from archaeology' *Proceedings of the Prehistoric Society* 41: 78–84.

Bintliff, J. L., 1977. *Natural environment and human settlement in Greece.* British Archaeological Reports International Series 528 (i and ii). Oxford.

Bintliff, J. L., 1991. 'Die Polis-Landschaften Griechenlands: Probleme und Aussichten der Bevölkerungsgeschichte' in E. Olshausen and H. Sonnabend (eds) *Raum und Bevölkerung in der antiken Stadtkultur* (Stuttgarter Kolloquium zur Historischen Geographie des Altertums 3): 149–202. Bonn.

Bintliff, J. L., B. E. Davies, C. F. Gaffney and A. Waters, 1990. 'Trace element accumulation in soils on and around ancient settlements in Greece' in S. Bottema, G. Entjes-Nieborg and W. van Zeist (eds) *Man's Role in the Shaping of the Eastern Mediterranean Landscape*: 159–72. Rotterdam.

Bintliff, J. L., and A. Snodgrass, 1988. 'Mediterranean survey and the city' *Antiquity* 62: 57-71

Blakeway, A., 1935. Review of F. Ollier, 'Le mirage spartiate' *Classical Review* 49: 184–5.

Blinkenberg, C., 1931. *Lindos. Fouilles de l'Acropole 1902–1914, I. Les Petits Objets.* Berlin.

Bloesch, H., 1940. *Formen Attischer Schalen.* Munich.

Bloesch, H. (ed.), 1982. *Greek Vases from the Hirschmann Collection.* Zurich.

Blouet, A., 1833. *Expédition Scientifique de Morée* vol. 2. Paris.

Boardman, J., 1963. 'Artemis Orthia and chronology' *BSA* 58: 1–7.

Boardman, J., and J. Hayes, 1966. *Excavations at Tocra 1963–1965: the Archaic Deposits 1.* London.

Boardman, J., and J. Hayes, 1973. *Excavations at Tocra, the Archaic Deposits 2 and Later Deposits.* London.

Boardman, J., 1967. *Excavations in Chios 1952–55. Greek Emporio.* London.

Boblaye, M. E. Pouillon, 1836. *Expédition Scientifique de Morée: Recherches Géographiques sur les Ruines de la Morée.* Paris.

Boehlau, J., 1898. *Aus ionischen und italischen Nekropolen.* Leipzig.

Boitani, F., 1990. 'Le ceramiche laconiche a Gravisca' *Bollettino d'Arte Supplemento al n. 64*: 19–67.

Bölte, F., 1929. 'Sparta (Geographie)', *RE* iiiA2, 1294–1374.

Bonanno, A., 1976. *Portraits and Other Heads on Roman Historical Reliefs up to the Age of Septimius Severus*. Oxford.

Bonfante, L., and E. Jaunzems, 1988. 'Clothing and ornament' in M. Grant and R. Kitzinger (eds) *Civilization of the Ancient Mediterranean: Greece and Rome* 1385–1413. New York.

Boring, T. A., 1979. *Literacy in Ancient Sparta*. Leiden.

Bosanquet, R. C., 1906a. 'Laconia II. Excavations at Sparta, 1906. 1. The season's work' *BSA* 12 [1905–06]: 277–83.

Bosanquet, R. C., 1906b. 'The sanctuary of Artemis Orthia' *BSA* 12 [1905–06]: 303–17.

Bosanquet, R. C., 1906c. 'Laconia II. Excavations at Sparta, 1906. 7. The cult of Orthia as illustrated by the finds' *BSA* 12 [1905–06]: 331–43.

Boschung, D., 1993. *Die Bildnisse des Augustus. Das römische Herrscherbild I.2.* Berlin.

Bouras, C., 1982. 'Ενα Βυζαντινό Λουτρό στην Λακεδαιμονία' *Archaiologike Ephemeris*: 99–112.

Bowersock, G. W., 1961. 'Eurycles of Sparta' *Journal of Roman Studies* 51: 112–18.

Bracker, J., 1968. 'Ein Trauerbildnis Hadrians aus Köln' *Antike Plastik* 8: 75–84.

Brijder, H. A. G., 1983. *Siana Cups I and Komast Cups*. Amsterdam.

Brijder, H. A. G., 1991. *Siana Cups II: the Heidelberg Painter*. Amsterdam.

Bringmann, K., 1975. 'Die große Rhetra und die Entstehung des spartanischen Kosmos' *Historia* 24: 513–38.

Brommer, F., 1941. 'Bilder der Midassage' *AA*: 49–52.

Broneer, O., 1959. 'Excavations at Isthmia' *Hesperia* 28: 298–343.

Bruit Zaidman, L. and P. Schmitt Pantel, 1992. *Religion in the Ancient Greek City*, ed./trs. P. Cartledge. Cambridge.

Buck, C. E., W. G. Cavanagh and C. D. Litton, 1988. 'The spatial analysis of site phosphate data' in *Computer Applications and Quantitative Methods in Archaeology, 1988* British Archaeological Reports International Series 446 (i): 151–60.

Buckler, C., 1986. 'The Myth of the Movable Skenai' *AJA* 90: 431–6.

Bulle, H., 1928. *Untersuchungen an griechischen Theatern* (Abhandlungen der bayerische Akademie der Wissenschaften, Phil.-Hist. Klasse, Band 33). Munich.

Bulle, H., 1937. *Das Theater zu Sparta*. Munich.

Cain, P., 1993. *Männerbildnisse neronisch-flavischer Zeit*. Munich.

Calligas, P. G., 1992. 'From the Amyklaion' in J. M. Sanders 1992: 31–48.

Carducci, C., 1933. 'Ritratto dell'imperatore Traiano' *Bulletino del Museo dell'Impero Romano* 4: 37–43.

Carpenter, T. H., 1986. *Dionysian Imagery in Archaic Greek Art*. Oxford.

Carter, J. B., 1989. Review of Pipili 1987. *AJA* 93: 473–6.

Cartledge, P. A., 1979. *Sparta and Lakonia*. London.

Cartledge, P. A., 1982. 'Sparta and Samos: A Special Relationship?' *Classical Quarterly* 32: 243–59.

Cartledge, P. A., 1985. 'The Greek religious festivals' in P. Easterling and J. Muir (eds) *Greek Religion and Society*: 98–127. Cambridge.

Cartledge P. A., 1987. *Agesilaos and the Crisis of Sparta*. London and Baltimore.

Cartledge, P. A., 1988. 'Review of M. Pipili, *Laconian Iconography of the Sixth Century* BC and M. Herfort-Koch, *Archaische Bronzeplastik Lakoniens*. *Classical Review* n.s. 38: 342–5.

Cartledge, P. A., 1995. ' "We are all Greeks"? Ancient (especially Herodotean) and modern contestations of Hellenism' *Bulletin of the Institute of Classical Studies* n.s. 2: 75–82.

Cartledge, P. A., 1996a. 'La politica'. in S. Settis (ed.) *I Greci I: Noi e I Greci*: 39–72. Turin.

Cartledge, P. A., 1996b. 'Putting the Greek Gods in Their Places' (Review-article of Alcock and Osborne 1994) *International History Review* 18: 104–12.

Cartledge, P. A., 1997. *The Greeks. A portrait of Self and Others* (rev. edn.). Oxford.

Cartledge, P. A., and A. J. S. Spawforth, 1989. *Hellenistic and Roman Sparta: a tale of two cities*. London and New York.

Catling, H. W., 1974. 'Arkadia-Lakonia: Sparta' *AR* 20: 14–15.

Catling, H. W., 1975a. 'Laconia: Sparta' *AR* 21: 12–15.

Catling, H. W., 1975b. 'Excavations of the British School at Athens at the Menelaion, Sparta, 1973–75' *Lakonikai Spoudai* 2: 258–69.

Catling, H. W., 1976a. 'Laconia: Sparta' *AR* 22: 13–15.

Catling, H. W., 1976b. 'New excavations at the Menelaion, Sparta' in U. Jantzen (ed.), *Neue Forschungen in griechischen Heiligtümern*. Tübingen.

Catling, H. W., 1977a. 'Excavations at the Menelaion, Sparta, 1973–76' *AR* 23: 24–42.

Catling, H. W., 1977b. 'Excavations at the Menelaion, 1976–77' *Lakonikai Spoudai* 3: 408–16.

Catling, H. W., 1978. 'Lakonia: Menelaion' *AR* 24: 31.

Catling, H. W., 1979a. 'Lakonia-Arkadia: Sparta, Menelaion, 1978–79' *AR* 25: 19–20.

Catling, H. W., 1979b. 'Excavations at the Menelaion, Sparta, 1973, 1974' *A. Delt.* 29 [1973–74] B2 *Chr.*: 302–12.

Catling, H. W., 1981. 'Arkadia-Lakonia: Sparta, Menelaion' *AR* 27: 16–19.

Catling, H. W., 1982. 'Excavations and Study at the Menelaion, Sparta, 1978–81' *Lakonikai Spoudai* 4: 28–43.

Catling, H. W., 1983a. 'Sparta. Excavations at the Menelaion' *A. Delt.* 30 [1975] B1 *Chr.*: 80–85.

Catling, H. W., 1983b. 'Study at the Menelaion, 1982–1983' *Lakonikai Spoudai* 7: 23–31.

Catling, H. W., 1984a. 'Sparta, Menelaion' *A. Delt.* 31 [1976] B1 *Chr.*: 79–80.

Catling, H. W., 1984b. 'Sparta, Menelaion' *A. Delt.* 32 [1977] B1 *Chr.*: 63–65.

Catling, H. W., 1985. 'Sparta. Excavations at the Menelaion' *A. Delt.* 33 [1978] B1 *Chr.*: 75–6.

Catling, H. W., 1986a. 'Arkadia-Lakonia. Sparta, Menelaion' *AR* 32: 29–30.

Catling, H. W., 1986b. 'Η Αγγλική Αρχαιολογική Σχολή Αθηνών στην Σπάρτη' *Lakonikai Spoudai* 8: 189–204.

Catling, H. W., 1988. 'Sparta, Menelaion' *A. Delt.* 35 [1980] B1 *Chr.*: 153–7.

Catling, H. W., 1989. 'Arkadia-Lakonia. Sparta, Akropolis. Sparta, Menelaion' *AR* 35: 35–6.

Catling, H. W., 1990a 'Lakonia. Aphyssou, Tsakona' *AR* 36: 22–4.
Catling, H.W., 1990b. 'A sanctuary of Zeus Messapeus: excavations at Aphyssou, Tsakona, 1989' *BSA* 85: 15–35.
Catling, H. W., 1990c. 'Zeus Messapeus near Sparta: an interim report' *Lakonikai Spoudai* 10: 276–95.
Catling, H. W., and E. A. Catling, 1981. 'Barbarian Pottery from the Mycenaean settlement at the Menelaion, Sparta' *BSA* 76: 71–82.
Catling, H. W., and H. Cavanagh, 1976 'Two inscribed bronzes from the Menelaion, Sparta' *Kadmos* 15: 145–57.
Catling, R. W. V., 1986 'Excavations at the Menelaion, 1985' *Lakonikai Spoudai* 8: 205–16.
Cavanagh, W. G., 1991. 'Surveys, cities and synoecism' in Rich and Wallace-Hadrill (eds): 97–118. London.
Cavanagh, W. G., 1995. 'Development of the Mycenaean State: Evidence from the Laconia Survey' in R. Laffineur (ed.) *Politeia* 82–8. Liège.
Cavanagh, W. G., and J. H. Crouwel, 1988. 'Lakonia Survey, 1988' *Lakonikai Spoudai* 9: 77–88.
Cavanagh, W. G., J. H. Crouwel, R. W. V. Catling, and D. G. J. Shipley, 1996. *Continuity and Change in a Greek Rural Landscape: the Lakonia Survey. II Archaeological Data*. British School at Athens, Supplementary Volume 27. London.
Cavanagh, W. G., J. H. Crouwel, R. W. V. Catling, and G. Shipley (eds), forthcoming. *Continuity and Change in a Greek Rural Landscape: The Laconia Survey. I: Methodology and Interpretation.* British School at Athens, Supplementary Volume 26. London.
Cavanagh, W. G., and R. R. Laxton, 1984. 'Lead figurines from the Menelaion and seriation' *BSA* 79: 23–36.
Cherry, J. F., 1990. 'The first colonisation of the Mediterranean islands: a review of recent research' *Journal of Mediterranean Archaeology* 3: 145–221.
Cherry, J. F., J. Davis, A. Demitrack, E. Mantzourani, T. F. Strasser and L. E. Talalay, 1988. 'Archaeological survey in an artefact-rich landscape: a Middle Neolithic example' *AJA* 92: 159–76.
Cherry, J. F., J. L. Davis and E. Mantzourani (eds), 1991. *Landscape Archaeology as Long Term History: Northern Keos in the Cycladic Islands from Earliest Settlement until Modern Times* (Monumenta Archaeologica 16). Los Angeles.
Chrimes K. M. T., 1952. *Ancient Sparta. A re-examination of the evidence*. Manchester.
Christ K. (ed.), 1986. *Sparta*. Darmstadt.
Christ, K., 1996. Review of C. M. Stibbe, *Das andere Sparta*. Frankfurter Allgemeine Zeitung 235 [9. 10. 1996]: 12. Mainz am Rhein.
Christou, C., 1957. 'Ἀνασκαφὴ Ἀφυσοῦ' *PAE* 1957: 214.
Christou, C., 1960. *Ἀρχαία Σπάρτη*. Sparta.
Christou, C., 1960a. 'Σπάρτη Ακροπολις' *Ergon*: 173.
Christou, C., 1960b. 'Ἀνασκαφὴ εἰς Ακροπολις Σπάρτης' *PAE*: 232.
Christou, C., 1963 'Ἀρχαιότητες Λακωνίας-Ἀρκαδίας' *A. Delt.* 17 [1961–62] B1 *Chr.*: 83–5.
Christou, C., 1964a. 'Σπαρτιάτικοι ἀρχαϊκοὶ τάφοι καὶ ἐπιτάφιος μετ' ἀνάγλυφου ἀμφορεύς τοῦ λακωνικοῦ ἐργαστηρίου' *A. Delt.* 19 A [1963–64] Mel.: 123–63
Christou, C., 1964b. 'Ἀνασκαφικαὶ ἔρευναι εἰς οἰκόπεδα Σπάρτης' *A. Delt.* 19 [1963–64] B *Chr.*: 135–41.
Clauss, M., 1983. *Sparta. Eine Einführung in seine Geschichte und Zivilisation.* **Munich.**
Coldstream, J. N., 1968. *Greek Geometric Pottery: a survey of ten local styles and their chronology*. London.
Coldstream, J. N., and G. L. Huxley, (eds) 1972. *Kythera. Excavations and Studies*. London.
Collinson, J. D., 1978. 'Alluvial sediments' in H. G. Reading (ed.) *Sedimentary environments and facies*: 20–62. Oxford.
Cook, J. M., and R. V. Nicholls, 1950. 'Laconia. Kalyvia Sokhás. Sparta' *BSA* 45: 261–98.
Cook, R. M., 1962. 'Spartan history and archaeology' *Classical Quarterly* 12: 156–8.
Cook, R. M., 1972. *Greek Painted Pottery* (2nd edition) London.
Cook, R. M., 1992. 'The Wild Goat and Fikellura Styles: Some Speculations' *Oxford Journal of Archaeology* 11: 255–63.
Coulson, W. D. E., 1985. 'The Dark Age Pottery of Sparta' *BSA* 80: 29–84.
Curci, F., *et al.*, 1994. *Museo Nazionale Archeologico di Taranto*. Taranto.
Daltrop, G., U. Hausmann and M. Wegner, 1966. *Die Flavier. Das römischer Herrscherbild* II.1. Berlin.
Datsouli-Stavridis, A., 1985. *Ρωμαϊκά πορτραίτα στο Εθνικό Αρχαιλογικό Μουσειο της Αθήνας*. Athens.
Datsouli-Stavridis, A., 1987. *Ρωμαϊκά πορτρ αίτα στο Μουσείο της Σπάρτης*. Athens.
Daverio-Rocchi, G. 1988. *Frontiera e confini nella Grecia antica*. Rome.
David, E., 1989. 'Laughter in Spartan Society' in Powell 1989: 1–25.
Dawkins, R. M., 1906. 'Laconia. II. Excavations at Sparta, 1906. 6. Remains of the Archaic Greek period' *BSA* 12 [1905–06]: 318–30.
Dawkins, R. M., 1907. 'Laconia. I. Excavations at Sparta, 1907. 4. The sanctuary of Artemis Orthia' *BSA* 13 [1906–07]: 44–108.
Dawkins, R.M., 1908. 'Laconia. I. Excavations at Sparta, 1908. 2. The sanctuary of Artemis Orthia—The excavation' *BSA* 14 [1907–08]: 4–29.
Dawkins, R. M., 1909. 'Laconia. I. Excavations at Sparta, 1909. 1. The sanctuary of Artemis Orthia' *BSA* 15 [1908–09]: 5–22.
Dawkins, R. M., 1910a. 'Laconia. I. Excavations at Sparta, 1910. 2. The Mycenaean city near the Menelaion' *BSA* 16 [1909–10]: 4–11.
Dawkins, R. M., 1910b. 'Laconia. I. Excavations at Sparta, 1910. 4. Artemis Orthia: the excavation of 1910' *BSA* 16 [1909–10]: 15–17.
Dawkins, R. M., 1910c. 'Laconia. I. Excavations at Sparta, 1910. 5. Artemis Orthia; the History of the Sanctuary' *BSA* 16 [1909–10]: 18–53.
Dawkins, R. M., 1910d. 'The Eleusinion at Kalyvia tes Sochás' *BSA* 16 [1909–10]: 12–14.
Dawkins, R. M., and J. P. Droop, 1911. 'Byzantine Pottery from Sparta' *BSA* 17 [1910–11]: 23–8.
Dawkins, R. M. (ed.), 1929. *The Sanctuary of Artemis Orthia at Sparta*. Society for the Promotion of Hellenic Studies, Supplementary Paper 5. London.
Delivorias, A. 1969. 'Ἀρχαιότητες και Μνημεία Αρκαδίας-Λακωνίας' *A. Delt.* 24 B *Chr.*: 130–41.

Delivorias, A., 1992. 'Λακωνικά Ανθέμια' in Palagia and Coulson 1989: 205–16.
Demakopoulou, K., 1965. 'Ἀνασκαφικαὶ ἔρευναι εἰς οἰκόπεδα Σπάρτης' *A. Delt.* 20 B *Chr.*: 170–8.
Demakopoulou, K. 1966. 'Ἀρχαιότητες Αρκαδίας-Λακωνίας' *A. Delt.* 21 B *Chr.*: 152–9.
Demakopoulou, K., 1967. 'Ἀνασκαφαὶ εἰς τὴν περιοχὴν τῆς Σπάρτης' *A. Delt.* 22 B *Chr.*: 200–203.
de Polignac, F. 1984. *La naissance de la cité grecque: cultes, espace et société VIIIe–VIIe siècles av. J.-C.* Paris.
de Polignac, F. 1994. 'Mediation, competition, and sovereignty: the evolution of rural sanctuaries in Geometric Greece' in Alcock and Osborne 1994: 3–18.
de Polignac, F. 1995. *Cults, Territory, and the Origins of the Greek City-State.* Chicago.
de Ste. Croix G. E. M., 1972. *The Origins of the Peloponnesian War.* London.
Desborough, V. R. d'A., 1952. *Protogeometric Pottery.* Oxford.
Diamant, S., 1974. *The Later Village Farming Stage in Southern Greece.* PhD. dissertation, University of Pennsylvania.
Dickins, G., 1905. 'Laconia. Thalamae. 1. Excavations. 2. Inscriptions' *BSA* 11 [1905–05]: 124–36.
Dickins, G., 1906a. 'Laconia. II. Excavations at Sparta, 1906. 4. The Great Altar near the Eurotas' *BSA* 12 [1905–06]: 295–302.
Dickins, G., 1906b. 'Laconia. II. Excavations at Sparta, 1906. 10. the Theatre' *BSA* 12 [1905–06]: 394–406.
Dickins, G., 1906c. 'Laconia. II. Excavations at Sparta, 1906. 13. Topographic conclusions' *BSA* 12 [1905–06]: 431–9.
Dickins, G., 1907a. 'Laconia. I. Excavations at Sparta, 1907. 7. The Hieron of Athena Chalkioikos' *BSA* 13 [1906–07]: 137–54.
Dickins, G., 1907b. 'Laconia. I. Excavations at Sparta, 1907. 9. A sanctuary on the Megalopolis road' *BSA* 13 [1906–07]: 169–73.
Dickins, G., 1908a. 'Excavations at Sparta, 1908: the hieron of Athena Chalkioikos' *BSA* 14 [1907–08]: 142–6.
Dickins, G., 1908b. 'The art of Sparta' *The Burlington Magazine* 14: 66–84.
Dickins, G., 1912. 'The Growth of Spartan Policy' *Journal of Hellenic Studies* 32: 1–42.
Dickins, G., 1913. 'The Growth of Spartan Policy. A Reply' *Journal of Hellenic Studies* 33: 111–12.
Dontas, G., 1969. 'LAKON KOMASTES' *BCH* 93: 39–55.
Dörpfeld, W., 1927. *Alt Ithaka.* Munich.
Dover, K. J., 1978. *Greek Homosexuality.* London.
Droop, J. P., 1907a. 'Laconia. I. Excavations at Sparta, 1907. 5. The early bronzes' *BSA* 13 [1906–07]: 109–17.
Droop, J. P., 1907b. 'Laconia. I. Excavations at Sparta, 1907. 6. The early pottery' *BSA* 13 [1906–07]: 118–36.
Droop, J. P., 1908. 'Laconia. I. Excavations at Sparta, 1908. 3. The Pottery' *BSA* 14 [1907–08]: 30–47.
Droop, J. P., 1909. 'Laconia. I. Excavations at Sparta 1909. 3. The Pottery' *BSA* 15 [1908–09]: 23–39.
Droop, J. P., 1928. 'Excavations at Sparta. 4. The native pottery from the Akropolis' *BSA* 28 [1926–27]: 49–81.
Droop, J. P., 1929. 'Bronzes' in Dawkins 1929: 196–202.
Ducat, J., 1990. *Les Hilotes.* Paris.
Eckstein, A. and F. Legner, 1969. *Antike Kleinkunst im Liebieghaus.* Frankfurt am Main.
Evers, C., 1994. *Les portraits d'Hadrien. Typologie et ateliers.* Brussels.
Farrell, J., 1908. 'Laconia. I. Excavations at Sparta, 1908. 4. Archaic terracottas from the sanctuary of Orthia' *BSA* 14 [1907–08]: 48–73.
Faustoferri, A., 1996. *Il trono di Amyklai e Sparta.* Perugia.
Fehr, B., 1971. *Orientalische und griechische Gelage.* Bonn.
Finley, M. I., 1975. *The Use and Abuse of History.* London.
Finley M. I., 1981a. 'Sparta and Spartan Society' in Finley 1981c : 21–40. London (=Finley 1975:161–77).
Finley, M. I., 1981b. 'The ancient city: from Fustel de Coulanges to Max Weber and beyond' in Finley 1981c: 3–24.
Finley, M. I. (ed.) 1981c, *Economy and Society in Ancient Greece.* London.
Finley, M. I., 1983. *Politics in the Ancient World.* Cambridge.
Finley, M. I., 1985. 'Town and country' in M. I. Finley, *The Ancient Economy.* 2nd edn., ch. V. London.
Fisher, N. R. E., 1989. 'Drink, hubris and the Promotion of Harmony in Sparta' in Powell 1989: 26–50.
Fisher, N. R. E. and H. van Wees (eds), forthcoming. *Archaic Greece: New Approaches and New Evidence.* London.
Fittschen, K., and P. Zanker, 1985. *Katalog der römischen Porträts in den Capitolinischen Museen und den anderen kommunalen Sammlungen der Stadt Rom* I. Beiträge zur Erschliessung hellenistischer und kaiserzeitlicher Skulptur und Architektur 3. Mainz am Rhein.
Fittschen, K., 1972. 'Das Bildprogram des Trajansbogens zu Benevent' *AA* 87: 742–88.
Fittschen, K., 1984. 'Eine Buste des Kaisers Hadrian aus Milreu in Portugal' *Madrider Mitteilungen* 25: 97–207.
Fitzhardinge, L. F., 1980. *The Spartans.* London.
Floren, J., and Fuchs, W. (eds), 1987. *Die griechische Plastik* I. *Die geometrische und archaische Plastik.* Munich.
Forbes, H. A., 1976. ' "We have a little of everything": the ecological basis of some agricultural practices in Methana, Trizinia' *Annals of the New York Academy of Sciences* 268: 236–50.
Forbes, H. A., 1989. 'Of grandfathers and grand theories: the hierarchical ordering of responses to hazard in a Greek rural community' in P. Halstead and J. O'Shea (eds) *Bad Year Economics: Cultural Responses to Risk and Uncertainty*: 87–97. Cambridge.
Forbes, H. A., 1995. 'The identification of pastoralist sites within the context of estate-based agriculture in ancient Greece: beyond the "transhumance versus agro-pastoralism" debate' *BSA* 90: 325–38.
Forrest, W. G., 1968. *A History of Sparta to 192 BC.* London.
Forster, E. S., 1904a. 'South-western Laconia' *BSA* 10 [1903–04]: 158–89.
Forster, E. S., 1904b. 'Inscriptions' *BSA* 10 [1903–04]: 167–89.
Forster, E. S., 1907. 'Laconia II: Gythium and the north–west coast of the Laconian Gulf' *BSA* 13 [1906–7]: 219–37.
Förtsch, R., 1994. *Kunstverwendung und Kunstlegitimation im archaischen und frühklassischen Sparta* (Habilitationsschrift, Köln).
Foxhall, L., 1990. 'The dependent tenant: land leasing and

labour in Italy and Greece' *Journal of Roman Studies* 80: 97–114.
Foxhall, L. 1992. 'The control of the Attic landscape' in B. Wells (ed.), *Agriculture in Ancient Greece*: 155–9. Stockholm.
French, E. B., 1990. 'Sparta, Akropolis' *AR* 36: 25–6.
French, E. B., 1991. 'Sparta, Classical City' *AR* 37: 28.
French, E. B., 1992. 'Sparta, Akropolis' *AR* 38: 19–21.
French, E. B., 1993. 'Sparta, Theatre' *AR* 39: 22.
French, E. B., 1994. 'Sparta' *AR* 40: 20.
Furumark, A. 1972 *The Chronology of Mycenaean Pottery* (2nd ed.). Stockholm.
Gaffney, C. F. and V. L. Gaffney, 1986. 'From Boeotia to Berkshire: an integrated approach to geophysics and rural field survey' *Prospezioni Archeologiche* 10: 65–70.
Gale, S. J., and P. G. Hoare, 1991. *Quaternary Sediments: Petrographic Methods for the Study of Unlithified Rocks*. London.
Gauer, W., 1975. *Die Tongefässe aus den Brunnen unter dem Stadion-Nordwall und im Südost-Gebiet*. Olympische Forschungen 8. Berlin.
Gauer, W., 1991. *Die Bronzegefässe von Olympia I*. Olympische Forschungen 21. Berlin.
Graindor, P., 1915. 'Les Cosmètes du Musée d'Athènes' *BCH* 39: 241–401.
Greifenhagen, A., 1929. *Eine attische schwarzfigurige Vasengattung und die Darstellung des Komos im VI. Jahrhundert*. Königsberg.
Gros, P., 1994a. 'Le schéma vitruvien du théâtre latin' *RA* : 57–80.
Gros, P., 1994b. 'Les théatres en Italie au 1er siècle de notre ère', in *L'Italie d'Auguste à Dioclétien. Colloque de l'École Française de Rome 198*: 285–307.
Gross, N. H., 1940. *Bildnisse Traians. Das römische Herrscherbild* II.2. Berlin.
Gschnitzer, F., 1991. 'Zum Verhältnis von Siedlung, Gemeinde und Staat in der griechischen Welt' in E. Olshausen and H. Sonnabend (eds), *Stuttgarter Kolloquium zur Historischen Geographie des Altertums* 3: 429–42. Bonn.
Halstead, P., 1987. 'Traditional and ancient rural economy in Mediterranean Europe: plus ça change?' *Journal of Hellenic Studies* 107: 77–87.
Halstead, P., 1996. Review of Sampson and Skoteini, *Tharrounia: the Cave, the Settlement, and the Cemetery* (1993) in *AJA* 100: 179–180.
Hammond, N. G. L., 1973. 'The creation of Classical Sparta', *Studies in Greek History*: 47–103. Oxford.
Hansen, M. H., 1987. *The Athenian Assembly in the Age of Demosthenes*. Oxford.
Hansen, M. H., 1993 (ed.). *The Ancient Greek City-State*. Copenhagen.
Hansen, M. H., 1995. 'Kome. A study in how the Greeks designated and classified settlements which were not poleis' in Hansen and Raaflaub 1995: 45–81.
Hansen, M. H. and K. A. Raaflaub, 1995 (eds). *Studies in the Ancient Greek Polis* (Historia Einzelschrift 95). Stuttgart.
Harding, A., G. Cadogan and R. J. Howell, 1969. 'Pavlopetri; an underwater Bronze Age town in Laconia' *BSA* 64: 113–42.
Harrison, J. E., 1908. *Prolegomena to the Study of Greek Religion*. Cambridge.
Harrison, E. B., 1953. *Athenian Agora I: Portrait Sculpture*. Princeton.
Hasluck, F. W., 1908. 'The promontory of Malea and Epidaurus Limera' 167–82 in Wace and Hasluck 1908: 161–82.
Hassel, F. J., 1966. *Die Trajansbogen in Benevent: ein Bauwerk des römischen Senats*. Mainz am Rhein.
Hayes, J. W., 1995. 'Pottery from the Construction Levels of the Upper Cavea' in Waywell and Wilkes 1995: 449–51.
Heath, M., 1988. 'Receiving the Komos: the Context and Performance of Epinician' *American Journal of Philology* 109: 180–95.
Hekler, A., 1921–24. 'Studien zur römischen Porträtskunst' *Jahreshefte des Österreichischen Archäologischen Instituts* 21–2: 172–202.
Henrichs, A., 1987. 'Myth Visualized: Dionysos and his Circle in Sixth-Century Attic Vase-Painting' in *Papers on the Amasis Painter and his World*: 92–124. Malibu.
Herfort-Koch, M., 1986. *Archaische Bronzeplastik Lakoniens*. Münster.
Hermary, A., 1986. 'Eros' in *Lexicon Iconographicum Mythologiae Classicae* III: 850–942. Zürich and Munich.
Heuss, A., 1979. 'Hellas', in A. Heuss and G. Mann: *Propyläen Weltgeschichte* 1–3 (2nd ed.). Gütersloh.
Hirsch, E. and M. O'Hanlon, 1995 (eds). *The Anthropology of Landscape: perspectives on place and space*. Oxford.
Hitzl, K., 1982. *Die Entstehung und Entwicklung des Volutenkraters von den frühesten Anfängen bis zur Ausprägung des kanonischen Stils in der attisch schwarzfigurigen Vasenmalerei*. Frankfurt am Main.
Hodkinson, S., 1983. 'Social order and the conflict of values in Classical Sparta' *Chiron* 13: 239–81.
Hodkinson, S., 1986.'Land tenure and inheritance in ancient Sparta' *Classical Quarterly* 36: 378–406.
Hodkinson, S., 1989. 'Inheritance, marriage and demography; perspectives upon the success and decline of classical Sparta' in Powell 1989: 79–121. London.
Hodkinson, S., 1992. 'Sharecropping and Sparta's economic exploitation of the helots' in Sanders 1992: 123–34.
Hodkinson, S., forthcoming. 'Lakonian artistic production and the problem of Spartan austerity' in Fisher and van Wees, forthcoming.
Holladay, A.J., 1977. 'Spartan austerity' *Classical Quarterly* 27: 111–26.
Hondius, J. J. E. and A. M. Hondius-van Haeften, 1921. 'Laconia II: notes on topography' *BSA* 24–5 [1919–21]: 144—50.
Hood, M. S. F., 1960. 'Archaeology in Greece, 1959–60' *AR* 6: 3–26.
Hood, M. S. F., 1961. 'Lakonia: Ayios Stephanos' *AR* 7: 32–33.
Hooker, J. T. 1976. *Mycenaean Greece*. London.
Hooker, J. T., 1980. *The Ancient Spartans*. London.
Hope Simpson, R., 1966. 'The seven cities offered by Agamemnon to Achilles' *BSA* 61: 113–131.
Hope Simpson, R., 1981. *Mycenaean Greece*. Park Ridge, New Jersey.
Hope Simpson, R., and O. T. P. K. Dickinson, 1979. *A Gazetteer of Aegean civilisation in the Bronze Age* 1: *The*

Mainland and Islands. Studies in Mediterranean Archaeology LII. Göteborg.

Hornbostel, W., 1984. 'Erwerbungen für die Antikenabteilung im Jahre 1983' *Jahrbuch des Museums für Kunst und Gewerbe Hamburg* 3: 143–98.

Hurst, V. J., 1977. 'Visual estimates of iron in saprolite' *Geological Society of America Bulletin* 88: 174–6.

Huxley, G. L., 1962. *Early Sparta*. London.

Iakovides, S., 1966. 'Περί τοῦ σχήματος τῶν λαξευτῶν τάφων εἰς τά Βολιμίδια Μεσσηνίας' in *Χαριστήριον εἰς Α Κ Ορλάνδον*: 98-111. Athens.

Isler, H. P., 1989. 'Vitruvs Regeln und die erhaltenen Theaterbauten' in *Munus non ingratum, Bulletin Antieke Beschaving, Supplement* 2: 141–53.

Jackson, A., 1992. 'Arms and armour at the panhellenic sanctuary of Poseidon at Isthmia' in W. Coulson and H. Kyrieleis (eds) *Proceedings of an International Symposium on the Olympic Games*: 141–4. Athens.

James, P. A., M. P. Atherton, A. M. Harvey, A. Firmin and A. Morrow, 1997. 'The physical environment of Methana: formation, exploitation and change' in C. Mee and H. A. Forbes (eds) *A Rough and Rocky Place: The Landscape and Settlement History of the Methana Peninsula, Greece*: 5–32. Liverpool.

James, P. A., C. B. Mee and G. J. Taylor, 1994 'Soil erosion and the archaeological landscape of Melos' *Journal of Field Archaeology* 21: 395–416.

Jameson, M. H., C. N. Runnels and T .H. van Andel, 1994. *A Greek Countryside: The Southern Argolid from Prehistory to the Present Day*. Stanford and Cambridge.

Jeffery L.H., 1990. *The local scripts of Archaic Greece*, 2nd edition, revised and enlarged by A. W. Johnston. Oxford.

Jones, A. H. M., 1967. *Sparta*. Oxford.

Jones, R. E., 1986. *Greek and Cypriot Pottery. A review of scientific studies*. British School at Athens, Fitch Laboratory Occasional Paper 1. Athens.

Jucker, H., 1984. 'Trajanstudien zu einem Chalzedonbüstchen im Antikenmuseum' *Jahrbuch der Berliner Museen* 26: 17–78.

Karouzou, S., 1955. 'Fragments d'un cratère à volutes' *BCH* 79: 177–204.

Kästner, V., 1990. 'Scheibenförmige Akrotere in Griechenland und Italien' *Hesperia* 59: 251–64.

Kavvadias, P., 1890–92. *Γλυπτὰ τοῦ Ἐθνικοῦ Μουσείου. Κατάλογος Περιγραφικός*. Athens.

Kennell, N. M., 1985. *The Public Institutions of Roman Sparta*. Unpublished PhD. thesis, Toronto.

Kennell, N. M., 1995. *The Gymnasium of Virtue. Education and Culture in Ancient Sparta*. Chapel Hill and London.

Kilian, K., 1988. 'The emergence of Wanax ideology in the Mycenaean palaces' *Oxford Journal of Archaeology* 7 (3): 291–302.

Kinch, K. F., 1914. *Vroulia*. Berlin.

Kirsten, E., 1956. *Die griechische Polis als geographisches Problem des Mittelmeerraumes*. Bonn.

Kirsten, E., 1984. *Landschaft und Geschichte in der antiken Welt*. Bonn.

Kleiner, D. E. E., 1983. *The Monument of Philopappos in Athens*. Rome.

Kleiner, D. E. E., 1986. 'Athens under the Romans: the patronage of emperors and kings' in C. B. McClendon (ed.) *Rome and the Provinces: Studies in Transformation of Art and Architecture in the Mediterranean World*: 8–20. New Haven.

Kleiner, D. E. E., 1992. *Roman Sculpture*. Yale.

Knell, H., 1991. *Vitruvs Architekturtheorie*: 2nd edn. 137–8. Darmstadt.

Kolbe, W., 1913 (ed.). *Inscriptiones Graecae* V.1. Berlin.

Korres, G. S., 1995. 'Παναγιώτης Σταματάκης, Ἀπόστολος εἰς Σπάρτην (1875)' *Ἐπιστημονικὴ Ἐπετήρις Φιλοσοφικῆς Σχολῆς Πανεπιστημίου Αθηνῶν* 1992–95: 495–508.

Kourinou, E., 1985. 'Ανασκαφικές Εργασίες', *A. Delt.* 40 B *Chr.*: 102.

Kourouniotes, K., 1911. ''Εξ Ἀττικῆς' *Archaiologike Ephemeris*: 246–56.

Kunze, E., 1958. *VI Bericht über die Ausgrabungen in Olympia*. Berlin.

Kunze, E., 1961. *VII Bericht über die Ausgrabungen in Olympia*. Berlin.

Kunze, E., 1967. *VIII Bericht über die Ausgrabungen in Olympia*. Berlin.

Kyrieleis, H., 1981. *Führer durch das Heraion von Samos*. Athens.

Kyrieleis, H., 1993. 'The Heraion at Samos' in N. Marinatos and R. Hägg (eds) *Greek Sanctuaries: New Approaches*: 125–54. London.

Lamb, W. W., 1927a. 'Excavations at Sparta, 1927. 5. Bronzes from the acropolis, 1924–1927' *BSA* 28 [1926–27]: 82–95.

Lamb, W. W., 1927b. 'Excavations at Sparta, 1906–1910. 6. Notes on some bronzes from the Orthia site' *BSA* 28 [1926–27]: 96–106.

Lamb, W. W., 1969. *Ancient Greek and Roman Bronzes* (reprint with additions of original 1929 edition). Chicago.

Lane, E. A., 1934. 'Lakonian Vase-painting' *BSA* 34 [1933–34]: 99–189.

Lane Fox, R., 1985. 'Aspects of inheritance in the Greek world' in P. Cartledge and F. D. Harvey (eds) *Crux: Essays in Greek History Presented to G. E. M. de Ste. Croix on his 75th Birthday*: 208–32. Exeter and London.

Langlotz, E., 1932. *Griechische Vasen in Würzburg*. Munich.

Lattanzi, E., 1968. *I ritratti dei Cosmeti nel Museo Nazionale di Atene*. Rome.

Lazenby J. F., 1985. *The Spartan Army*. Warminster.

Leake, W. M., 1830. *Travels in the Morea* I–III. London.

Leake, W. M., 1846. *Peloponnesiaca*. London.

Lembesi, A., 1985. *Το Ιερό του Ερμή και της Αφροδίτης στη Σύμη Βιάννου* I. *Χάλκινα Κρητικά Τορεύματα*. Athens.

Lemos, A. A., 1991. *Archaic Pottery of Chios: The Decorated Styles*. Oxford University Committee for Archaeology. Monograph no. 30. Oxford.

Leontis, A., 1995. *Topographies of Hellenism*. Ithaca and London.

Lewis, D. M., 1977. *Sparta and Persia*. Brill.

Lissarrague, F., 1990. 'Around the Krater: an Aspect of Banquet Imagery' in O. Murray (ed.) *Sympotica: a Symposium on the Symposion*: 196–209. Oxford.

Loraux, N., 1986. *The Invention of Athens. The Funeral Oration in the Classical City*. Cambridge, Mass.

Loraux, N., 1993. *The Children of Athena*. Princeton.

Loring, W., 1895. 'Some ancient routes in the Peloponnese' *Journal of Hellenic Studies* 15: 25–92.
Lotze, D., 1994. 'Bürger zweiter Klasse: Spartas Periöken. Ihre Stellung und Funktion im Staat der Lakedaimonier' *Sitzungsberichte der Akademie der Wissenschaften zu Erfurt, Geisteswissenschaftliche Klasse 1994*: 37–51.
Lullies, R., 1957. *Die Spitzamphora des Kleophradesmalers.* Opus Nobile No. 5. Bremen.
Mackenzie, D., 1897. 'Ancient sites on Melos' *BSA* 3: 71–88.
Malkin, I., 1994. *Myth and Territory in the Spartan Mediterranean.* Cambridge.
Marangou, L., 1969. *Lakonische Elfenbein- und Beinschnitzereien.* Tübingen.
Marinatos, S., 1952. 'Ἀνασκαφαὶ ἐν Πύλῳ' *PAE*: 473–96
Marinatos, S., 1953. 'Ἀνασκαφαὶ ἐν Πύλῳ' *PAE*: 238–50
Marinatos, S., 1954. 'Ἀνασκαφαὶ ἐν Πύλῳ' *PAE*: 299–306
Mattusch, C. C., 1988. *Greek Bronze Statuary.* Ithaca and London.
Megaw, A. H. S., 1964. 'Archaeology in Greece, 1963–64' *AR* 10: 3–30.
McDonald, W. A., W. D. E. Coulson and J. Rosser (eds), 1983. *Excavations at Nichoria in Southwest Greece* III: *Dark Age and Byzantine Occupation.* Minneapolis.
Mee, C. and W. G. Cavanagh, 1990. 'The spatial distribution of Mycenaean tombs' *BSA* 85: 225–43.
Meier, C., 1990. *The Greek Discovery of Politics.* Cambridge, Mass.
Meyer, H., 1991. *Antinoos.* Munich.
Moebius, H., 1968. *Die ornamente der griechischen Grabstelen klassischer und nachklassischer Zeit.* Munich.
Morris, I. M., 1987. *Burial and Ancient Society. The Rise of the Greek City-State.* Cambridge.
Morris, I. (ed.) 1994. *Classical Greece: Ancient Histories and Modern Archaeologies.* Cambridge.
Morris, I., forthcoming. 'Archaeology and archaic Greek history' in Fisher and van Wees, forthcoming.
Murray, O., 1991. 'War and the Symposion' in W. Slater (ed.) *Dining in a Classical Context*: 93–103. Ann Arbor.
Murray, O. and S. Price (eds), 1990. *The Greek City from Homer to Alexander.* Oxford.
Nafissi, M., 1991. *La Nascità del Kosmos. Sulla Storia e la Società di Sparta.* Perugia.
Neils, J. *et al.*. 1992 *Goddess and Polis. The Panathenaic Festival in Ancient Athens.* Dartmouth and Princeton.
Nicholls, R., 1950. 'Sparta' *BSA* 45: 282–98.
Oeconomus, G. P., 1921. *De profusionum receptaculis sepulcralibus inde ab antiquissimus temporibis usque ad nostram aetatem usitatis.* Athens.
Oldfield, F., B. A. Maher, J. Donoghue and J. Pierce, 1985. 'Particle-size related, mineral magnetic source sediment linkages in the Rhode River catchment, Maryland, USA' *Journal of the Geological Society of London* 142: 1035–46.
Omont, H., 1902. *Missions Archéologiques Françaises en Orient aux XVIIe et XVIIIe Siècles.* Paris.
Ormerod, H. A., 1910. 'Bardounia and north-eastern Maina' *BSA* 16 [1909–10]: 62–71.
Orsi, P., 1910. 'Di una anonima città siculo-greca a Monte S. Mauro presso Caltagirone' *Monumenti Antichi* 20: 806–15.
Osborne, R., 1985. 'Buildings and residence on the land in Classical and Hellenistic Greece: the contribution of epigraphy' *BSA* 80: 119-28.
Osborne, R., 1987. *Classical Landscape with Figures: The Ancient Greek City and its Countryside.* London.
Osborne, R. 1991. 'Pride and prejudice, sense and subsistence: exchange and society in the Greek city' in Rich and Wallace-Hadrill 1991: 119–45.
Osborne, R., 1992. ' "Is it a farm?": the definition of agricultural sites and settlements in ancient Greece' in B. Wells (ed.) *Agriculture in Ancient Greece*: 21–5. Stockholm.
Osborne, R. 1996. '*Classical Landscape* revisited' *Topoi* 6: 49–64.
Palagia, O., 1990. 'Seven pilasters of Herakles from Sparta' in S. Walker and A. Cameron (eds), *The Greek Renaissance in the Roman Empire*: 187–92. London.
Palagia, O., 1993 'A marble Athena Promachos from the akropolis of Sparta' in Palagia and Coulson, 1993: 167–75.
Palagia, O. and W. D. E. Coulson, (eds) 1993. *Sculpture from Arcadia and Laconia.* Oxford.
Panayotopoulou, A., 1989. 'Fragment de sol en mosaïque: La Toilette d'Aphrodite' in *Eros grec. Amour des dieux et des hommes.* (Catalogue de l'Exposition au Grand Palais, 6 novembre 1989–5 février 1990). Athens.
Panayotopoulou, A., 1994 'Les représentations de la Méduse dans les mosaïques de Grèce', *VI Coloquio Internacional sobre Mosaico Antiguo* (Palencia-Mérida, Octubre 1990): 369–82. Guadalajara.
Papamarinopoulos S., R. E. Jones and A. Gagalis, 1990. 'Geophysical survey and archaeological sites in Greece: a new initiative' in E. Pernicka and G. Wagner (eds) *Archaeometry '90* (Proceedings of the 27th International Symposium Heidelberg 1990): 777–86. Basel.
Paribeni, E., 1975. *Lavinium* II. *Le tredici are.* Rome.
Parker, R., 1989. 'Spartan Religion' in Powell 1989: 142–72. London.
Parlama, L., 1971. 'Θαλαμοειδὴς τάφος εἰς Ἀγραπιδοχώρι Ἠλείας' *Archaiologike Ephemeris Chr.*: 52–60.
Payne, H. G., 1931. *Necrocorinthia.* Oxford.
Payne, H. G., 1940. *Perachora* I. Oxford.
Pelagatti, P., 1955–56. 'La ceramica laconica del Museo di Taranto' *Annuario della Scuola Archeologica di Atene* 33–34 (n. s. 17–18): 7–44.
Pelagatti, P., 1989. 'Ceramica laconica in Sicilia e a Lipari' *Bulletino d'Arte* 54: 1–62.
Pelagatti, P., and C. M. Stibbe, 1988. 'Una forma poco conosciuta di vaso laconico: il cratere a campana' *Bulletino d'Arte* 52: 13–26.
Pelagatti, P. and Stibbe, C. M. (eds) 1990. *Lakonikà. Ricerche e Nuovi Materiali di Ceramica Laconica.* Bollettino d'Arte Supplemento al No. 64.
Pelon, O., 1976. *Tholoi, Tumuli et Cercles Funéraires.* Paris.
Pensabene, P., 1983. 'Osservazioni sulla diffusione dei marmi sul loro prezzo nella Roma imperiale' *Dialoghi di Archeologia* 3: 55–63.
Petrakos, B. C., 1992. 'Ο Παναγιώτης Σταματάκης ιδρυτής του Μουσείου Σπάρτης' *Lakonikai Spoudai* 11 (Festschrift D. V. Vagiakakos): 642–50.
Pettersson, M. 1992. *Cults of Apollo at Sparta. The Hyakinthia, the Gymnopaidiai and the Karneia.* Stockholm.
Phelps, W. W., 1975. The Neolithic Pottery Sequence in

Southern Greece. PhD. dissertation, University of London.
Phaklaris, P. B., 1990. *Archaia Kynouria*. Athens.
Philipp, H., 1981. *Bronzeschmuck aus Olympia*. Olympische Forschungen 13. Berlin.
Philippson, A., 1892. *Der Peloponnes: Versuch einer Landeskunde auf geologischer Grunde*. Berlin.
Philippson, A., 1959. *Die griechischen Landschaften*. Volume 3/2. Frankfurt am Main.
Piccirilli, L. 1984. 'Il santuario, la funzione guerriera della dea, la regalità: il caso di Atena Chalkioikos' in M. Sordi (ed.) *Santuari e la guerra nel mondo antico*: 3–19. Milan.
Pipili, M., 1987. *Laconian Iconography of the Sixth Century BC*. Oxford University Committee for Archaeology. Monograph no. 12. Oxford.
Powell, A. (ed.), 1989. *Classical Sparta: Techniques Behind Her Success*. London.
Powell, A., and S. Hodkinson (eds), 1994. *The Shadow of Sparta*. London.
Powell, A. D., 1995. 'The medieval occupation of the theatre' in Waywell, G. B., and J. J. Wilkes, 'Excavations at the ancient theatre of Sparta 1992–4: preliminary report' *BSA* 90: 445–7.
Rackham, O., 1983. 'Observations on the historical ecology of Boeotia' *BSA* 78: 291–351.
Raftopoulou, S., forthcoming a. 'Αρχαιότητες και Μνημεία Λακωνίας' *A. Delt.* 47 B [1992] *Chr.*
Raftopoulou, S., forthcoming b. 'Dark Age Burials from Sparta' *Acts of the 5th International Congress for the Peloponnese* (Nafplion 1995).
Rawson E. D., 1991. *The Spartan Tradition in European Thought*. Oxford.
Renard, J., 1989. *Le Site néolithique et helladique ancien de Kouphovouno (Laconia): fouilles de O.-W. von Vacano (1941)*. Aegaeum. Annales d'archéologie égéenne de l'Université de Liège, 4. Liège.
Rich, J. and A. Wallace-Hadrill (eds), 1991. *City and Country in the Ancient World*. London.
Robertson, N., 1992. *Festivals and Legends: the formation of Greek cities in the light of public ritual*. Toronto.
Roesch, P., 1985. 'Les taureaux de bronze du Kabirion de Thèbes et l'écriture archaïque béotienne' in J. M. Fossey and H. Giroux (eds) *Actes du III Congrès International sur la Béotie Antique, 1979*: 135–52. Amsterdam.
Rohde, E.,1927. *Psyche* (7th. ed.) Tübingen.
Rolley, C., 1969. *Les Statuettes de Bronze*. Fouilles de Delphes V.2. Paris.
Rolley, C., 1982. *Les Vases de Bronze de l'Archaïsme récent en Grande-Grèce*. Naples.
Rolley, C., 1986a. *Greek Bronzes* (English translation of French original, Fribourg). London.
Rolley, C., 1986b. 'Les bronzes grecs: recherches récentes' *Revue Archéologique*: 377–91.
Rolley, C., 1993. 'Les bronzes grecs et romains: recherches récentes' *Revue Archéologique*: 387–400.
Rotili, M., 1972. *L'Arco di Traiano a Benevento*. Rome.
Roy, J., 1971. 'Arcadia and Boeotia in Peloponnesian affairs 370–362 BC' *Historia* 20: 569–99.
Roy, J., 1996. 'The countryside in classical Greek drama, and isolated farms in dramatic landscapes' in Shipley and Salmon 1996: 98–118.
Runciman, W. G., 1982. 'Origins of states: the case of Archaic Greece' *Comparative Studies in Society and History* 24: 351–77.
Runciman, W. G. 1990. 'Doomed to extinction: the polis as an evolutionary dead-end' in Murray and Price (eds) 1990: 347–67.
Rutter, J. B., and S. H. Rutter, 1976. *The transition to Mycenaean; a stratified Middle Helladic II to Late Helladic IIA pottery sequence from Ayios Stephanos in Laconia*. Los Angeles.
Sabbadini, R., 1910. 'Ciriaco di Ancona e la sua descrizione autografa del Peloponneso trasmessa da Leonardo Botta' *Miscellanea Ceriani*: 183–243.
Sakellariou, M. B. 1989. *The Polis-State. Definition and Origin*. Athens.
Salzmann, D., 1982. *Untersuchungen zu den antiken Kieselmosaiken*. Archäologische Forschungen, Band 10. Berlin.
Sampson, A., 1992. 'Late neolithic remains at Tharrounia, Euboea: a model for the seasonal use of settlements and caves' *BSA* 87: 61–101.
Sanders, G. D. R., 1995. 'Pottery from medieval levels in the orchestra and lower cavea' in Waywell and Wilkes, 1995: 451–7.
Sanders, J. M. (ed.) 1992. *ΦΙΛΟΛΑΚΩΝ. Lakonian Studies in honour of Hector Catling*. London.
Sartre, M., 1979. 'Aspects économiques et aspects politiques de la frontière dans les cités grecques' *Ktema* 4: 213–24.
Schaus, G. P., 1978. Archaic Greek Pottery from the Demeter Sanctuary, Cyrene 1969–76: Minor Fabrics (PhD. dissertation, University of Pennsylvania 1978). University Microfilms: Ann Arbor.
Schaus, G. P., 1979. 'A Foreign Vase Painter in Sparta' *AJA* 83: 102–6.
Schaus, G. P., 1985. *The Extramural Sanctuary of Demeter and Persephone at Cyrene, Libya. Final Reports. Vol. II: The East Greek, Island and Laconian Pottery*. Philadelphia.
Schaus, G. P., 1986. 'Two Fikellura Vase Painters' *BSA* 81: 251–95.
Schleiffenbaum, H. E., 1991. *Der griechische Volutenkrater*. Frankfurt am Main.
Schmaltz, B., 1980. *Metallfiguren aus dem Kabirenheiligtum bei Theben* (Das Kabirenheiligtum bei Theben VI). Berlin.
Schnabel, H., 1910. *Kordax*. Munich.
Scranton, R. L., 1951. 'Monuments in the Lower Agora and North of the Archaic Temple' *Corinth* I, 3. Princeton.
Scutt, C. A. (1913) 'The Tsakonian dialect—I' *BSA* 19 [1912–13]: 133–73.
Scutt, C. A. (1913–14) 'The Tsakonian dialect—II' *BSA* 20 [1913–14]: 18–31.
Sear, F., 1990. 'Vitruvius and Roman Theater Design' *AJA* 94: 249–58.
Sear, F., 1993. 'The Scaenae frons of the Theater of Pompey' *AJA* 97: 687–701.
Seeberg, A., 1971. *Corinthian Komos Vases*. London.
Shear, T. L. 1933: 'The current excavations in the Athenian Agora' *AJA* 37: 305–12.
Shear, T. L., 1935: 'The Athenian Agora: The sculpture found in 1933' *Hesperia* 4: 411-413.

Shefton, B. B., 1954. 'Three Laconian Vase-Painters' *BSA* 49: 299–310.

Shefton, B. B., 1989. 'East Greek Influences in Sixth-Century Attic Vase-Painting and Some Laconian Trails' in *Greek Vases in the J. Paul Getty Museum 4* (= Occasional Papers on Antiquities 5): 41–72.

Shipley, G., 1992. 'PERIOIKOS: the discovery of classical Laconia' in Sanders 1992: 211–26.

Shipley, G., 1996. 'Ancient history and landscape histories' in Shipley and Salmon 1996: 1–15

Shipley, G. and J. Salmon, 1996 (eds). *Human Landscapes in Classical Antiquity. Environment and culture*. London and New York.

Simon, E., 1969. *Die Götter der Griechen*. Munich.

Simon, E., 1982. *The Ancient Theatre* (trans., C. E. Vafopoulou-Richardson). London.

Simon, C. G., 1986. The archaic votive offerings and cults of Ionia. PhD. dissertation, Berkeley.

Sismanidis, K., 1982. 'Νέος Μακεδονικός Τάφος στην Αγία Παρασκευή Θεσσαλονίκης' *AAA* 15: 267–84.

Snodgrass, A. M., 1977. *Archaeology and the Rise of the Greek State*. Cambridge.

Snodgrass, A. M., 1987. *An Archaeology of Greece: The Present State and Future Scope of a Discipline*. Berkeley.

Snodgrass, A. M., 1990a. 'The economics of dedication at Greek sanctuaries' in *Anathema: Regime delle Offerte e Vita dei Santuari nel Mediterraneo Antico*, special issue of *Scienze dell'Antichità* 3–4 [1989–90]: 287–94.

Snodgrass, A. M., 1990b. 'Survey archaeology and the rural landscape of the Greek city' in Murray and Price: 113–36.

Snodgrass, A. M. 1991. 'Structural history and classical archaeology' in J. Bintliff (ed.) *The Annales School and Archaeology*, 57–72. Leicester.

Snodgrass, A. M., 1993. 'The rise of the polis. The archaeological evidence' in Hansen 1993: 30–40.

Soteriades, G., 1910. 'Τὸ Πεδίον τῆς ἐν Σελλασίᾳ Μάχης' *BCH* 34: 5–57.

Soteriades, G., 1911. 'Anti-Sellasia' *BCH* 35: 87–107, 241–2.

Sotheby's, 1993. *Greek Vases from the Hirschmann Collection* (sale catalogue, December 9th). London.

Sparkes, B. A., and L. Talcott, 1970. *Black and Plain Pottery*. The Athenian Agora, Vol. XII. Princeton.

Spawforth, A. J. S., 1978. 'Balbilla, the Euryclids and memorials for a Greek magnate' *BSA* 75: 249–60.

Spawforth, A. J. S., 1980. 'Sparta and the family of Herodes Atticus' *BSA* 75: 203–20.

Spawforth, A. J. S., 1985. 'Families at Roman Sparta and Epidaurus: some prosopographical notes' *BSA* 80: 191–258.

Spyropoulos, T., 1980. 'Ανασκαφικές εργασίες', *A. Delt.* 35 B *Chr.*: 135–45.

Spyropoulos, T., 1989. 'Πελλανα', *A. Delt.* 37 B *Chr.*: 112–13.

Spyropoulos, T., 1981. 'Αρχαιότητες και Μνημεία Αρκαδίας-Λακωνίας' *A. Delt.* 36 B *Chr.*: 121–131.

Spyropoulos, T., 1982. 'Αρχαιότητες και Μνημεία Αρκαδίας-Λακωνίας' *A. Delt.* 37 B *Chr.*: 111–121.

Spyropoulos, T., 1983. 'Αρχαιότητες και Μνημεία Αρκαδίας-Λακωνίας' *A. Delt.* 38 B *Chr.*: 88–97.

Starr, C. G., 1965. 'The Credibility of Early Spartan History' *Historia* 14: 257–72.

Steinhauer, G., 1972. 'Αρχαιότητες και Μνημεία Λακωνίας-Αρκαδίας', *A. Delt.* 27 B *Chr.*: 242–51.

Steinhauer, G., 1973. 'Αρχαιότητες και Μνημεία Λακωνίας-Αρκαδίας', *A. Delt.* 28 B *Chr.*: 164–80.

Steinhauer, G., 1973–4. 'Αρχαιότητες και Μνημεία Λακωνίας-Αρκαδίας', *A. Delt.* 29 B *Chr.*: 283–301.

Steinhauer, G., 1975. 'Αρχαιότητες και Μνημεία Λακωνίας-Αρκαδίας', *A. Delt.* 30 B *Chr.*: 74–80.

Steinhauer, G., 1988. Γ. Ιούλιος Ευρυκλής· Συμβολή στην ιστορία της ρωμαϊκής Σπάρτης. Unpublished PhD. dissertation, Athens.

Steinhauer, G., 1992. 'An Illyrian Mercenary in Sparta under Nabis' in Sanders 1992: 239–45.

Stephanidou-Tiveriou, T., 1993. *Τραπεζοφόρα με πλαστική διακόσμηση. Η αττική ομάδα*. Athens

Stern, W. M., 1975. Studies in Hadrianic Private Portraiture. PhD. dissertation, Indiana.

Steuben, H. von, 1991. Review of Pipili 1987 in *Gnomon* 63: 340–3.

Stibbe, C. M., 1972. *Lakonische Vasenmaler des 6. Jh. v. Chr.* Amsterdam and London.

Stibbe, C. M., 1974. 'Il Cavaliere Laconico' *Mededelingen van het Nederlands Instituut te Rome* n. s. 1: 19–37.

Stibbe, C. M., 1976. 'Neue Fragmente lakonischer Schalen aus Cerveteri' *Mededelingen van het Nederlands Instituut te Rome* n. s. 3: 7–16.

Stibbe, C. M., 1978. 'Lakonische Kantharoi' *Mededelingen van het Nederlands Instituut te Rome* 40: 23–42.

Stibbe, C. M., 1986. 'Eine neue Schale des Allard Pierson-Malers' in H. A. G. Brijder, A. Drukker, C. W. Neeft (eds) *Enthousiasmos. Essays on Greek and Related Pottery Presented to J. M. Hemelrijk*: 29–34. Allard Pierson Series, 6. Amsterdam.

Stibbe, C. M., 1989. *Laconian Mixing Bowls*. Laconian Black-Glazed Pottery, Part 1. Amsterdam.

Stibbe, C. M., 1990. 'A Laconian Volute Krater from Sicily' *Xenia* 19: 5–18.

Stibbe, C. M., 1991a. 'Dionysos in Sparta' *Bulletin Antieke Beschaving* 66: 1–44.

Stibbe, C. M., 1991b. 'Bellerophon and the Chimaera on a Lakonian Cup by the Boreads Painter' in *Greek Vases in the J. Paul Getty Museum* 5 (Occasional Papers on Antiquities 7): 5–12.

Stibbe, C. M., 1992a. 'Archaic bronze hydriai' *Bulletin Antieke Beschaving* 67: 1–62.

Stibbe, C. M., 1992b. 'Dionysos mit einer Kithara?' in H. Froning *et al* (eds) *Kotinos: Festschrift für Erika Simon*: 139–45. Mainz am Rhein.

Stibbe, C. M., 1994. *Laconian Drinking Vessels and Other Open Shapes*. Laconian Black-Glazed Pottery, Part 2. Allard Pierson Series, Scripta minora, vol. 4. Amsterdam.

Stibbe, C. M., 1996. *Das andere Sparta*. Mainz am Rhein.

Stibbe, C. M., forthcoming. *Laconian Oil-flasks and other closed shapes*. Laconian Black-Glazed Pottery, Part 3. Amsterdam.

Stoddart, D. R., 1986. *On Geography*. Oxford.

Stubbs, H., 1950. 'Spartan austerity: a possible explanation' *Classical Quarterly* 44: 32–7.

Talcott, L. 1936. 'A Stand signed by Euthymides' *Hesperia* 5: 68.

Tausend, K. 1992. *Amphiktyonie und Symmachie. Formen zwischenstaatlicher Beziehungen im archaischen*

Griechenland (Historia Einzelschrift 73). Stuttgart.
Taylour, W. D., 1962 'Laconia: Ayios Stephanos' *A. Delt.* 16 [1960] *Chr.*: 104–05.
Taylour, W. D., *et al.* 1972. 'Excavations at Ayios Stephanos' *BSA* 67: 205–70.
Taylour, W. D., 1979. 'Excavations at Ayios Stephanos, 1973, 1974' *A. Delt.* 29 [1973–74] B1 *Chr.*: 312–14.
Thommen, L., 1996. *Lakedaimonion Politeia. Die Entstehung der spartanischen Verfassung* (Historia Einzelschrift 103). Stuttgart.
Thompson, R. and F. Oldfield, 1986. *Environmental Magnetism*. London.
Tillyard, H. J. W., 1905. 'Laconia. Geraki. 3. Inscriptions' *BSA* 11 [1904–05]: 105–12.
Tillyard, H. J. W., 1906. 'Laconia. II. Excavations at Sparta, 1906. 9. Inscriptions from the Artemision' *BSA* 12 [1905–06]: 351–93.
Tod, M. N., 1904. 'Teams of ball-players at Sparta' *BSA* 10 [1903–04]: 63–77.
Tod, M. N., 1907. 'Three new *sphaireis* inscriptions' *BSA* 13 [1906–07]: 212–18.
Tod, M. N., H. J. W. Tillyard and A. M. Woodward, 1907. 'Laconia. I. Excavations at Sparta, 1907. 10. Inscriptions' *BSA* 13 [1906–07]: 174–218.
Tod, M. N. and A. J. B. Wace, 1906. *A Catalogue of the Sparta Museum*. Oxford.
Tomlinson, R. A., 1976. *Greek Sanctuaries*. London.
Tomlinson, R. A., 1995 'Sparta: Theatre: Roman Stoa' *AR* 41: 15–16.
Torelli, M., 1992. 'Da Sparta a Villa Adriana: le terme dell' Arapissa, il gimnasio del Platanistas e il Teatro Maritimo' in *Stips votiva* (Festschrift Stibbe): 225-232. Amsterdam.
Toynbee, A. J., 1969. *Some Problems of Greek History* Oxford.
Traquair, R., 1906a. 'Laconia. I. Mediaeval fortresses' *BSA* 12 [1905–06]: 259–76.
Traquair, R., 1906b. 'Laconia. II. Excavations at Sparta, 1906. 12. The Roman stoa and the fortifications of the acropolis' *BSA* 12 [1905–06]: 415–30.
Travlos, J., 1971. *Pictorial Dictionary of Ancient Athens*. London.
Tsakos, K., 1980. 'Ενα ιερό της Αρτέμιδος στη Σάμο' *AAA* 13: 305–18.
Tsountas, C., 1889. '"Ερευναι ἐν τῇ Λακωνικῇ καὶ ὁ τάφος τοῦ Βαφείου ' *Archaiologike Ephemeris* 1889: 129-172.
Valmin, M. N., 1938. *The Swedish Messenia Expedition* III. Lund.
van Andel, T. and C. Runnels, 1987. *Beyond the Acropolis: a rural Greek past*. Stanford.
van Andel, T. and C. Runnels, 1995. 'The earliest farmers in Europe' *Antiquity* 69: 481–500.
van Andel, T., E. Zangger and A. Demitrack, 1990. 'Land use and soil erosion in prehistoric and historical Greece' *Journal of Field Archaeology* 17: 379–396.
van Berghem, J-W. and J. Fiselier, forthcoming. 'Interpreting site patterns using land evaluation' in Cavanagh *et al.*, forthcoming.
Vayakakos D. V. and I. G. Taïphakos, 1975. 'Λακωνικὴ Βιβλιογραφία'. *Lakonikai Spoudai* 2: 417–87
Venit, M. S., 1985. 'Laconian Black Figure in Egypt' *AJA* 89: 391–8.
Vermeule, C. C., 1968. *Roman Imperial Art in Greece and Asia Minor*. Cambridge, Mass.
Vermeule, E. T., 1964. *Greece in the Bronze Age*. Chicago.
Vita Finzi, C., 1969. *The Mediterranean Valleys: Geological Changes in Historical Times*. Cambridge.
von Bothmer, D., 1985. *The Amasis Painter and his World*. New York and London.
von Reden, S. V. I. A., forthcoming. 'The well-ordered polis: topographies of civic space' in Cartledge, Millett and von Reden (eds) *KOSMOS. Order, Conflict and Community in Classical Athens*. Cambridge.
Wace, A. J. B., 1905a. 'Laconia. Geraki. 2. Sculpture' *BSA* 11 [1904–05]: 99–105.
Wace, A. J. B., 1905b. 'Frankish sculptures at Parori and Geraki' *BSA* 11 [1904–05]: 139–45.
Wace, A. J. B., 1906a. 'Laconia. II. Excavations at Sparta, 1906. 2. The City Wall' *BSA* 12 [1905–06]: 284–88.
Wace, A. J. B., 1906b. 'Laconia. II. Excavations at Sparta, 1906. 3. The Heroön' *BSA* 12 [1905–06]: 288–94.
Wace, A. J. B., 1906c. 'Laconia. II. Excavations at Sparta, 1906. 8. The stamped tiles' *BSA* 12 [1905–06]: 344–50.
Wace, A. J. B., 1906d. 'The Roman Baths (Arapissa)' *BSA* 12 [1905–6]: 407–14.
Wace, A. J. B., 1907a. 'Laconia. I. Excavations at Sparta, 1907. 2. The City Wall' *BSA* 13 [1906–07]: 5–16.
Wace, A. J. B., 1907b. 'Laconia. I. Excavations at Sparta, 1907. 3. The stamped tiles' *BSA* 13 [1906–07]: 17–43.
Wace, A. J. B., 1909. 'Lakonia: excavations at Sparta, 1909. 6. The Menelaion. The lead figurines' *BSA* 15 [1908–09]: 127–41.
Wace, A. J. B., 1910. 'Laconia. III. Early pottery from Geraki' *BSA* 16 [1909–10]: 72–75.
Wace, A. J. B., 1929. 'Lead figurines' in Dawkins 1929: 249–284.
Wace, A. J. B., and G. Dickins, 1907. 'Laconia. I. Excavations at Sparta, 1907. 8. The Tombs' *BSA* 13 [1906–07]: 155–68.
Wace, A. J. B., and F. W. Hasluck, 1905a. 'Laconia. I. Excavations near Angelona' *BSA* 11 [1904–05]: 81–90.
Wace, A. J. B., and F. W. Hasluck, 1905b. 'Laconia. Geraki. 1. Excavations' *BSA* 11 [1904–05]: 91–99.
Wace, A. J. B. and F. W. Hasluck, 1908. 'Laconia. II: topography. South-eastern Laconia' *BSA* 14 [1907–8]: 161–82.
Wace, A. J. B. and F. W. Hasluck, 1909. 'Laconia II: topography. East-central Laconia' *BSA* 15 [1908–9]: 158–76.
Wace, A. J. B., M. S. Thompson and J. P. Droop, 1909. 'Excavations at Sparta 1909. 6. The Menelaion' *BSA* 15 [1908–09]: 108–57.
Wade-Gery, H. T., 1958. *Essays in Greek History*. Oxford.
Wagstaff, J. M., 1981. 'Buried assumptions: some problems in the interpretation of the "Younger Fill" raised by recent data from Greece' *Journal of Archaeological Science* 8: 247–64.
Wagstaff, J. M., 1992. 'Colonel Leake in Laconia' in Sanders 1992: 277–83.
Walbank, F. W., 1985. 'The problem of Greek nationality' in F. W. Walbank, *Selected Papers: essays in Greek and Roman history and historiography*: 1–19. Cambridge.
Walter-Karydi, E., 1973. *Samische Gefässe des 6. Jahrhunderts v. Chr.*, Samos VI.1. Bonn.

Warden, P. G., 1990. 'Part I: The small finds' in D. White (ed.) *The Extramural Sanctuary of Demeter and Persephone at Cyrene, Libya. Final Reports*, IV: 1–86. University of Pennsylvania, University Museum Monograph 67. Philadelphia.

Warren, P. M., 1992. 'Lapis Lacedaemonius' in Sanders 1992: 285–96.

Waterhouse, H. E., 1956. 'Prehistoric Laconia: a note' *BSA* 51: 168–71.

Waterhouse, H. E., and R. Hope Simpson, 1960. 'Prehistoric Laconia, Part I' *BSA* 55: 67–107.

Waterhouse, H. E., and R. Hope Simpson 1961 'Prehistoric Laconia, Part II' *BSA* 56: 114–75.

Waterhouse, H. E., 1986. *The British School at Athens; the first hundred years*. British School at Athens, Supplementary Volume 19. London.

Waywell, G. B., J. J. Wilkes, D. M. Bailey, and G. D. R. Sanders, 1993. 'Excavations at Sparta; the Roman Stoa, 1988–91. Preliminary report, Part 1' *BSA* 88: 219–86.

Waywell, G. B. and J. J. Wilkes, 1994. 'Excavations at Sparta: the Roman Stoa, 1988–91, Part 2' *BSA* 89: 377–432.

Waywell, G. B. and J. J. Wilkes, 1995. 'Excavations at the Ancient Theatre of Sparta 1992–4: Preliminary Report' *BSA* 90: 435–60.

Waywell, G. B. and J. J. Wilkes, 'Excavations at Sparta: the Roman stoa, 1988–91. Part 3' *BSA* 92: 401–34.

Waywell, S. E., 1979. 'Roman Mosaics in Greece', *AJA* 83: 293–321.

Weber, T., 1983. *Bronzekannen*. Frankfurt am Main.

Wegner, M., 1956. *Hadrian. Plotina. Marciana. Matidia. Sabina*. Das römische Herrscherbild II.3. Berlin.

Whitelaw, T. M., 1991. 'The ethnoarchaeology of recent rural settlement and land use in northwest Keos' in Cherry *et al.* 1991: 403–54.

Whitelaw, T. M., 1994. 'An ethnoarchaeological study of rural land-use in north-west Keos: insights and implications for the study of past Aegean landscapes' in P. N. Doukelis and L. G. Mendoni (eds) *Structures Rurales et Sociétés Antiques*: 163–86. Paris.

Whitehead, D., 1986. *The Demes of Attica 508/7 to ca. 250 BC*. Princeton.

Wilkinson, K. N., 1993. 'Investigations of past erosional and sedimentological processes at the Roman and Byzantine site of Sparta' *Papers from the Institute of Archaeology* 4: 9–24.

Wilkinson, K. N., 1997. 'The environment of Roman and Byzantine Sparta' 415–21 in G. B. Waywell and J. J. Wilkes 'Excavations at Sparta: the Roman Stoa, 1988–91. Part 3' *BSA* 92: 401–34.

Winter, N. A., 1993. *Greek Architectural Terracottas from the Prehistoric to the end of the Archaic period*. Oxford Monographs on Classical Archaeology. Oxford.

Woodward, A. M., 1907. 'Taenarum and south Maina' *BSA* 13 [1906–7]: 238–67.

Woodward, A. M., 1908. 'Laconia. I. Excavations at Sparta, 1908. 5. Inscriptions' *BSA* 14 [1907–08]: 74–141.

Woodward, A. M., 1909. 'Laconia. I. Excavations at Sparta, 1909. 4. Inscriptions' *BSA* 15 [1908–09]: 40–106.

Woodward, A. M., 1910. 'Laconia. I. Excavations at Sparta, 1910. 6. Inscriptions' *BSA* 16 [1909–10]: 54–61.

Woodward, A. M., 1925a. 'Excavations at Sparta, 1924–1925. 2. The Theatre' *BSA* 26 [1923–25]: 119–158.

Woodward, A. M., 1925b. 'Excavations at Sparta, 1924–25. 3. The Inscriptions' *BSA* 26 [1923–25]: 159–239.

Woodward, A. M., 1925c. 'Excavations at Sparta, 1924–25. 4. The Acropolis. The Finds' *BSA* 26 [1923–25]: 253–76.

Woodward, A. M., 1926a. 'Excavations at Sparta, 1926. II. The Theatre' *BSA* 27 [1925–26]: 175–209.

Woodward, A. M., 1926b. 'Excavations at Sparta, 1926. 3. The Inscriptions' *BSA* 27 [1925–26]: 210–54.

Woodward, A. M., 1927a. 'Excavations at Sparta, 1927. 2. The Theatre' *BSA* 28 [1926–27]: 3–36.

Woodward, A. M., 1927b. 'Excavations at Sparta. 3. The Acropolis, 1926–27' *BSA* 28 [1926–27]: 37–48.

Woodward, A. M., 1928. 'Excavations at Sparta, 1924–28: 2. The Inscriptions' *BSA* 29 [1927–28]: 2–56.

Woodward, A. M., 1930a. 'Excavations at Sparta, 1924–1928. I. The Theatre: Architectural remains' *BSA* 30 [1928–30]: 151–240.

Woodward, A. M., 1930b. 'Excavations at Sparta, 1924–27. II. Votive inscriptions from the Acropolis' *BSA* 30 [1928–30]: 241–54.

Woodward, A. M., and M. B. Hobling, 1926. 'Excavations at Sparta, 1924–25. 4. The Acropolis' *BSA* 26 [1923–25]: 240–52.

Woodward, A. M., and L. Robert, 1928. 'Excavations at Sparta 1924–28. Part II. Four Hellenistic decrees' *BSA* 29 [1927–28]: 57–74.

Woodward, J. M., 1928. 'Excavations at Sparta. 3. Terracottas, Plastic Vases, Reliefs' *BSA* 29 [1927–28]: 75–107.

Wright, J. C., 1987. 'Death and power at Mycenae: changing symbols in mortuary practice' in R. Laffineur (ed.) *Thanatos: Les Coutumes Funéraires en Égée à l'Age du Bronze*: 171-184. Liège.

Wycherley, R. E., 1978. *The Stones of Athens*. Princeton.

Xanalatou-Dergalin, E., and A. Kouloglou-Pervolarake, 1976. *Μονεμβασιά* (2nd. ed.). Athens.

Zancani Montuoro, P., 1954. 'L'agguato a Troilo nella ceramica laconica' *Bollettino d'Arte* 39: 289–95.

Zorides, P., 1982.'Δύο πορτραίτα του Αδριανού του τύπου "Rollockenfrisur" από τον Πειραιά και την Επίδαυρο' *AAA* 15: 115–24.

List of Contributors

Paul Cartledge,
Clare College,
Cambridge CB2 1TL.

Hector Catling,
Dunford House,
Lanford,
Lechlade,
Gloucestershire GL7 3LN.

William Cavanagh,
Department of Archaeology,
University of Nottingham,
University Park,
Nottingham NG7 2RD.

Reinhard Förtsch,
Archäeologisches Institut der Universität Köln,
Albertus-Magnus-Platz,
D-50923 Köln,
Germany.

Stephen Hodkinson,
Department of History,
University of Manchester,
Manchester M13 9PL.

Anna Karapanaiotou,
Archaeological Museum,
Tripoli 221-00,
Greece.

Christopher Mee,
School of Archaeology and Oriental Studies,
University of Liverpool,
14 Abercromby Square,
Liverpool L69 3BX.

Donald M. Nichol,
16 Courtyards,
Whittlesford Road,
Little Shelford,
Cambridge CB2 5ER.

Anastasia Panayotopoulou,
National Archaeological Museum,
Tossitsa 1,
Athens 106-82,
Greece.

Maria Pipili,
Academy of Athens,
Anagnostopoulou 14,
Athens 106-73,
Greece.

Stella Raftopoulou,
9 G. Athenassiadi Street,
Pendeli 152-36,
Greece.

Tyler Jo Smith,
Department of Art and Art History,
Virginia Tech College of Arts and Sciences,
201 Draper Road,
Blacksburg,
VA 24061-0103,
U.S.A.

Theodore Spyropoulos,
Archaeological Museum,
Tripoli 221-00,
Greece.

Conrad Stibbe,
Tondensestrasse 3,
6975 AB Tonden,
The Netherlands.

Susan Walker,
Department of Greek and Roman Antiquities,
British Museum,
London WC1B 3DG.

Geoffrey Waywell,
Institute of Classical Studies,
Senate House,
Malet Street,
London WC1E 7HU.

John Wilkes,
Institute of Archaeology,
31-34 Gordon Square,
London WC1H 0PY.

Keith Wilkinson,
King Alfred's College,
Winchester SO22 4NR.